ORPHEUS IN PARIS

LAEMLEIN
1850

OFFENBACH
1850

ORPHEUS IN ❊ PARIS

OFFENBACH
AND THE PARIS OF HIS TIME

BY

S. KRACAUER

TRANSLATED FROM THE GERMAN BY
GWENDA DAVID & ERIC MOSBACHER

*Que le lecteur ne se scandalise pas de
cette gravité dans le frivole.*
                                    BAUDELAIRE

NEW YORK
VIENNA HOUSE
1972

This 1972 VIENNA HOUSE edition is reprinted by
arrangement with the Estate of Elisabeth Kracauer.
International Standard Book Number: 0-8443-0093-4
Library of Congress Catalogue Number: 72-93827
Manufactured in the United States of America

CONTENTS

Contents

PART THREE

ILLUSTRATIONS

Illustrations [vi]

Part ONE

CHAPTER I

LIBERTY LEADS THE PEOPLE

In the Paris Salon of 1831 there was a picture round which crowds gathered daily, drawn to it less by the artist's technique than by his subject.

The artist was the already famous Eugène Delacroix, and the picture was called " Liberty Leads the People." [1] It was intended to represent an incident from the very recent past, the Revolution of July 1830. A half-naked young woman, wearing a red Phrygian cap, was to be seen leading a band of fighters forward to the assault, inspiring them with her own ardor. In one hand she held a musket, while with the other she held aloft the Republican tricolor, which fluttered in the smoke that obscured the sky. There was only one break in the smoke-cloud, through which it was possible to see the towers of Notre-Dame, over which there brooded a heavy, July sun. On the woman's right was a young man, a typical product of the Paris streets, armed with two pistols; on her left were top-hatted students and workers in caps and blouses. Was this new Joan of Arc a terrestrial being or a supernatural apparition? A dying worker crept towards her with his last strength, gazing upon her enraptured, as though he had been granted a miracle. In the midst of the fray and a moment before death he had set eyes on Liberty herself. But Liberty took no notice of him and, as though nothing could divert her, strode straight ahead, over the torn-up paving-stones and the many corpses that lay strewn upon the ground.

Perhaps a suspicion may have passed through the minds of

[1] *La Liberté guidant le peuple.*

some of those who came to gaze at it that this picture was not just a graphic representation of the three glorious days of July, but that it also lifted a corner of the veil that hid the future. For, in the decades that followed, the French people, following the call of Liberty, were indeed destined again and again to dream their republican dream. This picture of 1831 was by no means destined to fade into a mere historical painting associated with the events that gave rise to it. Just forty years later it was to reappear as a vision before the inner eye of a celebrated writer for the Paris stage, whose work the audiences of the entire world took to be the very quintessence of frivolity; as if to forewarn him that the time for jesting was over and that barricades and piles of corpses were about to be seen again in the Paris streets.

But many things were to happen between 1831 and that memorable evening at the Opéra when Ludovic Halévy, Offenbach's librettist, beheld the threatening vision.

Liberty led the people — but in the meantime the government was in the hands of Louis-Philippe, the elect of the wealthy bourgeoisie, whose leading representatives were a handful of powerful bankers. "Henceforward the bankers will rule," the banker Laffitte had remarked as he led the Duc d'Orléans in triumph to the Hôtel de Ville after the Chamber had hastily proclaimed him King. Laffitte knew what he was talking about. The July Revolution having put an end to the absolutism of the reign of Charles X and eliminated the old aristocracy, the way lay open for the aristocracy of finance. Moreover, the bankers and their political friends were enlightened people, of a liberal frame of mind, whose ideal was a constitutional monarchy on the English model. They wanted a king whose mere existence would keep the country quiet while Parliament did the governing. In this scheme of things they naturally contemplated playing the chief role themselves. For they were satisfied that while they controlled the rudder of the ship of state the value of securities would keep everlastingly rising on the Paris Bourse, thus contributing to the welfare of all mankind; or at least to that section of it that paid enough taxes to be entitled to the privilege of the vote. This privileged section of the community of course constituted only an infinitesimal fraction of the population of France.

Louis-Philippe was a corpulent old gentleman who made frantic efforts to maintain a popularity based on his willingness to sing the *Marseillaise* upon the slightest provocation. It was also recalled that on the occasion of the ceremony at the Hôtel de Ville he had received the tricolor from General Lafayette, who embraced him, exclaiming: " You are the best Republic! " To reinforce the profound impression thus made upon the public mind, Louis-Philippe was apt to emphasize his participation in the republican victories of Valmy and Jemappes. When he appeared in public it was not in the guise of a king by divine right, but as an ordinary citizen, taking the air in the evening after drawing the shutters and closing the shop. He wore a round felt hat instead of a crown and carried a homely umbrella instead of a scepter. He shook every hand that was offered him, greeted everybody he passed, laughed and gossiped, and assumed an air of harmless good-fellowship. Queen Marie-Amélie would occasionally accompany him on these politic excursions. Domestic bliss outshone the most brilliant candlelight.

Foreign newspaper correspondents, in sending descriptions of this republican simplicity to their native lands, seldom omitted to extol the royal skill at dissimulation. They did not trust the King's behavior and wrote of hidden aims. Nevertheless it became manifest right at the beginning of his reign that the sole object of his foreign policy was to keep the peace, even at the price of humiliating France — a policy that betrayed a statesmanly insight into the European balance of power. Moreover, it benefited business on the Bourse. " As for home affairs," Louis-Philippe announced soon after his accession, " we shall strive to keep to the *juste milieu.*" His abjuration of all constructive political thinking may well have been a consequence of his passive temperament; for if he was lacking in imagination he was certainly not lacking in intelligence. But the royal passivity, though it harmonized admirably with the Constitution, might well have suggested to the ignorant that there was no necessity whatsoever for a king. Since the stability of the throne was still precarious and Louis-Philippe was no rightful heir, he quickly became aware of the necessity of proving his own indispensability, and, for want of anything more substantial, filled the gap with the weight of his own person. " Louis-Philippe probably has a so-called system," one of the newspaper correspondents remarked, " but that system is himself and his family, and just enough monarchy to maintain his own position. Only he will never admit it."

There was no need for him to admit it, because it was evident to all beholders. And as he lacked the ability to rouse enthusiasm for his " golden mean," the extreme tendencies liberated by the revolution only flourished the more exuberantly. At the one extreme were the Legitimists, or Carlists — that is, the aristocratic coteries of the faubourg Saint-Germain, closely associated with the clergy. These feudal gentry regarded the bankers and their " Bourgeois King " as parvenus, and retired sulkily to their salons and châteaux, where they agitated to the best of their ability in seclusion. At the other extreme were the masses. The republicans in their low, broad-rimmed hats made no secret of the fact that they had not overthrown a king of the elder Bourbon line only to exchange him for a representative of the younger branch of the same family; particularly as it was obvious that he fully intended to act like a king. These were the real enemies of the new regime; and all those who were ashamed of the peace to which Louis-Philippe held firm in spite of the humiliations imposed upon him at the hands of England associated themselves with them. If the latter had had their way France would promptly have fought a war of revenge for Waterloo. Their warlike anger was nourished by memories of the glories of the Napoleonic era, which still lived on among the people. Veterans of the *Grande Armée* begged for sous in the streets in the name of Bonaparte, and grisettes sang the songs in which Béranger celebrated their idol's deeds. And, last but not least, the workers, who had vainly believed that the part they had played in the July fighting would be rewarded by an improvement in their lot, were seething with dissatisfaction. No improvement in their lot took place. Their wages remained low, their hours long, and the organizations in which they attempted to combine were increasingly threatened by the bourgeoisie who had swung themselves into the saddle with their aid.

Although the paving-stones had been replaced in the streets, there was as much unrest in Paris in the early years of the July Monarchy as though the revolution were still in progress. The barricades had been removed, but the freedom of the press remained, and countless satires and caricatures shocked and delighted the city, making sport of the " best of republics " and, above all, of the King and his round felt hat and umbrella. He was drawn as a tricolored parrot, that answered either " Valmy " or " Jemappes " to every question. Was his head not pear-shaped? All the pear-trees in France would not have sufficed to produce the multitude of pears that burgeoned on the walls and on the pages of the comic papers. But these products of the long-suppressed Parisian satirical spirit were but trifles in comparison with innumerable editorials and fiery speeches — such, for instance, as those made at public meetings by Blanqui, the eternal revolutionary, who had spent more years of his life in prison than at liberty. Blanqui was far from being an isolated zealot. The republican secret societies bestirred themselves, and early Socialist doctrines, in spite of their touching naïveté, started gaining adherents.

Every now and then some startling event provided an accompaniment to the spate of words: the hunger riots of the silk-weavers of Lyon (an entirely unpolitical movement, it is true); an attempt at a rising from the Right; anti-Government demonstrations; bloodthirsty republican rioting in the streets. Liberty's path was still strewn with corpses and obscured not only as usual by clouds of smoke, but also by rumors of all sorts, the result of the extreme opposing factions making common cause for reasons of opportunism. The Legitimists, by pretending for the time being to be enthusiastic republicans, hoped to hasten Louis-Philippe's downfall and take advantage of the subsequent confusion for their own ends; while the republicans, who had but few resources at their disposal, were not at all averse to the rich nobility's activity on their behalf. It was a miracle that the regime of the *juste milieu* did not succumb to this many-sided attack. But its defenders were fighting for the maintenance of profits and incomes, and their powers of resistance were visibly reinforced by general recognition of the fact that perpetual republican insurrectionism seriously prejudiced trade and commerce. The King, moreover, was a skilled calculator and tactician. When a rising was quelled, he would appear in the role of a conqueror, on horseback; when danger threatened, he would take his umbrella and go out, trusting the weather would soon clear up again.

The passions which seemed to threaten the country with perpetual civil war sprang from a volcanic soil, of which political upheavals were not the only symptom. The depths were opened, and from them arose elementary forces which shook habits and customs to their foundations. Paris was in turmoil. Caught up in the delirium, youths from the universities mingled with the people, and even the members of the older generation adopted the ways and manners of the young. Novelty and innovation became the rage, and license in speech and clothing the fashion. Carnival was celebrated in a manner that seriously shocked a number of prominent personalities of the time. Society seemed headed for a convulsion. At the end of March 1832 nature herself appeared to be calling a halt to these excesses. The cholera epidemic spread from England to Paris, but in spite of it, or rather because of it, no one thought of interrupting carnival.

At one of the masked balls a harlequin suddenly felt a queer coldness in his legs. He tore the mask from his face, which had turned a deep violet hue. The same thing befell a number of other pierrots and pierrettes. The unfortunates were hustled away to the hospital and buried a few days later in their carnival costumes, no doubt because of the rush.

In the course of the three months that followed, the plague cost about twenty thousand lives, and when it had run its course there was a brief pause, as if of exhaustion, before teeming life poured forth again from its nooks and crannies. Crime increased, anarchy spread. In the center of the city hawkers openly offered for sale pamphlets denouncing the crimes of the police, and tormented residents and passers-by with their din. The disorder was reflected in the blood-curdling dramas, full of nymphomaniacs, sleeping-drafts, bandits, poisons, and counter-poisons, produced at the Théâtre de la Porte-Saint-Martin. It was filled to overflowing every night. Gradually chaos grew, until it became so intolerable that the republicans sighed for a Legitimist king, and the Legitimists prayed for a republic. Prophecies of a speedy end were heard on every side.

Such was the state of Paris at the time of the young Offenbach's arrival. Yet in spite of all her horrors she succeeded unaccountably in winning her way into men's hearts. In those very years when the abyss seemed to be opening beneath her, Heinrich Heine called her " a lovely city of enchantment." And he would have been no poet, let alone a German poet, had he not tried to solve the riddle which she presented him — the riddle, that is to say, of her ability to reconcile him to the horror with which she filled him. In his book *Florentine Nights,* in which a young man of the name of Maximilian describes his experiences in the period following the July Revolution, he inquires into the matter. " It is an amazing thing," Maximilian states. " The greatest tragedies of world history are played in Paris; but the spectator of these great tragedies fares as I fared once at the Théâtre de la Porte-Saint-Martin, where I went to see *La Tour de Nesle.*[1] I happened

[1] A popular play by Alexandre Dumas.

to sit behind a lady wearing a hat of pink gauze; it was so big that it cut off my entire view of the stage. I saw the whole of the tragedy through the pink gauze of that hat, so that all the horrors of *La Tour de Nesle* appeared in a cheerful, rosy light. There is a rosy light of that kind in Paris, brightening all tragedies in the eyes of the close observer and preventing his pleasure in life from being spoiled. Even the tragedies one brings with one in one's own heart lose their horror in Paris, and pains are wonderfully softened. In the Paris air all wounds heal more quickly; there is something in it as generous, as open-handed, as amiable as the people itself."

CHAPTER II

INFANT PRODIGY

OFFENBACH's ancestry is lost in the darkness of the ghetto and cannot be traced back beyond his grandfather, who lived in Offenbach-on-Main. Juda Eberst, as he was called, was devoted to music and had a fine tenor voice. He made his living by giving music lessons, which are said often to have taken him to the house of the Rothchilds in neighboring Frankfurt.

His son, Isaac Juda Eberst, was initiated early into the traditions of Jewish musicianship. He also learned bookbinding, but it appealed to him far less than music. When he left Offenbach at the age of twenty to see what the world had to offer him, he quickly blossomed into a wandering musician, going from synagogue to synagogue as cantor, in the usual fashion of Jewish musicians, and fiddling at all the taverns he passed on the way. In the course of his wanderings he came in 1802 to Deutz, a suburb and entertainment center of Cologne. Deutz was full of dance-halls, gambling-rooms, and inns, and several Jewish tavern bands were established there, which could be useful to a man like Isaac Eberst. Glad at the opportunity of making a regular living, he settled at Deutz. As he was always known as *der Offenbacher* — the man from Offenbach — he called himself Offenbach for the sake of simplicity, and a few years later married Marianne Rindskopf, the daughter of an honorable Deutz money-changer and lottery-office keeper.

But hard times followed. During the Wars of Liberation the Deutz entertainment business collapsed and Isaac Offenbach, who was dependent on it for his livelihood, was forced to return once more to bookbinding. The work was uncongenial and in 1816 he moved with his family to Cologne, where he supported himself by teaching singing, the violin, the flute, and the guitar. He was remarkably versatile, for in addition to this he composed, wrote about religion, and dabbled in poetry. He was gifted with intelligence and a sense of humor and was devoted to the idea of Jewish emancipation. Though he had many rationalistic ideas, they did not in the least affect his naïve faith in God, which led him, in spite of the pitiful poverty in which he lived, to bring one child after another into the world.

On June 20, 1819 he celebrated the arrival of a second son, his seventh child, whom he named Jakob. Jakob's life began in a street filled with old-clothes-shops in the second-hand-dealers' quarter of Cologne, where musty smells mingled with the music that echoed all day long from his father's house. Young Jakob was taught the violin at the age of six and was composing little ditties by the time he was eight, and when he was nine, as his sister Julie relates, he was accidentally discovered to have been secretly and successfully practicing the cello, for which his arms were not yet long enough. This discovery resulted in his being taken to Herr Alexander, a good cellist of the older generation, who was known in Cologne as " the artist " because of his curious clothing. As soon as little Jakob had acquired the necessary technique, his hard-pressed father made use of him to form a trio, consisting of Jakob and his elder brother and a sister, Julius and Isabella.

The trio played opera selections and dance music at the restaurants and wine-bars of Cologne.

Old Offenbach sought to enhance the trio's drawing-power by advertising Jakob's age as even lower than it was, proclaiming him an infant prodigy. The youthful performers would often have to turn out twice a day, in the afternoon and in the evening. Old Offenbach now had ten children, and although he had become a cantor to the Jewish congregation of Cologne, with a fixed stipend and a house provided, he still had difficulty in making both ends meet.

But by making sacrifices he succeeded in continuing his children's musical education, in spite of their restaurant engagements. Jakob was his pride. As soon as it became clear that he had learned all that Herr Alexander had to offer him, he was handed over to the care of a younger and more up-to-date cellist, Bernhard Breuer, who also gave him composition lessons. Breuer had a reputation in Cologne, having written a great deal of music for the carnivals. But Jakob had no need of Breuer to learn the carnival songs.

The Cologne carnival, like that of Paris, of which echoes were again and again to recur in his operettas, was partly a product of the streets that Jakob loved to roam. The rapidity of his musical progress can be gauged by the fact that he very soon came to the end of all that Breuer had to teach him, which meant that Cologne had nothing left to offer. His father realized this and made what must undoubtedly have been a difficult decision, to send Jakob and Julius to Paris, to the Conservatoire. Paris was the only place where Jewish artists could make a name without obstacles being put in their way. For the old man dreamed of his son's future greatness.

Isaac Offenbach and his two sons started out on their journey in November 1833. As the stagecoach rattled away, Frau Offenbach went back into her kitchen, absent-mindedly rested her arm on the oven, and burst into tears. Little Jakob was only just fourteen, and Julius, though he was eighteen, was still a child, and when one thought of all the terrible things that might happen to two high-spirited boys in a place like Paris, that led so many people astray . . . If Julie had not come in and awakened her mother from her reverie in the nick of time, her whole arm would have been burned.

After a journey of four full days and nights the travelers reached their destination. As they drove wearily through the maze of noisy Paris streets — Offenbach had never seen so many streets and so many houses before — they felt they were being drawn into a labyrinth. Somewhere or other they came upon a fine street that was broader than the rest — that, with its trees and gardens, was rather like an avenue. This was Jakob's first sight of the Boulevards.

His father had no eyes for the city. He had one thought and one thought only: to get Jakob into the Conservatoire. So he went at once to see Cherubini, the celebrated Italian composer who was the director of that institution, not thinking he would have much difficulty in realizing his ambition, since the letters of recommendation he had with him unquestionably referred to the boy as an infant prodigy.

He had not, however, reckoned with Cherubini's fanatical pedantry. The seventy-three-year-old *maestro* permitted neither himself nor the professors and artists on his staff the slightest deviation from routine. He had a mania for punctuality, which caused him to be constantly looking at his watch, and his sense of duty was so severe that he seemed to mistake his musical academy for a fortress. His instinctive attitude to all petitions and requests addressed to him was that they were hostile attacks which must be repulsed. In Offenbach's case the repulse was all the quicker because of a paragraph in the Conservatoire regulations that banned foreigners. Ten years earlier this paragraph had actually caused him to turn away the twelve-year-old Liszt.

Fortunately Offenbach's father had experience in dealing with people in authority, for he was used to bargaining with the elders of the Jewish community of Cologne about the amount of his salary. Instead of taking Cherubini's no for final, he promptly embarked upon such a long and eloquent disquisition, pleading, arguing, imploring, and explaining, that Cherubini ended by consenting to give the infant prodigy an audition. The infant prodigy accordingly started playing a piece from sight. His success could not have been more complete. Cherubini interrupted him before he had finished. " You are a pupil of the Conservatoire! " he exclaimed.

Isaac Offenbach followed up his triumph by securing his boys a decent lodging and, faithful to the family tradition, found them places in a synagogue choir, which brought them in a little money. It was essential for them to earn something, because he could not entirely support them. They do not, however, seem to have been members of this choir for long. During his three months' stay in Paris, Isaac acted as a cantor several times, obviously with a view to a subsequent permanent transfer of himself and his family to Paris, but this transfer never took place. Then he went back to Cologne, leaving Jacques and Jules, as they very soon called themselves, to their own devices.

As little more will be heard of Jules, he deserves a digression. Not much is known about him, except that he gave violin lessons in Paris and played for some years in the orchestra of the Bouffes-Parisiens, the theater that his brother founded, managed, composed for, and made world-famous. What a fate! Wherever Jules went his brother's name followed him like a shadow, and throughout his life his role was confined to that of being Offenbach's brother. He was himself a shadow, doomed to be buried in silence. Bound inseparably to the younger brother whose shadow he was, he died a few days after the latter's death, as quietly and inevitably as though he had never had an independent existence of his own.

The new pupil of the Conservatoire found himself in a Paris in which life was no idyl. A law had just been enacted thanks to which the Government was at last able to get rid of the associations and secret societies which were undermining its authority. The answer to the passing of this law was a rising on the part of the workers of Lyon, who were supported by the republican clubs, which it took five days to quell. Barely had news of the rising reached Paris when rioting broke out there too, right in the heart of the city, where the Conservatoire was situated.

There were wholesale arrests, troops were called out in large numbers, the republicans defended themselves desperately, and it all ended in a massacre. But bullets might be flying in one street while musicians quietly went on with their work in the next.

Offenbach did not allow his studies at the Conservatoire to absorb him. On the contrary, he rather sought to avoid them, for he very soon discovered that Vaslin's cello class had little to offer him. He was at this time a tall, overgrown lad, smoldering with impatience, which lured him perpetually to acts of flightiness. He left the Conservatoire only a year after entering that institution. The irruption of this bright young comet into Cherubini's orderly constellation may well have increased the latter's mania for discipline.

Of the various possibilities open to an ex-pupil of the Conservatoire, a position in a theater orchestra appealed to him most. Several of his friends had found such positions, and if he followed their example it would enable him to get to know the theater from the inside.

There was much about the work that made it inviting.

He was instinctively drawn towards anything that even distantly resembled a stage; to have life and activity about him was a necessity of his being, and the theater was his predestined spiritual home. Restless as he was, he spent brief periods with two orchestras before finding a berth at the Opéra-Comique. Here his fellow-cellist was Hippolyte Seligmann, a lad two years older than he, and a brilliant and promising executant who had already been awarded a prize. He, too, was an ex-pupil of the Conservatoire and was receiving a final technical polishing from the celebrated virtuoso Norblin. It was probably due to his influence that Offenbach followed his example and studied under the same master.

Apart from the usual theatrical gossip, the two young musicians had plenty to talk about. Right at the beginning of their acquaintance came the first performance of Fromental Halévy's opera *La Juive,* a sensational success. All Paris was discussing whether this was due to the intrinsic merit of the music or to the magnificence of the production, and it was obviously necessary to go and see it in order to judge for oneself.

Offenbach decided to take a chance. One evening, long before the time for the curtain to go up, he took up a position just outside the Opéra and lay in wait for Halévy to appear. When he did appear he approached him and shyly asked him for a free ticket.

When such encounters are of importance, the participants often have some sort of inkling to that effect. Halévy examined this slender, curly-headed youth more closely and realized that he had seen him before, in the orchestra of the Opéra-Comique, where one of his works was running. A brief conversation followed, which made such a deep impression on Offenbach that twenty years later he was able to describe the whole scene in detail for the paper *L'Artiste.*

" 'Do you particularly want to see well? ' M. Halévy said.

" 'I wish above all to hear well, *maître.'*

" 'Then come with me and we shall listen to *La Juive* together, from a place which you see very badly, but which I always use when I want to judge the effect of the music, particularly the choruses.'

" We climbed to the gallery, where he was given a box from which I listened to the performance, all ears, without missing a single note of that magnificent score."

Had the young man not been so completely carried away by the music as to have no eyes for his surroundings, he might have noticed the atmosphere of social brilliance by which he was surrounded. The *beau monde* of the Era of the Golden Mean assembled nightly in this white and gold auditorium, which was illuminated by an enormous chandelier. The *élite* of this company consisted of the gentlemen of the recently founded Jockey Club, who either foregathered in their club box during the performance or spent their time paying compliments to the *ballerine*

in the *foyer de danse*. Offenbach's future public was in process
of formation on this very spot; for the members of the Jockey
Club were destined to be the most enthusiastic admirers of his
works in later years.

The director of the Opéra was the omnipotent Dr. Véron. Dr.
Véron possessed the calculating unscrupulousness that meets
good fortune half-way. Everything he touched turned to gold.
He believed in nothing but in getting the best out of life while
it lasted. He had started his career as a doctor and had occupied
a well-paid sinecure during the Restoration period, as physician
attached to the royal museums. He had bought the formula of a
patent medicine from its luckless inventor, and pushed it so successfully that within a short time it was bringing him in a hundred thousand francs a year. After this profitable maneuver he
had abandoned his profession for good and, with an extraordinary flair for the latent and undeveloped potentialities of journalism, founded a newspaper, *La Revue de Paris,* by which his
power had been considerably enhanced.

He seemed to be the very personification of money-making.
He changed his opinions as the wind blew and had no qualms
about deserting the camp of the royalists for that of the *juste
milieu* and leasing the Opéra as a supporter of Louis-Philippe.
Fortune, generally so fickle, continued to smile on him. No
sooner had he taken over the Opéra than Meyerbeer's *Robert le
Diable* came his way.

Fortune provided him with the prosperous social background
necessary for him to thrive, and he went ruthlessly ahead, not
shrinking from the most brazen expedients. Aided by the judi-
cious use of bribery, Dr. Véron developed the Opéra into a
gold-mine.

In some respects he resembled those Oriental despots who lay
about on soft cushions and lorded it over large harems on his
own stage. The voluptuousness of his operatic productions repaid
him well. His harem was the *corps-de-ballet.* The autocratic
fashion in which he exploited this selection of well-favored young

women was seen when he entertained his friends. One night at supper he caused an extra dish to be served. It was brought in on a silver salver by a gigantic butler and consisted of a naked *ballerina* decorated with green trimmings.

To be fair to Dr. Véron, it must be added that he was never stingy, but always gave the favorite of the evening a box of sugared almonds wrapped in a thousand-franc note.

This sybaritism, which, like its opposite, asceticism, often goes hand in hand with money, caused him to indulge in extravagant *mises en scène,* on which, as in the case of *La Juive,* he spent hundreds of thousands of francs. Others might have ruined themselves by such lavishness, but Dr. Véron had such an unerring flair for the inclinations of the public that the more money he put into his gold-mine, the more he drew out of it.

The result of Offenbach's visit to the Opéra was that Halévy started giving him lessons in composition. Halévy, as chorusmaster to the Opéra, was initiated into all the mysteries. It was good to be encouraged by such a man, particularly in view of the soporific effect of work in an orchestra.

However highly Offenbach may have rated the comic operas of Hérold, Adam, Auber, and others, it was not long before he knew the entire repertoire by heart, and nothing was more repugnant to his volatile temperament than repetition and monotony. Rehearsing and playing the same music over and over again — the *adagio* passages slowly and the *con molta espressione* passages with much expression — he found utterly intolerable. He often felt like jumbling all the *tempi* up together. In order to make life a little brighter he started indulging in practical jokes, in which Seligmann occasionally joined him. For instance, instead of following the score as they should have done, each would play alternate notes; or Offenbach would secretly tie several chairs and music-stands together and then make them dance during the performance. The disadvantage of all this, however, was that Offenbach's salary was eighty-three francs a month, and M. Valentino, the conductor, had a strong sense of discipline.

For disciplinary reasons and also, perhaps, for educative ones, he would fine the culprit for each offense. Offenbach regarded boredom as the greater evil, with the result that his salary often shrank to an alarming degree.

But by now he had friends, and there was no need to take these troubles too much to heart. For a time his closest friends were two brothers named Lütgen, who had settled in Paris some time before he had and were the sons of a Cologne violinist who was friendly with his father. They shared a garret in the rue des Martyrs, on the way to Montmartre, in one of those dwellings the upper regions of which have always been associated with poverty, the smell of cooking, and dreams of future glory. When funds were low, Offenbach and his room-mates would live on salad and potatoes. Jacques, as the youngest, was the one who did the shopping. This duty he found extremely uncongenial, as it conflicted with his natural pride. He made the ordeal more bearable by carrying home his purchases in an empty violin-case, which he took with him for the purpose, in order to save himself from what he regarded as public humiliation. With the potatoes effectively concealed in the violin-case, he could go about without feeling ashamed when girls looked at him, and life was bearable once more. It was lived in a Bohemia remote from the surrounding bourgeois banality, and remained unaffected even by the explosion of the infernal machine that Fieschi intended for Louis-Philippe on the occasion of a big parade of the National Guard. The King himself escaped, although there were many casualties.

CHAPTER III

MATERIAL FOR OPERETTAS

" HE needed movement and life all around him, having a terrible fear of solitude and quiet." That was what Albert Wolff, writer of *causeries* for *Le Figaro,* once said of his friend Offenbach. What was true of him in maturity was as true when he was a lad of sixteen, left to his own resources in a strange city. No one was more drawn than he towards the surface things of life or so receptive to the impressions that crowded in on every side.

The streets of Paris were filled with sights that might have been devised for the specific purpose of enthralling a young man who had played in a tavern band and felt at home in the midst of a throng. The boulevard du Temple, for example, to which Fieschi's attempted regicide had given a tragic notoriety, was the scene of a perpetual fair. Was it not a source of ever recurring delight to wander through the throng that surrounded the sword-swallowers, the human skeletons, the dwarfs, the giantesses; to watch an exhibition of performing fleas, then a learned dog parading his knowledge, then a young girl apparently being roasted alive? The freaks and the horrors, the mountebanks, the tumblers, the jugglers, and the acrobats, the exhibitions of legerdemain, the crowds, the perpetual din, exhausted every grade of emotion, from a pleasurable shivering in the spine to childish stupefaction. Behind the booths, the stalls, and the side-shows were a number of theaters next door to one another, and one of them, the Cirque Olympique, with its performing animals, its military and patriotic displays, and its resplendent pantomimes, outdid the fair itself. The whole street was devoted to entertainment, and it was not long before Offenbach himself contributed to it.

From here the Boulevards stretched westwards, through the business and commercial quarters, advancing by imperceptible degrees into the high-class shopping districts, where window-displays attracted a public with more money in its pockets. All along the route passers-by were continually pestered by an extraordinary collection of touts and beggars, whom Delphine de Girardin found so objectionable that she declared that it was positively dangerous to go for a walk. Indeed, the pedestrian was confronted with new obstructions at every step. There were beggars with monkeys on their shoulders, showmen with raree-shows and dioramas, children peddling shoelaces and mother-of-pearl buttons, men dressed up as Turks in blue blouses offering perfumed sweets that could be smelled from afar.

The main contingent consisted, of course, of singers and musicians, who were collectively responsible for a din that emulated the noise of the traffic and the clatter of the horses' hoofs. Towards noon the air would be filled with the vibrant notes of the harp, which later on in the day yielded pride of place to tambourines and triangles. The hurdy-gurdies, however, seemed to have no fixed hours. Who knows from what nooks and crannies this swarm of mendicants daily poured forth? Their numbers had been greatly multiplied by the 1830 Revolution, and they seemed to populate the streets like an advance-guard of anarchy. They used innumerable ruses to win public sympathy. A woman toothpick-seller who wore mourning showed no diminution in her grief and despair at the end of five years, and many of the blind men had perfect sight. All this was material for future operettas.

This picturesque mendicancy made a striking contrast to the elegance of the boulevard des Italiens, which was just becoming " the Boulevard " *par excellence.* Louis-Philippe had undertaken

a cleaning up of the Palais Royal, which had hitherto been a hive
of fashionable life. The further the cleaning-up process developed, the more fashionable did the Boulevards become. The hundreds of women who used the innumerable galleries and arcades
of the Palais Royal to pick up their gentlemen friends had already
been driven away, and the closing of the Palais Royal gambling-
rooms was due to take place at the end of 1837. From a resort of
pleasure it became a resort of high morality. This was enough to
cause the world of fashion to withdraw from its precincts and
migrate to the Boulevards, which entered upon the Palais Royal's
inheritance.

Each time Offenbach strolled along them he saw a spectacle
of wealth and brilliance that could not but be impressive to an
outsider. For the time being, the enchanted circles that dwelt
there remained closed to him and he only saw what everybody
else could see: the crowded terrace of the Café Tortoni, with innumerable carriages drawn up outside it, the shell-work of the
Chinese Baths, the façades of several luxurious restaurants, and
the young dandies, who looked very comic with fat cigars between their lips and top hats tilted right down over their eyes.
At any rate, they must have looked comic to a newcomer to the
city.

The dandies wore their hats like that because fashion demanded it. Fashion also demanded that each gentleman should
keep a " tiger " — that is, a groom whose stature had to be as
diminutive as possible and whose duty it was to follow everywhere at his master's heels. The ideal of these gentlemen with
well-lined purses was the so-called English " snob," and no
trouble was too great to live up to it. They took pains always
to look as phlegmatic and expressionless as possible, visited Lord
Seymour's armory, practiced pigeon-shooting, and made excursions to the Bois, from which they returned covered with dust.
But no matter where they roamed they invariably returned to
the Boulevards, to which they belonged. When not actually

there, they would generally be found in the neighboring alleys and passageways, which were well adapted to the purposes of conversation and making rendezvous.

Anyone who lost his way in these passages might well have been pardoned for supposing that he had entered a fairy grotto. The gilt decorations, the artificially illuminated flowers, pistols, bottles, and delicacies gleaned behind the plate glass like so many treasures. The city's magic seemed concentrated here. Remote from earth and sky, it seemed a realm exempt from natural laws, preserving marvelous illusions, like the stage.

Innumerable curious sightseers strolled through these streets on Sundays. Jules Vallès, one of the closest observers of the Paris of his time, said that all classes of the population received a common and uniform education in the streets — he called it their real education. Workers, laughing grisettes, soldiers, the petty bourgeoisie, who had few opportunities for strolling and gazing at shop-windows during the week and still regarded Louis-Philippe as a champion of the liberal cause, all took the opportunity of gazing their fill on Sundays.

Plenty of building was in progress. A huge statue of an elephant had been put up in the Place de la Bastille, and preparations were being made for erecting the obelisk in the Place de la Concorde. Nature was utterly remote. That, however, did not prevent a prosperous bourgeois from occasionally having his horses harnessed and going for a country excursion.

Offenbach was brought into renewed contact with Halévy during the rehearsals of the latter's charming opera *L'Éclaire,* which appeared at the Opéra-Comique towards the end of 1835. Wherever the young man went he left a trail of mischief in his wake, though he may not always have been the direct cause of it himself. It may or may not have been his fault that one day one of the singers lured him on to the stage in the middle of the performance. The penalty for this unrehearsed incident was a thirty-franc fine.

At carnival time, fortunately, there were no penalties for high spirits. How many memories of Cologne and home were awakened by that word! It was associated with merrymaking and music and color and flags and streamers and festivities of all kinds. The thrill that the mere mention of it awoke was redoubled at the prospect of taking part in the company of a whole gang of friends. Seligmann, the Lütgen brothers, Jules, friends from the Conservatoire, and the rest, most of them somewhat older than Jacques, were only too glad to make the sparks fly.

In later years the celebrations of the last three days of the Paris carnival, which ended with the traditional Bœuf Gras procession, were destined gradually to be withdrawn from the streets and to take place in dance-halls and such places. But in Offenbach's early years in Paris street festivities were still the rule. Their wildness proved that the revolutionary ferment had not altogether subsided. The streets swarmed with harlequins and columbines, pierrots and pierrettes, pantaloons and pulcinellos. Some dressed up as market porters, some wore costumes caricaturing the aristocratic society of the past regime, others appeared as comically attired warriors or rococo shepherds and shepherdesses and in this guise invaded the *grands boulevards,* the rue Saint-Honoré, the Place de la Vendôme, like swarms of locusts, engulfing the endless procession of carriages that from two o'clock onwards made its way through the dense, masked mob that thronged the streets.

The carriages, too, were filled to overflowing. Nothing on wheels, from the humblest cab to the most elegant carriage, was left in its stable on those three days. Should two vehicles happen to be caught side by side in a traffic block, their occupants would amuse themselves by exchanging remarks of the most hair-raising ribaldry at the top of their voices. Such ribaldry was entirely in accordance with the manners of the time. Besides, any exchange of sentiments expressed in less robust fashion would have been lost in the general uproar. Trumpets and bugles were used to intensify the din.

The sound of trumpets also issued from the windows of the Café Tortoni and the Café de Paris, which sheltered not a few guests who believed they were taking a full part in the popular revelry by furiously and persistently exercising their lungs. The only people who were really elevated above the throng were the gentlemen of the Jockey Club, enthroned on their balcony overlooking the Boulevards, puffing clouds of Havana cigar smoke into the air and allowing themselves to be gaped at by the masses.

But where was " Milord l'Arsouille "? " Milord l'Arsouille " was the name by which Lord Seymour was known to the masses. He would amuse himself at carnival time by scattering largesse wholesale among the people. In previous years he had either thrown it from the window or from his big four-horsed carriage in which he would appear in the company of a number of young men and women. *" Vive milord l'Arsouille! "* the crowd had shouted in enthusiasm. They took it for granted that it was Lord Seymour's face that was hidden behind their benefactor's mask; for popular repute held him to be the father of all eccentricities; all those, that is to say, that were not parented upon the half-crazy Marquis de St. Cricq.

Both the milord and the Marquis were well-known figures, and stories about them were rife. At carnival time they were particularly apt to be apocryphal.

The Marquis de St. Cricq possessed an inexhaustible fund of idiocy. One day at the Café Anglais, for instance, he slowly and deliberately poured salt into his tea and showed the most pained astonishment a few moments later at the remarkable taste. He then proceeded to haul the unfortunate waiter over the coals and actually made him taste the horrible stuff. On another occasion he put the salad-bowl on his head. Sometimes he would do several crazy things one after the other.

One day he hired a number of empty cabs and formed them into a procession. He then placed himself at the head of the procession, wearing clogs. Outside the Café Tortoni he called a halt. He then ordered three portions of ice cream to be brought him.

" MILORD L'ARSOUILLE "
From the painting by Gustave Doré

Cet homme à l'œil *vairon*, qui, certes, n'est pas beau,
Est connu dans la presse et dans la pharmacie,
Par la pâte-Regnault, le biberon–Darbo,
Et les *premiers-Paris* auxquels Thiers s'associe.
Son image est fidèle, et nous avons pris soin
D'y placer les produits qu'on doit à sa science ;
Même le biberon dont il aura besoin,
Car son journal tombe en enfance.

Dessiné par FABRITZIUS.   Gravé par MONTIGNEUL·

Courtesy, British Museum

DR. VÉRON

One of them he ate, and then, after long deliberation, filled his clogs with the other two.

On another occasion his eccentric behavior created a sensation at the Théâtre Français. It was a wet night, and he was angered by the favorable reception given to a play which he disliked. During the last act he slipped out of the theater for a few moments. To his fury and indignation, more volleys of applause greeted him on his return. " Go on clapping! You'll all get beautifully wet on your way home, you fools! " he shouted at the top of his voice. The prophecy came true, and it was not by accident either. For during his absence from the theater he had hired every single cab waiting outside it.

Later the Marquis was no longer allowed to go about alone, but invariably appeared in the company of a valet. White mutton-chop whiskers surrounded his reddish face, which glowed under the top hat he wore tilted over his eyes. He survived like a ghost from a bygone age and lived on into the times that paid homage to Offenbach's operettas.

But where was " Milord l'Arsouille "? He was a truly remarkable phenomenon. The man whom the crowds believed to be Lord Seymour was not really Lord Seymour at all, though scarcely anybody knew it, but an unfortunate young man of the name of La Battue. La Battue was the illegitimate son of an Englishman. He had inherited a fortune upon his father's death and now sought to purchase a cheap popularity by extravagant acts of folly. Apart from his prodigality at carnival time, he gave magnificent balls and paraded his various mistresses through the streets of Paris, disguised as odalisques. But in spite of all his efforts to lend an aura to the name of La Battue, the cries of " *Vive milord l'Arsouille!* " were all he ever achieved. The people had seemed to see through his pretensions, and in the end he had no longer been able to bear being continually mistaken for Lord Seymour, and had retired to Naples a year before, disillusioned and suffering from venereal disease; with the result that this year the masked throng waited in vain for their Crœsus. His windows remained shut and no largesse was flung to the crowd from his big carriage.

Lord Seymour himself, notwithstanding his wealth, would have been the last person to think of showering gold upon a crowd in the street. In spite of all his eccentricities, he differed widely from the figure that had been made of him. Legend had turned him into an incorrigible madcap, but in reality he was a splenetic, gloomy man whose most notable trait was a passion for sport. It was the latter, as well as the Anglomania prevalent in Paris at the time, that he had to thank for the role of *arbiter elegantiarum* that he played among the dandies. It was he who prompted them to an appreciation of the propriety of cigar-smoking. He was also a joint founder of the Jockey Club, and the armory at his house had developed into a kind of sporting academy. On top of this his biceps, according to contemporary reports, were as thick as a girl's waist. When any man of fashion caught a glimpse of them, the sight filled him with astonishment and dismay.

Even more intimidating than his powerful physique was the mind controlling it. Lord Seymour, in spite of all his frivolity, was a misanthrope — he hated people because he was perpetually afraid that they were duping him, and the practical jokes that he played were peculiar. The kind of thing that gave him pleasure was, for instance, to cause a guest unwittingly to swallow an emetic; or to give money to a man in want under conditions that were bound to torture and humiliate him. Such jokes were both crude and childish. But the alchemy of popular imagination had taken hold of Lord Seymour and fused him and La Battue into one, transforming the combination into a Puck, an Ariel.

When darkness fell the streets emptied, and very soon afterwards the masked balls started at all the theaters. The most famous, or rather the most notorious, was that at the Théâtre des Variétés. All the leading spirits of the carnival would gather there in fancy dress — rich man and poor man, streetwalker and student, actress and grisette. The reason why the ball at the Variétés was chosen by this extremely mixed throng was that it offered certain irresistible attractions, such as could not fail to appeal to Offenbach and his companions. The conductor at the Variétés was Musard, and they danced the cancan there.

Anyone looking today at illustrations of the masked balls of the time of Louis-Philippe will scarcely understand the enthusiasm and the excitement which they aroused. So many outlets for mass excitement have since been exploited that the old prints give the impression of very tame affairs indeed. They were nothing of the sort. They were no tamer than the old stagecoaches, which in some circumstances were very fast.

A few years ago a film was produced showing Napoleon hurrying to some distant theater of war in his traveling-coach. In miles per hour his speed was certainly very moderate. But what with mounted orderlies continually galloping up to him and galloping away again, and the Emperor himself opening dispatches and reading them and continually handing out orders without interrupting his journey for a single moment, the spectator received the impression that he was indeed covering the ground at enormous speed. Musard's masked balls must have been just as dynamic as Napoleon's progress. Writer after writer spoke of them as something infernal, using terms one would associate with some delirious event in which horror was mingled with delight. One eyewitness compared them to " civil war," and " massacre." Another spoke of the " howling of panthers," and a " gaiety that might easily be taken for frenzy."

The cancan danced at these witches' sabbaths was then only a few years old. It traced its descent back to a dance indulged in by the patrons of certains haunts that lay not only at the fringes of the city but at the fringes of society. It appears to have been introduced to these haunts by soldiers from Algeria, and doubtless it would never have been seen outside the low taverns that were its real home had not the *jeunesse dorée* adopted it in their pursuit of sensation. Tired of the everlasting round dances, the elegance of which had worn thin, they had taken with delight to the partly wild, partly indecent movements of the cancan, which they had adapted to their own purposes.

In 1832, the cholera year, a party, apparently led by " Milord l'Arsouille," alias La Battue, went to the Théâtre des Variétés and danced the cancan before the delighted throng. The result was a terrific scandal, with threats of police intervention. " The cancan, just like a new religion, did not spread without persecution," wrote Count d'Alton-Shée, one of the chief participants in its introduction, in a volume of reminiscences.

But the cancan came into favor in spite of the police. The Government may have regarded it as a not unwelcome safety-valve for riotous spirits.

The first law of the masked balls at the Théâtre des Variétés was riotousness. Sometimes a gang would gather at the top of the broad staircase that led from the dress-circle down to the dance-floor, link arms, and dash down the steps, sweeping aside everybody in their path. But incidents of that kind faded into insignificance compared with the cancan itself, the figures of which kept emerging from the general confusion.

" The couples dance it indecently close together, so close that even involuntary movements are almost inevitably improper," a German traveler named Ludwig Rellstab wrote, his tongue loosened by indignation. " But when one sees with what gestures and movements of the body the masked men approach the masked women, press close to them, and actually throw them backwards and forwards between themselves to the accompaniment of continual acclamation and laughter and ribald jokes, one can only be filled with disgust; nay, more, with horror and revulsion at this mass depravity, this flouting of all morality and shame. . . ."

Would that that had been all that Rellstab had to complain of! But, alas, he was compelled in consternation to confess that the cancan did not end there. It was capable of yet further depths of depravity.

" The beat of the music is hastened, the dancers' movements

become more rapid, more animated, more aggressive; and finally
the *contredanse* evolves into a great gallop, in which the dancers
form into double pairs, four in a row, and gallop madly round
the floor. Though at this stage individual indecent movements
are seen no longer, the dancers' behavior and facial expression
bear witness to a more intense voluptuousness, and the whole
effect of this gallop as it grows wilder and wilder is one of shocking bacchanalian license. For the music gets quicker and quicker,
until one finally sees masked women, like ecstatic mænads, with
flushed cheeks, breathlessly heaving breasts, parched lips, and
half-undone, flying hair, careering round the room, less on their
feet than being dragged along bodily, until with the last chord
they collapse breathlessly on the nearest seat."

The magician at the wave of whose wand these orgies were
kindled was Musard.

All revolutionary epochs throw up men who seem to be endowed with an instinctive power of responding to the heart-beats
of the mob, enabling them to play upon their emotions at will.
Musard, Napoléon Musard, or the great Musard, as he was also
called, was one of these. He had started as an orchestra violinist,
became a dance-music composer, and worked successfully for a
long time in London. He had then returned to Paris and quickly
made a name for himself as musical director of the balls and concerts at the Variétés. He was a little man, with a yellow, pock-
marked face, always dressed in black. He was always untidy and
unkempt. His grotesque appearance, however, actually promoted
his popularity, and at Christmas pastry-cooks used to make little
figures of Musard out of chocolate and gingerbread, and these
were eaten by the thousands. The greed with which the public
devoured them was in exact proportion to the impetuosity of his
sway.

A poet dedicated to him the lines:

Ce Musard infernal
C'est Satan qui conduit le bal!

Indeed, when he seized his baton he cast a spell that could only derive its force from the powers of the underworld. The music that he played was generally familiar. He would play extracts from *Robert le Diable* or other famous operas. But, torn from their context, in Musard's hands they seemed to acquire a new and independent existence, transformed into infernal quadrilles and gallops.

When Musard conducted, it was as though the elements were unleashed. While the tempest was at its height he would suddenly feel the need to show his power over it. He would spring to his feet, fling his magic wand to the ground, and for the first time show himself in all his greatness. Having abandoned his weapon, instead of giving up, he would resort to measures that were indeed remarkable. He would smash the stool on which he had been sitting, or walk to the edge of the platform and fire a pistol into the air. His satellites would seem to have been awaiting this signal for their ecstasy to reach its climax, and pandemonium would break loose. And Musard, Napoléon Musard, the great Musard, would be carried shoulder-high over the crowd of the possessed.

" That after a night like that the members of this bacchanalian throng should be utterly prostrate, mentally and physically, in the real sense of the word, is but the most immediate, more inevitable, and least grave consequence," Rellstab declared. " What is far more serious is that their whole moral and physical being is poisoned in the heyday of their youth."

The truth, however, was that they were not immediately poisoned, nor were they all prostrate next morning. On the contrary, Lord Seymour — the real one — Count d'Alton-Shée and others of their circle left the ball on the last night just as it was ending in order to go in the pale light of the dawn of Ash Wednesday to La Courtille, a high-lying suburb to the east of Paris, where there were innumerable taverns and places of amusement. Here, in accordance with annual ritual, the last dance began, at about six o'clock in the morning. This was something the young men about town did not want to miss, a sight to delight any connoisseur of human aberration. Groups of drunken dancers would waltz all the way from the top of the hill back into the city, stopping at all the taverns to right and to left, making the morning hideous with their clamor, and disregarding the daylight that pitilessly showed up their bedraggled fancy dress. By sharing in these saturnalia the gentlemen of the Jockey Club believed themselves to be setting a seal on their own higher profligacy. The dancers took four hours to wend their way from La Courtille to the boulevard du Temple, where they dispersed. Then, and only then, was it time for the dandies to go home and go to bed. But the same evening, freshly polished up and in clean white gloves, they turned up again in full force at the Café de Paris.

CHAPTER IV

THE FIRST WALTZ

MUCH as Offenbach disliked solitude and introspection, there were times when he could not avoid them; and when carnival was over, it was impossible for him not to be brought up against himself. The ecstasy of the last three days had reached such heights that those who had succumbed to its fever had been transported to realms far beyond the banality of every day. But now he had come to the end of the parabola — to land in the desolation of loneliness.

A document dating from Offenbach's old age gives us some clue to what loneliness meant to him when he was a lad of sixteen. Solitary again, his mind harked back to his youth in Paris and to the consolation he had derived from a tune of his childhood. It had been sung to him by his mother and sisters, as a lullaby to rock him to sleep, a slow, gentle waltz, of which he could only remember the first eight bars. Perhaps he had always fallen asleep at that point, or perhaps that was all of it that they knew themselves. But the poor fragment had the gift of conjuring up many memories.

" Those eight bars formed a whole world in themselves," he wrote. " When they came into my mind, I saw my father's house and heard the voices of my dear ones at home, for whom I longed. Exiled in Paris, where I earned my living as a cellist at the Opéra-Comique at an age at which other advanced children are just entering the fifth class, I was carefree about the future, but yearned for the past. Often I found the loneliness very bitter, and that waltz ended by taking on quite extraordinary dimensions in my life. It ceased to be an ordinary waltz and became almost a prayer, which I hummed to myself from morning to night, not as a prayer addressed to heaven, but because, when I played it, it seemed to me that my dear ones heard me, and then, when it returned to my mind later, I could have sworn that they were answering me."

This was a certain sign that Paris had not responded to the young man's deepest aspirations. Whether it was that friends failed him, or that he had some unhappy calf-love, or that the city and all its people seemed unfriendly, one cannot help concluding, if one is to judge by the intensity of his homesickness, that he went through a period of suffering and mental crisis, doubtless intensified by gloomy thoughts about his present and future prospects.

To be sure, Halévy had written a letter to his father, praising, both Jules and himself, declaring among other things that Jacques promised one day to earn laurels as a composer. His father would have liked to put the letter up in a public place for all the people of Cologne to see. But hopes of a glittering future did not relieve Jacques of the necessity of earning his living, and he found his bondage increasingly difficult to bear.

" During the three years I was riveted to my place in the orchestra, I was so discontented and unhappy," he wrote many years afterwards, " and I understand so well the irritation of rehearsing under an arrogant composer, that I have always regarded it as my duty to treat the artists to whom the performance of my music has been entrusted as gently and decently as possible." It was no wonder that he sought desperately for a way of escape from the bondage to which his poverty condemned him. For the time being, he could see one way only, to try his hand at composing dance music.

Not only was there a big demand for dance music, but the work was to his taste; it might enable him to make a name for himself quickly and become financially independent. Incidentally Seligmann, whose aspiration was also to escape as quickly as possible from the orchestra, had also recently started taking lessons in composition from Halévy.

This period in Offenbach's career coincided with the rise to notoriety of the cancan. Revolutionary-minded romantics used the dance to express their derision and contempt for the sanctimonious social conventions of the new regime, and for Louis-Philippe and his dynastic ambitions — the sorry result of their fighting at the barricades; while the young scions of the Legitimist aristocracy used it to show their disdain for the court balls and the bankers who attended them.

These young people, however, were careful not to become involved in any political agitation likely to prove dangerous; they were satisfied to turn ostentatious backs upon the regime, and to live their own Bohemian lives. Exiles in their own country, they devoted themselves to a life of pleasure as a way of escape from the shams all round them. Most of them had enough money to afford this, and so the cancan, into which their thwarted energies were directed, fulfilled a definite social function by providing an outlet for their hostility and a means of expression for their irony and their contempt.

One of the first to notice this was Heinrich Heine. " It sometimes seems to me," he wrote, " as if the cancan dancers . . . pour scorn on all those things that are held to be noblest and holiest in life, but which are so often exploited at the hands of the crafty and made ridiculous at the hands of blockheads that the people no longer believes in them as it used to in the old days. The people has so lost faith in the high ideals of which our political and literary Tartufes prate so much that they see in them nothing but empty phrases — *blague* as their saying is. This comfortless outlook is illustrated by Robert Macaire; [1] it is illustrated likewise by the popular dances, which must be regarded as the spirit of Robert Macaire put into mime. Anyone acquainted with

[1] Robert Macaire was the hero of an enormously successful play of the same name, first performed in Paris in 1834. It showed with complete cynicism that so-called leaders of society were often just as great rogues as the self-confessed rogue Macaire himself. Macaire had become a legendary figure.

the latter will be able to form some idea of these indescribable dances, which are satires not only of sex and society, but of everything that is good and beautiful, of all enthusiasms, patriotism, loyalty, faith, family feeling, heroism, and religion."

Heine exaggerated in this fashion because he forgot to take account of the French satirical spirit. Love of satire is a very French characteristic. But he saw plainly that the cancan was aimed at the destruction of false idols and the pricking of bubble reputations.

In later years Offenbach's operettas were to be aimed at that same thing. Offenbach was imbued with the same satirical spirit. It might therefore have been expected that he would succumb to the cancan immediately on making its acquaintance.

Nothing of the sort occurred. He passed the cancan by without even suspecting that he had anything in common with it. The reason was that he met it in its uncouth and primitive form, which by its impropriety still betrayed its obscure and dubious origin.

Crudity was incapable of appealing to Offenbach, for though satire was second nature to him, and satire was part of the cancan's function, its directness was contrary to his nature. Moreover, unlike the Bohemians, he did not live a sheltered life outside the bourgeois society of the time. He did not take that society very seriously, but he had to feel protected by it before he could make fun of it.

Fear of being driven from the safe, familiar world must certainly have intensified his homesickness, and the cancan was not the least of the things that awakened his longing for the tenderness of home. When the wild uproar of the dancing hordes surged over him, all he could do was to clutch like a drowning man at the old waltz-tune dating from his childhood.

It was not, however, a very substantial aid, and the need for something stronger may perhaps have fortified him in his decision to compose waltzes.

The waltz, which had once been held in as ill repute as the

cancan. was now, had long since conquered all grades of society. In spite of the reserve imposed in the faubourg Saint-Germain, it was danced in the exclusive drawing-rooms of the nobility as enthusiastically as at the public balls in winter and at the *café-concerts* in summer.

Thanks to the prosperity of the middle class, *café-concerts,* which combined music, dancing, refreshment, shelter, and fresh air, became more and more popular. The best proof of this was that Musard, who possessed an almost diabolical business flair, was opening a kind of concert hall on the boulevard Montmartre at the end of the year, on a site on which there were a number of fine old trees. According to rumor some of the trees were actually to be preserved inside the hall.

Musard, the lord of quadrilles and gallops, was certainly not the right man for such ethereal products as waltzes, apart from the fact that Offenbach and he were not congenial characters. So the young composer was compelled to look elsewhere. He had the not entirely unqualified good fortune of lighting upon Jullien, the twenty-four-year-old conductor and composer, who was concert director at the Jardin Turc and had risen during the summer like a comet in the skies.

The Jardin Turc was situated in the boulevard du Temple and had been well known for a long time. Its garden contained a café decorated in Oriental style, and as long as anybody could remember, it had been patronized by the innumerable respectable *rentiers* of the neighborhood, who enjoyed sitting over their cups of coffee on the elevated garden terrace, which afforded a view of the whole boulevard. But M. Besson, the proprietor, had introduced concerts two or three years before, and ever since then their peace had been somewhat disturbed — a fact which gave very much more pleasure to their daughters than it did to them. For the Jardin Turc developed from a sleepy backwater into a place of repute, and smart society began to frequent it. M. Besson knew that stopping still meant going back, and as he was bursting with enterprise he had decided to open the summer season of 1836 with a flourish, regardless of expense. He had modernized his garden, sacked his old conductor, increased his orchestra to sixty, and put Jullien in charge of it.

" If you want to see a handsome man, go and eat an ice in the Jardin Turc at Jullien's feet," was the saying in Paris. " But if you want to hear a musician, go and listen to Musard! " The slight injustice that this epigram did to Jullien must be put down to male irritation at female hero-worship of Jullien. The women had good reason to lose their hearts to him, for although, strictly speaking, he was not of divine descent, but the son of a military bandsman, he possessed dazzling good looks. There was something completely unapproachable about him, as though he were kept in a glass case. He might have been a hairdresser's or, still better, a tailor's dummy, for he owed his fetching appearance not only to hair so crimped and singed that it looked like a wig and to mustaches so beautiful that they almost seemed artificial, but to the perpetual smile that hovered about his features and the fantastic care and devotion he lavished upon the rest of his person. He always wore a suit cut in the very latest fashion, a sparkling diamond tie-pin, and yellow gloves — these last to avoid the painful impression that might have been created by the sight of his bare hands.

To see this Adonis conducting was a sight in itself. Now he would comport himself as daintily as a dancer interpreting music by the graceful and sinewy movements of his body; now he would assume the ferocity of a general on parade, picking out some unfortunate member of the orchestra and glaring at him irascibly as though suspecting some fault. But his idiosyncrasies as a conductor faded into insignificance in comparison with the sensation caused by his artistic creations. Almost immediately after his debut at the Jardin Turc a quadrille of his, adapted from Meyerbeer's exceedingly popular *Les Huguenots,* created a furore. All Paris flocked to the boulevard du Temple to hear it, M. Besson rubbed his hands, and people said that Jullien was going to put Musard in the shade.

There was no doubt that that was his ambition. Jullien introduced whole artillery salvos in answer to Musard's pistol-shots, and whatever Musard did, he tried to go one better. His standards were purely quantitative. But the public were probably attracted less by the sheer volume of sound than by Jullien's unusual combination of effects.

Jullien was one of the first to realize that the pleasure-seeking public desires the satisfaction of all its senses at once, and to draw practical conclusions from this discovery. He was a spiritual predecessor of the modern revue-producer, and to the acoustic thrills of his quadrilles he added the optical thrills of fireworks. The stentorian playing of the orchestra, interpolated with singing and continual cries and bangs, would be accompanied by a display of red, yellow, and green light-effects, in the midst of which Jullien himself appeared in all the glory of his chic. He provided such a violent contrast to the strident medley of sounds and colors that the bewildered audience took their conductor for a supernatural apparition in gloves. This remarkable attraction maintained its place in the program for weeks and was followed by a quadrille which roused a good deal of interest because the baying of a pack of hounds was very successfully imitated in it. A " sound-picture " entitled *Christmas Night at Rome* came next, showing a papal procession; Jullien was, of course, lavish with the chiming of bells in this show-piece, to say nothing of the subsidiary aid of illuminations.

Towards the end of the summer season Offenbach, perhaps with the aid of a recommendation from Halévy, whose composition classes Jullien had attended, succeeded in having a number of waltz-suites accepted and played at the Jardin Turc. One of them, the suite *Fleurs d'hiver,* was popular enough to be played at the Opéra and Opéra-Comique balls during the following winter. The musical paper *Le Ménestrel* declared that Offenbach was a talented young man. Shortly afterwards, however, it qualified this praise by some caustic remarks, implying that his behavior was that of a young man who believed himself to be on

Courtesy, Rischgitz

OFFENBACH
Caricature by Gill

Courtesy, Rischgitz

GRAND STAIRCASE OF THE PARIS OPÉRA

the point of dethroning Strauss and Lanner. But Offenbach was not to be defeated by a little sarcasm, and only applied himself the more readily to the work of composition. At the reopening of the Jardin Turc for the summer season of 1837 he was, of course, promptly on the spot.

The indefatigable M. Besson had a surprise in store for his clients this season. He had turned part of his garden into a subterranean covered gallery, illuminated by brilliant gaslight — gaslight being, of course, the very latest thing. This novelty, superimposed upon the magnetic attraction exercised by Jullien, resulted in the Jardin Turc becoming positively fashionable. Even though the dandies for some reason or other avoided the establishment, Offenbach had every reason to be thoroughly satisfied with the crowd that listened to his waltz *Rebecca* one fine June evening, walking up and down under the shady foliage or in the covered gallery.

But before Offenbach had time to enjoy his success the cup was dashed from his lips. His waltz was denounced by *Le Ménestrel* in no uncertain terms. Why? Because in composing it he had used tunes from Jewish religious ritual. " Was it absolutely necessary to burlesque melodies sanctified by religious observance in a wanton waltz? Not in the least. But nowadays it is necessary at all costs to be original." Such was the reproof administered by *Le Ménestrel*.

Offenbach undoubt lly aspired to early success, but he was certainly unconscious of having committed sacrilege. Only a year before, the Jardin Turc orchestra had played a piece of music that had been intended to represent the conflict between religious and earthly joys, and had coupled the *Dies Iræ* with a dance tune; so Offenbach was by no means original in combining the sacred and the profane. Certainly there was one big difference between Offenbach's waltz and Jullien's bravura piece of the year before. Offenbach did not leave religious melodies as religious melodies, but turned them into dance music; so that it was true that music that was sacred to the devout was converted to purposes of pro-

fane delight. But this lack of scruple was entirely consistent with
the traditions in which the young Offenbach had been reared.
Had his father ever had any hesitation in singing tunes from the
Freischütz in the synagogue?

The principal attraction of the season was not, of course, Offenbach's waltzes, but *Balthasar's Feast,* a most sensational production with which Jullien wished to outdo his quadrille from *Les
Huguenots* of the year before. But the higher he aspired, the
lower he fell. The chief role in his latest creation devolved upon
seven brilliantly colored transparents which gleamed so fantasti-
cally in the darkness that Jullien's orchestra, instead of being the
chief attraction, sank to being merely an accompaniment.

The construction of the device that produced this feast for the
eyes, which was called a " nocturnorama," had cost much breaking of heads. Jullien's artistic aberrations thus at least promoted
technical progress, which was just then shyly emerging from its
shell.

Almost contemporary with the appearance of the " nocturnorama " at the Jardin Turc, the first train traveled on the new railway between Paris and Saint-Germain. One of the passengers,
who remembered the experience with alarm to the end of his
days, recalled that for nearly one minute the train had traveled in
complete darkness. And gas-lamps started shedding luster all
along the Boulevards, at the same time showing up the rags of
innumerable beggars.

At the end of the summer season Offenbach had the good fortune to find suitable winter quarters for his waltzes, at the newly
started Concerts Saint-Honoré, at which both classical and dance
music were regularly played. The classical items were in charge
of Valentino, the stern Valentino who had conducted at the
Opéra-Comique only a year before and had imposed one fine
after another upon the unfortunate Offenbach. Thus old acquaintance was renewed.

Waltzes were the most popular dances in Paris that winter;
particularly Viennese waltzes, by reason of the fact that Johann

Strauss the elder conducted for several months in Paris that year. He won triumph after triumph. Auber threw him bunches of violets, Paganini shook hands with him, and the public waltzed. Offenbach and his music had chanced upon a favorable tide.

Nevertheless it became plain that waltzes alone would not be enough to give him his freedom; on the other hand it was absolutely vital for him to be free if he were ever to get to the top. So he made up his mind to leave the Opéra-Comique.

The decision does not seem to have been a very difficult one. Did a breach with Jullien follow the breach with the Opéra-Comique? Whether it did or no, the two saw each other no more. So far as Offenbach's future career was concerned, this was no loss. Instead of putting Musard, who had meanwhile become conductor of the Opéra balls, into the shade, his star visibly declined; and in 1838 he had to flee from Paris because of his debts. He settled in London, where he gave magnificent concerts and captivated the most prudish ladies by the inimitable charm with which he changed the gloves which a manservant brought him on a gilt tray at intervals throughout the evening. When London grew tired of him he went on tour, giving concerts in Scotland, Ireland, and America. He then returned to London and composed an opera, *Peter the Great,* which was a complete fiasco, and eventually ended up in Paris again, where he died mentally deranged in the heyday of the Second Empire.

CHAPTER V

THE SALONS

Offenbach took a big risk in giving up his appointment at the
Opéra-Comique without having anything else in view. He might
easily have found himself in the gutter had he not at the critical
moment made the acquaintance of a fellow-countryman, Friedrich von Flotow.

Flotow was the composer of the opera *Martha,* which is still
played today. It contains the popular Irish song *The Last Rose of
Summer.* Flotow was seven years older than Offenbach and came
of an ancient and aristocratic family in Mecklenburg, which had
been sufficiently broad-minded to allow him to become a musician. Like Offenbach he had received his artistic training in
Paris, where he had been living for nearly ten years. But his ap-
prenticeship had been spent under infinitely more favorable conditions. Offenbach possessed nothing in the world except his
talent, and all the dice seemed loaded against him, whereas
Flotow, ever since his arrival in Paris, had basked in an atmosphere of luxury and success; and he had talent into the bargain.
He was an extremely cultured young man, with not a financial
care in the world; and his name and his attractive personality
gave him the entrée everywhere. His compositions delighted the
granddaughters of the aged Lafayette, and he was a constant
visitor at innumerable aristocratic households, at which he played
the piano, talked, and made the acquaintance of scores of celebrities. Thus he was present, for example, on the memorable occasion at the Marquis de Custine's when George Sand, who arrived
in the company of Chopin, astonished everybody by asking for

a cigar and smoking it, strolling up and down in the garden.

Apart from his connections in high society, Flotow had a circle of intimate friends, among whom were a number of talented writers and composers. In short, he was a child of fortune whom the world took pleasure in spoiling. Only a year earlier a light opera of his had been produced at the Count de Castellane's private theater, to the unanimous applause of the elect.

Right at the beginning of their acquaintance Offenbach confided to him the details of his highly precarious financial state. He had only one pupil, and his father could only afford to send him a tiny allowance. In short, it was clear that he had barely enough to live on. To Flotow such poverty was unintelligible. Why did not Offenbach, like so many other musicians in a similar situation, simply give a concert? The doleful answer was that nobody knew him. Since he had not the entrée to any of the Paris salons, this was intelligible enough. Flotow could very well understand that. No one knew better than he how important the salons were for a man's career. It was certain that no young musician could count on success without frequenting them.

The salons in the time of Louis-Philippe still exercised an enormous influence. The complicated modern apparatus of publicity was only in the embryo stage, and to a considerable extent the salons still performed its functions. The salons constituted a world in themselves, with widespread ramifications.

In this world, as in the Restoration period, the nobility predominated. As soon as they recognized that the regime of Louis-Philippe was likely to endure, they had given up sulking in their châteaux, reopened their town houses, and even started giving parties again, under pressure from the younger generation, which had no intention of sacrificing its whole existence to cultivating regret for past glories.

The richer members of the bourgeoisie, wishing to extend their political victories into the social sphere, competed with them. Every box they secured at the Opéra was a trophy, each salon they opened was a fortress established on newly conquered soil.

The invasion of the bankers excited the hostility of the Legitimists of the faubourg Saint-Germain, who refused to receive
them, and hostilities degenerated into a protracted war of position. The nobility ridiculed the rising power of the bourgeoisie
but envied it, while the bourgeoisie ridiculed the nobility but
imitated them.

In spite of the tension between the two camps, however, there
was constant fraternization. As a consequence of the impover-
ishment of many feudal families on the one hand and the social
ascent of many bourgeois parvenus on the other, frequent inter-
marriages took place. The nobility stigmatized these as *mésalliances,* but willingly contracted them in order to restore the
luster of their tarnished coronets. Nevertheless the stock of the
nobility sank steadily during the July Monarchy. Whether because the bourgeoisie now felt themselves securely in the saddle
or because the supply of titles exceeded the demand, the new
rulers of society ceased finding it necessary to sacrifice a large
capital sum to secure their daughters' happiness. They found it
possible to acquire counts or barons as sons-in-law by guarantee-
ing them an annual income — on the installment plan, so to
speak.

The natural consequence of these mixed marriages was a re-
inforcement of the social conventions common to both sides.
The general rule was to go out as little as possible. But although the nobility followed the English fashion in professing
to despise domesticity, enormous gatherings in the salons were
highly popular.

The vogue for " routs," which had also been imported from
London, served to gratify this passion. A fashionable hostess
would invite hundreds of people to her house. Many of her guests
would, of course, be well known to her, but others would be
comparatively unknown. She in effect turned her home into a
kind of club, filling it with card-tables at which her guests would
sit and gamble without troubling very much about her. This
was what was called a " rout." It seems, however, that the social

round soon became altogether too overwhelming, for efforts were made to limit it by arranging fixed visiting-days.

The supreme ambition of the hostess of every salon was to offer her guests music. Music was the vogue. There was a universal obsession with it. A few political salons still survived, of course, and at these Thiers and Guizot were preferred to Meyerbeer and Rossini; and in some circles the music was so good that it actually seemed to be provided for its own sake. For instance, only musicians of real distinction were to be heard at Mme Orfila's, at Princess Belgiojoso's, at Countess Merlin's, and at Herr Kalkbrenner's (he was a German). The majority of the salons were not so particular, however. They did not bother their heads too much about whether the music was good or bad. The great thing was to provide music of some sort, and that was enough. Without music an evening would have been dreary and desolate.

The thing reached the proportions of an epidemic. Heine complained bitterly about it, and he regarded going to an evening party as a martyrdom. " Bands of youthful dilettanti, of whom one has learned by experience to expect the very worst, perform in every key and on all the instruments that have ever been invented," he wrote.

But what was often an ordeal for the consumers was of inestimable benefit to the producers. Once a musician had succeeded in gaining a foothold at a musical *soirée* such as was given by practically every rich or well-to-do family, the way to the salons lay open, and at the end of it there lay the dazzling prospect of the concert platform and fame as a virtuoso. The process was almost automatic. Flotow described it with the matter-of-factness of a kitchen recipe.

" One makes several appearances in the course of the winter," he wrote in his memoirs, " and then, at the beginning of Lent, one announces a concert and sends a dozen high-priced tickets, generally at ten francs, to the hostess of every salon at which one has played. That is the usual practice. It practically never happens that all, or even any, of the tickets are sent back. In fact often, when the musician is very popular, one or other household will apply for two or three times as many tickets as have been sent. The cost of such a concert is negligible. It is given on a profit-sharing basis, takes place in daylight, which saves the expense of lighting, and no heating is necessary, because the audience turn up in their outdoor clothes. Placards at street-corners are unnecessary, and in any case would serve no purpose. Nor is there any need for a box-office, and there is hardly even any need to have an attendant on duty at the door to collect the tickets. . . . The audience consist of habitués of the various salons and always give the virtuosos, whom they have already met, and the music that they play, most of which they already know, the warmest possible reception. Any artist who is ambitious can easily maintain himself in Paris in this agreeable fashion, without wasting much time or trouble over it."

That, under ideal conditions, was how things panned out. Flotow omitted, however, to add that many hostesses turned the ruling passion to their own advantage. They devised a system of blackmail that has often been exploited since. Mme X, for example, having two unmarried daughters to dispose of, would be particularly anxious to fill her salon. How was she to lure people to her house? The best bait would be a concert. Mme X therefore would decide to imitate high society and arrange a musical evening. The difficulty, however, was that the best musicians were expensive, and Mme X was determined not to pay a penny to anybody. Her policy would therefore be to attract ambitious beginners and unrecognized geniuses, all panting for recognition and an audience. She would promise them both, and pupils into the bargain; with the result that they thought themselves so lucky to be allowed to play at her house that they would never even mention the subject of remuneration. But instead of doing the right thing and quietly disappearing after their evening of triumph in her salon, the obstinate fellows would ungratefully survive and, in conformity with Flotow's recipe, impudently send her a dozen or so tickets for a concert arranged for their own benefit. This would, of course, cause Mme X, who after all was human, a good deal of chagrin. But it took more than that to make her depart from her economic principles. As a patron of the poor artist she would press all her visitors to buy tickets, and once more extricate herself from the quandary at no expense. In this mean but ingenious fashion she contrived to have her concert for nothing.

With all his worldliness, Flotow was a good-natured and helpful young man. When Offenbach opened his heart to him, he wasted no time on long discussions as to how admission to the best houses might theoretically be obtained, but declared forthwith that he would himself introduce him to all the salons which he frequented. He took Offenbach under his wing like a brother. Fortunately the next musical evening at which he was due to take part was at the house of the Countess Bertin de Vaux, whose *soirées* were considered to be serious artistic occasions. So no time need be lost. The Countess lent a favorable ear to Flotow's loyal propaganda. Her only stipulation was that his friend must content himself with a short piece on this occasion, as the program was already complete.

Although the Countess lived apart from her husband, who as the owner of the *Journal des Débats* and aide-de-camp to Louis-Philippe was a highly influential person, her house was a very important one. Offenbach was in the seventh heaven of delight. Unfortunately, when he and Flotow considered his repertoire, it transpired that all he had available were a few longish concert-pieces by Romberg. These would not possibly do. But he and Flotow were not composers for nothing. They set to and in a very short time had produced first one and then another sequence of harmonious trifles for piano and cello. The work was genuine collaboration. In the course of it Flotow could not sufficiently admire Offenbach's extraordinary facility at producing agreeable tunes. Flotow himself was a decided eclectic, with a definite tendency to work in collaboration with others.

The night of the *soirée* arrived. It was the first fashionable gathering that Offenbach had ever attended. He was only nineteen years old, and his gawky limbs must certainly have troubled him. But Flotow was at the piano, and his cello, that massive but trusty instrument, that lost all its clumsiness under his skillful manipulation, was in his hands. No sooner had he started playing than all timidity and awkwardness vanished. He did not feel in the least abashed by the flunkeys, the glittering suite of rooms, the elegant ladies and gentlemen, all the appurtenances, in fact, which would probably have crushed the spirit of most novices. On the contrary, they inspired him. For in the midst of the social hum he was in his element, and without a buzz of conversation all around him he lacked the air to breathe and to soar in.

" My friend was a great success," Flotow briefly noted in his memoirs, already quoted from, " and very soon he was a favorite at the house of the Countess de Vaux." After his debut at the Countess's, Offenbach made his bow at innumerable other salons in Flotow's company; they had to repeat their amiable little duet more than a hundred times. However small might be the artistic satisfaction to be derived from this pilgrimage, from the practical point of view it was invaluable. Offenbach learned to know the ways of high society at first hand, acclimatized himself to the changeable weather of the salon world, and assimilated an unlimited variety of situations, scenes, and characters with which he later populated the stage.

The most prominent feature of the scene that presented itself to his eyes in this new world to which he was introduced was the tremendous luxury that was developing, particularly among the wealthy bourgeoisie. The bankers, brokers, and merchants were getting richer and richer, and were gaining ground politically as well; and they wanted to enjoy their money and their power. What pleasure was there in possessions if they were not displayed? Ostentation became the fashion among the great and wealthy. Ostentation enhanced one's credit. They vied with one another in the splendor of their carriages, and transformed their dwellings into treasure-houses. The fundamental standard being the gold standard, they covered their walls and furniture with gilt. Consequently, when the chandeliers were lit in the evening — the chandeliers alone might cost anything up to twelve or fifteen thousand francs, — the whole place glittered and sparkled brilliantly. The chilly aspect of this magnificence was diminished by heavy curtains, which did not in the least detract from its splendor. The number of these fabulous draperies often provided a clue to the owner's income. They adorned the windows two or three deep and concealed doors and cupboards. In a good many houses there was certainly need for a curtain to be drawn over some things. Fashion decreed that the decorative scheme was not complete without a certain number of live animals. A pet dog would often be installed beside a sofa that had cost a hundred louis d'or, and tiny tortoises from Africa would reveal to the initiate that the family had a, friend or relative in Algiers, who kept them supplied with Arab burnooses and exotic perfumes.

The more at home Offenbach became in this atmosphere, the more plainly must he have become aware of the two rival trends at work in it. Both were the result of the fact that youth was offered no proper scope by the now securely consolidated regime of Louis-Philippe. It was always possible to earn money. But they had money in abundance, and earning more was not particularly attractive. It was possible to indulge in political opposition, either of the Right or of the Left, but the time for that either was over or had not yet come. As the Government was determined to avoid disputes with foreign countries, there was no chance of finding an outlet for their sense of frustration in a war. The result of all this was that the younger generation, in its restless searchings for an outlet for its pent-up energies, was thrown back upon its own resources.

One way was to plunge headlong into a life of pleasure, the devotees of which underwent the most extraordinary fatigues for its sake. During the season the day's work began with a big dinner followed by a concert and a ball. This would not always be the last stage of the evening's entertainment, for, in effect, the guests' main activities consisted in continually putting on and taking off their overcoats. At the conclusion of the winter campaign, instead of taking a well-earned rest, they tirelessly devoted themselves to a further round of pleasure, lasting well into the summer, when, with picnic parties added to their engagement lists, still greater demands were made on their time and energy.

Offenbach was brought into close contact with all this, even though he was not an active participant in it himself. But he had every opportunity of observing the game at close quarters. He saw the young dandies, who had no hesitation in entering a salon covered with dust and in dirty boots, and always made a bee-line for the smoking-room immediately after dinner — a form of behavior that in many circles was considered to be the height of smartness. He saw the society " lions," who by reason of their sensational achievements were the center of attraction at all the " routs " they condescended to attend, and, much to the annoyance of Mme de Girardin, were classed in the same category as the dandies. In one of her articles Mme de Girardin defined a " dandy " as " a man who wants to be noticed," while a " lion " was " one who is noticed." There were " lionesses " too.

Besides these Offenbach must necessarily have seen the innumerable young men, all looking exactly alike, half monkeys and half lap-dogs, who constituted the most harmless denizens of the salons and turned up at every function in herds, and whose main subject of conversation was the important question of whether they had been or were going to be present at other functions of a similar nature. " Were you at ——'s yesterday? " " Yes, I was. Frightful crush! Are you going to ——'s tonight? " " Yes. There'll be a terrible scrimmage there." And so on. The duration of the bombardment of question and answer which these forerunners of Bobinet and Gardefeu in Offenbach's *La Vie parisienne* kept up among themselves varied in exact proportion to the size of the reception they were attending.

While some made themselves slaves to pleasure in order to have something to do, or rather a substitute for something to do, others acted in a precisely opposite sense and compensated themselves for the impossibility of doing anything real in life by cultivating their inner sensibilities. They developed innumerable sentimental enthusiasms. Young poets were permitted to pose as geniuses even in the most aristocratic salons. Groups of young men and girls met to read the plays of Victor Hugo and the novels of George Sand and invariably showed themselves supremely affected by the experience.

This cultivation of somewhat facile emotionalism throws a light on the tremendous importance that music came to assume in the eyes of society. Its function, like that of romantic literature, was to compensate bourgeois youth, without embarrassing it politically, for the emptiness and meaningless of the atmosphere in which it lived — the atmosphere of the Golden Mean. The greater the outward triumph of materialism, the greater the inner need for emotional upsurgings. Music satisfied this yearning; not so much music in general as one form of it, the sentimental ballad, in particular. Sentimental ballads were the object of a positive cult, and in the salons there was no getting away from them. They plucked at one's heartstrings from behind the curtains, they sighed away into space past the gilded cornices, and reproduced the flood of emotion that wells up in a lover's breast. The lover in the ballad would marvel at the purity of his beloved's marble brow, ask himself why he should forever remain dumb and passive in her presence, or fervently beseech her to vouchsafe him a word to deliver him from his torturing uncertainties. A whole deluge of feeling was unloosed to vie with the flood of riches.

Like other satellites and dilettantes of the salons, Offenbach set to and turned out ballads of this sort.

A popular parody of them was current about this time. For the everlasting " I think of her " or " I think of thee " of the drawing-room ballad it substituted the refrain " I think of —

me." This base and commonplace sentiment, taken in conjunction with the yearning, languishing music, was extremely comic. Offenbach, however, was not responsible for it. His operettas, in which he ridiculed all these emotional orgies, still lay in the future. For the time being he was a naïve adherent of the popular pastoral school. This was perfectly natural and normal for his age. Two of his ballads were published by *Le Ménestrel,* which offered its readers one of these products of the salons every week. One of Offenbach's two contributions dealt dramatically with the theme of jealousy, while the other represented a series of fanciful visions imagined during a rustic idyl, their vagueness producing an extremely ladylike effect. This was not to be wondered at, for the words were by a certain Baroness de V. No doubt the name de Vaux was concealed behind that pseudonym. The composition of romantic ballads, in spite of their purely musical nature, incidentally often led to the consummation of romances of another kind.

Henceforward Offenbach often used the ballad-form. Ballads admitted of intimate personal expression, and the slightness of their construction probably attracted so determined an adversary of the sublime.

The fact that in other respects he set little value on the ballad as such is shown by a " critical causerie " he wrote in 1855. " At the daily sight of the 33,333,444,666,000 albums displayed in the windows of the music-shops," he wrote in disgust, " which have no other purpose than to beguile during the winter season the leisure of the salons dedicated to the ballad-cult, we may well exclaim: ' Album, why should I write anything for you? ' "

Offenbach's pilgrimage through the salons served its purpose. Before long he had so many patrons and patronesses that he was able to draw a correct conclusion from these favorable premises. He was not a man to hesitate a minute longer than was necessary when he could see a chance of success in the offing. Accordingly his first public concert took place at Pape's musical-instrument store at the end of January 1839 — earlier, that is, than Flotow had anticipated. Flotow, it will be remembered, had held out to him the prospect of being able to give a concert at the beginning of Lent. Jules took part in it too, and Jacques himself played a slow waltz of his own composition which was reminiscent of Chopin. The audience applauded, and *Le Ménestrel* praised his polished style.

Even Offenbach ought to have been satisfied. Instead he found himself confronted with a dilemma. Ought he to become a concert player or concentrate on the composition of waltzes and ballads? His real ambition was the theater. It was more than an ambition, it was a dream, an obsession that colored his whole existence. Under its influence he had never missed an opportunity of getting nearer to his goal. He had done his best to take advantage of the contacts brought him by his work at the Opéra-Comique, and in spite of his progress through the salons had steadily cultivated the society of singers and librettists. To do so cost him little effort. His cheerfulness, his good nature, his wit, and his mischief led him into the midst of theatrical Bohemia in the most natural way in the world. Whenever the initiates talked " shop " or discussed forthcoming productions he pricked up his ears. One day a crumb fell from the table which he instantly snapped up.

What an opportunity! He was commissioned to compose a number of items for a vaudeville piece, *Pascal et Chambord,* at the Palais Royal. According to the casual and cursory autobiographical notes that Offenbach left behind, it was Anicet Bourgeois, one of the two authors of the play, who asked him to do the work. This implies that he must already have had access to the inner circles of the theatrical world. For Bourgeois belonged to the vanguard of that shrewd band of commercial vaudeville writers who produced almost on a mass-production scale, generally in collaboration, employing methods as rationalized as those of Hollywood scenario-writers at the present day. Their work was a branch of industry rather than a profession. The plot of *Pascal et Chambord* included the usual love-story, this time placed in the period of the revolutionary wars, which enabled the current enthusiasm for Napoleon to be exploited at the conclusion. No words deserve to be wasted on it. All these vaudeville pieces contained songs, which were not just music-hall songs but were sung in the familiar operatic manner. To have special music composed for them was the very latest thing. This was a development that favored the rise of the operetta, for political satire had been one of the functions of vaudeville, and it was only waiting an opportunity to be revived.

The first night of *Pascal et Chambord* took place on March 2, 1839. It had turned out at rehearsals that Grassot, the popular comedian, had such a poor voice that Offenbach, greatly to his chagrin, had to cancel half his finale. Offenbach was on tenterhooks to know how his music would be received. With all the earnestness of his twenty years, he felt that his whole future depended on the outcome of the first performance. Not that his financial position was desperate now. Thanks to the salons, he had acquired a number of pupils in all parts of Paris, some of whom paid and some of whom did not. But long daily treks across Paris to give dull cello lessons were by no means the measure of his ambition. If *Pascal et Chambord* were a success . . .

It was not. Worse still, it was not even the sort of failure that is talked about. The audience remained perfectly unmoved, and the music evaporated into thin air. The piece had only a single echo. Grassot, whenever he met Offenbach in the street, would embrace him and sing at the top of his voice the last line of one of the songs in his part:

" The rascal can no longer escape me! "

Grassot was a comedian. But for Offenbach the fiasco was a bitter blow. The theater, which had been within his grasp, had eluded him, and his hopes of being able to make a living in Paris as a composer were, for the time being, over. If he did not take this failure over-tragically, it was because he already knew that he was born under a lucky star. True, luck was not to be relied on, and one could not dispense with one's own efforts. At the same time luck always kept something up its sleeve to surprise one with when one least expected it, and it might at any moment intervene to turn the greatest tragedy into the most riotous farce.

For instance, he had awakened one morning recently to discover that his total available capital amounted to five centimes. All day long he had been compelled to console himself with pleasurable anticipation of the dinner to which he had been invited — of course with his cello — by a certain Monsieur D. At last the longed-for moment arrived. When he rang the bell of Monsieur D.'s house, at which he turned up with a punctuality that can well be imagined, he was informed that the latter would unfortunately be unable to fulfill his engagement that evening. Perhaps the gentleman would care to do him and his wife the honor of calling in a week's time?

Offenbach had just sufficient strength left to reply that next week would suit him even better, and to stagger back to the Boulevards, with starvation staring him in the face. Near the Opéra arcade someone tapped him on the shoulder.

" Are you Monsieur Offenbach? "

" Yes."

" Please take these twenty francs."

The stranger explained that he owed this sum to Jules and asked him to be so good as to pass it on to him. Ten minutes after this unexpected development, which reminds one of the improbable happenings in *La Vie parisienne,* Offenbach was ensconced at the Café Anglais, convalescing with the aid of a partridge and a bottle of Saint-Julien. Doubtless he would never have invented the operetta had fate not beamed upon him from time to time, with the air of a prima donna graciously bestowing a favor upon one of her satellites.

The Palais Royal fiasco had a sobering effect on Offenbach. His theatrical ambitions had to be cast aside. His father's advice to remain loyal to his cello helped to reconcile him to this renunciation. Old Offenbach was a man of experience and dissuaded his son from flying too high, no doubt remembering the fate of Icarus. The young man accordingly remained upon earth and continued to frequent the salons and give lessons. He wrote several exercises for the cello at this time, thus showing that he took his duties as a music-master seriously. After all, renouncing a career as an opera-composer did not mean renouncing fame. Had he not already had his baptism of fire upon the concert platform? As he was apparently to be prevented from creating immortal masterpieces for the stage, he decided at least to make his name in the concert room.

Soon after the unlucky evening at the Palais Royal, Jacques and Jules went back to Cologne. Jacques had left home as a boy and came back as a man. His sister Julie describes their return:

" Mother went into the courtyard to meet her sons. Julius was the first to greet her with a kiss and a hug, while Jakob and his father greeted each other. Then he turned to his mother. ' But I don't know you! Are you my child? ' she exclaimed, and fainted. Jakob held her in his arms. ' Yes, mother. I am your child, your Jakob,' he reassured her."

How proud she must have felt at the concert her two sons gave at the big Cologne assembly rooms! Three months later they both went back to Paris. But after only ten months they returned to Cologne, this time in mourning. Twelve-year old Michel, the baby of the family, had succumbed to a sudden attack of typhoid fever, and their mother, unable to get over his death, was seriously ill herself. The doctor had said that her sons would be the best medicine for her, and they stayed with her for many months. Jacques exhausted his repertoire of jokes and pastimes in order to distract her and actually managed to make her smile, and she smiled so cheerfully that the brothers ventured to arrange a concert, the chief item being a *Grande Scène espagnole,* composed by Jacques in his parents' house. Spain was the spiritual home of the Paris Romantics; they believed a purer humanity was enshrined in that distant land. The Offenbachs' concert was highly praised by the *Kölnische Zeitung.* As though she had only been waiting for the satisfaction of knowing that her children were gaining the recognition that was their due, their mother died a week later. Jacques, like all young men of sensibility, broke into bad verse on the day of her death. The lines he wrote ended with the pious phrase: " God's will be done." His father, who also had a tendency to break into verse, contrived, from the depths of his sorrow and his hope, to compose a poem which he dedicated to his sons. Equipped with this effusion as with an amulet, they left Cologne for Paris at the end of November.

Thus the last bond that linked Offenbach with his boyhood was broken. That he was ripe for the separation is proved by two of his compositions dating from that year; the first was the *Boléro* from the *Grand Scène espagnole,* which delighted the Paris critics years later by its glowing passion, and the second was an entirely personal ballad, *Rends-moi mon âme.* The latter was dedicated to a friend, Roger, who later became famous as an operatic singer. He sang it so well that his singing of it survived in the memory of men who outlived Offenbach himself. These two compositions, so different in theme, exemplify the range of Offenbach's talent even at that time. Under a number of protective influences he had grown to maturity and was now ready to play an independent part in the world.

CHAPTER VI

THE BOULEVARDS, HOME
OF THE HOMELESS

Whenever Offenbach heard a concert was being arranged, he would hurry to ask for permission to play. As a rule this was readily granted, with no thought, however, of offering him any payment for his services. He was expected to be grateful for the opportunity of playing in public for nothing, so play for nothing he did. He was indefatigable, optimistic, importunate. In the course of his wanderings he picked up innumerable ditties, street-cries, hurdy-gurdy tunes, which mingled with the music effervescing in his own head. But eventually his health was affected, and once, when playing a languishing *adagio* in a drawing-room, he collapsed. The consequences of this mishap were far from disagreeable, for all the ladies present found it even more affecting than his playing. They gathered round him, palpitating with anxiety, fanned him with their elegant cambric handkerchiefs, and ended by nearly suffocating him. Among those present at this afflicting scene was a fellow-countryman of Offenbach's, also from Cologne. So envious was he of his rival's success that he dismissed the whole thing as a sham.

There would have been nothing surprising about it if it had been a sham. Duplicity of the kind was quite the usual thing. Paris was swarming with virtuosos, all of them consumed with ambition; the market was glutted, and competition so intense that extreme measures were necessary to draw attention to oneself and rise above the throng. *La Gazette musicale,* the leading mu-

sical paper, was lavish with personal details concerning the leading performers. For instance, in reporting a successful concert
given by one Döhler, at Marseille, it made great play with the
heart-rending pallor which was that pianist's legacy from a recent
illness. The description of Döhler's pallor produced the same
effect as Offenbach's unintentional fainting spell. Artists who did
not act as their own managers generally had a relative who took
charge of their press publicity for them, often the artist's own
father. One such father called at the office of *La Gazette musicale*
with a request that a story should be inserted describing some of
the noble traits in his son's character; his son, he stated, had given
a concert for the benefit of a poor widow and on another occasion had played for the benefit of a seventy-year-old schoolmaster
who had lost his only child. Unfortunately, however, the naïve
father admitted in the course of the interview that he himself had
never noticed any trace of nobility in his son's character. There
was nothing abnormal in Isaac Offenbach's urge to extol his son's
virtues.

Offenbach was one of many and had plenty of dangerous com-
petitors even within the limits of his own restricted field. Apart
from Seligmann, there was Batta, for instance, a Dutchman, who
was unexcelled at drawing sobs from his cello and used his boy-
ish charm to wheedle his way among the ladies. But in a few
years Offenbach managed to climb to the top of the tree in spite
of such competition. His success, attributable in the first place to
his exceptional gifts, was greatly assisted by the changes taking
place in the social environment. Many great artists have been
comparatively independent of the times in which they lived; not
so Offenbach. He had to be in perpetual contact with the world
about him in order to be creative at all. All who knew him bear
witness to the fact that he was the very personification of sociability. He plunged into social life because it alone supplied
him with the necessary tensions. He lived in the instant, react-
ing delicately to social changes and constantly adapting himself
to them. The speed with which he made a name was largely due

to the fact that at the moment of his debut a society was crystal-
lizing that satisfied the cravings of his being. He had only to be
himself for success to be there for the asking. His friend Albert
Wolff once said of his music that at least half of it reflected the
gay tumult of the Boulevards, like the shell which preserves
within itself the roaring of the waves; and a speaker at his graveside said rightly that, in spite of his German origin, he was not
only French but Parisian.

Just at the time he was making his first public appearances, the
Paris that was to adopt him as its own, the Paris of the Boulevards, was coming into being. His environment leaped to meet
him, and he kindled his genius on it. Such a fortunate coincidence might be described as luck, but luck of that kind is an
attribute of genius.

Society was just developing into its modern form, as the result
of industrial development, the consequence of innumerable inventions. Of these by far the most revolutionary was the railway,
which altered the face of the earth and the relations of mankind
and brought into being the vast and complicated ramifications of
the modern credit system. A thousand other inventions contributed to a revolution in ordinary life. New industries were born,
old ones expanded out of all measure. There was no one who
was not more or less directly affected by all these changes;
whether by gas-lighting or the invention of the daguerreotype or
electroplating, which lent the cutlery of the petty bourgeoisie a
glittering and deceptive resemblance to that of the great captains
of industry.

Thinkers began to appreciate some of the implications of this
development, and the first to realize its tremendous potential importance were the Saint-Simonists. They believed that the future
organization of society ought to be based purely on the requirements of industrial production, and that all traditional castes,
ranks, and privileges ought to be abolished. " Everything through
industry, everything for industry," was their motto. As a matter
of fact, their dream of the predominance of industry was already

LE BOULEVARD POISSONIÈRE, 1834

From the painting by Isidore Dagnan

LE BOULEVARD DES ITALIENS
From the painting by T. Boys

Courtesy, Rischgitz

coming true, though hardly in the manner that they envisaged. In the reign of Louis-Philippe finance and industry were visibly beginning to set the pace. A new force had arisen that threatened to deprive the old political forces of the importance they had hitherto enjoyed.

Princes, dukes, marquises, and counts became dummy directors of railway companies, owing this prominence purely to the confidence with which their names were likely to inspire the innocent investing public. One domain after another succumbed to the influence of economic interests.

In the period of early capitalism it looked as though industry were an instrument of social reconciliation. That, at any rate, was what the Saint-Simonists believed it to be. They made no distinction between the banks and the industrial undertakings that the banks financed, and indiscriminately lumped together all the preliminary steps that led to production under the one heading of "industry." They failed in exactly the same way to discriminate between the various potential lines of development that lay hidden in the economic future. In their eyes industrial production was a single, undifferentiated force capable of curing all society's ills.

In the early days of the Saint-Simonist movement, when it was still a "church," its adherents believed society should be organized on an authoritarian basis and that all its efforts should be concentrated on increasing production, making use of the widest possible expansion of the credit system for the purpose; production, they believed, would make an end of wars and improve the situation of the "most numerous and poorest class." Capitalism and Socialism vanished into one another in their undiscriminating eyes.

Were the Saint-Simonists idle dreamers? Not all of them, at any rate. Among them were pupils of the École Polytechnique, future magnates of industry and finance. Gradually, under the pressure of reality, they abandoned their religious speculations, and from 1840 onwards the last of them returned to ordinary civil life. They founded banks, built railways, and in 1846 formed a group to study the problem of building a Suez Canal. They sponsored great schemes and enterprises of the kind they had once aspired to for metaphysical reasons alone. They now resigned themselves to purely practical aims and went on believing themselves to be the leaders of a movement that would result in world peace and universal prosperity. Never for one moment did they suspect that they were introducing the age of class struggles. The effects of the development of modern industry were for the time being latent, so their consciences were at peace; and as they had unlimited hopes of the development of commerce and industry, commercialism became supreme in spheres where it had not reigned before.

One of these spheres was that of the press. Newspapers hitherto had been purely political organs, with circulations restricted to small groups of readers sharing the same views. Small circulations meant high subscription rates, and newspapers had to charge their readers eighty francs a month in order to be able to exist at all.

All this was changed by Émile de Girardin, who introduced a newspaper revolution. Girardin initiated the commercialization of the press. He had developed his business acumen in a stockbroker's office in which he had worked as a young man, and he hit on the brilliant idea of starting a newspaper on a new plan. He saw that a reduction in price would result in an increase in circulation, which in turn would result in an increase in advertising revenue. In 1836 this principle, which is that of the modern newspaper but was the object of widespread ridicule to his contemporaries, was put into practice for the first time in history when Girardin founded *La Presse*. Its subscription rate was forty francs a month, just half that usual at the time, and its advertisement rates were somewhat higher than those generally prevailing.

Contrary to the popular belief, great leaders of commerce and industry are not calculating cynics, but wholehearted idealists. Their ideals, of course, generally blend wonderfully well with their business interests. Girardin, for example, so far from being actuated by lust for gain, regarded himself rather as a public benefactor. According to a German visitor, his eyes betrayed " the powerful dynamics of his brain, the vehement ardor, the vivacity of an exuberant imagination." He differed from the Saint-Simonists in that he was a great advocate of freedom, but like them he aspired to bringing a maximum of happiness to the masses whom he sought to reach with his new paper. He was a political dreamer, exclusively concerned with social progress, and while he dreamed, the advertisement revenue flowed in. He encouraged advertising as an instrument for increasing national prosperity.

But, dazzled by the nobility of his ideals, he overlooked a highly important consequence of his newspaper revolution. By making newspapers dependent on advertising revenue he produced a state of affairs in which the ultimate controller of editorial policy was money. The commercialization of the press meant its withdrawal from the battle of rival opinions. Henceforward newspapers would only advocate opinions in so far as they were compatible with the economic interests of their proprietors. This, however, did not occur to Girardin and his contemporaries. What struck them was the fact that the press was now established in a kind of neutral zone, in which there were far fewer trammels on the free expression of opinion than there had been before. Significantly Girardin announced in his first number that he would give publicity to all legitimate opinions and attempt to reconcile conflicting views. (He omitted to mention that this broad-mindedness increased his circulation prospects.)

The forty-franc press, in providing a neutral platform for the free exchange of opinion, was obliged to make that platform as alluring a one as possible. A brisk demand arose for entertaining articles, stories, and gossip, and it was not long before the serialized novel made its appearance. Whole battalions of writers and poets, attracted by its ideal and material advantages, enlisted in the service of the press. Balzac, Dumas, Victor Hugo, Scribe,

George Sand, and many more worked for *La Presse* or *Le Siècle,* the circulation of which, thanks to such contributors, increased by leaps and bounds. Other newspapers refused to be left behind in the race, and a desperate scramble for authors began. Authors' fees, like circulations, rose to dizzy heights. The best-paid author was Eugène Sue, who was the first to realize that serial stories require a special technique. His *Les Mystères de Paris,* which appeared in the *Journal des Débats,* kept all Paris on tenterhooks for weeks, and on days when an installment failed to appear the whole city was left in a state of acute depression.

The advertisements did not fall far short of the reading-matter in entertainment value, and the advertising spirit became more and more typical of the age. It was no accident that virtuosos started competing for press notices, exposing the details of their private lives for the edification of the public. Competition in " putting things over " became intense. One resourceful young man who owned a small fashion paper paid *La Presse* a hundred francs a week for the privilege of printing a regular fashion article. He did not, of course, write the article himself, but had it written for him; but he recouped himself handsomely for his pains at the expense of the business men whose goods were praised in the course of the series. This young man, whose name was Henri de Villemessant, was destined to play a big part in Offenbach's life.

The newspaper boom led to a demand for journalists, and a new type came into being, bound to the economic principles of the modern newspaper. Girardin himself took these principles into account to the extent of giving *La Presse,* in spite of its professed indifference to questions of political principle, a kind of conservative, upper-bourgeois stamp. But for the time being all went smoothly, and no sense of strain was felt, because the growth of industry had not yet led to any pronounced development of social antagonisms. How pregnant with consequences were the economic ties into which journalism now entered was only to be revealed in the future. Meanwhile the journalists

reveled in their new-won "freedom." Released from the restraint of all sorts of traditional beliefs, they became Bohemians.
But the money on which they depended for their livelihood
sharpened their acumen, and they very clearly perceived that
many things that were held up to honor were hollow shams, and
many exalted ideals merely clues to economic interests. They
consequently became skeptics. The reverse side of the medal
was that they allowed themselves to be bought.

The attitude of neutrality that the forty-franc press originally
maintained towards the existing order was but a reflection of the
situation of industry as a whole. No one yet knew in which direction it was going. All its latest possibilities were still concealed. The continuation of economic prosperity and, above all,
the personal government of Louis-Philippe, caused this state of
affairs to endure.

In 1840 it looked as though a convulsion were about to take
place. England's Eastern policy sent Paris into a patriotic frenzy.
A European war seemed imminent, but the King wished at all
costs to avoid it, though, with the exception of the bankers, no
class of the population, not even his immediate entourage, was
in sympathy with him. Thiers, who was in favor of war, was
forced to resign, and Guizot was summoned to his place. With
Guizot, whom Louis-Philippe himself described as his mouth-
piece, there began a period the guiding principle of which was
the unalterability of the *status quo*. War might have had un-
predictable repercussions within the country, so he repeatedly
humiliated himself before England in order to avoid the slightest risk. He stubbornly refused to grant the electoral reforms that
the opposition demanded annually from 1841 onwards, fearing
that any alteration in the franchise would introduce an unknown
quantity into politics and upset the whole course of social development. An elaborate system of corruption, based on railway
concessions, state contracts, tobacco monopolies, promotions and
appointments, made the Chamber Guizot's accommodating tool.
"Guizot's France is a slumbering, yawning, inanimate France,"

Gutzkov wrote in 1842. The country remained in a state of stagnation for year after year. The social forces generated by industrial production were not yet evident, and the spirit fostered by the commercialized press developed undisturbed.

One of its most striking manifestations was in the little world of the Boulevards. Journalists — in fact all who had anything to do with the press — felt themselves irresistibly attracted to the Boulevards, where they met the dandies and the *jeunesse dorée*, whose mental outlook corresponded closely to their own in its avoidance of the *juste milieu* and the faubourg Saint-Germain.

On the Boulevards the dandies lived, so to speak, extraterritorially. They also resembled the journalists in that they refrained from attacking the existing order and merely confined themselves to maintaining an attitude of aloofness to it. Materially they were utterly dependent on it, and if they had openly rebelled they would have lost their incomes, a sacrifice they were unwilling to make. Their incomes permitted them to express their protest by leading a life of complete idleness. They got up at midday, had breakfast, paid a few calls, appeared on the Boulevards at about four o'clock, gossiped, and then went home to get ready for the evening, when real life began.

Enviable as it might seem to the outsider, this life of idleness and self-indulgence concealed boredom and revulsion, and their elegant superiority originated in an inner compulsion to cut themselves off from the banality that flourished so exuberantly all around them. "What an awful life! How tired I am of it," yawned Barbey d'Aurevilly, the biographer of Beau Brummell. The young men who devoted themselves to dandydom desired something better than the bourgeois banality of Louis-Philippe, and, there being no trace of human nobility in their environment, they relapsed into a snobbish cult of the self. It was not for nothing that Alfred de Musset attached importance to his adherence to the dandies, of whom Baudelaire said: ". . . they all nourish the spirit of opposition and revolt. They are all champions of that which is particularly valuable in human pride and are animated by the urge, which today is all too rare, to attack and destroy vulgarity." The *jeunesse dorée* united with the dandies. Characteristic of the life which they pursued was the fact that a large part of it was lived in the Jockey Club and other clubs. Clubs were the refuges of the homeless.

Consciousness of their hopeless aloofness led to a passion for gambling. As a distraction from the melancholy which always pursued them, members of the Jockey Club would make bets about the date of death of completely healthy fellow-members, about the speed of their horses or the chastity of their wives.

The soil had long been prepared for the assimilation of the journalists. The dandies had always sought the society of writers and artists, knowing that they were outsiders too. Alfred de Musset, it is true, was blackballed by the Jockey Club, but the world of fashion and the world of art and literature were linked by a thousand threads. " We had the great good fortune," Count d'Alton-Shée wrote in his memoirs, " to be the contemporaries, critics, admirers, and, what is more, the comrades and friends of famous men of all kinds: poets, speakers, writers, composers, and painters."

Not a few artists reciprocated the popularity they enjoyed in the fashionable world by taking an interest in horses and sharing in every vagary of fashion. Eugène Sue, before he compromised himself in the eyes of society, was looked upon as the paragon of dandies. No wonder that journalists soon formed the leaven of such a society. Not only did their mentality correspond to that which reigned upon the Boulevards, but they were servants of a master whom more and more poets, writers, and illustrators acknowledged as their master too.

The boundaries between journalists and authors faded into one another. On the one hand many professional newspaper critics, like Jules Janin or Sainte-Beuve, were in reality original authors, and on the other many famous writers and poets worked for newspapers for their daily bread. Théophile Gautier, under the pressure of necessity, devoted himself to journalism entirely.

Scarcely any authors managed to keep out of the newspapers altogether. In the last resort all writers were journalists. The conquest of the Boulevards by the journalists (in the narrower sense of the word) was facilitated by the power they exercised over public opinion. For they could make or break reputations. Members of the Théâtre Bohème, to whom the journalists had a thousand ties, appeared on the Boulevards in the journalists' wake. The typical *boulevardier* was a mixture of all these various ingredients. Apart from his dependence on money, he was a really free man, devoted to the enjoyment of life and the cultivation of his mind.

In 1843 a German traveler described the boulevard des Italiens as follows: " The lower story . . . consists of a plate-glass wall behind which the most varied riches are displayed — clothes, materials, furniture, gold, silver, and jewels. Places of entertainment, cafés and restaurants, no less sumptuously equipped, provide the only gaps in the continuity of this rich bazaar. Most of them appear to be built entirely of gilt and mirrors." The glitter of gilt and mirrors provided the *boulevardiers* with a suitable background. Their favorite resort at this time was the luxurious Café de Paris, at the corner of the boulevard des Italiens and the rue Taitbout. So distinguished were its waiters that the recent introduction of gas-lighting had thoroughly upset them. In the days of candlelight they had done their work absolutely noiselessly, but under the glare of gas they had started nervously clattering the plates. The genius of the chef of the Café de Paris adorned the simplest dishes. Could anything be more ordinary than casserole of veal? But at the Café de Paris casserole of veal was a work of art. Alexandre Dumas indulged in it three times a week.

The habitués of the Café de Paris jealously preserved their rights and saw to it that no unbidden guest entered the sacred precincts. They liked enjoying their privileges undisturbed. They constituted a clique, the aristocratic members of which included not only Lord Seymour but the Marquis du Hallays-Coëtquen, who was an expert on duels and on the *corps de ballet,*

OFFENBACH IN 1876

Courtesy, Rischgitz

ALEXANDRE DUMAS AND THÉOPHILE GAUTIER PASSING WITHOUT RECOGNIZING EACH OTHER — ONE THINKING HE SEES A BEAR, THE OTHER A RUSSIAN!

Caricature by Cham, 1858

on both of which subjects he was willing to discourse for hours. In addition to this he had a pornographic collection and a box at the Opéra, the notorious " devil's box " (*loge infernale*). It did not bear that name entirely without justification, for several of its regular occupants had died sudden deaths.

Another distinguished habitué was Major Frazer, who was in the habit of dressing half as a soldier and half as a civilian. He was a powerfully built little man, with surprisingly mild eyes, a heavily lined face, and fine fair hair and a beard, which he dyed black, because, he explained, dark hair only was popular in the first Russian regiment in which he had served. By birth a Scotsman, he had spent his youth at St. Petersburg, where an unfortunate love-affair had earned him the ill favor of the Czar. After being granted a pardon he had joined his family, who had settled in Portugal, and later had inherited a vast fortune, which he was now consuming in Paris, or rather on the Boulevards. He spoke nine languages, was adept at horses and conversation, smoked and drank incessantly, and took it amiss if he were not addressed as Major.

The most faithful customer, however, was the celebrated Dr. Véron. He was to be seen here every evening with unfailing regularity, laying down the law to a large circle of admiring friends. Having made a fortune of nearly a million francs as manager of the Opéra, he had retired and bought *Le Constitutionnel,* which had been in the market at a low price on account of its dwindling circulation. In it he contemplated publishing Eugène Sue's new novel, *The Wandering Jew,* for which he was prepared to pay the author a royalty of a hundred thousand francs; for which outlay he expected to recoup himself two or three times over. The little doctor, in shape as round as an egg, always sat at the same place at the café and was recognizable from afar by his enormous necktie, behind which he sought to conceal a scar on his neck, the existence of which, however, was common knowledge. His fastidious taste in food made him the terror of the chef. One of his sayings was: " You can only tell

next morning whether you dined well the night before." He was
a gourmet also in an erotic sense, and, as he never shrank from
expense in procuring himself physical comforts, he succeeded in
acquiring such dainty morsels as Rachel, the famous tragedienne.
He liked dining with his underlings — journalists, authors, and
critics. Generally he was accompanied by two of his closer friends,
Lautour-Mézeray and Armand Malitourne, both of whom were
experienced newspaper men. Latour-Mézeray invariably appeared with a five-franc white camellia in his buttonhole. The
brilliant idea of founding the world's first newspaper for children had been his, and a highly remunerative proposition it had
turned out to be. In contrast to him, Malitourne was a journalist
who disliked nothing more than writing; his incredible indolence
and the perpetually tired sound in his voice were presumably the
result of his mind having ceased to function before its time. He
and Dr. Véron had once jointly founded a ministerial paper,
but Malitourne's inactivity had led to its early demise. He was
able to frequent the Boulevards thanks to Dr. Véron's financial
support.

Roger de Beauvoir was another habitué of the Café de Paris
from whom there exuded a discreet odor of idleness. His real
name was Roger only, but pardonably believing that that simple
and commonplace patronymic did not do justice to his dazzling
personality, he had added to it the name of Beauvoir, his family
estate. In his younger years he had written a very promising
novel, which had given him the reputation of being the hope of
Romantic literature. Unfortunately that reputation pleased him
so well that he rested on his laurels and confined himself to the
kind of success that can be effortlessly acquired by a young man
who is both handsome and rich. With his black beard, his in-
fectious laughter, and his cheerful glance, he reminded his contemporaries of a Venetian nobleman, of Veronese's " Marriage
at Cana." He used to wear gold-embroidered waistcoats, carry a
rhinoceros-horn walking-stick, and drink champagne in the company of innumerable women. His wit was as sparkling as the

champagne, and he scattered epigrams at the expense of friend and foe alike. That, however, was the sum total of his achievements.

Where Roger was, Nestor Roqueplan could not be far away. Roqueplan, demigod of the Boulevards and all the fashionable journalists, had started as a journalist himself. He had contributed to the *Figaro* of the Restoration period and had later become a theatrical manager, without, however, neglecting journalism altogether. In the forties he was in control of the Théâtre des Variétés. His pride was to be a leader of fashion, his pleasure to play practical jokes. On one occasion he amused himself by introducing a number of people, as foreigners, to a lady he knew. Believing they understood no French, she expressed herself very candidly about them in their presence. Humor of that kind was as heartily applauded as the spirit of skepticism which Roqueplan displayed in his threefold capacity as journalist, theatrical manager, and *boulevardier*. Roqueplan wore his skepticism as a mask to cover a great kindness of heart. Few saw through the mask, but all the world knew of the unfailing regularity with which he was to be seen upon the Boulevards, evening after evening, either lounging on the terrace of the Café Tortoni, hat over one ear, embarking on an endless argument, or exchanging banter with the habitués of the Café de Paris, in company with Roger de Beauvoir, or telling anecdotes for hours on end.

Roqueplan originated the use of the term *lorettes* as a synonym for ladies of easy virtue. Many of these lived in the new houses in the reconstructed quarter surrounding the Church of Notre-Dame de Lorette. They did so for economic reasons. Flats in this neighborhood were cheap, the houses being damp. Conditions improved after the houses had been lived in for some time, and after fulfilling their mission the *lorettes* were evicted, to make way for more respectable tenants, who, of course, had to pay higher rents. Fortunately a building boom was in progress, so the *lorettes* never had any difficulty in finding new homes to dry.

The *lorette* took the place of the grisette, the little seamstress or laundress of the type celebrated by Murger and Paul de Kock, who uncomplainingly spent her life cooking and darning for some student or painter and felt herself richly repaid by his love; who, while she smiled at him, had pain in her heart, and whose native element was the idyllic Bohemia of the Latin Quarter, among the scions of the petty bourgeoisie, to whose excesses the Government closed a kindly eye, because it had not the slightest doubt that these high-spirited young men would grow up into excellent, God-fearing citizens who would have just as much interest in the maintenance of the existing order as their fathers before them. But times changed, the development of industry hit the petty bourgeoisie harder and harder, and the Bohemia of students, painters, and grisettes declined.

Not a few grisettes got into the habit of accepting money, moved from the Latin Quarter, and were transformed into *lorettes*. In the evenings they streamed on to the Boulevards, went to public dances, discovered a weakness for champagne, and fluttered longingly around the footlights. Their dream was to appear on the stage of one of the little theaters, but more often than not, when their dream came true, they had to pay for the privilege of offering their charms to the public. The stage was a jumping-off ground, with the aid of which they hoped to fulfill their yearning for splendor and luxury and their craving for the money that engendered them.

About that time Lola Montez, a young beginner, was dancing at the Théâtre de la Porte-Saint-Martin, and Thérèse Lachman, an ambitious Russian Jewess, who had started as a lady of the streets, had managed to gain admittance to the better-class dance-halls and, thanks to this step up the social ladder, was having an affair with Henri Herz, the famous pianist. In later years she was widely known at La Païva.

Though it was necessarily only the favored few who succeeded in scaling the giddy heights to which the great courtesans belonged, there were nevertheless a number of honorable intermediary stages, and those who belonged to the Boulevards' rank and file had climbed quite a considerable portion of the ladder. The Café de Paris hummed nightly with stories of their carousals.

Short as the Boulevards were, no real dandy would ever dream of taking a step beyond them. He would stroll from one end to the other and then back. " It is only a few steps from one end to the other; nevertheless they contain the whole world," said Alfred de Musset. He added contemptuously that beyond them barbarism began.

Beyond these civilized confines, however, there lived the common people. They were no longer satisfied with their role as supernumeraries in the social scheme. The workers had particular cause for resentment, for the gathering momentum of industrialization made their poverty increasingly intolerable. In 1842 a foreign observer wrote:

" In the midst of this hum of seemingly smooth and orderly activity four thousand workers who gather early every morning in the Place de la Grève, not knowing how they will be able to live through the day if they find no work, ten thousand who are uncertain of the morrow, twenty thousand who are uncertain of the following week, constitute the gangrene in the body-politic that might rapidly spread from the extremities of this city, the *barrières* and the *faubourgs*, and attack the vital parts, the alliance of power and wealth, honors and property." The gangrene certainly showed signs of its existence.

In the factories the workers sang songs that might have been composed in the nethermost pit, treated with contempt the law forbidding strikes, and devoured enormous quantities of revolutionary pamphlets. Well-known intellectuals sympathized with this early communistic movement. Eugène Sue described the sufferings of the people in his *Les Mystères de Paris,* the priest Lamennais wrote things that caused him to part from the Roman Church, and George Sand came out as an ardent upholder of the cause of the oppressed.

Socialist theories were evolved, under the influence of the ambiguous teachings of the Saint-Simonists, and served to give discontent an aim. The most enduring influence was that of Louis Blanc, who maintained that the right to work was a fundamental human right and that the state should carry this principle into practice by establishing national workshops. In intellectual circles it became the fashion to be well disposed towards Louis Blanc's theories, and he was generally held to be the coming man. But this fashion found no echo among the real bourgeoisie, who reacted to the disquieting ferment among the people by complaining bitterly of the growing spirit of materialism, and accused the masses of selfish pleasure-seeking, though, in view of the fabulous dividends distributed among the privileged, it was natural that the classes beneath them should also set their hearts on earthly pleasures. Plays such as *Les Pilules du diable* and *The Thousand and One Nights,* in which the laws of nature were violently interfered with by supernatural powers, were enormously successful. Nothing was more popular with the middle classes than a play in which the hero or heroine was rescued at the last moment by the intervention of a wizard; unless it were a melodrama at which they could have a good cry. The small tradesmen, the clerks, the innumerable people of one kind or another who were threatened with ruin by the economic revolution and lived in fear of being reduced to the state of the proletariat, found tears an enormous solace.

At the end of 1841 a German newspaper correspondent informed his readers that an enormous number of earnest, suffering, impatient, and threatening faces were to be seen in the streets of Paris. Inhabitants of that great city felt that the earth was trembling beneath their feet. They talked endlessly of the sovereignty of the people, were suspected of Socialist leanings, became enthusiastic devotees of the Napoleonic cult, under the influence of which they claimed that France should regain the left bank of the Rhine, and had no real respect for anything. Not that there was much about the atmosphere of the *juste milieu* that called for any particular respect.

De Musset described the area beyond the Boulevards as though it were utterly remote, but it was only thanks to Louis-Philippe's suppression of all signs of unrest among the people that he was able to talk in this fashion. Nevertheless there was a certain sense of disquiet in the air, which increased the *boulevardiers'* discomfort in the greater world about them.

Thus the miniature world which the *boulevardiers* created for themselves had its roots in economic developments, which included the commercialization of sex and of newspaper production; and superimposed on the economic factors was their deliberate shutting out of the outside world, with all its pregnant social developments. The Boulevards constituted a little world, but an artificial one, surrounded by invisible barriers. The ring of fortresses that began to rise around Paris at about the same time invites an obvious comparison, while a multitude of exiles from abroad enhanced the effect of unreality.

Polish, Spanish, and Italian aristocrats were among those who settled on the Boulevards. Some of them, such as Prince Belgiojoso, were political exiles, others had left their country for heaven knows what reasons.

There was, for instance, a stately Oriental, popularly known as " the Persian," who was to be seen stalking up and down the Boulevards all by himself for year after year and had never been known to talk to anybody.

Like the money on which it depended, the spirit of the Boulevards tended towards the destruction of myths, the " debunking " of oppressive authoritarianism. But in exposing to irony much that was traditional it proved its faithfulness to an old trait of the national character.

In 1858 Émile Montégut wrote: " This spirit is not, as has so often been repeated, a disintegrating element, an enemy of the social order and of divine and human laws. On the contrary . . . it is the implacable enemy of all pseudo-divine laws and all usurped rights. . . . Practiced as it is in detecting shams, it tears off masks and reveals the true faces behind them. All the great French writers were animated by the same spirit — Rabelais and

Montaigne, Pascal and Molière, Montesquieu and Voltaire. It is a spirit no lie can stand up against for long." As the world of the Boulevards was a relatively small one, its wit became more and more refined. It indulged in subtle allusions, extravagant arabesques. As long as prosperity lasted and no immediate danger loomed, its mood was high-spirited and gay.

It was no accident that Offenbach and the Boulevards were contemporary. They were related by their very nature. Offenbach was but another *émigré*. On the Boulevards he found his fellows and the atmosphere of liberty that he required, and consequently felt at home, just because the Boulevards were no home in the ordinary sense. There he found the spirit that attracted him and the kind of society in which he flourished. He made friends with journalists, whose volatility was closely related to his own. His volatility sprang from a remarkable gift for avoiding dangerous depths. A man like him could not cast anchor lightly. A striking characteristic of the world of the Boulevards was its lack of anchorages. Its situation was far from terra firma, in close proximity to that distant land that Offenbach had already apostrophized in his waltz *Rebecca*. It was for this proximity that Offenbach loved it. He had but to step off from the Boulevards and he had reached his goal.

CHAPTER VII

VIRTUOSO'S MARRIAGE

LIKE Paganini and the young Liszt, Offenbach the virtuoso neglected the true interpretation of masterpieces for the sake of brilliance of execution, which he regarded as an end in itself. In this he merely followed the fashion of his time. It was a fashion which can, perhaps, partly be related to the cultural reaction then prevalent in Europe. In the age of Metternich it was not permitted to touch the foundations of anything; and interpretation might be liable to awaken slumbering passions. Consequently in the practice of the arts all emphasis was laid upon technical brilliance.

Offenbach's was of a special kind. It did not just consist in the faultless execution of arpeggios, double stops, natural harmonics, and other familiar feats. Its true essence lay in a genius for imitation. A woman music-lover once said of him that he played every conceivable instrument except his own. Like the *boulevardiers,* who eschewed nature, he shunned the natural tones of the cello, preferring, as it were, artificial cultivation to primitive landscape. Instead of following where his instrument naturally led him, he preferred luring it from its somberness and coaxing capers out of it of a kind to which by nature it was little inclined. He made it imitate the bagpipes or the rattle or caused it to cheep and twitter like a bird. His audiences were as delighted as children at his cunning when his cello sparkled and effervesced like champagne and bubbled over with eccentric conceits. Such technique seemed miraculous, and when, contrary to the usual practice among virtuosos, the executant added a personal note to the performance by accompanying it with a small lecture, spiced with Boulevard wit, their delight was redoubled.

There is evidence in Offenbach's new compositions that he was now an habitué of the Boulevards. His own personality seemed not fully to develop until this final spur. In composition he now neglected the emotional effects for which he had previously striven, in favor of more light-hearted ones. He made his first effort in this direction in 1842, when he set to music six fables of La Fontaine. The critics, however, would have none of them. One critic regretted that Offenbach had forgotten the fable of the mountain in labor that brought forth a mouse, while another accused him of a lack of breeding and good taste. The presumption is that they were offended by Offenbach's poking fun at the fables' morals. The music in question has long since vanished, but it is known that he turned the fable of the cricket and the ant into a gay waltz, thus tending, at any rate in the minds of his more moral contemporaries, to enlist public sympathy on the side of the frivolous cricket instead of on that of the thrifty ant. In one of his operettas Offenbach also parodied and made fun of the fable of the cobbler who could not sing freely and happily unless he was poor.

In spite of his unfavorable press notices Offenbach felt convinced that this new genre to which he applied himself would find an echo on the Boulevards, and moreover that it held out hopes of theatrical success. His extensive contacts with journalists, singers, and librettists kept him in touch with public tastes and tendencies. He had been suppressing his aspirations to the stage for years and now decided to use Offenbach the virtuoso, who was widely respected, to launch Offenbach the theatrical composer, in whom nobody believed. If no stage was open to him, he must use the concert platform as a stage. In the spring of 1843 he arranged a concert on novel lines. The whole program was made up of his own compositions, and among them was a theatrical duet.

This " dramatic " concert took place at the Salle Herz, which belonged to Henri Herz, who was then living with Thérèse Lachman. Herz not only was an acknowledged pianist and Don Juan, but, with a business man as his partner, owned a famous piano factory, the profits of which substantially increased his income as a virtuoso and concert-hall proprietor. A musical industrialist on a grand scale, whenever anyone touched the keys of a pianoforte, it meant money tinkling for him. The future La Païva, in view of her pronounced love of music, can scarcely be blamed for giving herself to such a lord in the world of harmony.

Offenbach's concert aroused as much public interest as an important first night. The crowd that poured into the Salle Herz may possibly have been explained by the fact that Offenbach's friend Roger was one of the singers in the duet — Roger of the Opéra-Comique, whose elegant figure was as ravishing as his melodious voice.

The duet itself — entitled *Le Moine bourru* — was endowed with all the qualities of those comic duets with which Offenbach scored his first real triumphs at the Bouffes-Parisiens more than ten years later. But in 1843 Louis-Philippe was still on the throne, and the society that was to acclaim the operetta did not blossom forth until the days of the Second Empire. The libretto of the little scene was written by Edouard Plouvier, a former leather-dresser, who had worked himself up by his native talents. So fertile was the atmosphere of the Boulevards that many who ordinarily would never have seen a sentence of their own in print discovered a talent for writing. The truth was not that they wrote but that the Boulevards used them as a medium for self-expression. Plouvier's libretto was in entire accordance with their skeptical spirit, and satirized in particular the Romantics.

Romanticism was becoming more and more intolerable to enlightened spirits. Victor Hugo was a particularly profitable target, and his latest play, *Les Burgraves,* had just been a resounding failure. Plouvier was only one of many who parodied him. For the phantom mediæval monk at whom the satire of Offenbach's duet was directed bore an awkward resemblance to the spectral

monk that haunts Hugo's novel *Notre-Dame de Paris*. The heroes of the duet are two peaceable burgesses, Jehan and Pierre,
who meet in the street at night. Each believes the other to be the
eerie figure and is terrified accordingly. They both start singing
cheerful songs in order to give themselves courage, but eventually
recognize each other as neighbors, and make off for home together, rejoicing in the monk's non-existence. Offenbach showed
the soundness of his instincts in choosing this plot, for it gave him
his first opportunity of developing his own individual brand of
gaiety, the peculiar object of which was to dissipate groundless
fears and anxieties and to prick the bubbles of exaggeration, pomposity, violence, and oppression by which man is everlastingly
threatened. It was not for nothing that *Le Moine bourru* also
satirized grand opera.

As Offenbach did not confine himself to this one concert but
seized every possible opportunity of appearing in public, he soon
became a familiar figure. The public attitude to him showed that
people had an inkling that there was more in him than a mere
cello virtuoso. What excited people about him was that he seemed
a messenger from another, stranger world. Whether it was his
extreme thinness, which exaggerated his height, or whether it
was his hawk-like nose, his whole appearance was unreal. He
had long, wavy hair and a remarkably high-arched brow, and
when he started playing he looked more remarkable than ever.
He and his cello seemed fused into one, like a centaur, and he
seemed to be leaping through space on a magic steed. His audience felt that there was something demonic about him — a feeling that was accentuated by that curious glitter in his eyes that
led to a rumor that he had the evil eye. Alfred de Musset, who
had become a very heavy drinker, believed definitely in this theory, and the Boulevard press extracted a great deal of entertainment from this and similar superstitions.

One comic paper announced that Offenbach, having one day
suddenly caught sight of himself in a mirror in the street, saw
his own evil eye, whereupon he promptly got married three

months later. This kind of joke was, of course, evidence that in popular esteem he was regarded as somewhat uncanny.

Strange to say, the man to whom these rumors became attached, so far from having made any pose or pretense of being a Cagliostro, was one whose artistic practice was in complete harmony with the skeptical, satirical spirit of the Boulevards, a spirit which tended to ridicule the supernatural and reduce the diabolical to human proportions. What irony that the artist who was perhaps the supreme embodiment of that spirit should himself be associated with the uncanny and the supernatural! But there is an explanation of the paradox. For light and airy as the spirit of the Boulevards seemed, it contained a secret which Offenbach was destined to reveal. There was something Utopian about him, something that pointed towards the future. His music, his whole being, looked forward to a state of society in which all the powers of darkness had been abolished; a state of affairs to which the spirit of the Boulevards perhaps also pointed. If Offenbach was a magician, it was at any rate white magic that he practiced, casting out evil spirits and conjuring up a better human world.

Nadar, who could be malicious, neatly summed up the extraordinary vehemence of his movements, as well as his urge to rise from the ground and fly, when he called him a cross between a cock and a grasshopper. The journalist Vermersch, who wrote a poem in which he made the young Offenbach dream of future glory, was nearer the mark when he put the following words into his mouth:

> *J'aurai la fantaisie étrange des mers bleues*
> *Et la vivacité folle des hochequeues. . . .*

There was something bird-like about Offenbach that attracted people and at the same time made him seem strange to them. For he possessed a bird's quickness and elusiveness.

Such was the young man who arrived unexpectedly one evening at Mme Mitchell's salon and surprised and delighted all her guests. Mme Mitchell was a Spaniard who had had to leave Spain because her first husband, a Señor d'Alcain, had become involved in the Carlist disorders. Later she had married a Mr. John Mitchell, an Englishman, who was a bookseller, concert agent, and lessee of the French theater in London. Mme Mitchell had two children, Herminie and Pépito, by her first marriage. She was a warm-hearted and intelligent woman, who liked nothing better than a crowded salon.

One evening she arranged a particularly brilliant gathering in honor of a Carlist general who had heroically distinguished himself in the latest episode of the Spanish civil war. The general was the lion of the evening, and the satisfaction felt at his heroism was only mitigated by the host's failure to put in an appearance. Eventually there was a ring of the bell, and all eyes turned to the door, at which, however, not Mr. Mitchell but an unknown young man appeared who promptly reminded everybody of E. T. A. Hoffmann. The unknown young man was Offenbach. He quizzed the assembly through his eyeglass, made straight for Mme Mitchell, and introduced himself to her in a well-bred and self-possessed manner. Her husband, whose acquaintance he had made through a friend of both, had invited him, and so he had come. Mme Mitchell's guests were intrigued by this extraordinary-looking young man. They were beginning to feel the need for a little relief from the Spanish general, since large doses of heroism are apt in the long run to become tiresome; and as Offenbach liked entertaining people who wanted to be entertained, he started talking to them about everything that came into his head: about the Conservatoire, about the practical jokes he had played in the orchestra of the Opéra-Comique, and about his concerts. Herminie could have listened to him for hours.

Asked for a sample of his art, he carelessly touched the keys of a piano with one finger, producing, as if by inadvertence, the most delightful tunes, and sang snatches of song in a voice which, though hardly a voice, produced a charming effect. All the time he went on talking gaily, so that no one really knew when the talking ended and the music began. The whole gathering, Herminie not excluded, was enchanted by so much charm and wit, and by the time Mr. Mitchell turned up, everybody had forgotten the Carlist general.

After this triumphant evening Offenbach became a regular visitor at the Mitchells', and there was no denying that Herminie and he got on remarkably well. His visits to the house were only interrupted when he left Paris to take part in the musical festival at Douai in the summer of 1843 and later when he went to Cologne, where he gave two recitals.

His father, like an experienced publicity man, took care to communicate to the *Kölnische Zeitung,* long before his son reached home, the information that he was now *à la mode* in the Paris salons.

It may have been during this visit to Cologne that Jacques tried to trace the waltz with which his mother had rocked him to sleep in his childhood. One evening he started absent-mindedly humming the eight bars which were all that he could remember and that continually haunted him.

" Good gracious me! " his father exclaimed. " Do you still remember Zimmer's waltz? "

" Who is Zimmer? "

Zimmer, his father told him, was a young composer who had once been very much talked of but had suddenly disappeared from the scene. Offenbach's hopes were raised only to be dashed again. His father could not remember the end of the waltz, nor could it be traced at any of the music-shops at which he made inquiries next day. It seemed to have disappeared as completely as its composer.

Offenbach's father was not exaggerating in saying that his son was *à la mode* in the Paris salons. A ballad he wrote that year was all the rage. It spread through the music-loving salons like wildfire. To be sure, it owed its success mainly to the intriguing fact that not only was it entitled *A toi,* but it was unambiguously dedicated to Herminie d'Alcain, whose picture adorned the title-page. After such an unconcealed act of homage the two must surely be ripe for an engagement. But, as usual, there were difficulties. For the time being, Mme Mitchell would not hear of an engagement; after all, in spite of a few ballads and concerts, the young man's future prospects were still exceedingly vague.

These obstacles drove Offenbach to desperate efforts. He made a big provincial tour and did all in his power to put his Paris reputation on a sure footing.

Paris in the first few months of 1844 seemed more desirable than ever. Carnival was celebrated more deliriously than ever before. Men and women dined and supped in costume, as though the ordinary balls were not enough. Lovely women were to be seen everywhere, their loveliness enhanced by a touch of melancholy, which was the very latest thing. They danced the polka, which had just been imported from Bohemia, made striking figures against the dark background of the boxes at the theater, and self-sacrificingly plunged into the flood of concerts by which Paris was overwhelmed.

For his own concert, which took place in April, Offenbach, in obedience to the fashion, had composed a *danse bohémienne,* and moreover he played two bravura pieces that he had tried out in Cologne: a fantasia on themes from Rossini's operas and a ballet piece entitled *Musette,* in which he invoked the spirit of the seventeenth century with great brilliance. His concert was the climax of a hard winter's work, of which he had every right to feel proud. The paper *L'Artiste* described him and Seligmann, his former colleague at the Opéra-Comique, as "the most successful virtuosos of the season," and moreover announced with prophetic foresight that there was an inner bond between him and Alfred de Musset.

Conscious that the undisputed recognition that he had obtained offered a substantial guarantee for his future, Offenbach renewed his wooing of Herminie. His desire to set up a home of his own may have been reinforced by the positive epidemic of marriages then prevalent almong the virtuosos. So unanimously did they steer towards the altar that it looked as if they had all got tired of independence together. Thalberg married the daughter of the baritone at the Italian Opera, and another celebrity made a hurried match with a little seamstress. " The artistes have all gone a-wooing and are trilling hymeneals," Heinrich Heine wrote at the end of April 1844. Offenbach was no exception. As no adequate reason could be found for refusal, Mme Mitchell finally gave her consent, subject to two conditions which the family regarded as absolutely indispensable.

The first was that the brisk young lover must submit himself to a final test by appearing in London, which was untried territory for him, though all-important. Mr. Mitchell, of course, himself arranged the tour. Herminie's mother and stepfather wanted to be quite sure of the young man. Offenbach accordingly left for London in May, shortly after the opening of the Paris Industrial Exhibition, the mechanical and automatic exhibits of which caused the public to marvel. The hairdressers' dummies, for instance, lifted their wigs by themselves. Another Paris exhibition, years later, was also destined to mark an important milestone in Offenbach's life.

In London he was so successful and made so much money that the Mitchells finally capitulated, while Offenbach's father nearly burst with pride and made a positive nuisance of himself to the staff of the *Kölnische Zeitung,* upon whom he kept up an uninterrupted bombardment of puff paragraphs regarding his son's prowess. But in London Jacques's most vivid experience was — Paris. This visit to a foreign land taught him for the first time how much that unique city meant to him, and he yearned for it with a love that was to be expressed again and again in his operettas in later years. Overflowing with high spirits and pleasurable anticipation of his return, he unbosomed himself in a letter dated June 8, 1844, to his friend Émile Chevalet, a young official at the

War Ministry, who wrote novels, plays, and essays on political economy in his spare time. Incidentally the letter is also an excellent example of Offenbachian mischief.

"Last Thursday," he wrote, " I played before the Queen, Prince Albert, the Emperor of Russia, the King of Bavaria, etc.; in other words, before the whole elite of the court. I was a great success. However, in spite of all the honors that are heaped upon me here, I still prefer my beautiful Paris and spending my time among my real friends. Here everything is splendid, but cold. But in Paris all is graceful, humble — and warm; particularly when one has a few real friends. Therefore, my dear Émile, I am longing to shake you by the hand and to be in my good Paris again, which contains all that is dear to me and all that I love. You understand me, do you not, my dear Émile? . . . A few weeks ago I was invited to dinner by the Society of Musicians, whose president is the Duke of Cambridge. Naturally enough, my dear Émile, there was music after dinner. I played my *Musette* and they all made a tremendous noise and banged on the table for fully five minutes, shouting: ' Encore! Encore! ' at the top of their voices.

"I had to play the piece again. In short, you will see from all this that I have been as successful here as in Paris. Hence I am beginning to be just a little proud. When I am back in Paris, I shan't be able to go about with you any longer, I have got so used to associating only with lords, dukes, queens, kings, princes, and emperors! Emperors, my dear friend!!! I cannot lower myself by talking to a commoner, but you see, my dear friend, that I take advantage of the opportunity of writing to him. . . ."

The second condition imposed on the young man was that he must change his faith. Herminie had had a strict Catholic upbringing, which made this step essential. The Countess de Vaux was sufficiently concerned for his salvation to consent to act as his godmother. Did the old cantor in Cologne object? Old Offenbach believed in emancipation and was far too optimistic about the future of civilization to regard baptism as the radical breach with Jewry that it was in the eyes of the orthodox. Besides, the future of his all-beloved son was perhaps his chief article of faith. As for Jacques himself, his conversion did not worry him in the least. It was less a change of heart than an external concession, a formality. He never concealed his Jewish origin or spared monastic life his satire. To him a creed was no more than a backcloth. In his waltz *Rebecca* he had paid no heed to religious prejudices, for his eyes were set on a distant future in which all differences of creed had vanished. But he possessed a very genuine native piety. " I do not know what I have done to cause God to bestow so much happiness and so much melody upon me," he once stated in his years of maturity.

Jacques and Herminie were married on August 14, 1844 and moved into a modest home in the Passage Saulnier. Their combined ages were barely more than forty years.

CHAPTER VIII

ENNUI

At Offenbach's graveside Victorin Joncières, one of his friends, recalled the beginning of his marriage and spoke of the role played in his career by Herminie.

"She deserved well of her famous husband," he said. "For in the difficult times at the beginning of his career she skillfully maintained his courage, shared the ordeals of life with him without ever flagging, and comforted him with never failing tenderness and devotion."

Offenbach had very definitely arrived, at any rate as a virtuoso, and of course continued to devote himself to the cello. Soon after his marriage he wrote a study for four cellos which reminded his audiences of a conversation between four old men. But he had always regarded the concert platform as a makeshift, and a career as a virtuoso did not attract him. Marriage increased his dissatisfaction with it. The human fulfillment of marriage seemed to intensify his craving for artistic fulfillment, as though the happiness that Herminie gave him put him under an obligation to live in future for his true vocation alone. At all events from the time of his marriage onwards his inclination to the stage developed at the expense of his devotion to the cello. It was his passion to conquer the stage that led to the many difficulties of his debut. It caused him to fall between two stools. Without being really at home on the concert platform he had not yet achieved the stage. But for Herminie's constant support the ten-year-long struggle upon which he now embarked might well have led to disaster.

Few have been so dependent on environment as Offenbach, and it was due principally to this that his struggle was so weary and so long. At one stage of his career a favorable environment pushed him forward with a rush, and at the next it worked consistently against him. The manner of his adversity corresponded exactly to that of his good fortune.

The stagnation of the period of Louis-Philippe had laid the foundation of Offenbach's rapid ascent, but it actually jeopardized his further progress. The existing order, which to Guizot was sacrosanct, was seriously shaken by a whole series of economic disasters — a bad potato-blight, harvest failures, and a grave industrial and commercial crisis which spread from England to France.

The effect of all this was not directly revolutionary, but it shattered the last illusions on which the stability of the regime had been based. Offenbach had thrived in its shadow, but now it seemed as though the glamour of society were to be quenched. Things started appearing as they really were, and the crude materialism of the dominant bourgeoisie became plain for all to see. "The chief preoccupation of the most influential section of the population," a contemporary moralist announced in censorious tones, "and the sole aim at which all their energies are directed, are making money without working, contriving ways of exploiting human gullibility, and finding sufficient fools to exploit — in short, what is generally called fraud. Society is brilliant and corrupt; it believes in nothing and is empty itself; all it knows is material pleasures and the enjoyment of luxury."

The money-making had been open and unashamed, and it was common knowledge that one of the most successful speculators had been the King himself; encouraged by the royal example, speculation became the religion of the state, with the Bourse as its temple. The stocks and shares quoted on the Bourse had more than trebled in number since the beginning of the regime. The Government, having done its best to encourage speculative fever for the sake of absorbing the doubtful and disaffected, could not but be aware of the danger that threatened it when tens of thousands of people pulled long faces when *rentes* fell. Everyone reacted to the slightest fluctuations of the market, from the peers, big landlords, and deputies at the top of the tree right down to boys at school. Even women — dancers, singers, *grandes dames* — found Bourse quotations more exciting reading than novelettes. The cynical frankness with which people resorted to speculation unmistakably revealed that they had ceased to have any hopes of the regime itself.

Typical of the enervation of the time is the story of a man dressed in black who called on a well-known doctor and complained that he was suffering from a fatal illness. What illness? the doctor inquired. Depression, hypochondria, was the reply. He could bear neither himself nor anyone else. The doctor advised him to go to the Théâtre des Funambules and see the celebrated comedian Debureau, whose antics would quickly cure him. " I am Debureau," the man replied.

Though great comedians always tend towards melancholy, Debureau was typical of his period. The money-grubbing atmosphere of the *juste milieu* had become intolerably oppressive, and the prevalent state of mind led Lamartine to talk of the impending " revolution of contempt."

The only escape lay in distraction. Those who could not afford expensive pleasures played game after game of dominoes in the cafés, smoking cigars the while; or, like everybody else, sauntered aimlessly along the Boulevards. This was the period when the *flâneur* originated, the aimless saunterer who sought to conceal the gaping void around him and within him by imbibing a thousand casual impressions. Shop-window displays, prints, new buildings, smart clothes, elegant equipages, newspaper-sellers — he indiscriminately absorbed the spectacle of life that went on all around him. " He stopped at the Théâtre de la Porte-Saint-Martin," Flaubert wrote of Frédéric in his *Éducation sentimentale* — Frédéric had not left Paris for the summer — " to look at the play-bill; and, as he had nothing to do, he bought a ticket.

An old pantomime was being performed, and the theater was nearly empty. . . . The scene was a slave-market in Peking, with bells and gongs and robes and pointed hats and puns. Later, when the curtain fell, he wandered alone through the foyer and admired a big green landau at the foot of the steps, drawn by two grays. A coachman in short knee-breeches was holding them by the bridle. . . ." For the *flâneur* the sights of the city were like his dreams to a hashish-smoker.

It was impossible to walk along the Boulevards between half past eleven and one o'clock at night without coming across Nestor Roqueplan walking up and down in the midst of a throng of journalists and librettists. When it was time to go to bed he and Gustave Claudin, also a journalist, would take a cab and spend hours taking each other home in turn. As Claudin's supreme desire was to be well dressed from morning to night and as he hated the idea of going home and changing, which would have meant losing a few minutes on his precious Boulevards, he kept a hat, several pairs of shoes, and all the requisites of a well-dressed gentleman at each of his various haunts so that he had no need to go home when the desire to change overcame him.

Strolling and lounging were not the only products of the general hunger for distraction. A contemporary writer bitterly condemned the gossip indulged in by a section of the Boulevard press, and complained that the first preoccupation of many young people when they got up in the morning was the menu for their evening meal. It was characteristic of the time that the object of all forms of entertainment was entertainment only. The sole object was to kill time, not to give it a meaning.

General Tom Thumb, a dwarf who jumped in a comical manner and sent all Paris into ecstasies of delight, was perfectly adequate for this time-killing purpose, and Marie Sergent, called " Queen Pomaré " after the Queen of Tahiti, found no difficulty in these conditions in earning herself a day's glory with a polka to which she gave an individual note by adding a touch of the cancan. She appeared at the fashionable restaurant kept by the Mabille brothers on the Champs-Élysées, where she performed her polka solo to resounding applause. At the theater, apart from lavish pantomimes, which offered satisfaction to all the senses, the fashion was for light revues, with current allusions that pleasantly tickled the senses.

Was this not a propitious time for Offenbach? One might have expected a ready welcome for operetta. Offenbach himself knew exactly what he owed to boredom. " My dream was always to found a mutual insurance society for the combating of boredom," he often used to say; and it was out of this dream that he created the operetta.

A revue by Clairville, produced at the Vaudeville in 1846, provided a striking proof that the times were coming half-way to meet him. The revue was called *Les Dieux d'Olympe à Paris,* and its plot was this: The immortals, being bored to death on Olympus, come to Paris on pleasure bent. Its motif being the conquest of boredom by unbridled pleasure, it might almost be regarded as a precursor of Offenbach's great operettas. Folly himself proclaims the gospel of unbridled pleasure to the gods and urges them to leave Olympus, and while they are in the midst of a champagne party in Paris, Minerva, the goddess of wisdom, who is by this time a little tipsy, advises the immortal assembly to give no ear to the monotonous preaching of virtue, but to be reasonable and drink and sing happily.

This was the mood of the operetta of the Second Empire, and it must certainly have stimulated Offenbach's pining for the stage. But though the atmosphere electrified him, for the time being the operetta still eluded him. In the first place several essential conditions were lacking; in the second place the successful period of Clairville's revue and other similar productions was too brief for Offenbach to have a chance. It started during a period of euphoria just before the end, ill-adapted to usher in the operetta, which required an unclouded sky and, as in the later years of the Second Empire, was quickly banished by the shadows of approaching doom.

Offenbach, however, utilized the fleeting moment to compose his first real burlesque, and burlesque was one of operetta's principal ingredients. Skits on important plays had delighted Paris since time immemorial. In a burlesque of Victor Hugo's *Les Burgraves,* produced at the Palais Royal, the actors parodied that tragedy's interminable monologues by looking at their watches every now and then and imploring the public to have patience, for it was not yet over.

Offenbach picked on Félicien David's symphonic ode *Le Désert,* one of the most noted productions of musical Romanticism. Its first performance, in 1846, had caused such excitement that when it was over, the audience had remained in the vestibule discussing it for a whole hour. Its theme was a poet's eulogy of the desert as the image of eternity, coupled with his pity for the townsman imprisoned between stone walls. This piece of sentimentalism was explained by the fact that David was a Saint-Simonist, and the Saint-Simonists were then engaged in studying their pet project of building a Suez Canal, with the result that all eyes were turned towards the desert. Offenbach, as a true *boulevardier,* must have felt irresistibly tempted to mock a work which sang the praises of nature because of its glorious views and thus ran counter to all the instincts of the Café de Paris. His burlesque was produced before more than two hundred guests at the Countess de Vaux's salon — it was just about the time of Clairville's revue — and caused hurricanes of laughter. David's highfalutin poet was turned into a Parisian of the name of Citrouillard, whose relation to the original was that of Sancho Panza to Don Quixote. Citrouillard complained bitterly about the climate and the lack of cafés in the desert and had so little appreciation of the majesty of night that at its approach he trembled for fear of tigers. The sentimentality of David's music was remorselessly exposed.

But the Opéra-Comique meant far more to Offenbach than

any salon success. The stage on which he had set his heart was that on which the works of Auber, Adam, Thomas, and Donizetti were produced, the stage below which he himself had sat as a humble, unknown member of the orchestra. This early dream was firmly planted in him and never left him throughout his life. He was convinced that the Opéra-Comique was the only proper place for the comic operas maturing within him; but incomparably stronger than this conviction was the blind, youthful longing, to which his protracted struggle with the Opéra-Comique gave an embittered intensity.

As the defenders of the fortress showed not the slightest sign of giving in, Offenbach renewed his attack with increased vigor. His forces consisted of seven new operatic fragments which he marshaled at a concert on April 24, 1846, two months after his burlesque of *Le Désert*. Among them were a Spanish ballad, *Sarah la blonde,* and *Meunière et fermière,* a comic duet, the words of which were again written by Plouvier.

In the latter two countrywomen, neighbors, start a friendly conversation, which gradually becomes quarrelsome and gets more so until they finally come to blows. The music is reminiscent of Auber, and the whole thing is a complete operetta scene in itself. Offenbach, moreover, did not confine himself merely to demonstrating his talents, but enlisted newspaper support on his behalf, in order not to leave M. Basset, the director of the Opéra-Comique, the slightest loophole.

There can have been few journalists in Paris to whom he did not talk of the Opéra-Comique, and his advances to M. Basset have a certain resemblance to the naïve audacity of Charlie Chaplin's advances to the circus manager in *The Circus*. The musical critic of *La France musicale* did his duty by Offenbach particularly well, for he declared that he had come away from his beautiful concert with full confidence that this talented composer would soon be given a libretto by the Opéra-Comique. He added that *La France musicale* would be much surprised if this did not happen.

M. Basset, driven into a corner by these and similar maneuvers, was compelled to give in. He gave the unwelcome intruder an adaptation of a one-act vaudeville piece, *L'Alcôve,* which had been successful at the Palais Royal in 1833. Offenbach wrote the music for it in a few months, glad at having opened a breach in the Opéra-Comique's defenses. His friend Roger promised to play the chief role, and he felt confident that M. Basset was now on the point of putting the whole Opéra-Comique at his disposal.

Armed with his score, he went to see him. He was told that the director was not in. When was the best time to find him? Perhaps the morning would be best, the attendant replied, or perhaps the evening; unless perhaps the gentleman preferred coming at midday.

Offenbach indefatigably waited upon M. Basset at all times of the day for weeks and months, but never found him in. He caused paragraphs to be put in the papers, but that made no difference either. There was no doubt that personal animosity was at work, but it was not that alone. The Opéra-Comique, as the result of its whole tradition, had a conception of comic opera that differed radically from Offenbach's, and very intelligibly recoiled from experiments, particularly in these troubled times; and Offenbach would have been an experiment. The music that he was now writing had no pronounced social function, but was simply light music. But according to the ideas of the Opéra-Comique it was excessively light music.

Midwinter came, and Offenbach was still being put off with excuses. As he could not live on them, he started giving recitals again. He played at the salons of Mme Orfila and the Princess Belgiojoso, who now regarded it as an honor to have him in her house.

Princess Belgiojoso was passionately devoted to the cause of Italian freedom, which caused her to be regarded as an eccentric. But that was not the only reason why she was so regarded. Another was that she liked collecting people of the most varied social status about her. Her ambitions were not satisfied by being ad-

mired by one stratum of society alone. On one occasion she organized a charity concert, in which Offenbach took part, and the
best place she could find for it was the Mabille dance-hall. In
the opinion of a man of the world who knew her, her real object in organizing the whole affair was to mix with courtesans.
That, if true, would have meant only that she was conforming
to the general tendency of the times. More and more courtesans
were to be seen at the races and on other public occasions, and
society women lost no opportunity of measuring themselves
against their rivals. When Marie Duplessis, the Lady of the
Camellias, died, they competed so frantically for her most intimate toilet articles that they pushed them up to perfectly fantastic prices. The salon was advancing into the street, and the
street was pushing its way into the salon.

In view of Offenbach's slender stock of patience, it meant a
great deal that he allowed himself to be kept waiting by the
Opéra-Comique until the spring of 1847. Then he had enough
of it. He turned his back on M. Basset and arranged to have his
musical setting of *L'Alcôve* produced on his own account, in the
shape of a *concert d'un genre neuf,* which took place on April 27,
1847 in the presence of an extremely fashionable audience. They
had their money's worth. The little opera was one of those
military pieces, so popular at the time, celebrating past days of
martial glory; its plot was laid in the time of the revolutionary
wars, and it contrasted a cowardly braggart of a republican
named Sauvageot with an upright and honorable nobleman.
This division of light and shade was well adapted to the taste
of his audience, and in writing his music Offenbach had followed the Opéra-Comique style, which did not, however, prevent his typical humor from breaking through in the passages
devoted to Sauvageot. *La France musicale* once more came out
very strongly on Offenbach's behalf. " On leaving the hall everyone was humming the prettiest tunes from his opera and won-
dering why on earth he should be left to wait in vain upon the
threshold of a temple that has been opened to so many medi-

LE BAL MABILLE

CARICATURE OF OFFENBACH

ocrities." M. Basset ignored this hint as he had ignored all previous ones. However, the praise lavished on the little work by Adolphe Adam, composer of *Le Postillon de Longjumeau,* who had just obtained the license for the Théâtre Lyrique, provided some compensation. As though to make good the injustice done to him by the Opéra-Comique, Adam commissioned him to write a comic opera, which he promised to produce soon after his theater opened.

But scarcely had Offenbach's luck turned when political events chased it away again. Social forces that had hitherto been dammed overflowed and swamped the regime of the *juste milieu.* The proletariat was on the move; and this time it was no longer willing to follow tamely in the footsteps of the bourgeoisie, as it had been in 1830. It took up Louis Blanc's claim for the right to work and demanded the suppression of machinery and the abolition of private property.

More important, however, was the opposition that came from within the bourgeoisie itself. Louis-Philippe's regime was not overthrown from without, it collapsed from within. In the course of 1847 a campaign of banquets for electoral reform began on the initiative of the Orléanists. Large sections of the bourgeoisie, whose economic situation was becoming more and more acute, could no longer be expected to remain without political representation; and the fact that it was only possible for business to develop in the shadow of the aristocracy of finance, and that corruption had passed all bounds, made the tension even more acute. In short, dissatisfaction was so rife among the bourgeoisie that it got very much on the nerves of such as Dr. Véron. He and his like had nothing to complain of. Hence in his opinion everything was satisfactory as it was, and he subsequently wrote in his memoirs that " when the February Revolution broke out, it was because people had grown tired of happiness, both in the political world and among the bourgeoisie."

The bourgeoisie, however, had no intention of abdicating; perhaps all that had happened was that they had grown thoroughly tired of a system which was embodied in such types as Dr. Véron and was so destitute of meaning, substance, and faith in itself that it gave in without a struggle.

The King summed up this attitude in his words to Guizot: " Even if we both call on everything we possessed — you your courage, your eloquence, and your devotion to the public good; and I my endurance and my experience of men and things — we shall never be able to effect anything in France, and a day will come when my children will have no bread."

Such resignation was not likely to achieve much. It remained possible for a short time yet to shut one's eyes and close one's ears, but then it was all over. When all the castles in the air had exploded and all the means of distraction had been exhausted, the disillusioned bourgeoisie finally turned their backs on the Government and plunged into the rapidly swelling republican tide.

Republicanism was resurgent. A wave of lyrical poetry had started in 1845, surrounding it with a romantic halo and lending it power over men's hearts. Romanticism had deserted the sinking ship and sought refuge with the opposition. A number of worker-poets made their appearance, and even Mme de Girardin could not refrain from praising some of them. The best of them was undoubtedly Pierre Dupont, who sang of country life, the poverty of the people, and the beauty of the social revolution. According to Baudelaire these poems owed their appeal to their " infinite yearning " for a republic.

Offenbach did not feel tempted to set them to music, and just when Dupont was writing very topical verses about the lot of the workers, whose toil began daily at cock-crow, Offenbach published a far from topical ballad addressed to a young girl coming home from the ball at about the same hour. Like the *boulevardiers,* he withdrew into the background as soon as things grew serious and the invisible barriers that protected the Boulevards collapsed. Although the *boulevardiers* were instinctively critical of the existing regime, all of them, with the exception of Count d'Alton-Shée, who declared himself a republican, were opposed to a democratic revolution, which would presumably rob them of their privileged position. They needed security if their own brand of Bohemianism were to flourish; therefore they abdicated in the face of a situation to which they themselves had contributed by reason of their fostering of the critical spirit. Many of them were only too conscious of being useless and played out.

It was therefore only natural that Offenbach's comic opera never appeared. The Théâtre Lyrique was opened under Adam's management in November 1847, and the production was postponed again and again. At last, in January 1848, it was announced that it really was going to be staged. But the plans were balked by the appearance of another drama, on a wider stage. The action took place in the streets, with barricades and corpses for scenery.

Freedom led the people.

Entr'acte 1848

ENTR'ACTE 1848

WHEN the revolution broke out, Offenbach, like many others, took to his heels. In a city without music and without Boulevard life he had nothing to lose and still less to gain. As a musician he was dependent on a public. The revolution drove his public away.

No one could possibly have suspected that the result of this revolution would be a society that would acclaim Offenbach. On the contrary, during the first few months it actually looked as though the republican dream were coming true; it even looked as though the aspirations of the working class were going to be fulfilled. The kingdom of heaven seemed to have come. Industrialists insisted on being called by the honorable name of "workers," bankers cried "*Vive la République!*" citizens of wealth and position deliberately neglected their clothing, ostensibly out of pure sympathy for the proletariat, and everyone waxed enthusiastic about the liberation of Poland and the national risings in Germany and Austria. The lion had lain down with the lamb.

But it was only the lamb that believed that the paradise would last. The Republic was founded with proletarian assistance, but it very soon became clear that it was an essentially bourgeois republic, the interests of which were directly opposed to the aspirations of the proletariat. To be sure, the Provisional Government, under pressure from the workers, organized "national workshops" to combat unemployment. These establishments were by no means in harmony with Louis Blanc's theories, being specifically designed for the purpose of reducing them to ridicule. The bourgeoisie, anxious for the failure of this pseudo-Socialist experiment, sabotaged it and hastened the economic ruin that came inevitably in its wake. The consequence was a crisis, for which, of course, the proletariat were blamed. Thus the proletariat ended by having both petty bourgeoisie and peasants against them. From moral isolation to forcible suppression was but a step.

On June 21, 1848 the constituent National Assembly enacted a decree prescribing the dissolution of the national workshops. Its conditions were so hard that the Paris workers took to arms in desperation. The battle between them and the militia and troops of the line commanded by General Cavaignac lasted four days, during which Mme de Girardin found herself greatly depressed by the unrestrained gaiety with which the birds sang in the deserted Champs-Élysées. After the victory of the Republic over the proletariat, many workers were massacred and thousands deported.

If the days of June left the workers exasperated and embittered, they gave the bourgeoisie a nasty shock. Animated by their zeal for liberty, they had overthrown Louis-Philippe and set up a democracy, naïvely leaving class antagonisms out of account. And then, when they believed themselves firmly in the saddle, they had suddenly discovered that democracy opened the way to the now self-conscious proletariat to seize the power in its turn. The bourgeoisie therefore brutally struck the proletariat down. But in doing so it flew in the face of its own principles and destroyed democracy. The breach of the bourgeoisie with the proletariat was also a breach with its own conscience.

A violent reaction then set in. The erstwhile democrats behaved like a lot of children who have strayed into a darkened room, had a bad fright, and run away in terror. The Catholics, Legitimists, and Orléanists, united into the Party of Order, and the peasants who were its allies, aspired to a restoration, and the desire for " order " and a " strong man " was heard on every side. The bourgeois desire for a strong man was the result of shock. The events and experiences that had led to it, the whole role played by the proletariat, their own alliance with it, and the reasons why they had liquidated it were deliberately repressed into the unconscious, where they formed a complex. People simply refused to face the facts, which they shamelessly suppressed and falsified. The nature and power of the complex is well illustrated by a conversation between the young republican Juliette Adam and her grandfather which she herself reports in her memoirs. It was this complex that led to the Second Empire.

" My grandfather," she wrote, " who was scarcely able to control his indignation, asked me angrily:

" ' So you are for the insurgents? '

" ' I am for a hundred thousand unfortunates, grandfather, who, perhaps incautiously, were promised work and are now faced with a brusque and merciless threat of being deprived of it.'

" ' But they are murderers.'

" ' Whom have they murdered? '

" ' They are thieves.'

" ' What have they stolen? '

" ' They are terrorizing the whole country.'

" ' Oh, yes, they are called criminals and madmen, so that they may be killed off. In the end, perhaps, the result will be that they really will spread terror. . . .'

" ' It is time Prince Louis intervened,' my grandfather retorted. ' Otherwise ideas like yours will bring us to the madhouse, Juliette.' "

The extravagant hopes that were placed upon Prince Louis Napoleon were another proof that the country was suffering severely from shock. Practically all that was known about the Prince was that he was the nephew of the great Napoleon, and that, relying upon the magic of his name, he had undertaken two pitiful attempts at insurrection. His name inspired him with a mystic belief that he had a star to follow, and he exploited like an adventurer the aura that surrounded it. He moved in international circles, incessantly plotting and conspiring, raising money from doubtful sources to procure himself even more doubtful followers. His dreams were highly colored and romantic. He was in favor of social reforms for the benefit of the working classes within the framework of a Cæsarean democracy. He also desired a revision of the treaties of 1815 and the carrying out of the principle of nationality. These ideas were not formulated in a program nor did they possess the power to create a Bonapartist movement. But in spite of all that, at the general election he defeated his opponent, the seasoned General Cavaignac, by an enormous majority. The surprising thing was that members of all parties voted for him. The wire-pullers of the Party of Order, with Thiers at their head, supported him because they secretly believed that he would not last long. The workers voted for him because they hated Cavaignac. The peasants regarded him as the future national dictator.

Only a phantom could be the object of such varied and inconsistent expectations. It was not the fact that he was known but the fact that he was unknown that rocketed Louis Napoleon to the skies. The masses, under the influence of shock, were still engaged in a rapid flight from reality, and their longing for a strong man concealed a neurotic aversion from facing reality. The very vagueness of the figure of Louis Napoleon, into which they could read almost anything they liked, made him infinitely more attractive than any clear-cut personality. Louis Napoleon had the incredible luck to hit upon a society that was looking for a phantom.

Meanwhile, where was Offenbach? In the critical days of February he took Herminie and his little daughter to Cologne. He was an *émigré*, emigrating to his native place. His return was the very opposite of a triumphal progress, because he came back as poor as the prodigal son. According to an unconfirmed report, he was so hard up that Herminie had to sacrifice her slender savings on the way. He is said shortly afterwards to have gambled his last florins at the Homburg casino, and actually to have

FLIGHT OF LOUIS-PHILIPPE
Revolution, 1848

THE PEOPLE IN THE TUILERIES
Revolution, 1848

Courtesy, British Museum

won. His winnings cannot have been great, for when he reached Cologne he went to live with his wife and child in a furnished room which contained nothing but a few sticks of furniture and a jingling old piano.

If Offenbach believed he would be able to live quietly in his native city till the troublous times were over, he made a big mistake. The revolution, with its most unmusical noises, followed upon his heels and seemed, indeed, to recognize no frontiers. Cologne, like Paris, was in an extraordinary state of ferment, the result of sudden and overwhelming democratic freedom, coupled with waves of patriotic emotion generated by the chimera of national unity. The whole city was in a state of uplift.

Offenbach had jumped out of the frying-pan into the fire. In earlier days his father had been able to help him, but the old man was nearly seventy now and needed help himself. Nevertheless Offenbach had to live somehow, and as there seemed to be no escape from the European madhouse, he adapted himself to the situation. Fortunately the course of the revolution in Cologne flowed into complacent, even musical channels. Innumerable glee clubs and volunteer bands sprang into existence, called forth by the gentle spring wind of democracy, and they found themselves faced with a severe shortage of songs. The whole German revolution was accomplished to the sound of songs, and while the people sang, the princes made their preparations to stifle it at leisure. Offenbach must have felt sorely tempted to burlesque the musical outpourings of the citizen-soldiers, but he preferred to keep in step and work for the available market. He composed a *Song of the German Boys,* bursting with insufferable military pathos, and *The German Fatherland,* a song in honor of the German girl, who was said to be incapable of Latin guile. Offenbach seized every opportunity of getting into the limelight. He excelled at patriotic songs and serenades and found his way into the inner circles. The *Kölnische Zeitung* called him " with pride our very own." So much was he " their very own " that he played at the farewell banquet to the retiring mayor and reverted to his original signature of Jakob.

The comedy reached its height with the celebrations on August 14, 1848, in honor of the six hundredth anniversary of the laying of the foundation-stone of Cologne Cathedral. The celebrations were given a national character by the presence of the King of Prussia, the Vice-Regent, the Archduke John of Austria, and a deputation from the Parliament then in session at Frankfurt. The Cologne Men's Choral Society was called upon to play a very prominent part in the proceedings. At that most notable performance Offenbach played his cello. Wedged in among the singers in the crowded Cathedral, he played his fantasia from the works of Rossini, which could not be described as exactly German, to the greater glory of German liberty and unity. The scene was as stirring and as comic as German democracy itself.

Perhaps Offenbach was aware of the absurdity of his role, but he was singularly naïve, and piety towards his aged father, to whom democracy doubtless meant the completion of Jewish emancipation, may have caused him to take it seriously. Self-interest, an unconfessed sense of mischief, and a trace of genuine conviction may all have been inextricably mingled.

At the end of this exciting year Offenbach busied himself with the preparation of a German version of his *L'Alcôve*. It was produced in Cologne in January 1849, but the press took no further notice of it. Meanwhile peace had been established in Paris, so back to Paris he went.

Part TWO

CHAPTER I

COUP D'ÉTAT

OFFENBACH had been away from Paris for a whole year. Upon his return he tried to pick up the thread where it had been interrupted a year before, as the Opéra-Comique in particular soon became aware. He once more laid siege to it with his accustomed guile, but M. Perrin, the new director, held out as obstinately as his predecessor. Under the pressure of grim necessity Offenbach plunged for the hundredth time into the same old round of salons and concerts. But he did score one success. He received an invitation to the Élysée, where he was applauded by the Prince-President. It was his first meeting with the future Emperor. But in spite of this and other social triumphs, success as an executant satisfied him so little that he started neglecting his playing. One of the musical papers criticized him for triviality and deplored his apparent satisfaction with pleasing the bourgeoisie and aristocracy.

This public enjoyed Offenbach's light-heartedness all the more because it had other troubles at the moment. Having successfully got rid of the workers, it now had the petty bourgeoisie to reckon with. The latter, in their economic distress and their anxiety not to be sacrificed on the altar of the wealthy bourgeoisie, were wholeheartedly republican and democratic, while for equally cogent reasons the serried ranks of the wealthy bourgeoisie drawn up in the Party of Order were anti-republican and anti-democratic. At the elections for the Legislative Assembly the Party of Order, thanks to its alliance with the Prince-President, its financial resources, and the after-effects of the bloodthirsty days of June, obtained an absolute majority. This triumph of reaction resulted in the radical petty bourgeoisie uniting with the Socialists, whom they had fought so bitterly only a short time before, to form the party of the Mountain. The Legislative Assembly met on May 29, 1849, and only two weeks later the tension between Right and Left flared up into an open conflict, which ended with a defeat of the Mountain and the elimination of its leaders. Reaction was now supreme. Its first task was to put the clock back and wipe out all traces of republicanism, for it had had enough of democracy and all the bourgeois liberties thanks to which it had climbed into the saddle. As the by-elections in the spring of 1850 showed that Socialism had by no means been extinguished, but was actually making headway in the army and among the peasants, Parliament proceeded to abolish universal suffrage and the liberty of the press. This condemned the bourgeois Left and the proletariat alike to political impotence. The republican dream was over. Henceforward the only question was who was going to take over its mantle; the Party of Order, which was heading straight for a monarchy, or the Prince-President, who did not relish the prospect of relinquishing power when his period of office expired.

These were bad times for Offenbach. He was unhappy and could not bring himself to compose anything. Thus another year passed.

At the end of April 1850 his father died. Not long afterwards Offenbach was sitting one morning at the Café Cardinal, which was the recognized meeting-place of everyone connected with the stage. Had he not been sunk in thought, he could not have failed to notice the entry of a man who came in and sat down at a neighboring table. He had a handsome and commanding presence, curly hair, a fan-shaped beard, and a smiling mien. Arsène Houssaye had every reason to smile. After a romantic, Bohemian boyhood, he had effortlessly achieved every possible kind of success: women, friends, literary success, all the pleasures of a carefree life. He was not a man to plumb life to its depths, but he enjoyed it with taste. He was a cultured dilettante, a connoisseur. Rachel had just had him appointed director of the Comédie Française, and she was certainly right in believing that this amateur had the gifts required to restore the fortunes of that ancient institution, which were at a low ebb.

The need for diplomacy and resourcefulness had been seen immediately after his appointment. For the players, jealous of their independence, had violently objected to a director who was given authoritative jurisdiction over them, and they were so mistrustful of Rachel's intrigues that they had gone on strike. Thus Houssaye had been forced to look for substitutes, negotiate, improvise, before he had properly begun.

Just at this critical period chance willed it that he should walk into the Café Cardinal. No sooner did he catch sight of Offenbach, whom he had met at many salons and of whose artistic gifts he had the highest opinion, than it struck him that he had not yet even considered the question of his orchestra. Nominally the Comédie Française possessed an orchestra, but it was impossible to pretend that it really deserved the name. It was in as precarious a state as the ill-fated Republic itself and consisted of a few musicians who played from time to time when a musical accompaniment was required, though this formality was often omitted even when the text demanded it. They also played during the intermission because that was the custom, although it never occurred to anyone to listen. Houssaye decided that something must be done about this and approached Offenbach.

" Would you like to revolutionize the Comédie Française? " he said.

" Certainly. I'm a man who likes to be in the midst of things."

Houssaye offered him the post of conductor at the Comédie Française at a yearly salary of six thousand francs. Modest though the position was, Offenbach did not even hesitate before accepting it. He would have accepted anything for the sake of escaping from bondage to the salons; and he would show the world what he had in him yet.

Full of the best intentions, he promptly enlarged the existing Comédie Française orchestra, engaged several competent musicians, undertook a variety of reforms, and exploited the opportunity of playing his own compositions as much as possible. One of his methods of forcing people to listen to the music was to appear at the conductor's desk in evening dress and white gloves, which was unusual at that place. He might have been conducting at the Opéra.

Houssaye was delighted at all this zeal, which gave new life to the Comédie Française. This was just what he had expected. "Offenbach did wonders," he wrote in his memoirs. "How many operas and operettas did he not play during the intermissions!" Houssaye was also attracted by the conductor's gay and cheerful temperament, though, looking back in later years, he says that Offenbach was not always cheerful, but was often troubled by extra-marital love-affairs. It is more than likely that he greatly exaggerated these, for he himself was favored with a superfluity of amorous adventures, and as he set great store by himself, he instinctively pictured his friends after his own image.

But the approbation of the director and the satisfaction felt by the more appreciative section of the audience at Offenbach's efforts to make his entr'actes harmonize with the events on the stage availed him little. The actors resented Offenbach's innovations as an intrusion, and as they also shared in the theater's profits, they objected to the fact that a number of the best seats had to be sacrificed to make room for the enlarged orchestra, apart from the fact that they were not in the least interested in anything so inferior as music. Was there to be no difference between the Comédie Française and a music hall? In their childish vanity the players sabotaged the music in every way they could. The result was the outbreak of a guerrilla warfare between them and Offenbach, which gave the latter no little cause for complaint in his autobiographical notes.

" Scarcely had I installed myself," he wrote, " when I saw how vain my struggle would be against the preconceived notion that at the Théâtre Français the music must be impossible and the orchestra appalling. The stockholders in particular took this for granted. I had arranged for the curtain not to go up until after the bell had been rung, as is the practice even in second-rate theaters, but every evening insuperable difficulties arose. Once the stockholders were upon the stage, they refused to wait, while the stage manager refused to raise the curtain, saying that he had Houssaye's specific instructions. And the result was endless vexation, unpleasantness, and dissension."

If the curtain had only been Offenbach's sole disappointment! He was destined to find out to his cost that there were important differences between actors and singers. At the beginning of his career as a conductor preparations were being made for the production of Alfred de Musset's *Le Chandelier,* the chief character in which is Fortunio, a fledgling lawyer who is in love with his client's wife. Fortunio believes his love is returned and sings her a love-song, without, however, suspecting that she is having an affair with a young officer and is only using him, Fortunio, to put her husband off the scent. But she is caught in her own trap and ends by succumbing to Fortunio's charms and the magic of his song.

One day a young man was in Houssaye's office when de Musset himself walked in and asked Houssaye to ask Offenbach to put the song to music the next time he saw him. The young man, of whom de Musset had taken no notice, was Offenbach. Houssaye introduced them, and Offenbach wrote the music the same day, bearing in mind the soft, gentle voice with which the actor Delaunay played the part of Fortunio. Having heard his voice, it was impossible not to believe that he would have a lovely tenor. Next morning Delaunay arrived to try the music. Offenbach sat down at the piano, but stopped after a few bars and sadly folded up his manuscript. Delaunay's voice was a deep bass. Offenbach's music had to be scrapped.

Offenbach's setting was as tender as the poem itself. Fortunio says that not for a kingdom would he tell the name of his beloved. His beloved was undoubtedly the lawyer's wife, to whom the song was addressed. But his words are in reality addressed to the invisible, unattainable, ideal she. The music is also addressed to the infinite and belongs to the never-never land to which Offenbach belonged, the only country in which he had any real roots.

As for de Musset, as the years went by he became more and more detached from the world of reality and by the time that he met Offenbach he was a very sick man. He had taken to absinthe and was visibly going downhill, and indulged in caprices that showed how slight was his contact with real life. When Dr. Véron asked him for an article for *Le Constitutionnel,* he demanded the fantastic fee of four thousand francs, which he promptly squandered in a single evening. For some reason he believed Offenbach to be a bird of ill omen, and after their meeting in Houssaye's office he always avoided him.

Offenbach's nature was by no means bureaucratic. As the players at the Comédie Française remained intractable, he gradually gave in and only conducted when it was absolutely essential. But he never allowed the music of his orchestra to suffer because of his own artistic frustration. On the contrary, responsibility acted on him like a spur.

Offenbach always willingly made sacrifices to help others. He secured better pay for his musicians, who received two thousand francs a year, and, remembering his own poverty when he had been in the orchestra at the Opéra-Comique, lent them money whenever they asked for it. One evening he confessed to Herminie that he had only one hundred and fifty francs left out of his monthly salary. He could not resist other people's misfortunes, and he was completely indifferent to possessions himself.

While Offenbach was engaged in drudgery at the Comédie Française, the society that was to acclaim his operettas was coming into being. The masses had chosen a phantom for their

President, but the phantom played his cards with skill. He produced one trump after another. He organized gangs of supporters among the Paris rabble, who used bludgeons as a powerful argument on his behalf; he bought up newspapers, packed municipal and Government offices with his own adherents, and made a whole series of skillfully organized provincial tours in order to enhance his popularity. Dangerous opponents, such as General Changarnier, who was a strong parliamentarian, were adroitly eliminated. Nevertheless the outcome of all this would have been doubtful had not the overwhelming majority of the bourgeoisie, in their fear of the Socialists, sided with him and against Parliament.

Parliament itself, indeed, seemed to regard the assertion of its own independence as more important than the restoration of a strong regime. The Party of Order tried again and again to check Louis Napoleon's autocratic tendencies and even went so far as to ally themselves with the parties of the Left, a maneuver which tended to strengthen the Republic rather than lead to a monarchy. But the bourgeoisie, indignant at the dissension between Parliament and the executive power, stabbed their own Parliament in the back.

They were in a tremendous hurry. Félix Arvers, who had been one of the celebrities of the Boulevards in the time of Louis-Philippe, wrote a letter bursting with enthusiasm for Louis Napoleon to his friend Alfred Tattet, at whose side he had fought at the barricades in 1830. His significant conclusion was that " the total suppression of the Republic " was essential for the return of prosperity. The bankers, the industrialists, and, above all, the great majority of the bourgeoisie endorsed this opinion. These people had one interest and one interest only: to be able to get on with their business, undisturbed by politics. During the July Monarchy they had been just as materialistic. But a revolution had intervened, and a mood of callous self-interest had replaced their previous naïve idealism. In their blindfold haste to accept the dictatorship of Louis Napoleon and deny their own revolution, they had stifled their conscience and replaced it by a complex.

In 1851 everybody knew that a dictatorship was inevitably and rapidly approaching, though nobody knew exactly how it would come. A whole host of adventurers, sharks, and careerists who hoped to benefit from it appeared as its harbingers.

The times were very favorable indeed for Thérèse Lachman, who had long since discarded Henri Herz, who was now living in poverty in America. She lived in grand style and associated with a slightly disreputable clique of magnates, German millionaires, and English lords. It was in these circles that she one day met a Portuguese nobleman in reduced circumstances, by name the Marquis de Paiva-Aranjo. Believing that such a well-sounding name would be an excellent investment, she quite literally bought it, by paying the poor Marquis's debts. The only trouble was that she had to accept the Marquis into the bargain. But she managed to get rid of him only two years after their marriage, and it was then a simple matter to set herself up as La Païva.

Another individual who managed to keep his head above water was Dr. Véron, whose capacity for adapting himself to the most varied regimes was truly exceptional. To be sure, with the passage of years he had lost some of his former elasticity. When the Minister Faucher brusquely refused a favor he asked for Rachel, he let loose a furious attack on him in *Le Constitutionnel*. He was too vain to imitate the crawling obsequiousness of the younger generation. This little episode did not, however, prevent M. Faucher from occasionally dining choicely at Dr. Véron's château at Auteuil. The tremendous impression made on such a well-informed man of the world as Count Horace de Viel-Castel by the uncanny power exercised behind the scenes by Dr. Véron is therefore readily intelligible. The Count was positively hypnotized; and he had good reason to be, for Dr. Véron's power survived kingdoms, revolutions, and republics.

Tirelessly as Persigny, Louis Napoleon's oldest and most faithful adherent, drove him forward upon the road he had embarked upon, he lacked the capacity to move in the highest spheres and render them subservient to his will. As a whipper-in he rendered priceless services; as a statesman he was like a provincial actor on a metropolitan stage. Louis Napoleon was lucky that at the decisive stage of his struggle for power he was able to enlist the support of Count de Morny, who, as the natural son of Queen Hortense and General de Flahaut, was his half-brother.

Having grown up among the grandees of the Empire and the elite of the *ancien régime,* Morny, ever since his childhood, had moved in exalted circles, in which cynicism was second nature and a well-mannered rogue was considered preferable to an honest man of uncouth behavior. Morny was a product of that world. He distinguished himself as an officer in the African expedition, but abandoned his military career before the age of thirty and settled in Paris, where he joined the Jockey Club, became friendly with Count d'Alton-Shée, and tried to raise the tone of the court of Louis-Philippe. But, unlike most of his tribe, he had not the slightest intention of idling his life away in vice and frivolity. He set himself to explore the inner workings of society with an acuteness entirely unhampered by any political or humanitarian ideals; and his investigations satisfied him that the future belonged to finance and industry. So he bought a sugar factory at Clermont-Ferrand, and, being aware of the fruitful effects of reciprocity between finance and politics, secured a seat in the Chamber of Deputies. His new political influence was most opportunely supplemented by his influence in society, where he derived considerable assistance from his mistress, the Countess Le Hon.

The result was that he acquired widespread business interests that extended from his beet-sugar enterprise to a share in Dr. Véron's *Le Constitutionnel*. These enterprises flourished exceedingly, and Morny was enabled to indulge his tastes and collect valuable pictures. But æsthetic interests did not in the least distract him from his practical ones. On the contrary, they rather enhanced his quickness of vision and sureness of touch. Towards the end of the July Monarchy he proposed a bold series of social reforms which, if promptly adopted, might perhaps have prevented the collapse of the regime. The sole reason why he was progressive on this occasion was that he deemed it to be expedient. A few years later he offered Louis Napoleon his support for the same reason. His finances had been shaken by the revolution, and it did not take him long to discover on which side his bread was buttered. Louis Napoleon appreciated his new ally at his full value, although it disturbed him slightly to see him always with a hydrangea [1] in his buttonhole, as if to demonstrate to all the world that he, too, was Queen Hortense's son. Louis Napoleon did not like sharing his mother with anybody.

When Parliament refused to revise the Constitution in order to legalize an extension of the Prince-President's term of office, a *coup d'état* became inevitable. Every step taken at the Élysée pointed in that direction; for instance, Parliament was asked at the eleventh hour to restore universal suffrage, the sole purpose being to win the workers for the future Emperor; and resolute supporters were put in all the key positions. Saint-Arnaud, the new Minister of War, was specially summoned from Africa because of the lack of suitable generals in France; not long before he had been specially put in charge of an African expedition against the Kabyles in order to give him a little artificial popularity. As soon as the stage was set, it was possible for the farce to begin. The bourgeoisie were afraid of reality, victims of a complex, which Louis Napoleon and his supporters unscrupulously exploited for their own purposes. Count de Viel-Castel gives a clue to the frivolity of the whole affair by saying that the band of conspirators reminded him of a carnival party.

By order of the Prince-President the *coup d'état* took place on December 2, 1851, an auspicious date because it was the anniversary of the Battle of Austerlitz and the coronation of the great Napoleon. Where responsibility is lacking, astrology generally steps in to take its place. The stage-management was in the hands

[1] In French, *hortensia*.

of Morny, as Minister of the Interior, and the performance was technically without a flaw. After a final conference at the Élysée on the evening of December 1, Morny went to the Opéra-Comique, where he chatted and smiled disarmingly and seemed mainly interested in inspecting an extremely attractive young blonde in a box through his eyeglass. During the night, proclamations were printed announcing the dissolution of Parliament and the holding of a plebiscite, while all the persons whom Morny regarded as being potentially dangerous were arrested.

When the people of Paris awoke next morning, it seemed as if hobgoblins had been working during their sleep. The bourgeois republicans tried to prevail upon the workers to resist the *coup d'état* by force, but the workers, having certain experiences behind them, not unjustifiably decided that this was an affair of the bourgeoisie, and went on playing billiards. Barricades were few and isolated, but at one of them on the following day Victor Baudin, a republican deputy, sacrificed his life in an effort to rouse the masses from their indifference. As the conspirators were of opinion that a *coup d'état* was not complete unless there were a real armed insurrection to put down, it was a source of great satisfaction to them that on December 4 a movement developed that half looked like developing into a rising, thus making military intervention possible. Several hundred persons, mainly curious spectators, were shot down on the spot. The farce had to be a bloody one, otherwise its true nature would have been seen through too quickly.

" Everything is quiet here," Offenbach wrote a day after the massacre to his sister Netta, in Cologne, whose daughter was at a Paris boarding-school. " Everything is quiet here, so we have just sent Julius to see little Isabelle. She is quite well, and very pleased at having been present at a revolution, though at a safe distance. We, too, are all as well as could be. I hope that Paris will again live in joy and glamour as it did before."

CHAPTER II

JOY AND GLAMOUR

Joy and glamour was also the motto of Louis Napoleon. In his zeal for it he instituted a ruthless reign of terror directed against all who might disturb it. Immediately after the *coup d'état* tens of thousands of Socialists, republicans, and members of secret societies were summarily arrested and sent into exile or deported like common criminals. The sufferers were certainly not the bourgeoisie, who spoke of the reign of terror as necessary police action, though of course somewhat harsh.

Louis Napoleon had no choice but to proclaim a policy of joy and glamour if he were to maintain himself in power. For he was faced with a variety of insoluble paradoxes. The interests of the peasants were profoundly divergent from those of the bourgeoisie, yet he represented them both. The material progress made by the bourgeoisie was inevitably destined to constitute a menace to him, yet he was compelled to favor them. Both the bourgeoisie and the peasants desired the suppression of the proletariat, but he was compelled to woo the workers' support if his dictatorship was to endure. One of the most important groups supporting him was the Roman Catholics. But as an upholder of the nationality principle he was bound sooner or later to come into conflict with the Pope.

The dictator's policy was therefore conditioned from the first by the necessity of stifling all these incompatibilities. As he had neither the capacity for carrying out reforms or introducing social changes nor the intention of doing so, his sole ambition being to maintain himself in power, his only possible course was perpetually to maneuver and tack. Steps he took to benefit the workers were resented by the bourgeoisie, and concessions had to be made to placate them. These in turn made other adjustments necessary, and thus a kind of endless cycle was set up. No amount of political dexterity of this kind would, however, have sufficed by itself. Louis Napoleon saw clearly the need for banishing all sense of realism, all capability of seeing things as they really were and detecting the paradoxes and antagonisms latent within the new regime. His object was to keep the country in a perpetual state of hysteria, prevent it from ever having time for cool reflection.

Hence the motto of joy and glamour — the joy was to intoxicate and the glamour to dazzle. Hence, too, the lavish expenditure that Louis Napoleon embarked upon. The Presidential Palace was the scene of a perpetual round of fêtes, and sumptuous splendor characterized the Prince-President's hastily improvised court. The purpose of this magnificence was not only to fascinate the people but to satisfy the appetites of his innumerable supporters and accomplices. Sinecures rained down upon them like manna. Thanks to a grant of twelve million francs, Louis Napoleon was also able to make suitable provision for his relatives. The latter did not amount to very much.

If old Jerome, who as King of Westphalia had made a not inconsiderable contribution to the increase in that country's birthrate, possessed the sentimental value that attaches to a family relic, his son, Prince Jerome Napoleon, was not an asset in any sense of the word. The only exception to the general worthlessness of the family was Princess Matilda, Prince Napoleon's sister, who had been not long married to the Russian Prince Anatole Demidoff, whose wealth enabled her to devote herself to the cultivation of art, literature, and society. She gratified the wishes of her cousin, the Prince-President, by agreeing to act as hostess at the Élysée. This was a good and sufficient reason for Offenbach to dedicate to her a collection of his tunes, entitled *Les Voix mystérieuses,* including Fortunio's song.

Louis Napoleon took the living relics of his great uncle under his wing less out of piety than because he believed it would facilitate his entering upon the whole inheritance, as he now aspired to do. With the skill of an experienced plotter he took step after step in the direction of the imperial throne. At a ceremony on the Champ de Mars, which roused the ridicule of his opponents, he presented the army with Napoleonic eagles, and once more made a series of provincial tours. More and more often was he met with the cry of "*Vive l'Empereur!*" Underlying every step he took was the knowledge that the title of Emperor would be an ideal instrument for rousing mass hysteria, and that by it the prestige of his dictatorship would be immeasurably enhanced.

But he also knew that in the long run even the name of Emperor would not suffice to disguise the contradictions with which his dictatorship was faced at every step. The effects of even the most brilliant piece of play-acting are necessarily shortlived. Other measures were required to cast a really enduring spell upon the people. Something had to be found that would affect the masses in their daily lives; to give a new, homogeneous impulse to their way of thinking and acting, to release and at the same time to fetter energies that otherwise might be dangerously directed.

It was from considerations such as these that Louis Napoleon favored the Saint-Simonists, who, though they still believed that the best guarantee of social progress and lower-class prosperity was unrestricted industrial progress, had now abandoned theory and confined themselves to purely practical aims. The dictator's advances to the Saint-Simonists were reciprocated. Enfantin, once the head of the long-dead Saint-Simonist school, stated that the *coup d'état* was an act of Providence; indeed, the need for a dictatorship had long been a part of the Saint-Simonist creed. Louis Napoleon was impelled towards the Saint-Simonists by the hope that they would inspire the whole population. Loan banks and joint stock companies that enticed the money from the pockets of the people, put it into circulation, and created work; gigantic public-works schemes, giving employment to thousands — all this must be put across on a grand scale if the industrial upsurge were to stifle all opposition.

A remarkable result of it was that Louis Napoleon, whose sole object was to bolster up his own power by deluding the people with chimerical visions, nevertheless inadvertently became a real instrument of progress. The times were ripe for large-scale commercial and financial developments, for the opening up of new channels of international trade and finance; in short, for capitalist development on a world-wide scale. Only the final impulse was lacking, and Louis Napoleon supplied it. And though his sole motive was to distract the attention of the masses from political realities, his actions had a number of useful economic and social consequences.

In the first year of his dictatorship the resources of the whole nation were mobilized at his bidding. The Government distributed railway concessions, encouraged the shipping industry on a grand scale, won the peasants by laying down departmental roads, reformed the public pawnshops, granted funds for the building of better workers' dwellings, and actually set about rebuilding Paris. The rapidity with which decree followed decree, and the glamour that surrounded all these schemes, robbed people of either the desire or the leisure to grieve for their lost liberty. That was precisely what they were intended to do. Commerce and finance vied with each other in seizing the opportunities held out to them. In the course of 1853 there were established the Crédit Foncier, the Crédit Mobilier, founded by the brothers Péreire for the purpose of financing the railways, and the Bon Marché, the first of the big Paris stores.

The pace of these developments was unhealthy and intemperate, and since the intention behind them was to create an illusion, their illusory nature was often very nearly revealed.

" After the *coup d'état* people started talking in millions," Arsène Houssaye states in his memoirs, " and everyone began to dream of his own millions. What an abundance of sudden wealth! The reality exceeded the dream." Houssaye's own dream came true in triumphant fashion. He made 825,000 francs in a single operation on the Bourse, then lost it all within three days, started playing the market again, and finally, child of fortune that he was, brought his capital up to the desired million. He was not the man to put any unnecessary obstacles in the way of his good fortune. Scarcely had Louis Napoleon returned from his tour of the provinces, during which he coined the famous slogan: " The Empire is peace," when Houssaye composed a *Hymn to the Emperor of Peace* and had it declaimed by Rachel on the occasion of a gala performance arranged in Louis Napoleon's honor at the Théâtre Français. Only three or four years before, immediately after the revolution, Rachel had sung the *Marseillaise* on the same stage. She was now at the zenith of her fame and often entertained Count de Morny to dinner.

Count de Morny had resigned his position as Minister of the Interior, as a protest against the confiscation of the Orléanists' property. The Orléanists were friends of his, and he regarded loyalty to them as important. This behavior was, of course, its own reward; but it also enabled him to devote himself to his own finances for a time. They were once more thriving. This interval out of office was very lucrative. He and Dr. Véron made more than a clear half-million each by selling *Le Constitutionnel* to the financier Mirès.

On December 2, 1852, exactly one year after the *coup d'état,* the seal was set on the dictatorship by Louis Napoleon's coronation as Emperor, following a vote of the Senate and one of those plebiscites which Louis Napoleon, the first of the modern dictators, exploited in such masterly fashion.

The fantastic had come true. But now that he had unlimited power, instead of emerging from the haze that surrounded him, he disappeared more and more behind the smoke-clouds of his innumerable cigarettes. He would spend his time in silent and solitary brooding. Sometimes he resembled a sleepwalker pursued by hallucinations, and his suite tried vainly to discover what voices he was listening to. He seemed to be terrified of waking up and finding himself in the gray light of an ordinary day. As the bourgeoisie had no desire to be awakened, everything was all right; at any rate as long as the general slumber was not abruptly disturbed. The Emperor, in order to make it more profound, put the finishing touch to the dream-structure by taking unto himself an Empress.

The Countess Eugenia de Montijo, a Spanish lady, whose mother's past was not entirely beyond suspicion, had succeeded in winning him without herself falling a victim to his charms in the usual fashion; so that he had to do the right thing by her and marry her. He justified his decision in a speech he made to the three organs of government, flattering his subjects by saying that he, being an upstart himself — that is, a ruler by the people's will — had no ambition to obtrude himself upon the old dynasties. When, therefore, on January 30, 1853, her wedding day, Eugénie, seated at the Emperor's side, drove through the new rue de Rivoli on the way to Notre-Dame in all the finery of her white satin dress and her crown diadem, the crowd rejoiced at this climax of splendor and had no suspicion but that joy incarnate had descended upon earth.

Offenbach was not one of the jubilant ones. He was now repeating, though on a higher level, the ordeal of his earlier days at the Opéra-Comique — the ordeal of not being independent. Houssaye, who liked to flit like a bee from talent to talent, entrusted the musical setting of the choruses in Ponsard's tragedy *Ulysses* not to him but to the unknown Gounod. A slight like that hurt. For want of artistic satisfaction, Offenbach sought at least to gain social advantages from his position. So he had himself introduced by Berlioz to Jules Janin, the omnipotent dramatic critic, and started frequenting his salon. It did him no good. So many other people got their chances in these days; would his chance never come? However, Paris held out to the last against its future idol. And although as a theatrical conductor he was admitted to the inner circles of the theatrical world, he still had to give concerts in order to have his stage music played at all.

He had considerable hopes of the concert he was due to give in May 1853, at which singers from the Opéra-Comique were presenting his latest work, *Le Trésor à Mathurin;* he thought he was entitled to assume that in their own interests they would persuade their director, M. Perrin, to accept it. His expectations were, of course, based on the merits of the little piece, a one-act pastoral, the choruses and finale of which had a dramatic twist. The libretto was by Léon Battu, one of Offenbach's Boulevard friends. Its ingredients included the chiming of bells, lights in the darkness, and love again, while the charm and grace of Offenbach's music brought Mozart to mind. With all this it could not fail to be a success. The result of the evening was that the skirmish between Offenbach and the Opéra-Comique was resumed, with results as negative as before. Offenbach had yet to learn that in order to be successful one must already have been a success, and that one's first success is governed by a thousand incalculable factors. Four years later he had the satisfaction of seeing this spurned piece leap to world fame under the title of *Le Mariage aux Lanternes*.

Small signs of courtly favor were an inadequate compensation for the failure of his concert to achieve its real purpose. A gay schottische he had played in an intermission at the Théâtre Français pleased Prince Jerome so well that he insisted on an encore and next day sent the composer a letter of thanks, as well as an expensive diamond tie-pin. But recognition such as this arose from the mood of a moment and died with it.

A more important fact was that his one-act comic opera *Pepito,* which he had dedicated, in spite of all his disappointments, to Mme Perrin, the wife of the director to whom all his aspirations were directed, was produced at the Théâtre de Variétés. The Variétés was at least a real theater. The action of *Pepito* takes place in Spain, or more particularly in Elizondo; the hero is a young dandy transplanted from Madrid to that rural spot; and

the plot contains several love-affairs and has a happy ending. It
it a pleasing little work, half-way between an opera and an
operetta. Jules Janin wrote about it in a friendly fashion and deplored the coyness of the Opéra-Comique. Nevertheless the
Opéra-Comique remained unmoved. Six months later Offenbach
consoled himself for the meager success of *Pepito* by arranging
a private performance of it in his own home. He played the chief
male role himself, notwithstanding his impossible bass voice.
Two hundred guests were crammed into the narrow rooms,
almost touching the ceiling with their heads. Singers, journalists,
librettists, and littérateurs liked coming here, for they enjoyed
the cheerfulness and friendliness of Offenbach's house. And as
for their host, the more crowded his rooms were, the more people
he had around him, the happier, the more secure he felt.

In the meantime the social life typical of the Second Empire
was beginning to blossom. Its pattern was the court, whose luxury propagated its kind. Plenty of joy and glamour could be
conjured up with the twenty-five million francs of the Imperial
civil list. Napoleon used to say that luxury brought money into
circulation among the people, using this spurious argument to
conceal its real object. The Empress Eugénie adored the magnificence her husband paraded in order to assert his power. She was
young and more beautiful than the most beautiful women by
whom she was surrounded, and when the Tuileries re-echoed
with the gay tumult of the court balls she outshone the most glittering chandeliers and rapturously accepted the homage that was
paid her. Besides acting as the center of attraction on these and
other festive occasions, she was active in charity work, and
helped the Emperor to attract to the court poets, artists, and men
of learning, who are, of course, a court's indispensable adjunct.
The Emperor and Empress found not a few who were willing to
oblige in fulfilling their ambitions in this respect.

One of the Emperor's favorite projects was the rebuilding of
Paris. Like all dictators, his dread of perishability led him to
erect monuments. He was a strange mixture of calculation and

fantasy. One of his motives for beautifying his capital was that of sustaining and increasing the magic associated with his name; but he was also actuated by purely practical aims, such as the combating of unemployment, the improvement of hygiene, and the betterment of traffic conditions; and last but not least, broad, straight streets made insurrections more difficult, because they could be swept by artillery, and macadamized roads increased the difficulty of putting up barricades.

In Baron Haussmann the Emperor found the right man for the job. Different regimes favor different types. The regime of Napoleon III favored men who got down to work without any excessive scruples, seized chances where they found them, and looked neither too far forward nor too far back. Looking back might have been too dangerous. Haussmann, appointed Prefect of the Seine in 1853, was a man of this stamp. He possessed the robust optimism of all prefects, a robust constitution capable of standing up to the most riotous drinking bouts, a flair for essentials combined with a ruthless lack of consideration for details and an autocratic temperament disinclined to any kind of parliamentary negotiation. All these characteristics were invaluable for the reconstruction of Paris.

One of his first tasks was the building of the Palace of Industry in the Champs-Élysées. The Emperor dreamed of a world exhibition on the pattern of the Great Exhibition in London.

The spell cast over the bourgeoisie was intensified at the sight of the vast piles of debris, the new buildings going up, the scaffolding, the destruction of old streets giving place to the building of new. Many people who did not wish to be left out of the running started recalling their Corsican descent, and daughters and nieces of dignitaries of the era of the great Napoleon enjoyed a boom on the marriage market. *Gleichschaltung* was a feature of the dictatorship of Louis Napoleon no less than of more modern dictatorships. In harmony with the inspiration from above, less interest was taken in politics than in the Empress's toilet, the finer points of court ceremonial, events in society, and, first and foremost, business.

That business was booming there could be no doubt. But as the regime was based on a flight from reality, there was a visible diminution in the capacity for distinguishing between real and fictitious values. Wider and wider circles succumbed to the snare and illusion of financial speculation. The regime set its imprint upon the whole population. The Emperor's cult of the stars filtered right down to the drawing-rooms of the petty bourgeoisie, and spiritualism prospered. The court set a universal fashion for table-rapping and conversing with the dead. When one has turned one's face against reality, one is bound to take the supernatural at its face value.

A play, *Les Filles de marbre*, by Lambert Thiboust, which caused a sensation at the Vaudeville in 1853, pointed a moral for the new times. It was an answer to *Camille*, by Alexandre Dumas *fils*, which had appeared only a year before. Dumas's courtesan romantically sacrificed herself for her lover, while Thiboust's ice-cold cocottes unscrupulously ruined their lovers instead of saving them. They had no love for anything but money. Hearts had closed, and the glamour was based on the will to forget.

Among the men thrown up like froth by the teeming waves of this new society was Henri de Villemessant, who was destined soon to become a powerful ally of Offenbach. Villemessant was the embodiment of the very spirit of the Boulevards. Like Offenbach, he was drawn to the surface things of life, but unlike Offenbach, he had no deeper roots. He was a native of Rouen and, like a good many others who rose to prominence in the Second Empire, was of illegitimate birth. After marrying, having two daughters, and ending his career as a provincial business man in the bankruptcy court before the age of thirty, he noisily established himself in a hotel in Paris and made the acquaintance of a newspaper employee who frequently took him to his office and let him watch the paper being made ready for press. In this world of proofs and printer's ink he discovered his vocation.

He had no illusions about journalism being a means of self-expression or anything like that, but regarded the press as an instrument which, if properly applied, offered unlimited scope for publicity and ballyhoo. Villemessant's resourcefulness in inventing " stunts " was illustrated in his very first journalistic enterprise, *Sylphide,* a fashion journal. Thus he organized a concert and supper for his subscribers and printed stories the sole object of which was to give publicity to the name of some fashion house or other. It is uncertain whether his paper meant more to him than the ballyhoo attached to it or vice versa. However, he carried his activities to such extremes that the paper failed and he was sent to the debtors' prison at Clichy. But he was not a man to be defeated by such things as bankruptcies, distraints, court proceedings, or duels. On the contrary, he found them stimulating. He lived without a thought for the morrow and would drop a thing as soon as his enthusiasm for it dwindled — that is, as soon as it ceased to be topical. The Revolution of 1848 had offended all his parvenu instincts, and he had reacted to it by starting a newspaper, *La Lanterne,* in which he came out as a furious royalist and obligingly informed his readers that the republicans constituted a plebeian and ungentlemanly rabble. After two months of unbridled scurrility *La Lanterne* was suppressed, whereupon Villemessant appeared upon the Boulevards like an avenging fury and started snatching republican newspapers from the hands of the newspaper-sellers, hurling them to the ground and trampling on them. He was naturally arrested. He founded more newspapers and caused more sensations and only quieted down after the *coup d'état,* convinced at last that this was the dawn of a brilliant era, full of " stunts " and glory.

At first, however, the newspaper world was very adversely affected. All discussion of public affairs was forbidden by the dictatorship, so that the press was forced back on the discussion of private affairs if it was to survive at all. It was on this transformation that Villemessant based his hopes, proposing to rescue the public from its boredom by supplying it with spicy gossip about leading personalities, revealing back-stage secrets, retailing the gossip of the Boulevards, and catering continually to the desire for variety and entertainment. As it was forbidden to plunge into the depths, the surface of life must be reflected in as many ways as possible, and the surface was Villemessant's element. Nothing was sweeter to him than frequenting the Boulevards, surrounded by friends, going from café to café, gathering news, opinions, feelings, ideas. The first number of his new weekly, *Le Figaro,* appeared on April 2, 1854.

Although he had repeatedly come across Offenbach, their acquaintance was for some time superficial. Offenbach had fallen back so far that it seemed as if, on the very eve of his triumph, he had unconsciously obeyed the proverb: *Reculer pour mieux sauter*. He was profoundly depressed and often thought of giving up the struggle.

"The golden future of which I dreamed is not approaching," he lamented in a letter to his sister Netta, dated May 9, 1854. Incidentally, the purpose of this letter was also to deter his younger sister Julie from paying a visit to Paris. It was a pitiful tale of woe. He announced that he intended to emigrate to America in the autumn, in order to make some money, for he could no longer afford to pay for his wife's clothes, because the increasing luxury meant higher prices for everything, apart from which this year's concert had been far less remunerative than earlier ones, as everyone was economizing. The cause of all the trouble was "this accursed war," by which he meant the Crimean War. The Emperor had engaged in it for the same reason that had led him to encourage industrial production, because he wished to broaden the foundations of his power.

Instead of going to America, to the gold-mines or to the red Indians, Offenbach of course remained on the Boulevards. It seemed as though all his efforts were in vain. He sought to win the favor of the female associates of the Comédie Française by publishing a collection of dances entitled *Décaméron dramatique,* each dance being named after a different actress. The first was a *grande valse* dedicated to Rachel, which seemed very frivolous compared to the classical tragedies which were the favorite fare at the Théâtre Français. Offenbach suffered greatly from the never ceasing flood of tragedies, and the decision he made in secret to get back at all this antique stage lumber some day is only too intelligible. In his hours of involuntary leisure he had recently started writing musical criticism for Houssaye's paper, *L'Artiste*. His articles were lively and witty, and, as in his later operettas, anything that was pompous and inflated was his special target.

" The scores of many of our composers," he stated in an article that appeared in January 1855, " resemble the most fashionable ladies on the Boulevards, in that their crinolines are excessively luxuriant. In suitable light they look substantial enough and show pretty colors, but looked at closely, in deshabille or at the piano, as the case may be, they are phantoms; phantoms inflated with wind and noise."

But at last the time for makeshifts was drawing to a close, and Offenbach, at the moment of his profoundest depression, stood at the threshold of his fame.

CHAPTER III

THE BOUFFES

" I REMAINED at the Théâtre Français for five years," Offenbach states in his fragmentary autobiographical notes. " It was then that the idea came to me of starting a musical theater myself, because of the continued impossibility of getting my work produced by anybody else. I said to myself that the Opéra-Comique was no longer the home of comic opera, and that the idea of really gay, cheerful, witty music — in short, the idea of music with life in it — was gradually being forgotten. The composers who wrote for the Opéra-Comique wrote little grand operas. I felt sure that there was something that could be done by the young musicians who, like myself, were being kept waiting in idleness outside the portals of the lyrical theater."

As a result of the Government ban on politics, the theater was becoming more and more the center of social life; in fact, the theatrical business was booming; and Offenbach's desire for a stage of his own was all the more sharp because another composer had been quicker than he and was having a successful run of musical plays at his own little theater. Offenbach cannot have failed to experience a feeling of resentment at someone else's having stolen a march on him.

The composer who did so was Hervé, whose real name was Florimond Ronger, an extremely gifted individual, somewhat younger than Offenbach. He earned his living sometimes as an actor and sometimes as an organist, and he was an impulsive and highly eccentric person. His extraordinary character may perhaps have been due to his mixed French and Spanish blood. His first compositions for the stage were partly after the fashion of Offenbach's comic duets and were partly based on an exploitation of material that Offenbach was only to use later. The first thing to which he set his hand was the cancan.

While he was a conductor at the Palais Royal he wrote *La Gargouillada,* a burlesque of Italian opera, in which he made play with the comic contrast between the players' few stereotyped gestures and the dramatic progress of the plot. *La Gargouillada* won him the favor of Morny, who regarded it as politically expedient that the Parisians should be diverted. He would have liked to compose such entertaining trifles himself. It was thanks to his influence that Hervé was granted a theatrical license.

Because of a Napoleonic decree which had never been repealed, every theater in Paris had a special genre prescribed to it by law, and practically every genre had, of course, long since been allotted. Consequently newcomers in the theatrical field found their freedom of action very severely restricted; that is, if they were lucky enough to be granted a license at all. Hervé established himself in a concert hall in the boulevard du Temple, and his license only allowed him to produce one-act shows with two characters. Hervé often acted as librettist, composer, and actor combined. After his opening at the beginning of 1854 he produced one musical playlet after another, and very soon his little theater came to be known as " Les Folies Nouvelles." He himself came to be known as *le compositeur toqué* ("the cracked composer"), which was the title of one of his productions. The name suited him admirably. The ingenious way in which he evaded the restrictions caused great amusement. As he was only allowed two characters on the stage, he would make the third a corpse — a singing corpse. A corpse was not a character within the meaning of the act. Jests of this kind were highly appreciated by the *demi-monde,* which formed the mainstay of his public.

Offenbach, whether he liked it or not, was faced with the fact that Hervé had got in first. He must also have been keenly aware that in spite of superficial resemblances there was an abyss between Hervé and himself. He could move freely in musical spheres that must forever remain closed to " the cracked composer," and the one-act playlets which provided an entirely sufficient outlet for Hervé's talents would very soon have turned out to be an intolerably inadequate vehicle for his own genius. But there was a more important difference between the two than that. When Hervé jested, he merely drew on the contents of his own chaotic, protean, kaleidoscopic personality, of which his humor was an echo. Not that it was undirected; but it did not spring from a native insight into human sensibilities and was merely the reflection of his own baroque temperament. By comparison, Offenbach's humor had a positive, almost an objective purpose, the exposure of " phantoms inflated with wind and noise." Unlike Offenbach's creations, which were penetrated with intelligence and wit, Hervé's outpourings were completely untamed. Both made brilliant jests, and both were oddities; but the gaiety of Offenbach was as unrestrained as that of a bird.

As long as a theater of his own remained only a passionate aspiration, the Folies Nouvelles exercised a magnetic attraction over him. After all, the Folies Nouvelles were meant for gay trifles such as his. So at the beginning of 1855 he called upon Hervé, paid him exaggerated compliments, and finally produced a score entitled *Oyayaie ou la Reine des Îles*. The libretto was by Jules Moinaux, who had been his collaborator in *Pepito*.

Hervé was pleased by Offenbach's compliments, received him kindly, and only two days later informed him that *Oyayaie* was accepted. It was sufficiently grotesque to appeal to him. The plot was as follows: Râcle-à-Mort, a double-bass-player discharged from the Théâtre Ambigu, falls among cannibals, who divest him of everything except his hat, his collar, his tie and his shoes and in this guise lead him to their Queen, Oyayaie. Oyayaie, though delighted by her prisoner's musical accomplishments, is overcome at the sight of him by an enormous appetite. Râcle-à-Mort, who has no desire to satisfy either love or hunger, makes a last-

minute escape and rows away on his double-bass. Like most of
the pieces produced at the Folies Nouvelles, it was sheer nonsense. But it satisfied the demands of the public, whose chief re-
quirement was distraction.

Now that the society susceptible to him was flourishing, Offenbach's luck promptly turned. Shortly before the opening of the
Universal Exposition somebody mentioned in his presence that
there was a little theater near the Palace of Industry which would
undoubtedly be well frequented while the exposition was in progress, particularly on rainy days, when thousands of visitors would
be looking in vain for cabs or shelter. Was there a theater there
at all? Most people had forgotten the fact. But there it was, a tiny
little wooden structure hidden between two trees on the Champs-
Élysées. It had been erected by the city of Paris after the Revolution for the conjurer Lacaze, a valient National Guard.

Offenbach jumped at the chance and promptly made inquiries.
He discovered that the little theater had been standing empty for
a long time, but was going to be leased again in connection with
the exposition. He immediately applied for the license. His only
hope, of course, was to pull all the wires and rally all the influence behind him that he could. It was not for nothing that as
conductor at the Théâtre Français he had come into contact with
innumerable highly-placed personages. First he secured the back-
ing of Prince Jerome, who had been so delighted by his schottische, and of Count de Morny; and he implored all the actresses
whose goodwill he had secured by reason of his *Décaméron
dramatique* to intercede for him with all their influential friends.
The tiny theater had taken his fancy, though its relation to a
real one was that of one of his own comic sketches to a full-
length comic opera.

Before any decision was made, the exposition was opened. By
it the Emperor hoped to confirm his power anew. The exhibition was intended to be a mirror of human progress, a triumphant
display of achievement, in which all the civilized peoples of the
world were to vie with one another; and its object was to dazzle

the nation. But though it was intended as a drug for the people, it served, nevertheless, the progressive purposes of world economy and the increasing demands of industry. As in most of the Emperor's enterprises, unreal motives and real necessities were inextricably mingled.

The opening ceremony took place in the Palace of Industry on May 15, 1855, a cold, gray, wet day. The Palace of Industry was a striking mixture of boldness and timidity, with modern iron construction coyly hiding behind Corinthian columns, allegorical groups, and other attributes of the Stone Age. As hardly any unpacking had yet been done, the triumphant display of human achievement remained temporarily invisible.

The Emperor took his place on an improvised throne beneath the iron girders and, ignoring the fact that a war was in progress in the Crimea, announced that it was with pleasure that he dedicated this Temple of Peace. After a tour of the empty rooms, the final march from *William Tell* was played as a sign that the ceremony was over.

A few weeks later Offenbach triumphed over twenty rivals and was made lessee of the miniature theater, his license allowing him to produce pantomimes and short musical sketches with three characters. Now he need no longer dissipate his talents, but could at last devote himself to something he felt unreservedly worth while. But first the business details had to be attended to. A company was formed, and Offenbach was given a free hand as managing director. He was to be paid a fixed salary, independently of royalties. Villemessant, who suspected that the new venture would be a fertile source of amusement, hovered behind the scenes. Offenbach had promised to be topical, so he had made friends with him and lavished extravagant advance publicity upon the venture in the columns of *Le Figaro*. No doubt the fact that he had been promised a fixed percentage on the net profits acted as a fillip to his purely æsthetic anticipations. Offenbach had inherited from his father a conviction that the power of the press cannot be overestimated.

However, the arrangement of these financial details was the least of the preparations that Offenbach had to undertake, all within three weeks. For in order to have the full benefit of the crowds that would flock to the exposition, the opening of the Bouffes-Parisiens, which was the name by which the little theater was henceforward to be known, was announced for July 5. Offenbach had twenty days in which to collect his cast, recruit his authors, arrange his program, order his scenery, supervise the rehearsals, to say nothing of composing in the odd moments that were left; and this, remember, in the days before the telephone. At the same time his *Oyayaie* was running at the Folies Nouvelles, with Hervé in the leading role. Offenbach, in his element at last, dashed here, there, and everywhere, adroitly surmounting all obstacles.

When the authors whom he asked to write the prologue let him down and he could not find anyone else willing to undertake the task, he was obliged to have recourse to an entirely unknown author, who was only twenty-two years old. His name was Ludovic Halévy, and he worked in a Government office.

Ludovic Halévy was one of nature's favorites. He was born in the venerable Institut de France, the home of the French Academy, where his mother, father, and grandfather lived. His grandfather, Hippolyte Lebas, was the Institut architect and had a spacious official home at his disposal. Ludovic's childhood was of the kind that is generally only described in fairy-tales. It was spent in a realm of endless corridors and courtyards, in the midst of a community of painters, architects, and engravers, all winners of the Prix de Rome, who worked away in the quietness of the Institut, helped and encouraged younger pupils, played lotto, and talked passionately about the beauties of the Eternal City. In this carefree and unassuming atmosphere the child unconsciously absorbed invaluable traditions and was initiated, among other things, into the strange and wonderful world of the theater.

His father, Léon, a great connoisseur of antiquity, wrote tragedies for the Théâtre Français and vaudevilles for the Théâtre

des Variétés, and his uncle, Fromental Halévy, was the composer to whom Offenbach already owed so much encouragement.
Playwright and composer were both the sons of a German-
Jewish immigrant, a cantor in the synagogue like Offenbach's
father, and they liked nothing better than taking young Ludovic
to the theater. The result was that he grew up with the theater
in his bones. Before he left school, the revolution closed an epoch
in which all the blessings of peace were showered upon him. But
the esteem in which his family was held shielded him from every
difficulty. On leaving school he was taken straight into the Government service, and while still a fledgling he accompanied the
councilor Villemain on a tour of the provinces which the latter
undertook in 1854 on behalf of the Government to sound popular feeling in different parts of the country. In the course of his
travels Halévy took pains to see that Villemain never missed
his beloved game of whist; and this put him in such a good
mood that in his report to the Government he had no words
of praise high enough for the loyal feelings of the population.
As for Halévy himself, he returned to Paris with the manuscript
of a comedy in his pocket. His ambition was to be a playwright,
not a Government official.

Offenbach knew Halévy by sight from the Théâtre Français;
and one day during the frantic three weeks before the opening
of the Bouffes-Parisiens he took a cab to the Ministry and went
to see him. After broaching the subject in flattering and general
terms, he implored him to help him out of his difficulty. Halévy
was of course delighted at this opportunity of real authorship,
and consented on the spot.

" All right," said Offenbach. " Please start right away. Just a
little one-act play, with songs — about anything you like . . .
only there's just one thing; you must put in a hundred lines I've
got here; they must go right in the middle of the act, in the place
of honor."

Offenbach pressed a sheet of paper into Halévy's hands and
explained that the lines had been written by a friend of his,

Méry, and that they were to be spoken by a character representing Fantasy.

"One of your characters must be called Fantasy. You don't mind, do you?"

"Not at all, not at all."

"When Méry got to the prose part his courage failed him," Offenbach explained. "So I asked Lambert Thiboust, but he let me down too. Now you will replace Thiboust."

"With pleasure."

"There's just one thing," Offenbach said once more, and proceeded to explain that Thiboust, even though he had let him down, had written a song which he, Offenbach, had already put to music.

Halévy began to feel somewhat alarmed.

"The song," Offenbach explained, "is written for Bilboquet.[1] So you'll have to make Bilboquet the second character in your prologue."

"Very well. I like Bilboquet very much."

"As for the third character — oh, yes, I forgot to tell you, I am only allowed to put on plays with three characters. . . ."

"So there'll be one character I shall have to create myself," Halévy said, feeling there was a ray of hope.

Offenbach smiled.

"Create?" he said. "Well . . . good gracious me, I must explain the situation. The part of Fantasy will be played by Mademoiselle Macé, and Bilboquet will be played by a first-class provincial actor whom I have just engaged, of the name of Pradeau. . . . Well, the third character will be played by Derudder, who is also a member of my cast — Derudder, the famous mime! So of course his role must be completely silent. . . . By the way, Derudder is the best Polichinelle that can possibly be imagined. You won't mind making him Polichinelle, will you?"

---

[1] Bilboquet was originally the chief character in a play called *Les Saltimbanques,* which was frequently played about 1838, and had since become a legendary figure.

Halévy was in despair. Only one character was left to him, and a dumb one at that. Nevertheless, he agreed to do what Offenbach asked, and that was how the famous partnership began.

Apart from the prologue, the program of the opening night of the Bouffes-Parisiens included a pantomime, full of themes from Rossini, a sentimental country idyl, entitled *La Nuit blanche,* and a musical farce, *Les Deux Aveugles,* written by Jules Moinaux, a skit on the tricks indulged in by the begging fraternity.

The last was by no means so far-fetched as might appear. Paris was infested every summer by swarms of beggars who spent the rest of the year as independent men of leisure in the bosom of their families. The heroes of the piece are Patachon, a fat trumpet-player, and Giraffier, an emaciated guitar-player. Both of them sham blindness in order to excite sympathy. These two human wrecks, instead of being treated sympathetically, are shown up in all their abjectness. They accidentally take up stations on the same bridge and start quarreling about a sou that rolls along the pavement between them. Each tries to drive the other away by telling the most hair-raising stories about himself, and finally they decide to settle the question as to which of them is to go by a game of cards, in the course of which they both cheat in the most outrageous fashion. The game is only interrupted at the sound of approaching footsteps, when they abandon their rivalry in the hope of gain. Words and music outdo each other in extracting hilarious effects from this somewhat sordid theme.

Those present at the dress rehearsal felt uncomfortable about this item from the moment the curtain went up. Villemessant, who had a personal interest in the new theater, declared that he was shocked, and implored the authors to withdraw it. He had a high opinion of the delicacy of feeling of the readers of *Le Figaro* and highly disapproved of such patent cynicism. Like all practical men of his type, he regarded it as tactless to make a display of the cynicism which he himself, of course, exemplified in real life. Halévy, who was still inexperienced and innocent in the ways of the world, also prophesied that the piece would be a failure. The singer Berthelier, however, who took the part of Giraffier, did not agree. But the fact that this was his first stage role, and that he was obviously anxious not to lose it, heavily discounted the favor that the piece found in his eyes. Berthelier had been singing the song-hit of the season, *Vive la France!* at a *café-concert* when Offenbach engaged him. Offenbach was the only one who had implicit faith in the *bouffonnerie's* success. The impulse to show up sham in any form was so deeply ingrained in him that he simply could not understand why there should be any hesitation in making fun of beggars.

The Bouffes-Parisiens opened punctually on July 5, 1855, with results that not only justified Offenbach's expectations but immeasurably surpassed them. Villemessant, in spite of his expert knowledge of public taste, had been entirely wrong. He had omitted to take into calculation the fact that what the hysteria-ridden public wanted was above all to be amused, and moreover that this burlesque of mendicancy was bound to be welcome to them as a reflection of their own irresponsibility. The first-night audience clapped and cheered. They rocked and roared with laughter at Pradeau's look of solemn imbecility as Patachon, at Berthelier's Marseille dialect, which made a visit to the Canne-bière superfluous. Whether it was their separate virtues or the combination of the two, their boasting, or their mean and pitiful tricks as beggars, from that moment they became famous. This was success — success that came like a hurricane and swept away everything in its path. Patachon and Giraffier reappeared in all the theatrical revues, and Offenbach's music was played at every ball. In particular his *Boléro,* which he had turned into a waltz and given the beggars to sing on hearing pedestrians approaching, became the rage at the dances at the Jardin d'Hiver, next door to the Bouffes.

The little theater, which was compared to a kiosk or a choco-late-box, became the rage. The tiers of seats climbed so steeply

that a comic paper described them as a ladder with human be-
ings clinging to the rungs. At the top was a row of boxes so
small that you could not take your coat off inside them unless
you opened not only the door but the window outside in the
corridor as well. In fine weather an uncovered terrace was used
as a foyer, and from it could be seen the wooden horses of the
merry-go-rounds revolving under the trees. The glamour of success lay over the Bouffes from the first, and the result was that
the primitive seating-arrangements actually became a popular
attraction, and the cramped space was prized for its intimacy.
The " House full " notice was displayed on night after night, and
when Mme Offenbach went to see the show she had to be content to sit on the stairs.

Paris was crowded with provincial and foreign visitors. The
Emperor had promoted the exposition to stimulate world economy and postpone, if possible forever, the date when the nation
would return to a more sober mood, and lo! the world, exceed-
ing his expectations, sent him swarms of foreigners whose presence redoubled the prevailing frenzy. For the foreigners in Paris
succumbed to it just like the natives. They spent money like
water, and their mere presence was a stimulus. Paris became a
tower of Babel. All sense of reality was lost.

The visitors dutifully admired the machinery in the Palace
of Industry, marveled at the huge enlarged photographs of minute insects, paid due tribute to the wonders of the Indian, Egyptian, Chinese, and Turkish pavilions, and wandered through the
international art exhibition, which included Théodore Rousseau
and Kaulbach and roused general interest as the first of its kind.
Foreigners were to be seen everywhere in the streets, gazing at
the sights of the city, large areas of which were in the hands of
the builders and roadmakers.

They themselves were objects of curiosity in the eyes of the
natives. According to an article in one of the papers, their trousers were too short and their coats too long, and they went about
gaping at everything with their noses in the air, surrounded by

swarms of little boys and girls and nurses and babies. The sign
" English spoken " appeared at many shops and buildings.

The foreigners were, of course, mainly in search of pleasure.
Officers returning from the Crimea, and politicians belonging
to the opposition, complained that Paris was enjoying itself
while men were dying in the trenches before Sebastopol, but
the Emperor had his reasons for wishing it to be so. These
were good days for the Boulevards, which had been a haunt
of foreigners and homeless ones in the time of Louis-Philippe.
The hotels had to turn people away, restaurants were often
sold out, and the new *café-concerts* flourished. Strangers of any
distinction were invited to the Tuileries, danced at the balls
given by Baron Haussmann at the Hôtel de Ville, and thronged
the fêtes at the Jardin d'Hiver. Théophile Gautier declared in
one of his articles that scarcely a Parisian was to be seen at the
theater.

Offenbach was fortunate in that the opening of the Bouffes
coincided with the beginning of the international era, and that
his genre corresponded exactly with the foreigners' secret wishes.
It was not for nothing that their taste was the same as that of
the French public. What was more important, Offenbach offered
them something that was not to be found elsewhere — a kind
of music that was directly intelligible to them. Its gaiety and
tenderness, instead of being expressed in a strong local idiom,
were rooted in a distant land in which all mankind was at home.
Was not Offenbach himself an alien? Offenbach's music, like
Charlie Chaplin's films, was an international phenomenon in
an age of international development, in which great hopes were
entertained of permanent reconciliation between the peoples.
In these circumstances it was inevitable that a crowd of idle
pleasure-seekers should float to the surface.

Offenbach, as if to cement the bond between him and the
foreigners, devoted a comic musical sketch to them, *Le Rêve
d'une nuit d'été,* which appeared at the Bouffes as early as the
end of July. The chief characters were two Englishmen, who

QUEEN VICTORIA AT THE TUILERIES
August 1855

DEPARTURE OF H.M. THE QUEEN OF ENGLAND FROM PARIS

August 27, 1855

Courtesy, Rischgitz

were exactly like each other in every possible way, and were seeking the favor of the same woman at the Balle Mabille. Offenbach made fun of their favorite expression: "Very good," and made them sing a panegyric of Paris life.

Joy and glamour reached their zenith in August, when Queen Victoria and Prince Albert paid a ceremonial visit to the Emperor. The Emperor had good reason to rejoice, because this state visit set the outward seal on his power. Queen Victoria, with perfect courtesy, spent some time in contemplation beside Napoleon's tomb in the Invalides and enjoyed the glitter of Paris without allowing herself to be dazzled. She possessed sufficient insight and realism to mistrust so much magnificence.

" All so gay, the people cheering the Emperor as he walked up and down in the little garden," she wrote in her Journals. " And yet how recently has blood flowed, a whole dynasty been swept away, and how uncertain is everything still! All is so beautiful here, all seems now so prosperous, the Emperor seems so fit for his place, and yet how little security one feels for the future! "

Chance willed it that Bismarck should be present at the big ball at Versailles that was given in the Queen's honor — Bismarck, who was to execute the sentence that the nation had pronounced upon itself in delivering its destiny into the hands of Louis Napoleon.

In the midst of all these festivities no one noticed the arrival of a girl from the provinces who came to Paris in search of fame and fortune. She was twenty-two years old, her name was Hortense Schneider, and she was the daughter of a German master tailor who had settled in Bordeaux, married a Frenchwoman, and subsequently succumbed to drink. It was rather remarkable that, like Offenbach and Ludovic Halévy, she had German forbears; the operetta in fact, was an *émigré* product.

At the age of three Hortense was singing songs; at the age of twelve she threatened to commit suicide unless she were allowed to go on the stage, whereupon she was promptly apprenticed either to a milliner or in a flower-shop. However, she had her own way in the end, studied singing for several years, and joined a small provincial troupe, with whom she was so badly paid that she was compelled to take a lover. It did not take her long to ruin him. When she arrived in Paris she had a long, narrow face with reddish golden hair and looked delicate, even ill. Immediately after her arrival she went to see the singer Berthelier, to whom she had an introduction. Berthelier took her to the Restaurant Dinochau, a haunt of journalistic and literary Bohemia. He showed her Baudelaire and Murger and then took her home to his room, where they had to be very careful, since it was only separated from his mother's by a thin partition. Hortense had no luck with the director of the Variétés, so Berthelier sent her to see Offenbach at his home. Scarcely had she sung a few notes when Offenbach shut the piano with a bang and asked her whether she intended to go on studying to perfect her singing. Hortense thought it advisable to reply that she did.

" Miserable wretch! " Offenbach exclaimed in his execrable French. " If you dare take it into your head to do anything so monstrous I shall tear up your contract! Because I'm engaging you at two hundred francs a month. Do you understand? "

This was the usual tone in the theater. Hortense Schneider's debut at the Bouffes took place on August 31 in *Le Violoneux,* a sentimental piece with words by Mestépès and Chevalet, based on a Breton legend, which enjoyed great public favor. Hortense Schneider was praised by *Le Figaro* for her grace and polish. Darcier, as an old village musician, held the audience enraptured by the tears in his voice, and Offenbach's music was highly praised for its wit and feeling.

Only two months after the Bouffes was founded it had become a recognized institution. The Paris stage was unthinkable without it. So successful were the *bouffonneries* that the pantomimes were quickly dropped. The box-office receipts often amounted to twelve hundred francs, and Offenbach was able at last to abandon his old stand-by, conducting at the Théâtre Français.

In October he produced *Madame Papillon,* in which Pradeau excelled as an old lady from the provinces in search of love. The words were by Halévy. But the big attraction remained *Les Deux Aveugles,* whose drawing-power seemed inexhaustible. It reached its four hundredth performance, and at the beginning of the following year the Emperor ordered a command performance in the Tuileries during the Peace Congress which terminated the Crimean War.

Cold weather came, and the wooden horses of the merry-go-rounds under the trees revolved no more. At the end of November the World Exhibition was closed. It was time to find winter quarters for the Bouffes.

CHAPTER IV

THE MOZART OF THE CHAMPS–ÉLYSÉES

THE THEATER chosen was the Théâtre des Jeunes Élèves. Like the little wooden hut on the Champs-Élysées, before passing into Offenbach's hands it had been devoted exclusively to the arts of magic and mystery. It lay in the heart of the city, near the Italian Opéra, and it still exists today. M. Comte, its former proprietor, had invariably introduced his performances by promising to make all the ladies present vanish before the last curtain. When the show was over he would recall his promise and cause a magnificent bouquet of roses to appear out of nowhere. " Are the ladies not all united in this bouquet? " he would then ask.

Offenbach had the derelict little theater hastily redecorated, regardless of the expense, which was about eighty thousand francs. The place was scarcely bigger than the summer home of the Bouffes had been.

Having been freshly gilded, carpeted, and upholstered, it opened two days before the end of the auspicious year 1855 with *Ba-ta-clan,* a *chinoiserie musicale,* with libretto by Ludovic Halévy. It had the indiscriminate quality of a dream, a higgledy-piggledy of memories and wish-pictures. But it might also perhaps be regarded as the utterance of a man who had suddenly become aware that the frenzied world about him was itself a dream-world, withdrawing ever farther from reality, a man who, though still half-dreaming, was slowly beginning to rub his eyes.

Offenbach's *chinoiserie* was an echo of the World Exhibition, with its mingling of the most varied nationalities. The action took place at the court of Fé-ni-han, the absolute ruler of a petty kingdom containing twenty-seven subjects. Some of these subjects were disaffected, however, and were plotting to overthrow him; for as a result of his imperfect knowledge of the Chinese language he had inadvertently caused five citizens to be impaled, though his real intention had been to bestow a special honor upon them. He turned out to be a Parisian; and the two principal members of his entourage, Ké-ki-ka-ko and Fé-an-nich-ton, turned out to be shipwrecked Parisians too, the former being a ruined man of fashion and the latter an ex-star of the music halls. Pining for their little suppers at the Maison Dorée and the balls at the Opéra, the two resolved to flee. But their plans were discovered, and they were brought before Fé-ni-han, with whom a long discussion ensued. Poor Fé-ni-han was pining for Paris himself, but he was far too afraid of the plotters to allow them to go. In the end Ko-ko-ri-ko, who was the chief of the plotters as well as the captain of the guard — Offenbach was still only allowed four characters — revealed himself to be a Frenchman too, and, as he hankered greatly after Fé-ni-han's throne, he facilitated the flight of his three compatriots.

This was the first work of real collaboration between Offenbach and Ludovic Halévy, and in it the chief ingredients of the later and greater operettas are already perceptible. In the first place, power is a joke and court life mere mummery. For in reality (or so Offenbach and Halévy seem to imply) the most idolized ruler is often nothing but a dressed-up Fé-ni-han or Ko-ko-ri-ko. He who would could see topical allusions in *Ba-ta-clan*. It dealt as unceremoniously with grand opera as it did with the glamour and pomp that surround a tyrant; for grand opera also exercised a dictatorship over the public mind, and it was legitimate to suspect that, like other dictatorships, it, too, was a fraud. The "Chinese" sung and spoken by the characters in *Ba-ta-clan* was a senseless Franco-Italian gibberish, and the effect was a complete parody of Italian opera, with a ferocious rolling of " r's " and elaborate trills signifying nothing.

Meyerbeer fared no better at Offenbach's hands. Offenbach took passages from *Les Huguenots* and planted them so artfully in his " Chinese " atmosphere that their empty, trashy nature was promptly exposed. " Phantoms inflated with wind and noise " collapsed like pricked bubbles. Moreover, there was a rebels' song, sung by the plotters to hearten themselves in the struggle against their tyrant, a kind of Chinese *Marseillaise,* aimed at degenerate grand opera as well as at Fé-ni-han's absolutism.

But all this was meant only in jest. As if to prove it, Fé-ni-han himself sang the rebels' song. Grand opera remained in its place, and tyrants could sleep in peace. The veil was lifted just long enough to allow a glimpse at a possible better order of things, but it immediately fell again. In spite of all the burlesque, Offenbach's music remained an end in itself; moreover, the emphasis lay less on the satire than on the gaiety which was the result of it and which had an independent existence of its own, by no means depending solely on the humor extracted from parody. The critical function of the humor was only incidental. In the scene in which the ex-actress and society man hark back to their days in Paris, pleasure is exalted for its own sake.

> *Souvenirs charmants*
> *D'une vie*
> *Qui suivait gaîment*
> *La folie . . .*

The pair sing and dance, inspired by the thought of Paris, and the orchestra plays waltzes and a cancan.

> *Valsons!*
> *Polkons!*
> *Sautons!*
> *Dansons!*

In this passage Offenbach proclaims the gospel of pleasure for the first time. As in the later operettas, gaiety is closely associated with dancing, and Paris is above all a haunt of pleasure.

" People laughed, clapped, shouted as at a miracle," Jules Janin wrote after the first night. He added that the exuberance of the whole thing gave people of all ages an irresistible urge to dance, and he called Offenbach a master. The music was sung everywhere, in streets and workshops. It was played at the Opéra balls. Such was its popularity that a *café-concert* assumed the name of *Ba-ta-clan* to attract custom.

That Offenbach was himself to a great extent aware of the implications contained in his work is shown by an article he wrote in July 1856, shortly before announcing a prize to be awarded by the Bouffes to the composer of a suitable operetta. He contrasted the style favored by the Bouffes with that in vogue at the Opéra-Comique, of course to the advantage of the former. Using the most polite language and walking warily in order not to offend anybody, he pointed out to the Opéra-Comique, that institution which he both loved and hated, that there was nothing whatever in common between the "big comic opera" it exclusively favored and the light and gracious comic opera of the eighteenth century. He likened the old comic opera of Philidor and Monsigny to a little brook running between green banks. Should a little brook grow into a broad river, it could certainly be called a development, but nevertheless it was no longer the same thing. And as for his own *bouffonneries,* which the Opéra-Comique continually rejected, he stated that he associated himself with the eighteenth-century tradition and defined the object of the Bouffes as the revival of *" le genre primitif et gai,"* the resuscitation of the forgotten French spirit of gaiety, which was to be sought for in vain at the Opéra-Comique.

In 1844 Heine had heard Monsigny's *Le Déserteur,* one of the operas to which Offenbach referred. " This is real French music," Heine had written at that time, " the gayest grace, the most innocent sweetness, a freshness as of the scent of wild flowers, verisimilitude, even poetry." Offenbach's aim could scarcely be described better.

It was not for nothing that Offenbach used many familiar, traditional tunes in his compositions, tunes which, like fairy-tales, belong neither to any specific culture nor to any specific age. The Jewish musicians of whom he had been told by his father wandered from place to place playing traditional popular tunes to the greater glory of God.

At the same time he criticized the grandiose in music. In speaking of the old comic operas he had used the simile of a brook which ripples along clearly and brightly over the stones. You could see the bottom of a brook, but who knew what dirt and filth might be carried along in the turgid waters of a big river?

"In an opera which lasts only three quarters of an hour, in which only four characters are allowed and an orchestra of at most thirty persons is employed, one must have ideas and tunes that are as genuine as hard cash (*de la mélodie argent comptant*). It is also worthy of note that with a small orchestra, such as incidentally sufficed for Mozart and Cimarosa, it is very difficult to cover up mistakes and ineptitudes such as an orchestra of eighty players can gloss over without difficulty."

In his expression of preference for small-scale opera Offenbach was thinking less of the small scale which was imposed on him by circumstances than of the fact that it was the opposite of the pompous and inflated. He objected to dressing up his music in crinolines. He often found a few bars sufficient to indicate a whole scene. As against grand opera, he was David slaying Goliath with a sling.

The prize that Offenbach proposed served the purpose of once more drawing public attention to the Bouffes; it also encouraged those composers who lacked the desire or capacity to put to music the obscure and bulky librettos prized by the Opéra-Comique. The list of judges was an impressive one, including Fromental Halévy, Scribe, and other celebrities. All French com-

posers and foreigners long resident in France were eligible, provided that none of their works had been produced either at the
Opéra or at the Opéra-Comique. After a preliminary examina-
tion to sift the sheep from the goats, the six surviving candidates
were given a comic libretto, *Le Docteur Miracle,* which had been
written, somewhat carelessly, by Ludovic Halévy and Léon Battu.
The winners were two young men who later became world-
famous, Charles Lecocq and Georges Bizet.

Lecocq intensely disliked having any rivals and was angered
at the delay that took place in paying out the prize money,
which consisted of twelve hundred francs and a gold medal worth
three hundred francs. On top of this several alterations in his
score were suggested, with the result that he bore Offenbach a
grudge for the rest of his life. *Le Docteur Miracle* was duly produced at the Bouffes at the beginning of 1857, both in Lecocq's
version and in Bizet's, but both were complete failures.

During the two or three years that followed the production
of *Ba-ta-clan* Offenbach's compositions followed each other upon
the stage of the Bouffes in an unending stream. The many writers of the Boulevards showered more librettos upon him than it
was possible to use, and his own fertility was inexhaustible. The
librettos of that time are yellow and faded now, but then they
were bright and novel and gay.

In one of them a young man, kept a prisoner by an innkeeper
because he cannot pay the reckoning, buys himself off by giving
mine host's niece singing lessons; the singing lessons, however,
develop into love lessons. In another a young Tyrolese, believing
he has won the big prize in a sweepstakes, becomes intolerably
arrogant, only to learn that he has not won it at all; he is finally
rescued from the humiliation of his imaginary loss by a substantial gift from a wealthy uncle. In another an ex-equestrienne in
a circus tries to extricate herself from her difficulties by offering
herself as a prize in a lottery, with the result that she becomes the
wife of a cousin of hers who entered the lottery without suspecting her identity; and the sum he paid for her turns out to be

exactly equivalent to that of an inheritance of which he had previously cheated her. In others the situation is that of a girl torn
between two lovers — a nursemaid having to choose between a
chimney-sweep and a laborer — or a more aristocratic damsel
having to choose between two cavaliers in an Auvergne tavern,
in whose company she trills operatic phrases. From time to time
the gaiety degenerates into clowning. Grotesque cannibal chief-
tains put Oyayaie completely in the shade, and grown-ups are
made to behave like children. But such aberrations are rare, for
Offenbach was less a clown than a mocking-bird piping from the
roof-tops at the eccentricities perceptible below.

He made an operetta of the music he had once composed for
La Fontaine's fable *Le Savetier et le financier,* turning the idealist
cobbler of the fable into a materialist. In *Tromb-al-Cazar* he
satirized the romantic bandits of grand opera. In *Croquefer, ou
le dernier des Paladins,* he burlesqued the heroes of medieval
romance, though his satire did not strip his victims bare of all
nobility; his method was not to slay by satire, but to dissolve in
laughter. In *Croquefer* the hero, Mousse-à-Mort, is condemned
to dumbness, but circumvents this obstacle by causing his pages
to show scrolls with *" Grande canaille"* or other suitable expressions written on them when he wishes to cause offense.

In the operetta *Mesdames de la Halle,* the first in which Offenbach was permitted to use choruses and any number of characters
he chose, he parodied traditional melodrama. The scene is laid
most realistically in the neighborhood of the Halles, and the plot
concerns the amorous skirmishings of Ciboulette, a charming
flower-girl, a kitchen-hand who is equally charming, a number
of market women who are all in love with him, and a lovesick
drum-major of the name of Raflafla. The tender feelings aroused
are partially canalized towards the end by the discovery that one
of the market women is Ciboulette's mother, while the drum-
major is her father.

These early librettos offer us a succession of characters, situations, and scenes many of which seem to have sprung from the

Paris in which Offenbach spent his youth. The accompanying music reduced grand opera and the powers that be to absurdity. Offenbach exposed them long before their natural decline set in, and the strange thing was that his work of disenchantment, because of its gaiety, became an enchantment in its turn.

How delighted the Parisians were when in the midst of a smashing military finale they suddenly detected the notes of a well-known children's song! Sometimes Offenbach would prick a romantic bubble by the introduction of some startling banality. A scene of great pathos would suddenly be interrupted by a gay waltz; the poison poured into Croquefer's wine turns out to be a strong purgative. " *O ciel! grands dieux! que sens-je?* " the victims sing, while the music most expressively imitates the nature of their sensations.

Offenbach gave plenty of rein to his talent for imitation. He composed a " farmyard waltz," full of the barking of dogs and the quacking of geese, recalling the times of the Jardin Turc. Byplay of this kind and the occasional cheap humor of anachronism were, however, never allowed to overwhelm the main theme. In *Croquefer,* as in *Ba-ta-clan,* the satire was transfused into a stream of gaiety. Fleur-de-Soufre, imprisoned in Croquefer's tower, dreams of the Opéra balls in Paris, while the orchestra plays soft dance music; and the gaiety reaches its climax in a thrilling gallop, which was so daring that audiences found it frightening.

Offenbach sometimes tired of it all and wanted to be just as serious as his victims. An operetta, *Les Trois Baisers du diable,* belongs to this period, and according to *Le Ménestrel* its effect was horrible and uncanny; it was certainly a pointer towards *The Tales of Hoffmann.* The public, however, only expected to be amused at the Bouffes and mistook the piece for a satire, so the experiment was not repeated.

In an announcement to the press in 1857 Offenbach stated that in spite of being perpetually busy casting, rehearsing, and producing, as well as reading the continual flow of manuscripts and scores that were sent to him, he had so far composed and produced five pantomimes, several cantatas, and no fewer than twenty operettas. He possessed an extraordinary and unerring sense of the theater, without which all this activity would have been impossible. Offenbach was a man who pined in solitude, and the theater was the opposite of solitude. He never completed any of his works until he saw them on the stage. At rehearsals he did not cling to a finished text, but used them to give final form to a text that was only provisional. No matter how good the music, it would be ruthlessly blue-penciled if it turned out not to be lively enough for the stage. " *Une bedide goupure* " was a phrase constantly used by Offenbach in his execrable French.

His productions had to be as taut as his own theatrical impulse. He kept a relentless eye on the dramatic continuity of his scenes and tolerated no digressions of any kind whatever. The innumerable waltzes, gallops, drinking songs to be found throughout his operettas are not interspersed at random, but are where they are because the development of the plot requires it. As the years passed, Offenbach concentrated less and less on individual items in his score and more and more on the total effect. He chose quick tempi and laid emphasis on rhythm. In view of the importance he attached to action it was natural that he should work in the closest collaboration with his librettists. " Poet and composer must live together in spiritual wedlock," he once said. He did not make the lives of his temporary partners easy; but they often tended to agree with him when he cut passages which were mere padding, or, with a sure eye for stage-effect, detected weaknesses of construction. His criticisms even extended to verbal details.

One result of the way he worked was that unless he had at least a part of the libretto before his eyes, he could not compose properly at all; and as he composed more quickly than the librettists could write, he was continually pestering them for more.

His extraordinary theatrical instinct was also shown by his flair

for human material. He discovered future stars in unknown beginners with the most uncanny sense. He discovered Berthelier,
Pradeau, Hortense Schneider.

As soon as Hortense was firmly established on the road to
fame, she exchanged Berthelier, who could no longer be useful
to her, for a nobleman who set her up in a fine home and
provided her with her first carriage and her first diamonds. In
return, before she left him she presented him with a child that
was not his but somebody else's. It was not that she was fickle;
but she was the victim of a strong temperament; and besides
she liked the glitter of diamonds. As Offenbach refused to gratify
her continual demands for increases in salary, out of sheer caprice
she obtained an appointment at the Variétés, which, after entering upon a liaison with the young Duc Ludovic de Gramont-
Caderousse, she soon exchanged for the Palais Royal, where she
climbed to still greater heights of popularity.

Offenbach found a substitute for her in Lise Tautin. This
young woman possessed a seductiveness based on a voice of
metallic suppleness as well as considerable power as an actress;
she was as skillful at comedy as she was at more or less indecent
innuendo. In contrast to her carefree exuberance on the stage,
however, in her private life she was just like a romantic little
grisette; any lover who was more or less indifferent to her and
treated her badly was good enough for her. Another success
of Offenbach's was the comedian Léonce, who had a passion
for extemporization, played with every risqué word like a cat
with a mouse, to the huge delight of the public, and performed
upon the cello like a master. In private life he was a hypochon-
driac who, when he appeared in the street in dark glasses and
a white tie, looked more like an undertaker or a bailiff than
an actor. Léonce and Désiré were inseparable; Désiré's eccentricities certainly needed something to keep a check on them, but
on the stage they always roused storms of laughter. In short,
Offenbach knew all the tricks of the trade. " You know," he
once wrote indignantly to a friend who sent an ugly singer to

see him, " that in my little theater the public sits very close to the stage, and consequently the women have to be even more beautiful than elsewhere."

The mass of work that Offenbach took upon himself made it inevitable that he should turn out a large number of hasty sketches. Some of his operettas are merely the equivalent of musical journalism. The facility with which he created reinforced his inclination to satisfy the great demand for his work in summary fashion. Saint-Saëns observed that his scores swarmed with microscopic little notes, like flies' feet, and out of sheer hurry barely touched the paper. There was a connection between the hastiness of Offenbach's work — that is, on those occasions when it is evident — and the bond that tied him to the surface of life. A few phrases that he wrote at the age of fifty-five, looking back on his immense output and a whole lifetime of experience, illustrate how strongly he tended by nature to take into account the transitoriness, the impermanence of things. " The new piece causes the old one to be forgotten," he wrote. " The two are not compared or put side by side, and no analogies are sought between them; it is rather like a series of pictures, shown one after another in a magic lantern; when once the show is over, the most striking success weighs no more in the mind of the spectator than the rankest failure."

The Bouffes rapidly acquired a faithful and regular public, including such prominent personages as Morny, the Count de Castellane, and innumerable pleasure-loving young men. The illustrious Meyerbeer himself became an habitué.

Meyerbeer was perfectly well aware that in the last resort Offenbach's parodies increased the fame of his own works, and as a man of the world he was far too shrewd to fall out with this jester. Instead of taking the jokes amiss, he took every opportunity of stating that he had a very high opinion indeed of Offenbach's talents. His visits to the Bouffes were carried out according to a fixed and invariable ritual. He regularly ordered an orchestra seat for himself for the second night of every new production and presented himself punctually with his ticket; whereupon he would be led to a box which had been specially reserved for him, in which Offenbach would unfailingly visit him during the performance. The conversation between the two would invariably consist of a mutual exchange of compliments. As not a few of the habitués were possessed of considerable wit, innumerable *bons mots* and anecdotes would be exchanged in the foyer and promptly spread like lightning along the Boulevards.

The foyer merely consisted of a space where the corridor became a little wider, and contained four worn-out benches, a piano, and a clock which did not go, and the available space was still further restricted by the new fashion of crinolines for program-sellers. Fortunately the Passage Choiseul was immediately outside the theater and could be used for strolling up and down in during the intermissions. It also contained a fruit-stand, from which it was the thing to buy oranges. As a result the auditorium used to smell like an orange-grove.

Very soon the little theater became one of the sights of Paris that no foreign visitor could possibly afford to miss. William Makepeace Thackeray, after seeing the first night of *Le Savetier et le financier* at the end of September 1856, was convinced that Offenbach had a great future, and Tolstoy, who went to the Bouffes a few months later, noted in his diary: " This is really French; the comedy is so wholesome and spontaneous that everything is permitted it."

Much as he would have liked to, Offenbach could obviously not fill the whole repertoire at the Bouffes with his own works alone. It was necessary to supplement them; so he took advantage of the opportunity of occasionally producing works by famous authors, thus compelling those critics who had so far ignored him to pay attention to his theater. When Adolphe Adam died, at the beginning of 1856, he produced his *Les Pantins de Violette,* in which there are plenty of pierrots, columbines, and magicians.

Shortly afterwards he produced Mozart's little opera *The Im-*

presario in an arrangement of his own. He regarded Mozart with what he once described as " religious veneration," and no doubt he felt there was an inner relationship between him and his idol. Others thought so too.

Offenbach secured from Rossini permission to reproduce one of the latter's youthful works, *Bruschino,* a comic opera which in its time had been hissed off the stage at Venice. Rossini said, half pleased, half sad, that he considered himself lucky to be able to do anything for " the Mozart of the Champs-Élysées." *Bruschino* was once more a complete failure, however, though this time criticism was modified by the respect felt for its composer. This second failure was not in the least surprising, because the composition of *Bruschino* had been an act of sabotage in the first place. To get back at the director of the San Mosé Theater at Venice, who had given him a bad libretto, Rossini had written a score that deliberately exaggerated all the libretto's defects. The old man now permitted Offenbach to revive this youthful indiscretion, but declined to attend the first night, not wishing to appear publicly as an accomplice.

Since the whole world did not come to Paris every year, but still wanted to hear Offenbach, he started going on international tours. The first of these took place in 1857. Armed with all the show-pieces of his repertoire, he had a season in London with his troupe, which was fifty strong. While in England the Bouffes were invited to Twickenham, where Marie-Amélie, widow of the long-dead Louis-Philippe, made her home. At Twickenham they performed the military operetta *Dragonette,* in which a soldier who had been suspected of being a coward and a deserter succeeds in capturing flags from the enemy and returns with them, to be acclaimed a hero. At the words of the finale: " *Chantons en chœur: vive la France!* " tears came into Marie-Amélie's eyes. Offenbach, who dined at the royal table, said in a letter to his wife that this visit taught him how near laughter was to tears.

After his visit to London, Offenbach had a season at Lyon.

At the end of the summer he arranged a charity fête at the seaside resort of Étretat, which was having such a good season that he could scarcely find accommodation for his cast. In the following year he paid a triumphant visit to Berlin, with *Le Mariage aux Lanternes* as part of his repertoire, as well as to Bad Ems, which was much frequented by French visitors, and where a theater had been built in the *Kurpark,* the diminutive size of which served as an agreeable reminder of the Bouffes' original home on the Champs-Élysées.

When society re-forms after an upheaval the men who were its leading lights and the institutions which once flourished tend rapidly to vanish into obscurity, though outwardly untouched. Just at the time when the Bouffes were rising to fame an epidemic of deaths took place among the celebrities of the previous generation. Among those who died were Musard, Heine, Eugène Sue, Rachel, and Alfred de Musset. " They gamble without passion, love without passion, dissipate without pleasure," Alfred de Musset wrote of the youth of the new age before he died. The replacement of passion by the contemporary vogue of artificially produced excitement was indeed characteristic of a bourgeoisie that had unceremoniously jettisoned all its real feelings.

Even the Café de Paris, which had been the center of the social scene in the time of Louis-Philippe, closed down. It could not withstand the competition of noisier and more lively places which were more in accordance with the tastes of the time. The Café de Paris's last guests were Dr. Véron and his crony Malitourne, who, when supper was over, made a speech of farewell to the proprietor which moved Dr. Véron so much that he dropped a tear on his napkin. Notwithstanding his emotion, however, Dr. Véron had no thought of abdicating himself. He sat in the Corps Législatif as a Government supporter and published his memoirs under the title of *Mémoires d'un bourgeois de Paris.* Rumor had it that they were written by Malitourne.

A few ghosts still haunted the Boulevards. After spending

eight years at Boulogne, Lord Seymour, who had scuttled hastily away during the revolution, returned to Paris, where he continued to vegetate for some time yet. His form was bloated, his passion for gymnastics, cigars, and horses had waned. Unlike him, however, " the Persian " continued his dumb existence in every way unchanged. When the Persian Ambassador first visited the Opéra in 1857 and his eyes fell on his mysterious fellow-countryman, the Parisians hoped for a sensation. But the two men, after fixedly gazing at each other, made not the slightest sign to indicate that they knew each other.

The society of the Second Empire took no notice of the relics, the corpses, and the ruins. The current abhorrence of reality was illustrated by the hostility encountered by the new trend towards realism in literature. Flaubert was prosecuted because of *Madame Bovary*. The age demanded banquets and feasts and intoxicating revels, thrills that lifted the moment from the commonplace and drowned the agitation of the Socialists, the republicans, and the students. Opportunities for celebration constantly occurred — there were the Peace Congress, the christening of the Prince Imperial. Those at the center of things felt instinctively that only noise and excitement could prevent social antagonisms coming to the surface with disastrous consequences. The rebuilding of Paris, the frantic tearing down of old buildings and the setting up of new, were part of it all, just as were the innumerable *mésalliances* that now took place.

A Marquis married a horse-dealer's daughter, a girl of noble birth her father's coachman. The society men of the new age went in for luxury on a parvenu scale. Raphael Bischoffsheim, for instance, would invite journalists, playwrights, actresses, and celebrities of the *demi-monde* to gigantic suppers, followed by dancing that went on all night. Morny sailed in splendor over the waters to represent the Emperor at the coronation of Czar Alexander at St. Petersburg and, after carrying out his duties there with great éclat, married a Princess Troubetskoy. Since the end of 1854 he had been President of the Corps Législatif, and he fulfilled the functions of this office with a most worldly composure. He had plenty of time left to write plays for the court theater and to look after his private business interests. The Bourse hummed when Morny was said to be in the market.

In this Paris Offenbach floated like a cork upon the waters. His royalties grew, which only meant that he spent and gave away his money more light-heartedly than ever. There must be no troubles anywhere in his neighborhood. He now lived in style in the rue Laffitte, near the palace of the Rothschilds, but the accommodation was still insufficient on his Friday evenings.

Offenbach's Friday evenings, which were invariably devoted to entertaining, had originated during his days as a conductor and were now so famous that all Paris talked of them. They were not always just cheerful, informal gatherings, but occasionally blossomed forth into greater magnificence, when the rooms would be packed to suffocation and the supper tables would overflow on to the landings. At one such party, which took place in February 1857, " in celebration of the imminent end of the world," Léo Delibes danced a solo polka — the young Delibes who, to the indignation of all serious composers, wrote librettos for the little theaters instead of competing as he should have done for the Prix de Rome.

As this party was a huge success, it was followed only a month later by a fancy-dress ball at which Gustave Doré walked in on his hands. The celebrated draftsman had picked up the knack from the numerous clowns and acrobats who frequented his studio. Later on in the evening Offenbach's " farmyard waltz " was played, followed by some amateur theatricals. The play was *L'Enfant Trouvère,* with Offenbach himself playing the chief role, Ludovic Halévy as a page, and Bizet at the piano. Amateur theatricals were extremely fashionable and served as some compensation for the silence imposed by the dictatorship.

Next year Offenbach organized a ball at the Bouffes, under his old legend of a " mutual insurance society for the combating of boredom." The program bade the ladies encourage the young men by fiery glances, and " improper dances " were " obligatory," while " those who indulged in them would promptly be shown the door."

Apart from his Friday evenings, parties invariably took place at Offenbach's house after every first night. These were known as *" Les soupers de Jacques."*

Far from being detrimental to Offenbach's work, these parties stimulated him. In the midst of a crowded social gathering Offenbach would suddenly become absorbed and begin to cover sheets of paper with innumerable little flies' feet. Others might have required deep peace, but the concentration and poise necessary for composition would come to him in the midst of a buzz of conversation. For that very reason the Boulevards were a necessity to him.

He lunched regularly at the Restaurant Peters, at a table reserved for Villemessant and his staff. At the third mouthful he would light a cigar, with the aid of which he would steer his way via an egg dish and a cutlet towards a cup of coffee, in which he invariably dipped a cake bought previously at a pastrycook's. He found the conversation of his journalist friends as stimulating and inspiring as the hum of activity behind the scenes at the theater. He deserted the Restaurant Peters for a time when M. Peters, the proprietor, hit upon the unlucky idea of introducing a tame bear for the better entertainment of his clients. This was too much for Offenbach, and he only returned after the bear had taken its departure.

There was a great deal in common between writing operettas and running a newspaper. Villemessant, like Offenbach, abhorred monotony, and his aim was to make every issue of his paper as bright and entertaining as possible. He, too, pined in solitude and could only breathe freely when he was in the midst of a throng. He was a man who liked to be thought charitable. Occasionally caprice would lead him to take some poor devil from the street, reclothe him from head to foot, and give him ten francs for a hot dinner into the bargain. But he was a man of a coarser mold than Offenbach, and their outer resemblances concealed fundamental differences.

Villemessant was obsessed by his newspaper. At the café he would tell stories he was thinking of printing in his next issue, and those that failed to take on he dropped like hot coals. He was perpetually on the alert to hear what people on the Boulevards were saying about the articles written by his staff. When an article was praised he overwhelmed its author with marks of favor; but when an article was blamed he would hurry back to his office, kick up a tremendous row, and sack the poor journalist responsible on the spot. Sometimes his method of getting rid of an undesired member of his staff was to present him with a handsome walking-stick, as a hint that he should walk out with it. On second thoughts he generally regretted his severity, but the newspaper was his fetish.

He introduced a number of journalistic innovations, such as bringing out special editions on special occasions, such as the death of Rachel. He was the first to feature " news in brief," and to arrange the reading-matter in such a fashion that the reader always knew that he would find the same feature in the same place. His constant preoccupation was to divine or create public demand. He soon turned *Le Figaro* into a half-weekly and started two other papers in quick succession, one a fashion journal and the other devoted to the provision of news only. *"Elle est bien bonne"* was the phrase that was always falling from his lips. It could take on every conceivable shade of meaning.

No end to this gay existence seemed in sight. Yet clouds were on the horizon, distant and unnoticeable as yet, which were destined to result in a return to a more sober mood. After a certain interval during which he remained faithful to Eugénie, the Emperor resumed his amorous adventurings, fancying he would not have to answer for them before the gods. The consequence was that Eugénie made the fateful decision to intervene in high politics.

Difficulties arose. The more pressing the Italian question became, the more acute grew the conflict between the principle of nationality and the Catholic interests. On the one hand the Emperor relied on the clergy, to whom he had bound himself by numerous concessions, while on the other the Napoleonic tradition and his own past forced him to ally himself with Victor Emmanuel, who came forward as the champion of Italian freedom and the unification of Italy. This brought him into conflict not only with Austria but with the temporal power of the Pope. Eugénie, with her rigid Catholic upbringing, was an ardent defender of the Catholic cause, while the beautiful Countess Castiglione, an emissary of Cavour, tried to woo the Emperor, who was captivated by her, for the Italians. Disappointed at the Emperor's long delay, Orsini, an Italian patriot, tried to assassinate the Emperor in January 1858, by throwing a bomb at him outside the Opéra. Though this attempt was not the first of its kind, it caused the greatest havoc and led to an intensification of the dictatorship, but in the long run it tended to hasten the Italian alliance. The Emperor hoped later to conciliate the Pope by a compromise.

Reality, with its many conflicts and antagonisms, loomed nearer in the economic sphere as well. The Emperor was a free-trader, because the glamour so useful to the maintenance of his power was best served by the promotion of world trade. But the industrialists clung firmly to protection; in this their interests were at one with a section of the working class, who feared their wages would suffer if duties were removed. The greatly increased cost of living, which went hand in hand with increased gold-production, made the prospect of lower wages even more alarming.

In the meantime, however, all these various conflicts remained latent, and joy and glamour were unabated. But soon reality would be knocking at the door.

CHAPTER V

ORPHEUS IN THE UNDERWORLD

ALTHOUGH Offenbach's operettas played to full houses, his theater did not prosper. The reason was that he was a bad businessman. Like the cricket in the fable he set to music, it never occurred to him to set aside anything for a rainy day. Personally he had no great use for money. His wants were relatively small. But the gaiety which it was his ambition to spread by means of his theater seemed inseparable in his eyes from an atmosphere of luxury and sumptuous furnishings. His theater was meant to be a kind of foretaste of paradise, and in paradise there must be superfluity. He had been over-lavish in expense on costumes and effects for *Mesdames de la Halle,* but when two seats were slightly damaged he had no hesitation in replacing the seats in the whole auditorium. To have haggled about a little thing like that would have been as impossible for him as to have refused help to a friend, or even a stranger, in need.

The result of this uncommercial outlook became plain as early as 1858. Although the box-office takings were high, the expenses were far higher. And as his creditors were not willing to sacrifice their money for unprofitable products of the imagination, they put the bailiffs in. To escape the persecutions of these gentry, whose appearance is never humorous except in operettas, Offenbach went to stay with friends, traveled secretly from place to place, in fact resorted to all the expedients to which debtors have had recourse ever since debtors began. It was clear that nothing could save him except a success greater than any he had yet enjoyed. So he set all his hopes upon the new operetta, *Orpheus in the Underworld,* on which he was now at work. He even worked at it in the hotel bedrooms in which he compulsorily sojourned while in flight from his creditors.

The idea of turning the story of Orpheus into a satire on the gods of Olympus had been in the air for a considerable time. Ludovic Halévy and Hector Crémieux had sketched out a libretto based on it two years before, but it had come to nothing, because as long as Offenbach's license only allowed him to put four characters on the stage, it was hardly possible to do justice to all the Olympians. The idea was apparently Offenbach's own. Some envious spirits accused him of plagiarizing from the Cologne poet Karl Cramer. But even if the idea did come from a carnival play seen in his native town, that was only one of the many sources from which he might have taken it. Italian comedians and comic poets in Vienna had long since applied the legend of Orpheus to the purposes of parody, including parody of grand opera. Artistic creation does not take place in the void. It must have something for its raw material. The artist does not create out of nothing, but rather transforms something already in existence.

As soon as the last restrictions on his license were withdrawn and the Bouffes was finally allowed to put on what it liked, Offenbach reverted to the idea of an operetta based on the old legend. Threats of distraint were not the only difficulty he had to face. Before the libretto was more than half written Ludovic Halévy was appointed general secretary in the Ministry for Algeria — an extraordinary promotion that unfortunately prevented him from working as a librettist, particularly for such a frivolous theater as the Bouffes. He did not then suspect that his withdrawal from the work, which of course involved a substantial reduction in his royalties, meant a renunciation on his part of tens of thousands of francs. Offenbach was greatly distressed at his withdrawal. He wrote him a letter recalling their first work in collaboration, the prologue for the opening of the Bouffes, and appealed to him at least to finish *Orpheus,* which promised to be

a masterpiece. In describing it as a masterpiece he was referring
not to the libretto but to his own music, by which he was thrilled
to the marrow. The urgent nature of Offenbach's appeal was
largely due to the fact that Crémieux, his new librettist, was much
addicted to melancholy reverie and, unlike Halévy, wrote at a
snail's pace, which drove Offenbach to distraction. No matter
how you bullied or cajoled him, Crémieux refused to be hurried.
As Halévy preferred writing librettos to his work in a Government office, he yielded to Offenbach's entreaties to the extent of
agreeing to supply passages in case of need, provided his name
was not mentioned. His name was mentioned, however, for
Offenbach and Crémieux dedicated the operetta to him.

Rehearsals were already in progress when Offenbach engaged
Bache, an actor who had just left the Comédie Française. In his
anxiety to omit nothing that might tend to increase his chances
of success, Offenbach might, of course, have created a role specially for him. It is far more probable, however, in view of his
unerring theatrical instinct, to assume that he engaged him to
improve the balance of the piece. Bache was incapable of appearing on the stage without making an unforgettable impression. His height and his leanness were sufficiently striking in
themselves. He was a melancholiac, and seemed to be wandering
on the border-line of madness. Therein lay his strange and peculiar individuality.

His behavior was most eccentric. Sometimes he was to be seen
striding along the Boulevards carrying an enormous kitchen
knife. This was a sure sign that he had been invited out to
dinner. He was unable to believe that any other knife would cut.
On the stage he heard inaudible voices, prompting him to deliver
his lines now with exaggerated slowness and emphasis, now at
breakneck speed, the words toppling over one another in his
anxiety to get them out. But his inexplicable crescendos and
diminuendos endeared him to the public, who believed his va-
garies to be deliberate, and the fact that his voice was unbroken,
like a boy's, and that in moments of fervor he looked rather like

a high-strung giraffe, made him funnier than ever. Indeed, so strange was his behavior on the stage that he might have been a visitor from another planet. In *Orpheus* he played the important role of John Styx.

The *Journal amusant* carried a description of the bustle that went on in the manager's office at the Bouffes on the day of the première of *Orpheus*. In spite of its exaggerations, it cannot have been very far from the truth. At least it gives one an idea of how the Parisians of his time pictured the Mozart of the Champs-Élyseés. The description is as follows:

Just when Offenbach was making some alterations in the score for the piccolo someone came in and told him that Mlle Tautin, who was playing the part of Eurydice, was insisting on being provided with a real tiger-skin; otherwise she would be utterly incapable of producing the necessary bacchanalian frenzy. Then a number of Germans trooped in and, in their capacity as his fellow-countrymen, started pestering Offenbach for free seats. As soon as they had been shown out, Offenbach was informed that the piccolo had an attack of fever and would be unable to play that night. Then three mysterious-looking gentlemen appeared and disappeared again; evidently the bailiffs. Then a commissionaire handed in an anonymous letter the writer of which, evidently the author of a rejected masterpiece, threatened to make a disturbance during the first performance. Then the janitor came in and announced that the gas-pipe in the street had just burst. Then Offenbach was informed that the Ministry of the Interior insisted on some more cuts being made in the text, and Villemessant appeared in the doorway and asked Offenbach to act as his second in a duel. And so it went on.

Works of any real originality take some time to give rise to those misunderstandings which cause them to become a public sensation. The first performance of *Orphée aux Enfers,* which took place on October 21, 1858, was a disappointment. It was not a failure, but neither was it the success that Offenbach required. The audience applauded Bache's melancholy humor and his lines: " When I was still a prince in Arcadia . . ." and they were duly edified by the beauty of the blonde Venus and admired the Babylonian splendor of the final scene in the underworld, with its vaults, palaces, and pillared halls, the sight of which, together with the superb costumes, many of which were designed by Gustave Doré, must have filled Offenbach's creditors with dismay. The first-night audience took in innumerable details, but missed the point of the whole. And as for the critics, with a few exceptions they tended to disapprove.

In their non-comprehension some of them condemned the piece outright. One composer-critic whose own work had been produced at the Bouffes expressed surprise at anyone having stumbled on such an unfortunate idea as that of attempting to produce a musical satire of this kind, and he said that those who found this sort of thing humorous were lucky. Offenbach, in the hope of making the best of a bad job, made some of his celebrated *bedides goupures,* the result of which, in conjunction with the witty improvisations of Léonce as Pluto and Désiré as Jupiter, was a heightening of the humorous effects. There were quite a lot of people who found the piece to their taste after all. Gods in carnival costume, scattering jokes and witticisms in the jargon of the Boulevards, were decidedly entertaining. The box-office receipts gradually increased. There was a modest hope that, after all, *Orpheus* might perhaps reach its eightieth performance.

Then, a month and a half after the first night, a thunderbolt fell. It was hurled by Jules Janin, the Jupiter of criticism, from his Olympus, the *Journal des Débats.* He had condescended once more to pay a visit to the Bouffes, and what he saw, so he stated, beggared description. Instead of the amiable and carefree gaiety which in the past he had praised, there was now rife there a spirit of irreverence that bordered on blasphemy. The venerated figures of Orpheus and Eurydice were being dragged in the dust by people who did not shrink from profaning antiquity and desecrating the gods. In short, *Orpheus* was a profanation of " holy and glorious antiquity," a crime for which there ought to be condign punishment.

Janin's thunderbolt, so far from striking the evil-doer dead, served rather as a flash of lightning brilliantly illuminating him. The operetta had hitherto been held to be a harmless piece of entertainment, but now it appeared in a lurid light. Offenbach and Crémieux hastened to exploit this unexpected stroke of fortune. They made a vigorous reply in *Le Figaro* to Janin's onslaught; in fact they succeeded in getting the last laugh.

There is a passage in *Orpheus* in which Pluto repeats a highflown tirade, which he maintains he has read somewhere, in praise of the wonders of Olympus. He does so in order to divert Jupiter from interest in his own realm. This passage always caused a great deal of amusement. " Here is a scent of goddesses and nymphs, a delicious aroma of myrtle and vervain, nectar and ambrosia. One hears the cooing of doves, the songs of Apollo, the Muses of Lesbos! . . . Here are the nymphs! . . . Here are the Muses! . . . The Graces are not far away. . . ." Crémieux revealed that these phrases had appeared word for word in an article written six months previously by no other than Jules Janin in connection with a ballet. They showed conclusively that the defender of " holy and glorious antiquity " was inspired by the object of his veneration to nothing but empty verbiage.

The Bouffes benefited by these controversial fireworks. All Paris became convinced that mighty issues were at stake, and everyone felt it incumbent on him to see *Orpheus* and judge for himself.

In Janin's eyes the operetta was a desecration of antiquity. But this was far from being the first occasion on which such desecration had taken place. Why, then, did *Orpheus* so distress him? French literature of the previous two hundred years contained countless satires on antiquity. In 1829 Mlle Mars had organized a masked ball at which the gods and goddesses appeared in carnival costume just as they did at the Bouffes. Everyone knew

Daumier's mythological caricatures, which, in the words of Baudelaire, made Achilles, Odysseus, and the rest look like a lot of
played-out tragic actors, inclined to take pinches of snuff at moments when no one was looking. At the beginning of the Second
Empire satire at the expense of the great figures of antiquity had
actually become a fashion, no doubt providing an outlet for the
suppressed impulse to protest against the dictatorship. At the end
of 1858 the Goncourt brothers drew attention to the astonishing
modernity of the old scoffer Lucian, whom they described as a
predecessor of Heine, the same Heine whom Xavier Aubryet in
his notice of *Orpheus* described as being related to Offenbach.

Satire on antiquity being a current practice, Janin's indignation must really have been based on something else. This is what
it was: Offenbach's operetta, though in play, laid bare the foundations of contemporary society and gave the bourgeoisie an opportunity of seeing themselves as they really were. The bourgeoisie had drunk of the waters of Lethe in order to drown the
memory of their past, but this operetta threatened to bring them
up against themselves again. That was the danger that filled
Janin with such panic fury. But he dared not confess the real
cause to himself. For if such feelings had come to the surface it
would have been a heavy blow to the contemporary regime. He
therefore necessarily suppressed the real reason why he was
shocked, and instead of accusing *Orpheus* of sacrilege against
contemporary society, he accused it of sacrilege against the gods.
Janin's indignation was unconscious and real. His attributing it
to a desecration of antiquity was a misunderstanding on the plane
of consciousness.

Offenbach, developing a theme he had already touched on in
Ba-ta-clan, had indeed thrown a light on the background against
which the impressive spectacle of the dictatorship was being unfolded. It was easy to detect contemporary allusions, what with
Jupiter, the father of the gods, who was after every pretty woman
he set eyes on; his wife, Juno, who was consumed with jealousy;
and the court camarilla of the gods, who followed the example

of their overlord. No less drastic was the exposure of the shifty expedients by which the apparatus of power was kept intact. In order to escape punishment for the rape of Eurydice, Pluto incited the gods against Jupiter, and Jupiter himself did not shrink from the meanest and most dishonest devices in order to maintain himself in power or to attain some private end. His reign corrupted Olympus just as that of their dictator did the bourgeoisie. No sooner did Jupiter propose taking the gods with him to the underworld than they forgot their rancor against him and started singing his praises, forgetting everything except their own passion for amusement and distraction. The inhabitants of the earth fell victims to the same pettiness. Like the gods, Orpheus and Eurydice also sought happiness outside the marriage tie and were not exactly amenable to the precepts of morality. In short, the operetta made a mock of all the glamour that surrounded the apparatus of power. Behind all the impressive display of the Second Empire the old appetites and lusts lived on.

There was only one power before which gods and men, and Jupiter himself, trembled. The Napoleonic dictatorship deliberately wooed and indeed relied on the favor of the masses and was therefore more susceptible than any other regime to public opinion — that wayward, fickle entity that a prince compared to a temperamental woman, who would remain motionless on her sofa for days on end and then, in a moment of passion, would tear to pieces everything on which she could lay her fingers. Offenbach's librettists had the bright idea of replacing the chorus of classical tragedy by Public Opinion. Public Opinion in *Orpheus* stood for the *appearance* of honor, loyalty, and faith; in other words, for social convention.

Public Opinion bade Orpheus beg Eurydice back from Jupiter, and when he hesitated, being glad at having at last got rid of her, she spurred him on with the words: " Come! Honor calls you! " It would have been impossible to state more pointedly that honor only persisted as a convention. And as for Jupiter, he yielded to convention knowing full well that it was the only thing that held both Olympian and terrestrial society together, at the same time allowing himself every license under its cover. It was nothing but a convenient façade. " Everything for decorum and through decorum," he preaches to his gods. In the end he uses the crudest trickery to force Orpheus to renounce Eurydice and sends Public Opinion empty-handed away; from which it is abundantly clear that Public Opinion can be manipulated with impunity by the powers that be.

But were conventions and sensual appetites the sum total of existence? The character of John Styx was a reminder of a life that contained something more.

" When I was still a prince in Arcadia . . ." John Styx sang, recalling a time when he had been free and proud and had known love that was more than an illusion. John Styx was far from being merely an extra character who just happened to be put in because a suitable actor had become available. On the contrary, he provided the necessary counterfoil to his iniquitous environ-ment. Without him there would not even be a memory of a better life. The sadness of his song is the sadness of one to whom the present means nothing, the past everything. It was thor-oughly natural that this unfortunate, who had once been a prince in Arcadia, a realm in which everything was topsyturvy, should now be degraded to be a servant. There was a tragic element about his shadowy existence; but as a consequence of the angle from which it was observed, it was made to appear extremely comic. For where illusion rules, reality becomes a mockery.

At one point, however, the dissolute Olympians seemed about to smash through the make-believe. Satiated with the everlasting azure of heaven, they had had enough of sipping nectar and ambrosia. In this passage Offenbach seemed to be calling upon his contemporaries to awaken. You live in the azure of material prosperity, the operetta seemed to say, and are perpetually cele-brating festivals at which nectar and ambrosia flow in streams.

Confess that you are just as bored as the gods, and follow the lead that they are giving. What was the lead the gods were giving? They were setting about making a revolution.

> *Abattons cette tyrannie,*
> *Ce régime est fastidieux,*

they sang, threatening Jupiter in chorus. And so that their anger might be given a thorough contemporary note, the orchestra struck up the *Marseillaise,* which in the days of the Second Empire was very definitely a revolutionary song. The challenge was plain enough.

Such daring was possible only because the whole thing was an illusion, a mirage. Jupiter had no difficulty whatever in taming the venal gods; at this point the operetta, reminiscent of *Ba-ta-clan* once more, reverted to the glorification of pleasure as such. It became an affirmation of the life of pleasure, to be ecstatically enjoyed.

An alternative might have been revolution; ecstatic pleasure was the refuge of him who objected to the veil being torn from reality. But was it only a refuge? In the big final scene in the underworld the frenzy rose to dionysiac heights. Eurydice's hymn to Bacchus set the keynote:

> *Evohé! Bacchus m'inspire,*
> *Je sens en moi*
> *Son saint délire,*
> *Evohé! Bacchus est roi!*

This, in the words of a contemporary, was no song to be hummed gaily by a bonneted grisette, but the song of a frenzied bacchante, clad in a tiger-skin, with vine-leaves in her hair; no tavern tune, but the impassioned hymn of an ecstatic cult. The land of innocent gaiety had been left far behind, and the little brook flowing between green banks had swollen into an impetuous torrent. For a moment the unleashed elements were held in check by a minuet dating from the time of Offenbach's grandfather, and then they discharged themselves into a wild rhythm, danced with furious abandon by all the gods and goddesses.

"Did it not seem as though at the first sound of this delirious orchestra a whole society suddenly sprang into being and dashed madly into the midst of the dance?" Francisque Sarcey wrote. "This music would be enough to awaken the dead. . . . At the first stroke of the bow which set the gods of Olympus and the underworld in motion it seemed as though the whole throng were seized with a mighty impulse, and as though the whole century, with its governments, institutions, customs, and laws, were plunged into the whirl of a tremendous, all-embracing saraband."

This dance was the resuscitation of the old cancan of the period that followed the Revolution of 1830, the cancan in which the untamed passions of the people mingled with the unrest of nobles and bourgeoisie. Nor could it deny its heritage. For though its glamorous frenzy served the ends of Imperial policy and suited the tastes of the generation, it also contained elements of danger. For it led straight to dionysiac orgies which could only end in self-destruction. If the *Marseillaise* was a direct attack on the dictatorship, this dance was an indirect attack.

It was Offenbach's score that put all this across the footlights, introduced the *Marseillaise,* brought out the character of John Styx, invoked the god Bacchus, and spun out the libretto into an infinity of humorous and satirical allusions. It parodied Gluck, made fun of the absurd Comédie Française convention of causing what a later age would call a "signature tune" to be played when a god or goddess came upon the stage. Nevertheless neither the satirical, critical function of the music nor its humorous function ever became exclusively predominant. It reflected the exotic Greek landscape, and sad or tender melodies alternated with gay ones. In Offenbach tenderness and gaiety, bright wit and genuine feeling lived harmoniously side by side. That was perhaps his most noticeable characteristic. A kind of inverted magician, he took it as his mission to unmask the hollow phantoms which tyrannize over mankind; but he gave his blessing to every genuine human emotion that he met on the way.

There is no doubt that it was Jules Janin who, without wishing to, established the fame and fortunes of *Orpheus*. The audiences who were attracted to the Bouffes by his attack naturally assumed that there must be something quite specially remarkable about a production on which such a wholesale onslaught had been made. They reacted to Janin's ridiculous ardor on behalf of classical mythology by refusing to see any signs of unseemly irreverence in the operetta and finally made up their minds that it must be a masterpiece. They also, of course, shut their minds to the real sacrilege perpetrated by Offenbach. To have admitted that it was an attack on the callousness of the bourgeoisie and that it flitted perilously near reality would have been too dangerous. So they had no alternative but to misunderstand. They therefore took it to be a buttress of the contemporary regime, a kind of hymn to the greater glory of the Second Empire.

The operetta was certainly sufficiently ambiguous to render this misunderstanding pardonable. All that was necessary was to disregard the contemporary satire as an entertaining piece of nonsense, to isolate the character of John Styx, and to lay all emphasis on the scenes of ecstasy, and the operetta would appear in the desired light. The authors themselves liked to see it that way.

Orpheus in the Underworld became more than an operetta; it became a token, a portent of the times. After about the eightieth performance crowds flocked to see it in an unending stream. It played to capacity for night after night. Offenbach was saved. The glory that only he achieves who gives a whole generation what it wants surrounded his name. The music of *Orpheus* set all Paris dancing. The light infantry marched to it, and its waltzes and gallops became the rage, from the Tuileries to the smallest suburban taverns. Incidentally the cancan also offered a welcome opportunity of seeing the pretty legs that were hidden beneath the crinolines. Offenbach as usual gave a supper in honor

BACCHANAL FROM *Orphée aux Enfers*
From the painting by Gustave Doré

IN THE CHAMPS-ÉLYSÉES

Lithograph by Daumier, 1855, in the Bibliothèque des Beaux-Arts

of the two hundredth performance. Some enthusiasts went to
see *Orpheus* again and again; one of them went forty-five times
in succession. Such pertinacity, however, was generally characteristic only of those mortals who enjoyed the favor of one of the
goddesses or bacchantes. Such intimacies, of course, made the
bond between audience and stage all the closer.

After the two hundred and twenty-eighth performance the
players were so exhausted that *Orpheus* had to be taken off.
However, at the end of April 1860 it was staged again at a gala
evening at the Italian Opéra, which was then a center of sumptuous social life. The Emperor had consented to be present on the
express condition that *Orpheus* was on the program. The house
was sold out within a few hours of the announcement being
made, in spite of Offenbach's insistence on the audience being
rigorously sifted, for fear of a plot against the Emperor's life.
The evening's profit was twenty-two thousand francs, besides a
costly bronze from the Tuileries, together with a note from the
Emperor saying that he would never forget the delightful evening he owed to *Orpheus*.

With Orpheus the genre of the *offenbachiade* was created.
Offenbach's later great operettas all derived from this one. The
controversy to which *Orpheus* gave rise broke out again and
again. *Orpheus* was exalted as a unique picture of the age; it
was denounced, as Janin had denounced it, as an instrument of
decadence. One German musical critic described the score of
Orpheus in 1863 as "brothel music" (the word *Kulturbol-
schewismus* had not yet been invented), while Nietzsche saw in
Offenbach's music "the supreme form of wit." Judgments varied
in accordance with the social conditions from which they arose.
And to this day the controversy about the true meaning and
value of the *offenbachiade* continues.

Offenbach naturally determined to follow up his success. To
avoid repeating himself he chose a medieval subject, the legend
of Genevieve. The first performance of *Geneviève de Brabant*
took place in November 1859, with a large contingent of police

on duty to control the crowd at the doors. Well as the music was liked, the operetta was given a cool reception, and after fifty performances it was taken off. The fault lay with the libretto of Jaime and Tréfeu, which was not a closely knit texture, but contained long passages of pointless and irrelevant jokes. However, it was the first of Offenbach's real court satires, introducing as it did the stupid Prince Sifroid, the intriguer Golo, and the furious warrior Charles Martel, all characters that were to appear again and again in the future. Moreover it contained some lines devoted to the subject of gambling, the very topical nature of which was a pointer towards the later great operetta *La Vie parisienne*. Offenbach subsequently had the libretto completely revised with Crémieux's help, and the revival, which took place in 1867, owed its success to its satire on the gendarmes and the pomposity of minor officialdom.

CHAPTER VI

OPERETTA WORLD

THE OPERETTA would never have been born had the society of
the time not itself been operetta-like; had it not been living in a
dream-world, obstinately refusing to wake up and face reality.

At the beginning of the Second Empire the bourgeoisie was so
effectively isolated that scarcely a breath of air from the outside
world came to ruffle its composure. The dictatorship forbade all
expression of opinion and stifled all political life. The control
was so strict that the bourgeoisie withdrew more and more into
private life; and private life was just as empty as public life. The
bourgeois flight from reality was in entire harmony with its dislike of nature and the elements, a dislike it shared with the *boulevardiers* of the time of Louis-Philippe. " To me nature is an
enemy," the Goncourts stated in their diary; and the witty
Laurant-Jan remarked that the sight of a wall covered with
posters was more precious to him than the most beautiful sight
in nature.

Not even war brought the bourgeoisie up against reality. For
the wars of the Second Empire were fought in distant lands, and
the echoes that were heard in Paris were indistinct and confused.
Even in the economic sphere emphasis lay more on speculation
and finance than on solid industrial development.

But in spite of all these barriers set against the inroads of reality, the operetta-like qualities of Second Empire society could
scarcely have flourished so exuberantly had not relatively wide
sections of the population been assured of material prosperity.
Second Empire society, moreover, was exclusively a town prod-

uct. Only in Paris were there present all the elements, material and verbal, that made the operetta possible. Paris was the home of that peculiarly Parisian product the *bon mot*. It enabled them all, the powers that be and their genuine and opportunist supporters as well as the doubters and critics, to trip lightly and heedlessly over the pitfalls that were the inevitable consequence of the dictatorship and its breach with reality.

The model of all the courts in Offenbach's operettas was that of the Tuileries. When the Archduke Maximilian, later Emperor of Mexico, who was brought up in the courtly traditions of the Habsburgs, paid a visit to the Imperial pair, the upstart character of the Paris court made a painful impression on him. " There is something amateurish and theatrical about the whole thing," he wrote home to Schönbrunn, " and the various roles are played by officials who are not very sure of their parts." The excessive magnificence of the royal household, with its Life Guards, palace prefects, chamberlains and masters of ceremonies, the swarm of attendant adventurers, and the general style of life made the whole thing even more parvenu-like.

The courtiers who took pains to copy faithfully the Emperor's mustaches, slouching walk, and far-away eyes might have been the creatures of a librettist's imagination. Their pattern and prototype was Count de Tascher, whose astonishing imitative powers turned the court into a kind of cabaret. At the Emperor's request he would cluck and waddle like a turkey-cock or give a striking imitation of a raging storm or the sun glowing on a hot day, or alternatively assume the elegiac appearance of the moon. Not one of the elements was safe from him. By way of a change the court would play charades, in which mythological characters were very popular. The Greek gods in Offenbach's *La Belle Hélène* also filled in their time with games of charades. The passion for this kind of entertainment betrayed the shallow nature of court life, which had appeared suddenly out of the blue and might disappear just as suddenly. It was as artificial, as superficial, as impermanent as the courts that occur in the works of Offenbach. *" Oh, c'est aussi un de ces rois constitutionnels! "* the Empress once said of the Prince of Wales. That was the language of an operetta monarch.

" We shall rule this land with a purse in one hand and a whip in the other," Persigny had said to the Countess Le Hon shortly before the *coup d'état*. The whip generally turned out to be superfluous, because money did the work. In this atmosphere money was not regarded as the just reward of labor, but as the magic wand, the open sesame that with a " Hey presto! " promised the effortless acquisition of boundless delights, and spirited reality away. People idolized and yearned for it.

In his novel *L'Argent* Zola describes the walks taken in the evening by the financier Saccard. He passes along the rue Vivienne, one of the principal streets in the Bourse quarter. " Gentle, crystalline music, like the voices of fairies, floated up from the earth and enveloped him, and he recognized the music of gold, the perpetual tinkle peculiar to this quarter of the city devoted to trade and speculation, the music that he had heard that same morning. The end of the day was the same as its beginning." At the end of the rue Vivienne there lay the Bourse, of which Offenbach sang in *Le Savetier et le financier:*

> *Il est rue Vivienne*
> *Un grand monument,*
> *Dont la forme ancienne*
> *Plaît infiniment. . . .*
> *Ça hausse ou ça baisse,*
> *Voilà l'important,*
> *Et chacun s'empresse*
> *Dans le mouvement. . . .*

" *. . . Et chacun s'empresse dans le mouvement. . . .*" The truth, however, was not so much that members of the public were falling over each other's heels in their anxiety to speculate upon the Bourse. It was rather that the new magnates of finance applied their skill to wooing the money from their pockets. They recognized that the anonymous masses could be reached via the newspapers, and therefore they combined their operations on the Bourse with deliberate newspaper propaganda. Innumerable financial papers sprang up, and they were given away almost for nothing, because their real purpose was to catch " suckers."

Two speculators on the grand scale, Polydore Millaud and Jules Mirès, who worked in partnership until after the beginning of the Second Empire, exploited the instrument of the press with particular success. After dissolving partnership each continued his operations on an even vaster scale. While Millaud gave financial tips in *La Presse,* which he had inherited from Girardin, the mighty Mirès group showed its lack of prejudice by subsidizing newspapers of the most conflicting kind. Mirès, compared to whom Dr. Véron was an angel, was an utterly unscrupulous gambler. He owned mines, built blast-furnaces, secured the concession for the Rome railways, had his finger in the pie in the building of the new harbor at Marseille, arranged foreign loans. This comet of finance reached his zenith in 1860, in which year he succeeded in buying Prince Alphonse de Polignac as a husband for his daughter. Was he not a prince himself? In his heyday this nervous, active little man lived in splendor worthy of a prince of the underworld. Like Millaud and other plutocrats, he liked assuming the role of a Mæcenas. However, the boundary between patronage and corruption was often obliterated.

Mirès and the Péreire brothers, following the example of the Rothschilds, would from time to time cause an unexpected shower, not of gold but of securities, to descend on numbers of well-known poets, journalists, and playwrights, without involving any direct obligation in return. The scene in *Orpheus in the Underworld* in which the gods, after plotting against Jupiter, start enthusiastically singing his praises as soon as he holds out to them a definite prospect of amusement was certainly not without precedent in real life.

" *Ça hausse ou ça baisse, voilà l'important. . . .*" Why bother with prosaic reality when castles gleaming in the air looked solid enough? The development of world economy conjured up visions of wealth and an attitude to it that is reflected over and over again in Offenbach's operettas. Winning tickets in lotteries and sudden and dramatic changes of fortune are part of the stock-in-trade of his early work. Sudden changes of fortune were just as characteristic of the world about him, for members of the ruling caste speculated in the hope of strokes of fortune worthy of his operettas.

Berryer described the Crédit Mobilier as "the biggest gambling-hell in Europe." An author said it was like watching jugglers at a circus, juggling with shiny metal balls, which went up and down and up and down and up and down again.

Just as might have been expected, the speculative fever led to incidents that would have been entirely in place in one of Offenbach's works. Soon after the *coup d'état* the Emperor reproved Saint-Arnaud, his War Minister, for having suffered severe losses on the Bourse. Saint-Arnaud tried to excuse himself, saying that in reality his losses had been very slight. He then asked the Emperor who had told him of this trifling matter. The Emperor said that it was Fould, another of his Ministers.

"Fould!" exclaimed Saint-Arnaud. "But, Your Majesty, Fould, who denounces me, was a bear when I was a bull. The only difference between us was that I was convinced that your regime would result in increased confidence, and I lost. But Fould reckoned on a panic, and he gained."

The Emperor had no choice but to pay Saint-Arnaud's debts. He had to do the same a few years later for his Foreign Minister, Count Walewski. Fould himself, as a shrewd financier, seldom speculated unwisely, and it was his firm conviction that the only source of real wealth was hard work.

As hard work seemed a relatively unproductive source of wealth, it was unpopular, and a state of mind was fostered in which speculation proper was confused with speculation on the gullibility of others. Thus the reconstruction of Paris led not only to an enormous amount of speculation in property, but also to an entirely new branch of commerce, the object of which was to exploit the public funds and bamboozle the expropriation committee. Small traders and shopkeepers were naturally anxious to make as much profit as possible from their enforced removal. Special businesses therefore sprang into existence to assist them. The expropriated trader would be supplied with false books and inventories, and, in case of need, his premises would turn out to have been newly redecorated and refurnished; while during the visit of the committee to the premises a constant stream of unexpected customers would pour in, to show how good business really was.

In the general atmosphere of delirium the delicate distinction between commercial transactions that encouraged swindling and commercial transactions that were swindling was apt to evaporate.

Saccard, the hero of Zola's *L'Argent,* tried to justify speculation to a skeptical woman friend. "Let me see," he said. "Do you believe — how shall I express it? — that one can beget many children without desire? For every hundred children that one fails to beget, at most one is actually born. In other words, achievement is the result of excess, is it not? . . . Well, then, without speculation no business would be done." Treacherous as the comparison was, it reveals the connection between the speculation and the voluptuousness that prevailed in the society of the Second Empire and in *Orpheus in the Underworld* alike. Napoleon-Jupiter, if asked about his relations with his wife, would have answered something like this: " During the first six months of our union I remained faithful to her, but now I feel the need of occasional little diversions, in spite of which I am always glad to return to her."

In 1860 one of these little diversions was Mme de C. At any rate it was known that the Emperor paid her a great deal of attention. Moreover, according to the Count de Viel-Castel, her husband, the Marquis de C., who had been a simple naval lieutenant before the Italian War, had been subsequently promoted

to the rank of commander without visible cause; not long afterwards he had given up his naval career and gone to N. as First
Secretary of the French Embassy there; and he had ended by
being advanced to the Senate.

Ludovic Halévy himself tells a story illustrating how the love-
affairs of a Pluto might interfere with the mechanism of state.
The hero of this story, the date of which was the latter part of
the Second Empire, was likewise a naval lieutenant, who was in
love with an enchanting member of the *corps de ballet*. Another
of her admirers was the banker Reynald, but she was too attached
to her naval lieutenant to pay attention to his advances. Reynald
took the rebuff so much to heart that he actually started neglecting his business. His wife was far more disturbed at this than
she was by the dancer, so she advised him to get the Government
to send the lieutenant a long way off. As the banker financed
two papers which supported the Government, the Government
was willing to oblige him, and the lieutenant was assigned to the
frigate *Penelope,* which was sent on a voyage round the world.

By the time the *Penelope* had reached the South Seas, the little
dancer, having dependants to support, had yielded to the banker's
blandishments. But the poor banker felt so uncertain of his acquisition that he paid another visit to the Ministry of Marine and
succeeded in having the *Penelope* sent to Mexico to support the
French army there, though this step was quite unnecessary from
the military point of view. In the course of the debate on the
Mexican expedition in the Corps Législatif he made a speech
patriotically declaring that the expedition must under no circumstances be abandoned. The possibility that he might place his
two papers at the service of the opposition enabled him to delay
the return of his rival to Paris for six whole years; and when the
unfortunate lieutenant finally returned, the dancer gave him his
congé, saying that, alas, she had grown used to the banker;
whereupon the latter presented her with a house in the avenue
de l'Impératrice. His business was once more flourishing, and
so his wife was content.

In spite of, or rather because of this mode of life, Jupiter's exhortation to the gods: "Let us preserve appearances, for all depends on that!" was strictly observed. Moral hypocrisy was the order of the day. No matter how public opinion was defied in secret, the outer façade must be kept intact. The preservation of appearances has, of course, been a necessity at all times and in all ages, but in the Second Empire appearances played a quite special role. A dialogue in Daudet's novel *Le Nabab* vividly illustrates the conventions of the period. It takes place between a fashionable physician, Dr. Jenkins, who is a sanctimonious rogue, and a decayed Marquis.

"'My dear Marquis,' the doctor said in conclusion. 'Explanations between men of honor are always unambiguous.'

"'Honor is a big word, Jenkins,' the Marquis replied. 'Let us rather say men of good behavior. That is sufficient.'"

To the Marquis de Monpavon, a second John Styx, honor is only a memory, and decorum is all that matters.

Even in military affairs decorum was all that mattered. Superb uniforms were used to hide the grim earnest of soldiering, even more, perhaps, than at any other time. The *guides* wore a green jacket with five rows of buttons and a bearskin with a feather. In fact their uniforms competed easily with those of the stage. The attitude to war held in the Paris of the Second Empire was that, though, of course, it involved inevitable sacrifices, it brought glory, sent up the values of securities on the Bourse, and provided opportunities for magnificent processions and parades.

Gaston Jollivet, who was a child at the time, describes the return of the troops from the Crimea. When the victorious army marched triumphantly into Paris, he says, one of the particular heroes was a colonel of Zouaves whose head was enveloped in bandages from brow to chin. "His jaw had been shattered at the assault on Malakoff. Nothing could be seen of his face except his eyes. This was the only sad note of the day. Right at the beginning of the procession a cheerful note was struck by a huge drum-major who was several inches taller than the average of his colleagues. This enormous man smiled at the crowds with an air of great self-satisfaction. He raised his eyes to our window, and when he saw my aunt he made a gallant flourish with his cane."

A happy incident like that, so worthy of the gallant drum-major Raflafla in *Mesdames de la Halle,* of course completely eclipsed the unfortunate colonel with his smashed jaw. War itself was no more than an incident in an operetta. "Your son will enjoy himself. Young people are so fond of war!" were the words the Empress used to console Mme de Sancy, whose son took part in the Italian campaign. "He will have successes of every sort. The girls of Italy are said not to be entirely insensible to French charm. Console yourself," she added with a smile; "he will give mighty saber-blows to our enemies, and perhaps contribute to increasing the Italian population as well!"

Such words were worthy of one of Ludovic Halévy's prima donnas. And who but Offenbach would have dared invent the scene that took place at the Emperor's own departure for Italy? When he passed along the Boulevards in pomp and panoply at the head of his troops he happened to notice a photographer's — photography was new and very fashionable at the time — and he was suddenly overwhelmed with the desire to be photographed just once more. So he ordered a halt. And while he posed before the camera the whole army waited behind him.

The wealth gained by speculation might vanish tomorrow as easily as it had come yesterday; so its possessors reveled in luxury, in order at least to enjoy today. And as they desired to ignore both the past and the future, they cast themselves headlong not just into enjoying themselves but into enjoying themselves deliriously. The pattern on which they based their lives was, in fact, that of so many of Offenbach's finales.

At court there was an extraordinary fashion for *tableaux vivants,* the object of which was to seize and eternalize the fleeting moment; and after the *tableaux vivants* were over, the company would plunge into the whirl of a masked ball, at which Offenbach's music fulfilled the same function as at the theater. At one of these masked balls the Empress appeared darkly veiled as Night, streaked with a Milky Way of diamonds. One lady's fancy dress represented the Bosporus in the light of the evening sun, and another labeled herself the Sea of Marmora on a misty day.

At the beginning of 1857 the speculator Millaud, whose nickname on the Boulevards was Millaud-Million, was led by his fondness for gold to having the interior of his house gilded throughout. To celebrate the completion of this symphony, he gave an enormous party, which began with a dinner of one hundred and fifty covers, at which the guests included two ex-ministers, a general, a dozen bankers, the directors of the big and little theaters, Villemessant and other leading figures in the world of journalism, apart from such celebrities as Lamartine, Gautier, and Houssaye. Eight hundred additional guests attended the reception that followed, and the entertainment included the singing of some simple songs by Berthelier, as well as a number of choral and operatic fragments. The concert was intended to symbolize the harmonious mingling of the various sections of the population. Later in the evening supper was served, after which a real saturnalia broke loose. A week later Mirès, not to be outdone, gave a ball which Lamartine enjoyed even more. Once Lamartine had been the hero of the French people and had promised liberty to all the oppressed. But nobody now spared a thought for the beginning or the end.

Cares, nevertheless, were growing. Perhaps the Emperor's experience in the Italian campaign, which he conducted as an ally of Victor Emmanuel against the Austrians, was a premonition. He was so shaken by the sight of the dead and wounded on the battlefield of Magenta that the spectacle may perhaps have made him even more eager to stop the war than he would otherwise have been. It was his first contact with naked and undisguised reality; for he had not seen the dead of December 2. From now

on he was able to escape reality no longer. The Italian campaign
earned him the enmity of the conservatives, and above all of the
Catholics, who rightly felt that the now inevitable unification
of Italy would mean the abolition of the temporal power of the
Pope. The result was a thoroughgoing political regrouping. As
the props which had hitherto held up his throne were now withdrawn, he was forced to try and woo the support of the republican
masses, who had favored the war against reactionary Austria for
the same reason that the Catholics and the conservatives had opposed it. Directly after his return from Italy he declared a political amnesty, which brought many revolutionary-minded men
back to Paris, and issued decrees which were aimed at reawaken-
ing parliamentary life.

He could no longer adhere to the principle on which he had
hitherto relied. That principle had been to stifle all the contradictions and antagonisms of social reality by the conjuring up
of joy and glamour. To this principle he had faithfully adhered.
But there came a time when he had to readmit the reality he
had deliberately banished; and to maintain himself in power he
found himself obliged to be disloyal to the principle that had
made his power possible. The paradox was speedily detected.
Prosper Mérimée violently criticized his liberal reforms and said
it was absurd to give the Corps Législatif and the Senate the right
to discuss " addresses " without giving them the right to hold
the royal ministers accountable. The absurdity could only be put
right by the granting of more liberal reforms. In short, the innovations the Emperor introduced to bolster up his power necessarily undermined it.

The Emperor's star shone less brightly as soon as he felt himself delivered up to the mercies of two irreconcilable principles.
His self-confidence diminished, his flair started to fail him. Just
as he had not dared to carry the Italian campaign through to
the end, so did he again and again decide to pursue courses which
very soon afterwards he abandoned. His autocratic impulses

pulled him one way, the consequences of his autocratic policies the other. What was he when he could no longer blindly follow his own star? A well-intentioned, sympathetic man to whom it was agony to have to make a decision. He aged visibly and suffered gravely from lassitude, fatigue, and abdominal pains that no doctor could cure. If his entourage had previously thought him a visionary, they now regarded him as irresolute and strange.

The situation was not improved by the inevitable results of excessive speculation, to which many fell victims. The dismay caused by financial disasters found an echo in the republican camp and spread to many conservative-minded people. In 1857, a year of crisis, a series of big financial trials started, under the influence of the opposition to the Saint-Simonist democratization of credit; they disclosed an enormous amount of corruption and sharp practice, such as fraudulent bankruptcies, abuse of confidence, and artificial driving up of prices. An enormous sensation was caused by the trial of Mirès, which started in 1861 and dragged on for years. When Mirès, who obstinately defended the excesses of speculation, quoted his patronage of the arts in self-defense, the public prosecutor replied that his good deeds must be discounted, because he had carried them out with the savings of housemaids and coachmen. Several plays attacking the Bourse caused sensations, and even the Emperor tried to exercise a restraining influence on its excesses.

As for the workers, they had streamed into Paris in masses, attracted by the opportunity of getting work on the great building projects, and their class-consciousness was reinforced by reason of the fact that they were driven by higher rents from the quarters in the center of the city in which they had hitherto lived cheek by jowl with the bourgeoisie; and in the comparative isolation of the suburbs they came more and more to realize their community of interests. In accordance with the new course which the Emperor had embarked upon, he granted them certain concessions. But these did not cause them to renounce their republican aims or their social program.

Nothing would be more mistaken than to suppose that all these difficulties meant any diminution in the operetta-like life of Second Empire society. On the contrary, it was only now that delirium was really let loose, as if to chase away the mounting shadows.

CHAPTER VII

TWO TYPES OF FRIVOLITY

TOWARDS the middle of February 1860, barely three months after the production of *Geneviève de Brabant,* and in the midst of carnival, Offenbach produced his revue *Le Carnaval des revues.* The libretto was by Grangé, Gille, and Halévy. Such revues were a regular institution in Paris and were usually performed about New Year's. Barbey d'Aurevilly was no doubt perfectly right in saying of them that "their object was to appeal to everybody's lowest instincts," but that was certainly not Offenbach's object. His revue consisted of a series of pictures of Paris life set to an accompaniment of the most popular tunes from the repertoire of the Bouffes. The only topical note was provided by the last-minute insertion of a scene entitled "*Le Musicien de l'avenir,*" which was a satire on Richard Wagner.

Satirizing Richard Wagner was certainly topical. The German composer, after innumerable difficulties, had at last succeeded in having three concerts of his work given at the Italian Opéra. They failed to bring Paris to his feet. Nevertheless they roused a furious controversy, in which even non-musical Paris joined, and thus the name of Wagner became speedily known.

Scarcely had Wagner vanished from the boards of the Italian Opéra when, greatly to the delight of the town, he reappeared at the Bouffes in Offenbach's satire. The scene was laid in Elysium, and the plot consisted of a confrontation of Wagner with Grétry, Weber, Mozart, and Gluck. Wagner was made to behave impudently to these masters, telling them it was time they were scrapped as so much useless lumber, and ended by giving two specimens of his own work. The first was a " *symphonie de l'avenir*," in which Wagner counted each *leitmotiv* as it occurred, and the second a grotesque " *tyrolienne de l'avenir*." The four masters, indignant at being offered such fare, thereupon forcibly expelled this apostle of the music of the future from the temple of art. In all this Offenbach betrayed only a slight knowledge of Wagner's work, and it therefore could scarcely be said that his satire truly hit its target. Nevertheless it was talked about a great deal and was put on the program of the gala evening at which the Emperor insisted on hearing *Orpheus*. For Wagner Offenbach's satire meant but one more of the many blows he suffered at the hands of ridicule.

No doubt one of the reasons why Offenbach attacked him was that he detected a fundamental hostility between Wagner's music and his own. Wagner and he indeed represented mutually exclusive worlds. Wagner sought to lay his audience under a fervent spell, clothing his music in a mantle of asceticism, while Offenbach was the quintessence of tenderness and gaiety. Wagner used mythology and saga to create musical dramas which in spite of, or because of, their pessimism in the last resort aggravated the political impotence of the German bourgeoisie, while Offenbach exploited the same or similar raw material to make satires in which he playfully put topsyturvy political conditions to rights. The former used the heavy rumblings of metaphysics to lull people to sleep; the latter chased away all metaphysical fogs that interfered with ecstatic, delirious enjoyment, the object of which was by no means to dull the senses only. Wagner was an architect who piled edifice upon edifice; Offenbach, a destroyer of bogies that stifled the free play of all good impulses. Wagner strove after monumental effects and tried to elevate art into a religion; Offenbach's ambitions were more modest; he shunned everything that smacked of being an inflated phantom, and left art in its place. In Wagner there was a great yearning for emancipation; but Offenbach was as emancipated and free as a bird. The passion with which people sided for one or for the other showed that a conflict of two principles was at stake within one and the same historical situation. Alfred von Wolzogen, an anti-Wagnerian, who was opposed to the " new German " trend in music, hailed *Orpheus* enthusiastically as soon as it appeared, while Nietzsche valued the works of Offenbach highly as an antidote to the spirit of Bayreuth.

In his horror of dark and elementary forces Offenbach rejected Wagner with an abruptness that was rare for him. " To be erudite and boring is not the equivalent of art; it is more important to be piquant and rich in melodies." That is what Offenbach wrote in *L'Artiste* immediately after the first performance of *Tannhäuser* in Paris, on March 13, 1861. Auber was in entire agreement with him. " How evil it would be if that were music! " he announced. Baudelaire, however, was in the other camp. But perhaps the leading Wagnerian was the Princess von Metternich, who conducted zealous propaganda for *Tannhäuser* as the result of her German feelings and broke her fan in the heat of a discussion at the first night. The broken fan was the event of the evening. The Princess and her husband, who had been Austrian Ambassador in Paris since the Italian War, enjoyed the special favor of the Empress, who hoped to be able to serve the Papal cause by securing an alliance with Catholic Austria. " She is not beautiful, she is worse," people used to say of Pauline Metternich. Her outspokenness was of a kind that only a truly *grande dame* could carry off.

The sensation caused by the first night of *Tannhäuser* so impressed itself upon people's minds that several years later Offenbach thought of parodying the tournament on the Wartburg in *La Belle Hélène*. He abandoned the idea, however, no doubt feeling that one's attitude to Wagner could only be hostile or adoring, and nothing between. Besides, he hardly ever parodied a single work or scene, but nearly always parodied several operas at the same time, as though to show that his barbs were aimed at the whole species. His hostility towards Wagner did not diminish with time. Only a year before his death, though he respected

RICHARD WAGNER "SPLITTING AN EAR-DRUM"
Caricature by Gill

COUNT DE MORNY

Meyerbeer and admired Berlioz, he said that Wagner was a Gorgon's head which led young composers astray.

If Offenbach's ethereal temperament was incapable of appreciating the significance of Wagner, Wagner was less unfitted to appreciate Offenbach. After the first performance of *Tannhäuser* he met Hervé at the house of a friend of both; Hervé's operettas delighted him and were able temporarily to dissipate his habitual gloom. But to Offenbach, who had held him up to ridicule and was again to cross his path in Vienna at a later date, he was pitiless. He regarded *Orpheus* with horror, said that the warmth that exuded from Offenbach's music was that of " a dung-heap on which all the swine in Europe wallowed," called him " the most international individual in the world," and wrote the following lines of doggerel about him:

> *O wie süss und angenehm,*
> *Und dabei für die Füsse so recht bequem!*
> *Krak! Krak! Krakerakrak!*
> *O herrlicher Jack von Offenback!* [1]

Not till after Offenbach's death did Wagner's rancor diminish. Then, in 1882, in the clarity of old age, he admitted in a letter that there was a resemblance between Offenbach and the divine Mozart, and that he might have been like Mozart. And thus the phrase coined by Rossini, who called Offenbach the " Mozart of the Champs-Élysées," received corroboration.

A fruitful encounter took place just after the first night of another operetta of Offenbach's, the pastoral *Daphnis and Chloë,* which took place on March 27, 1860, and seemed to have been taken straight from a Gobelin tapestry. Offenbach asked Halévy for a libretto for a high personage who desired to compose a little operetta. This high personage was no other than His Excellency Count de Morny, President of the Corps Législatif. Halévy, with his father's help, wrote the libretto and thought no

[1] Oh, how comfy and how sweet, and how grateful to the feet! Krak! Krak! Krakerakrak! is noble Jack von Offenback!

more of the matter. But a few weeks later Offenbach informed him that M. de Morny had an idea for a *bouffonnerie,* the working out of which he desired to entrust to Halévy, and that therefore he wished to make his acquaintance.

Morny's wish was, of course, a command. Their first meeting took place in Offenbach's presence, and each was immediately captivated by the other; Halévy was impressed at finding himself in the presence of the Emperor's stepbrother, while Morny felt for Halévy the respect of the amateur for the professional. Halévy quickly sketched out a scenario on the basis of Morny's idea and read it to him without delay, very conscious the whole time that his new collaborator had been the stage manager of the *coup d'état* and the lover of the Countess Le Hon. Moreover Morny's collaboration was genuine, because the alterations he suggested were very sensible, quite apart from the fact that he contributed a number of witty lines.

Very soon afterwards Halévy once more presented himself at the Presidential Palace with the libretto complete. The little sketch was entitled *Monsieur Choufleuri restera chez lui le. . . .* It betrayed traces of de Musset's influence and was a satire on the bourgeois salons of the time of Louis-Philippe, seen from the angle of a *grand seigneur.* The plot was as follows: Choufleuri, a rich parvenu, tries to elevate himself in society by engaging three famous Italian singers named Sontag, Rubini, and Tamburini to appear at a musical evening, to which he sends out invitations to all the ambassadors and ministers. The Italian singers let him down, however, and the ministers and ambassadors fail to appear. Thus M. Choufleuri is faced with the prospect of being made to look foolish in the eyes of all his guests. But his daughter Ernestine has a brilliant idea. Against her father's wishes, she is in love with Babylas, a hopeful young composer, who lives in a neighboring garret and communicates with her by a musical code. She sends for him, and between them they persuade M. Choufleuri to join them in pretending to be the Italian trio. This, of course, provides an opportunity for plenty of parody of grand opera. The result is that the artful girl's triumph is as complete as it could possibly have been. M. Choufleuri's musical evening is a success, as his guests of course take the false singers for the true. But he is compelled to give Babylas his daughter's hand in compensation, with fifty thousand francs' dowry into the bargain.

The remarkable fact that Morny, one of the leading statesmen of his time, and Halévy, a high Government official, collaborated in writing librettos for operettas throws light on the Second Empire spirit of frivolity. This frivolity did not just consist in drowning reality by delirious pleasure-seeking; its true essence was seen when reality was plainly recognized, as it was by Morny, but treated frivolously all the same. The Emperor adopted the same attitude when he said: " People grumble that everything does not always go well under my regime. How could it be otherwise? The Empress is a Legitimist, Morny is an Orléanist, I am a republican. There is only one Bonapartist, and that is Persigny, and he is mad! "

At the time of his meeting with Halévy, Morny was at the zenith of his power. A humorist said of him that he united *" le chic et le chèque." Grand seigneur* and speculator at the same time, it was he who made Deauville a fashionable resort. He presided over the sessions of the Corps Législatif with such political tact that he gained even the respect of the opposition. He conducted his own business and the business of the state with the same sophisticated nonchalance.

Alphonse Daudet, who as a young man was his private secretary, relates that one morning he brought his chief a few banal verses which he had written at his request. The Minister of the Interior and the Minister of Police were waiting outside in the anteroom. Morny, in his skull cap and his ample dressing-gown, looked just like a cardinal secretary of state. But now, bitten by the operetta bug, he absolutely insisted on trying out the music for which Daudet's verses were written, with the result that he, Daudet, and Lépine, who was also present, seized all the footstools in the room and started making a terrible hubbub. Meanwhile the Minister of the Interior and the Minister of Police were completely forgotten.

Morny's frivolity was rooted in cynicism. If he believed in anything, it was that men were basically evil, for he saw nothing but hypocrisy in various degrees all around him. He kept a number of apes in cages in the vestibule of the Presidential Palace, and he found them inexhaustibly entertaining. They seemed to him to reveal the true nature of man; his unbridled appetites, his imitativeness, his passion to play a role. The Imperial dignitaries, the money magnates, the representatives of the privileged classes, all the flatterers by whom he was surrounded, seemed to him exactly like his apes. Instead of being astonished or indignant at the resemblance, he took it perfectly for granted.

The only thing he insisted on was that appearances be preserved. Appearances were as important to him as to Jupiter or the Marquis de Monpavon. In Morny's eyes appearances, like good manners, were meant to conceal the disgusting nature of man. He found nothing more repugnant than associating with people who had no manners. Their presence affected him with physical revulsion. He permitted himself at most a certain familiarity with brokers on the Bourse, just sufficient, incidentally, to win their confidence, which could be useful. But brokers were not society people, and in society he behaved with elaborate ceremonial. His expression was that of a bored idol; his contributions to conversation were confined to half-phrases, which he would only complete and elaborate when he chanced upon someone worthy·of his mettle. Then his talk would sparkle. His intimates complained that he was continually preaching correctness of behavior and giving them lectures on etiquette. The cynic in him undoubtedly feared that the dam of convention might burst and submerge his little world in the flood. It was not for nothing that he felt highly gratified at the dukedom the Emperor gave him in 1862. This new honor increased his sense of security in the face of a world of obtrusive and threatening apes.

His devotion to the operetta, which held up to ridicule the behavior of mankind, is therefore readily intelligible. The real *offenbachiade,* however, was not based on Morny's type of frivolity, but on Halévy's, which was fundamentally different.

Halévy was a great observer, and what he observed he stored within him. As a child the violently contrasting impressions he had imbibed in the corridors of the Institut de France and behind the scenes at the Opéra had not bewildered him; and in later life the habit of listening to everything and collecting experiences everywhere did not desert him. On the Boulevards he would pick out some curious-looking individual who looked as if he might be interesting, and follow him until he knew absolutely everything about him. He would devote equal attention to studying the flirtations of habitués and ballet-girls in the *foyer de danse.*

A man with an inexhaustible sense of wonder, he strolled through life observing the worlds of art, fashion, and politics, and his exploration of Second Empire society certainly gave him a greater knowledge of it than most of his contemporaries. He knew its shams, its realities, and its corruption, saw how the strings were pulled behind the scenes to move the marionettes hither and thither, and he succumbed to none of the current illusions himself. The standard by which he judged humanity was the standard in himself.

It was significant that from his earliest youth he was an intimate friend of Anatole Prévost-Paradol. Prévost-Paradol, who was somewhat older than he, had, after early struggles, joined the staff of the *Journal des Débats,* on which he proved himself a brilliant political writer. An Orléanist by conviction, he also wrote articles attacking the Empire in the *Courrier du Dimanche,* and his criticisms were greatly feared. He was not, however, exclusively a politician. His political convictions were the result of moral concepts, which he made an attempt to state in his *Études sur les moralistes français,* published in 1864. He was a man with a high conception of the grandeur and independence of man. His influence in this direction was exercised upon Halévy in their school and university years. At the age of eighteen he sent Halévy a letter recommending him to read the *Annals* of Tacitus. " From this book one learns to remain free in the midst of slaves, to challenge tyranny in the name of freedom and one's will, to count on oneself and on oneself alone; to be master of one's life and to pay less attention to one's life than to one's virtue. You have need of such powerful teachings. If your light, gay character is trained in that school, it has everything to gain."

Halévy was trained in that school. Though he was the very opposite of dogmatic and intolerant, he had an unfailing eye for what he considered right and wrong. His later prose works show that he paid less attention to the political or moral principles that a man professed than to his actual conduct. Such an outlook might be ascribed to bourgeois individualism; but that is by no means the whole story. Halévy's practice was the same as his principles, and there was absolutely no conflict between them. His ideals were the natural expression of the man. Like Offenbach, he was straightforward and honest, and, in spite of a lifetime in the theater, he was more of a family man than a Bohemian. In judging the operetta it is important to note that its creators did not live the lives of their heroes. The operetta was only denounced as immoral because the prevalent immorality objected violently to being shown up.

Halévy's nature prevented him from succumbing to the frigid cynicism of a Morny, but there were other directions along which he might have, but did not, travel. He did not succumb to the revulsion with which Félicia Ruys, one of the chief characters in Daudet's *Le Nabab,* reacted towards " the fashionable masquerade, that agglomeration of hypocrisy, greed, and vile and filthy conventions," nor was he moved, as Henri Rochefort was some years later, to rebellion against the prevalent regime. He was prevented by his sense of irony. It was this sense of irony that was the real source of his frivolity and the determining factor in setting the *offenbachiade* upon the path that it took — namely, social satire and the sanctioning of intoxicating pleasure. Halévy's irony was not based on contempt for humanity or on any fundamental skepticism as to the possibility of real human progress; it was based on his observation that progress is not easy and that even with the best of intentions it is not easy to do good. He had seen too far behind the scenes not to feel that honesty and purity of motive were rare, and that therefore outward changes, alterations of political institutions and government systems, meant relatively little. How, then, could he accept the idea of progress when those who believed in it based their arguments on the character of man? The fact that he saw the past in glowing colors made him all the less inclined to believe in progress in the future.

For him the Golden Age was the age of his childhood. In the speech on Count d'Haussonville he made in 1886 on the occasion of his election to the Academy he declared that in the eighteen years of the July Monarchy France had been able " to taste the joys of life and at the same time remain a great nation, loved and respected by all Europe "; and he added that he had only " happy and brilliant memories " of that time. Socialists, for example, would not have accepted this interpretation of history; but Halévy, like Prévost-Paradol and many others, surrounded the past epoch with a golden halo. Halévy's frivolity was based on an irony that in turn was based on a sense that paradise was lost.

He was an observer of life rather than an active and passionate participant in it; and his melancholy was only the shadow of a wisdom that bade him be gentle, mild, and good and forbade him to shirk the present for the sake of the past; for good occasionally did appear in the world, and sometimes real joy and beauty blossomed. He took what was available without pining for what was not. Thus he was able to be happy in spite of his melancholy, and as melancholy was the constant companion of his happiness, he was able to preserve it from decay. His good fortune remained with him right into his old age, and so real and genuine was it that he was able to display it as a gift. " People have often reproached me for being a happy man," he said in his address, to the Academy, " and I have never disputed it, seeing that the reproach was thoroughly justified."

Having thus explained the nature of the frivolity native to the operetta, we can proceed to define a little more closely the place of the operetta itself. Offenbach's music made it a promise of paradise. Halévy too, in the irony he stamped upon it, set his face towards a paradise; but it was a paradise lost. Thus the operetta oscillated between a lost and a promised paradise; but the latter was a fleeting apparition, a teasing will-o'-the-wisp that vanished if a rude hand tried to seize it. The republicans who revealed in its satire and the debauchees to whom the scenes of delirium made such an appeal were both equally deceived. With its innumerable frivolous ambiguities, the operetta snapped its fingers at both. Its real home was not among mankind at all. It winged its way in and out of time, impalpable and intangible. The unreality of the Second Empire allowed it to spread its plumage.

Only a few months after the completion of their joint work the friendship between Morny and Halévy had become close enough for the latter to be able to ask the former an important favor. One day he read in the *Moniteur* the decree of November 24, 1860, by which the Ministry for Algeria, in which he worked, was abolished. The same decree gave the Corps Législatif the right of discussing addresses. Special reports of the discussions, subject to confirmation by the President of the Corps Législatif, were to be supplied by special functionaries (*secrétaires-rédacteurs*). No sooner had Halévy read all this than he drove straight to the Presidential Palace to see Morny. Morny asked him to call again later, as he was very busy owing to the decree. Halévy said that it was the decree that he had come to talk to him about and briefly explained his mission. The position on which his livelihood depended had been abolished and he was not satisfied by the various alternatives that were open to him. Morny had doubtless been under the impression that his visitor had called about something serious, such as an idea for a libretto, for instance, and pooh-poohed Halévy's concern about such a trivial matter as his career. That was a mere bagatelle, he explained. It was perfectly obvious that he would find his friend a good job. If necessary, he would simply approach the Emperor. Halévy replied that there was no need to approach the Emperor, because all he asked for was the post of *secrétaire-rédacteur* in the Corps Législatif, and that was a post at Morny's disposal.

" You are appointed," Morny said, astonished at the modesty of the request. " And now leave me, I am very busy."

The post Halévy thus secured gave him a vantage-point from which he had an unparalleled opportunity of observing the inner workings of political life at first hand, besides bringing him into yet closer contact with Morny, the President of the Corps Législatif. During the same year chance also brought him into contact with Henri Meilhac, a former schoolfellow of his, who had been in the book trade and had also been an artist on a comic paper before devoting himself to literature. Meilhac was the quintessential *boulevardier*. His irony was unbounded, and when he was not devoting himself to the pleasure of sleep, his chief interest in life was to be a *flâneur*. Fortunately in the course of his lounging and strolling innumerable scenes and situations occurred to him, which with equal ease and effortlessness he was able to turn into plays and librettos. Henceforward he and Halévy were inseparable collaborators, and the result was innumerable *offenbachiades,* comedies, and plays.

Meanwhile the profits of *Orpheus* had enabled Offenbach to build himself a summer house at Étretat, which was then in vogue. The Villa d'Orphée, as it was called, became a rendezvous for all his friends and acquaintances. The operetta also brought him official recognition of all kinds. He became a naturalized French citizen at the beginning of 1860, his application being endorsed by Morny. In the following year he was awarded the ribbon of the Legion of Honor.

Offenbach had now traveled a long way. Ten years before,

he had been a mere theatrical conductor. Now he was a famous composer whose works could no longer be kept out of the big theaters. Once more with Morny's influence behind him, his two-act ballet, *Le Papillon,* which was based on an idea of the former prima ballerina, Maria Taglioni, was produced at the Opéra on November 26, 1860. The guardians of the temple among the critics regarded it as a desecration that a place devoted to the cult of Meyerbeer, Halévy, and Auber should be profaned by dance music, which they denounced as vain and frivolous. The audience, however, did not seem to share their objections, for the ballet was performed forty-two times and actually put in the same bill with *Tannhäuser.* Thus chance made strange bedfellows. *Le Papillon* contained a " *Valse des rayons* " which was very popular and established the reputation of the dancer Emma Livry.

Alas, how transitory is the glory of even the greatest stars of ballet! Maria Taglioni, whose glory had already faded, sank to becoming a teacher of dancing and deportment in England, and Emma Livry, the pride of the *corps de ballet,* went too near the footlights one day during rehearsals, whereupon her dress caught fire and she was enveloped in flames. This was only two years after her debut in *Le Papillon.* A fireman threw a damp rug round her, and, wrapped in it, she fell on her knees and prayed. Not till six months later was she released from her agony.

The " *Valse des rayons* " had an extraordinary career. Offenbach used it twice more in other works, and then it was lost and forgotten for many years. But in 1908 it was suddenly rediscovered and used for an apache dance at the Moulin Rouge, after which it became a show-piece of the hand-organs and hurdy-gurdies all over Europe, droning its way remorselessly from tavern to tavern.

Even the Opéra-Comique abandoned its coyness towards the creator of *Orpheus.* Offenbach's dream seemed to be coming true. But he tempted the gods by seeking to fulfill it before the appointed time. His comic opera *Barkouf,* produced for the first time on Christmas Eve 1860, was such a failure that it was almost a disaster. The fault was principally due to the libretto, by Scribe. Scribe had the effontery to make the plot center on a dog. A dog at the Opéra-Comique! And music that imitated a dog's barking! The hostile critics described it as a *chiennerie,* and Berlioz in his indignation recalled Offenbach's German origin and put him and Wagner into the same boat. " Something is definitely disturbed in the brain of some musicians," he wrote. " The wind that blows through Germany has made them mad." In order to rescue his work from oblivion, Offenbach revised it after the War of 1870 and turned the dog into an ox. But even the ox met with no roar of applause.

However, another thing that Offenbach desired to retrieve from oblivion succeeded so miraculously that he was richly compensated for his failure at the Opéra-Comique. He resurrected Fortunio's song, which he had composed years before for de Musset's *Le Chandelier,* in an operetta, *La Chanson de Fortunio,* which was given an enthusiastic reception barely a fortnight later.

Halévy and Crémieux continued de Musset's work in his spirit. In *La Chanson de Fortunio* the role of the original Fortunio passed to a young clerk, Valentin. Mme Pfotzer made her debut in the part. Fortunio himself has become a jealous old lawyer, and his song, which has been lost and forgotten, has become a legend. In his youth, it is said, no woman had been able to resist the magic power of Fortunio's song. What has happened to it now? It is ferreted out among a lot of dusty legal documents, and henceforward all the action centers on it. Valentin sings it to Fortunio's young wife; the other clerks sing it to their girls. And where love is real it turns out to have preserved its potency. The triumph of youth over crabbed and selfish old age, bright and innocent gaiety, the sweetness of the hours in which heart opens to heart, and a trace of nostalgia for the past, regret as tender as foliage bathed in sunshine — all these elements are united in the little work. Meyerbeer said he wished he had written it, and Xavier Aubryet declared that he had rather be a free sparrow like Offenbach than a stuffed eagle like Berlioz.

Fortunio's song was followed by a comic opera, *The Bridge of Sighs,* the scene of which was laid in medieval Venice. During the run of this tuneful burlesque of melodrama, with its assassinations, masks, serenades, and scenes of jealousy, the sight of Morny's carriage outside the Bouffes caused passers-by to gape with respectful admiration every afternoon. Morny was supervising the rehearsals of his *Monsieur Choufleuri* with a devotion that he seldom showed for affairs of state. As soon as he felt himself an author, his frivolity vanished in the face of a naïve passion for literary renown. The first performance of *Monsieur Choufleuri* took place on May 31, 1861, in the Presidential Palace; in the presence of as many ministers and ambassadors as had refused to attend the musical evening of M. Choufleuri. Was it Morny the man of the world or Morny the author who paid one last visit to the actors behind the scenes before the curtain went up and asked to be shown the snuff-box that Désiré, who was playing the part of Choufleuri, was going to use on the stage? In a tone of reproach he said: " But consider, my dear Désiré, that you are to play the part of a rich bourgeois in the play! " He thereupon handed him a choice gold snuff-box, and used similar winning ways to fire the other actors.

Monsieur Choufleuri, the author of which was said to be a certain Saint-Rémy, though all Paris knew whose identity the pseudonym concealed, opened the winter season of the Bouffes. The Bouffes was no longer under Offenbach's management. Offenbach had by now recognized what a bad business man he was, so he had handed over the management to Varney. At one of the performances Léonce, in the role of Mme Balandard, one of Choufleuri's guests, roused the amorous feelings of a provincial spectator, who sent him a magnificent bouquet, as well as an invitation to dinner in his box. Great was his dismay when instead of the lady he had expected a serious-looking gentleman in blue spectacles turned up.

The production of operettas now settled down along a middle course. Offenbach had reached a pitch of fame and success such that he no longer needed to make extreme efforts. In one of the operettas of this period, *Le Voyage de MM. Dunanan père et fils,* two provincials are deceived into thinking that Paris is not Paris but Venice, which they had set out to visit. The ground was being prepared for *La Vie parisienne* — the Paris life that was an intoxication of all the senses, the Paris that was a place of delirium.

CHAPTER VIII

COURTESANS, RAKES, JOURNALISTS

HORTENSE SCHNEIDER, yielding to one of her caprices, once consented to play at the enormous Châtelet Theater before popular audiences very different from her own. But she repented of this rash decision and ruefully returned to the Variétés. " I need my own public," she complained.

Her public consisted of courtesans, men of fashion, Boulevard journalists, with a sprinkling of financial magnates, politicians, foreigners, and other miscellaneous individuals. " A strong smell of powder and perfume floats down to the orchestra seats," a German visitor wrote, " which are filled with many gentlemen who have come straight from dinner, and a few little ladies, all exuding a faint odor of champagne, which floats up to the stage. Intoxication above, intoxication below."

In his moral indignation this German visitor seems to have overlooked the boxes, in which the grandest and most expensive ladies sat enthroned, their coiffure rising tier upon tier, their ear-rings dangling down to their snow-white shoulders. In this world everybody knew everybody else, and, as a consequence of the intimate relations between the gentlemen and the actresses, stage and audience constituted an indivisible whole. This general intimacy made it possible for the audience to converse loudly and exchange witticisms during the performance without the slightest embarrassment. If an actress chanced to overhear something said in the front rows, she would be quite capable of stopping in the middle of a sentence and not going on until she had finished laughing. To most of the actresses the stage was merely a means towards another end. The whole house was so highly charged with personal cross-currents that it was like an electric battery. Thus the slightest allusion was assured a full response. That was the subtle, electric atmosphere that Hortense Schneider required.

When Francisque Sarcey described the public that was swept away by the bacchanalian dance in *Orpheus* as a collection of *déracinés,* he was referring to the world of fashionable Bohemia that rejoiced in the operetta. In comparison with the old Bohemia of the days of the July Monarchy, the new Bohemia of the Second Empire was far less exclusive. A man who had money to fling about was admitted without too many questions being asked. This greater lack of discrimination was merely the result of the general spirit of intoxication. But though the Bohemians had become far less exclusive, they remained a class apart, an entity distinct from the great mass of the bourgeoisie. But for the existence of this class part, the frivolity of the operetta would scarcely have made such an impression.

It was, in fact, to this class that the mixture of satire and ecstasy of Offenbach's operettas principally appealed. These people lived a life apart from the dominant society of their time, though they were completely dependent on it. They were outsiders, whether because the salons were closed to them or because they deliberately withdrew from bourgeois society. The fact that they were outsiders on the one hand drove them to mock at the dictatorship and on the other drew the sting from their mockery and made it harmless. When the operetta took the plunge into bacchanalia it conveyed the exact feelings of the Bohemians. For, much as they liked to see the absurdities of the current regime exposed, they were perfectly well aware that they were indebted to it for their gilded freedom, and therefore, in their own interests, recoiled from criticism into delirious acceptance of it. Their Bohemian frivolity was the direct result of their social situation.

From the beginning of the sixties onwards — in other words,

from the moment when the Emperor began his attempted *rapprochement* with the Left and started trying to compromise with the reality that he had previously denied — the special place of the Bohemians in the scheme of things became more pronounced. Political tension grew, opposition increased, and the clouds grew higher and higher on the European horizon, while the Emperor merely vacillated and hesitated. Meanwhile the world of fashionable Bohemia glittered and shone in a zone of complete and utter indifference, in which all conflicts and antagonisms seemed to have been abolished.

The home of the Bohemians was the Boulevards, which had already served as the home of the homeless in the time of Louis-Philippe. Here the outsiders devoted themselves to the life of pleasure as of yore, and the atmosphere was pregnant with their spirit. But in the meantime life on the Boulevards had undergone a leveling process and taken on a cosmopolitan air which the dandies of bygone days would never have thought possible. The transformation which had taken place was the result of improvements in communication and travel facilities, the transition to world economy, and the whole political policy of the regime.

The reason why the courtesans occupied such a powerful position in the Second Empire was that the money and the speculation were meant for them. Like all money gained by gambling, it was apt to go as easily as it had come. The great object was therefore to enjoy it quickly. As a means of enjoyment the courtesans stood in the front rank. By the lavish and extravagant style in which they lived they saw to it that their patrons' money was consumed at a rapid rate. In an epoch of feverish speculation, they constituted the most sought-after commodity on the love-market. Though they mercilessly fleeced their clients before abandoning them, they were actuated less by heartlessness than by pitiless market fluctuations. Mercenary creatures that they were, they modeled their behavior closely on that of the money age in which they lived. They often acted as agents for brokers and financiers, working on a commission basis among their clientele.

Many of these creatures came from the depths. Often they had been discovered by *entremetteuses* who made a business of launching beautiful girls in the fashionable world. They would hire their protégées all that was needed for a satisfactory start, from underclothing to jewels and dresses, including an adequate supply of banknotes, which were not, of course, intended to be spent, but were exclusively designed to create an impression of means. The fact that the *entremetteuses* were known as " ogresses " gives some sort of clue to the high dividends they drew from the undertakings they financed.

A courtesan's surroundings would be in entire accordance with the requirements of her trade. Her rooms would be full of elegantly upholstered armchairs and couches. There would be curtains everywhere, and a heavy damask canopy over the bed. One of the better-known cocottes used black satin sheets to show up the whiteness of her skin. The lady's-maid who invariably presided over all this hothouse vegetation generally collected so many tips from clients and tradesmen that she was able to put aside a tidy sum for her old age, even though her wages tended to be very irregularly paid. Her mistress, however, generally enjoyed a less secure old age. But how could she be expected to think of the distant future? She was like the cricket, that lived for the day only.

Scarcely had she awakened, at midday at the very earliest, from her slumbers beneath her damask canopy when her first visitors of the day would enter; her manicurist, her laundress, her modiste, her creditors. These business details having been completed — the arduous business of letter-writing would be part of them — she would drive to the Bois, go and see her dressmaker, or keep some secret rendezvous; unless she went to an afternoon tea-party and took the opportunity of dropping into her bookseller's on the way, for it was essential to be *au fait* with the latest

novels. The evening routine would begin with a theater, followed by a visit to the Café Anglais, where she would remain
until dawn. Dusty visits to her family would have to be fitted in
between.

For intellectual and artistic pleasures the courtesans had not
much taste. Their spelling was nearly always very shaky, and
they generally refused to take any notice of a man who was not
a member of the Jockey Club. One man of fashion took his mistress for a carriage tour of Italy, and at Sorrento she insisted on
having the hood drawn so that the game of piquet she was playing with her lover need not be disturbed. She had already won
ten thousand francs from him in the neighborhood of Amalfi.
When Renan's *Life of Jesus* appeared and was a sensational success, a joke became current on the Boulevards to the effect that
one day a cocotte had refused to go driving in the Bois with one
of her friends because she had been completely absorbed by the
fascinating story and could not bear to stop until she had found
out how it ended. As in these circumstances conversation on
festive occasions tended to be rapidly exhausted, the courtesans
gladly turned to more frivolous pursuits. One of them vastly
entertained the guests at a dinner by pouring cold soup over her
neighbor's bald pate. This action caused far greater pleasure than
the most brilliant witticism.

When the representatives of the *demi-monde* and of the *grand
monde* were seen side by side at the races at Longchamp or in
any other public place, thanks to the efforts that the latter made
to imitate the former it was almost impossible to distinguish between them. The use of enormous quantities of cosmetics lent
them all an equal air of artificiality, which their crinolines intensified. This artificiality made the task of distinguishing between them immeasurably more difficult. Both the cosmetics and
the crinolines were consistent with the political tendencies of the
day; for they sought to smother physical realities as effectively
as the regime of Napoleon III sought to smother social realities.
Also, of course, the crinoline gave a clue to the wealth of its

wearer. The more joy and glamour the Empire radiated, the wider became the circumference of the crinoline. It did not begin to diminish till 1866.

An abyss separated the *demi-monde* from the republican masses. The latter regarded the courtesans as part and parcel of the upper class and abhorred their luxury and immorality. Similarly they regarded Offenbach as nothing but *le grand corrupteur*. They did not see the ambiguous nature of the relationship of fashionable Bohemia to the dictatorship and ignored the fact that the courtesans reduced many to beggary who from their own standpoint deserved no better fate. Did the courtesans themselves realize their own disintegrating function? It was no accident that they appreciated the frivolity of the operettas so highly.

At the head of the one hundred courtesans who constituted the top flight was a small group of about one dozen who were known as *la garde* and formed a closed caste of their own. These were the aristocracy of the *demi-monde*. They lived as blithely as the lilies of the field, because there would always be some millionaire who would clothe and feed them. The leading spirit among them was Adèle Courtois, at whose house the others would frequently hold gay and friendly meetings. Adèle Courtois, though past her first youth, still set the fashion for all the rest, thanks to her talent for clothes, her conversational gifts, and her long-standing and almost marital liaison with a wealthy foreign diplomat. The next most brilliant star in this little constellation was Anna Deslions, the favorite of the men of fashion. With her mop of black hair, she looked like an Italian boy, and her velvet glances were like warm caresses. When she granted a night to a favored suitor she invariably sent her night attire to him in advance, choosing a color-scheme in accordance with the happy man's taste. The cost of this toilet, which was generally between 2,500 and 3,000 francs, gives one some idea of what must have been the price of the woman herself. Her surroundings were no less luxurious. When the Goncourt brothers inspected her bedroom, which was bedecked with red satin, they were filled with horror when they came upon a picture of laborers sweating in a field — a scene which was in shocking contrast to the purposes to which this room was put.

Stars of similar brilliance glittered in the vicinity. Giulia Barucci, a beautiful brunette of Italian origin, possessed jewelry worth more than a million francs and refused no man who was a member of any of the smart clubs; so good-natured was she that she occasionally lent her house to society women who wished to meet their lovers in secret. One of her colleagues, Marguérite Bellanger, actually became the Emperor's mistress in 1863. Ludovic Halévy, who said that Marguérite Bellanger had the smallest feet in Paris, once helped her to secure a picture which he believed would amuse the Emperor. It was a picture of a naked woman tempting St. Anthony.

Among the actresses who were inseparable from *la garde* were the dazzling Léonide Leblanc and Blanche Pierson. The latter looked like a chaste visionary. Another who started her career on the stage was Juliette Beau. After appearing in Offenbach's *Daphnis and Chloë* and exciting the interest of the connoisseurs by her look of innocence, she abandoned the stage and captivated a wealthy foreigner who ended by marrying her, whereupon she disappeared from the scene. But such happy endings were rare.

Another member of this sisterhood was Cora Pearl, who was a truly remarkable phenomenon. She was an Englishwoman, whose real name was Emma Crouch. In spite of her lack of refinement, she was able to keep in the very front rank throughout the Second Empire because she possessed such a talent for voluptuous eccentricities that Prince Gorchakov described her as the acme of sensual delight. She was a pioneer of artificial beauty treatment. With the help of essences, salves, and powders imported from England, she succeeded in transforming her physical appearance as radically as she had transformed her name. Her iridescent eyelashes, her smoothly polished brow, her strangely gleaming eyes, her milky, red, or silvery skin — she was able to produce any shade required — were extensively copied by society.

Another remarkable phenomenon was a blonde dancer known as Rigolboche, who became the rage at the dance-halls and on the Paris stage. She was ugly, had a coarse voice, and expressed herself with alarming realism, but all this vanished when she danced a cancan of her own devising, with supple hips and gestures that were an inimitable combination of boldness and grace. "To Rigolboche dancing is a sacrament that releases her completely from the world," wrote a critic intoxicated by her performance. Indeed, in rousing renewed interest in the cancan she was seconding the efforts of the operetta. So great was her popularity that her memoirs were published. They were written for her by two talented authors. She was photographed in every conceivable costume and pose.

But the one who flew higher than all her like was La Païva, who attained the Olympus, or rather the Valhalla, of courtesans while still alive. In about 1860 there arrived in Paris Count Guido Henckel von Donnersmarck, one of the richest mine-owners in Germany, whose fortune amounted to millions. He was a big, powerful man, and his appetite, thirst, and beard were all of similarly vast dimensions. His only wish in Paris was to enjoy himself, and La Païva saw to it that he did.

She was a favorite of fortune, and it was her merit that she recognized her fortune and held fast to it. Although she was ten years older than the Count, she managed to attach herself to him permanently. She lived with him both in a new Renaissance-style palace and a real, ancient historical castle, and thus she would have been perfectly satisfied and content had it not been for her insatiable social ambitions, the intensity of which was only equaled by the rancor she bore the high Parisian society that obstinately refused to receive her. The little court of artists, writers, and scholars that she gathered round her by no means compensated her for being shut out of the Tuileries and not being on speaking terms with Princess Matilda.

The clique of society men attached to the great courtesans consisted of about a hundred fashionable gentlemen who nearly all belonged to the nobility and exercised unquestioned authority in all matters of fashion and etiquette. Their frivolity expressed itself in the contempt they felt for the bourgeoisie, and the life they lived consisted in a deliberate defiance of bourgeois conventions and an obstinate refusal to do any kind of serious work. Among them were many officers of the Emperor's horse guards, who exercised an irresistible attraction over the demi-monde, thanks to the double appeal of their brilliant uniforms and their social rank.

The Duc de Gramont-Caderousse called some of his intimates *Cocodès,* and this nickname was used as a description of all the members of the clique; their mistresses were therefore inevitably known as *cocodettes.* No *cocodès* could possibly not be a member of the Jockey Club, and not one of them but from time to time took advantage of the discreet services of Isabella, who was both flower-seller and *entremetteuse.* Decked in the colors of the last Derby winner, Isabella sold her flowers for year after year outside the Jockey Club during the daytime and at the entrance to the Café Anglais during the evening. The chief interests in life of these fashionable gentry were cards, horses, and duels, as in the days of Louis-Philippe. But the precincts had widened. The paddock at Longchamp was now a scene of sumptuous elegance; and when Daniel Wilson gave one of his famous dinners every lady found a five-hundred-franc note under her napkin for her to stake at baccarat or lansquenet afterwards. Now and then the gentlemen would take exercise by rowing for an hour or so in the evening sun; and occasionally they would transfer the scene of their inactivity to Epsom, Ascot, or Baden for the races.

Round the circle of the elite there fluttered innumerable rich young men who wanted to sow their wild oats before settling down and often burned their fingers badly in the process. Many foreigners mingled in this society, the most prominent being Russian noblemen. They paid their mistresses well, but treated them like serfs, in accordance with the practice at home. The *coco-*

dettes regarded all foreigners as barbarians and only tolerated them for purely commercial reasons.

Wealthy members of the bourgeoisie were tolerated for the same reasons. Although the bourgeoisie were always kept in the background, they were really indispensable figures in the social scene. One middle-aged gentleman who had enough money to be able to sate a courtesan's lavish tastes felt he had indeed triumphed over the society men who despised him. But as he felt inferior to them all the same, he only visited the expensive dwelling in which he had established his mistress at fixed hours, when he could be certain of not meeting any of his fashionable rivals. In order not to lose the regular income she drew from him, the woman very sensibly avoided deceiving him with anyone of his own class, thus giving him a reassuring feeling that he was being treated very well indeed.

Most of the *cocodès* were gifted with resounding names; Baron d'Auriol, Count d'Hérisson, M. de Rennepon, the handsome Paul Démidoff, Masséna, the Duc de Rivoli, the Prince d'Orange (who was always known as Prince Lemon) — the list could be indefinitely extended. Some of them, like Khalil-Bey, devoted themselves entirely to debauchery; others did so more restrainedly, not wishing to wear themselves out before their time. Bryan, for instance, dabbled in the arts and collected books and engravings.

The undisputed leader of the *jeunesse dorée* was the Duc de Gramont-Caderousse. In 1857, when he was about twenty-four years old and met Hortense Schneider, he had already tried his hand at diplomacy and lost over a million francs at cards. As he had inherited a fortune of several millions, there was still plenty left for him to squander.

He gave up his diplomatic career suddenly on learning that he was a consumptive, and devoted himself to a life of debauchery in anticipation of an early death.

He and Hortense Schneider were well suited to each other.

Gramont-Caderousse was a slender young man with curly, fair hair, an animated yet cold expression, lips on which there hovered a perpetual smile, eyes which were gentle yet awakened no trust, and surprisingly nervous hands. Hortense Schneider, true to her temperament, desired pleasure in rich measure and was ready for any excess that did not interfere with her art, and she was drawn towards anything that glittered.

What a life the two led! Instead of simply presenting his mistress with a carriage, Gramont-Caderousse caused a giant Easter egg to be sent to her house, containing a carriage, two horses, and a coachman. Another time they drove in grand style to the ancestral château of Caderousse to attend the dedication of some bells which he had presented to the village church. Hortense behaved as though she were the Duke's fiancée in the priest's presence and played the role of girlish innocence as brilliantly as she would have done on the stage of the Palais Royal.

There is no doubt that in so far as she was capable of love she loved him. A year after their first meeting — by this time he had started coughing badly and was constantly spitting blood — she secretly gave birth to a son at Bordeaux. This was evidently a result of their liaison. The baby boy turned out to be an imbecile. There is no doubt, either, that although she was a woman to whom possessions meant much, she lent Gramont-Caderousse money when he was deeply in debt. He spent it — and she knew it — on other women, permitting himself this indulgence all the more readily because she herself always ridiculed monogamy. Anna Deslions and he were very intimate. Was Hortense merely another mistress to him? Knowing himself to be a condemned man, he valiantly defended himself against an emotion which had no business in his life. He obstinately sabotaged it and did everything to keep Hortense Schneider away from him, just because he really loved her. But he always returned to her, and there was no end to the scenes of jealousy with which she plagued him.

His proud and crazy determination not to succumb tamely to

his insidious disease but to anticipate it by self-destruction was the dominant factor in his life. If he had to succumb, well and good. But at least let him die in a blaze that would create a sensation among the survivors. In spite of his lungs he rode in all the races, at Chantilly, at Baden, and at Spa. Before the horses had had time to cool down he had bathed and changed and was leading the dance. At the Tuileries he was valued as an adventurer who lent new glamour to the adventurous regime. Other adventurers struggled for wealth or power or to discover new countries; he strove only to live wildly and to defy his illness. The quiet, contemplative life was abhorrent to him, as the prerogative of men with certain and assured lives, and he therefore kicked up a terrible racket wherever he went, thoroughly justifying the name — the Prince des Halles — by which he was known to hotel pages and waiters.

One day he bet some friends that he would get himself arrested without having committed any punishable offense. He dressed as a tramp, entered a café on the Boulevards, ordered champagne, and threw forty thousand-franc notes down on the table to prove that he could pay; whereupon the police were called. "I am the Duc de Gramont-Caderousse," he declared at the police station, thanking everybody for having helped him to win his bet.

His life consisted in playing one prank after another. Once, when Blanche Pierson and one of her colleagues were required to act in a comedy called *Cotillon* at the Vaudeville, they decided that their parts were unworthy of them. Gramont-Caderousse and his friends therefore went to the theater and kept up a constant barrage of hissing and booing on the first and second nights. On the third night Gramont-Caderousse, as the ringleader, was ejected by the police, but the audience took his part so violently that he returned in triumph a few minutes later. The play had to be taken off.

His inordinate desire to cheat the fate that threatened him often had serious results. Several affairs of honor he became involved in passed off bloodlessly, but in a duel he fought in the autumn of 1862 he forced his opponent, a sporting journalist named Dillon, to fight with sabers, a weapon Dillon did not know how to use. Dillon was helpless, and Gramont-Caderousse killed him, as though wishing to commit a crime to avenge himself for his own death sentence. Maybe there was a touch of horror in the admiration with which he was henceforth regarded by the fashionable world. The young *cocodès* dreamed of being able to greet him in the street, and women fell for him even more readily. His liaison with Mme de Persigny was common knowledge. If he treated her as though she were merely one of his cocottes, she behaved just like one herself; rumor had it that she involved him in a public scene in a dance-hall.

He was a berserker in the clothing of a man of fashion. His friends urged him to restraint. But they were helpless to stop his headlong race towards self-destruction. He bathed in cold rivers, passed the nights at the Café Anglais, and rode continually. In 1864, when his illness was far advanced, he was at last persuaded to go to Egypt. It is uncertain whether Hortense Schneider's pleadings influenced him to make this belated attempt to save himself.

Philibert Audebrand, a journalist of the period, describes a café in which in 1861 journalists of the most diverse opinions gathered: Bonapartists, republicans, and constitutional monarchists. Instead of dividing up into groups, they all mingled together and attracted an increasing number of writers, novelists, and professional men to join them. Such harmony was only possible because after ten years of oppressive dictatorship all political beliefs and aspirations had lost their former urgency. It may also have been the result of contemplating the innumerable changes of regime that had taken place in the past half-century in France.

These journalists knew too much to be able to go on behaving as party doctrinaires. So they put politics into the background, concluded an armistice, marked out a neutral zone, and set about pleasurably observing the gay life that was flourishing all around them. " Cato no longer stabs himself with his dagger," Aude-brand wrote; " he sits at a café table, drinks, smokes, and stoically looks and listens." The passionate sincerity of 1848 had been transformed into a worldly skepticism. Under its influence the journalists for the time being regarded the sound and fury of the prevalent regime with frivolous unconcern. But for the time be-ing only. For beneath the veil of frivolity political antagonisms still survived; and at the first serious crisis they would once more come to the surface.

Not one of these Boulevard journalists, whether famous or not, but had worked for *Le Figaro*. Villemessant, whose noisy and active life consisted, according to a remark of Aurélien Scholl, of " tears and anecdotes, outbursts of anger, and advertisements," formed a whole generation of journalists. In his passion to be constantly offering the public something new and something bet-ter, he used every talented young man he could lay his hands on and struck sparks out of him. And if he brutally flung him aside when he had no more use for him, he had at least awakened him and offered him incomparable opportunities. In *Le Figaro,* which constantly sang Offenbach's praises, a mirror was held up to the Boulevards.

Aurélien Scholl wrote for *Le Figaro* before he founded his own satirical journal *Le Nain jaune,* which the world of fashion took to be a literary portent of the first importance. Scholl was the personification of the Boulevards of the Second Empire. His be-lief that it was not absolutely necessary to be a bad writer just because one attached importance to what was chic seemed to be the result of exhaustive self-analysis. With his monocle stuck in his eye, he was to be seen lunching with the Duc de Gramont-Caderousse; he was to be seen at Baden and later at Monte Carlo. He took his apéritif at the Café Tortoni, where he would be ob-served listening appreciatively to the long-winded anecdotage of an old gentleman from whom he succeeded in eliciting fresh items of gossip every day. These he would reproduce for the amusement of his readers, safe in the knowledge that the old gentleman had declared that he never read the papers. Like others of his stamp, he had no choice but to fritter away his considerable talents on frivolous newspaper stories and articles. His were distinguished by a polemical spirit which gave no hint that he would ever develop into a republican.

Henri Rochefort, like Scholl, had not yet heard his call at the beginning of the sixties. He wrote harmless plays for the Palais Royal, in collaboration with Albert Wolff, his colleague on the *Figaro*. Wolff was one of Offenbach's best friends, and like him came from Cologne. He let himself be carried away by the froth of the Boulevards, which he idolized — his writings were nothing but artificial froth themselves — but Rochefort was rooted in firmer soil. He was the son of the Marquis de Rochefort-Luçay and had become a vaudevillist after the July Revolution. Like Halévy, from his earliest youth he had been initiated into what went on behind the scenes. He started his career in one of the departments of the Hôtel de Ville, but spent his time scribbling dramatic criticisms on official notepaper. From this it was but a step to working for *Le Figaro* and writing librettos. According to Daudet's description of him, even in those early years his disheveled hair, his black eyes, his beetling brow, and his pointed beard made him look like a skeptical Don Quixote or a gentle Mephistopheles; and he had at his command a cold, biting wit, which invariably struck his opponent at his weakest spot. No wonder that Villemessant, who was a friend to all the world, decided that there was something uncanny about this extraordinary man, who emphasized his leanness by wearing a dark, tight-fitting suit. Villemessant never dared treat him like the rest of the *Figaro* staff.

The Empire was theatrical; and it was a playwright, Rochefort, who discovered it to be his duty to combat its illusions in reality's name. The authors of all the serious accusatory moral plays aimed at the Empire contributed less to its downfall than this vaudevillist who fitted in with the phase of frivolity.

Xavier Aubryet, who was a star of the Boulevard press, like Wolff and Scholl, was another who could not endure being away from the Boulevards for long. He cut short a visit to Italy on the ground that he had seen enough Madonnas in the picture galleries. He abominated the trivial bourgeois world. But his only reaction against it was an affected pose, behind which an instinctive leaning towards authoritarianism was concealed. It was so strong that he once observed that freedom was nowhere more oppressed than under a republic. His preciosity of expression caused him to be called a literary *cocodette*. He was a thin, gentle man of middle-class origin, who often mistook extravagance for elegance, which was one of his ideals. He wrote his articles and books in the midst of the noises of the street, sitting at café tables, because he was afraid that he might miss something on the Boulevards if he wrote at home. If no paper was at hand to write on, he would start talking and go rambling on in endless monologues, which were certainly calculated to annoy Villemessant, who was much too fond of talking himself to put up with a competitor. As the fees for his newspaper articles had no relation to the standard of luxury he loved, he supplemented his income by selling champagne, so that it was not only as a friend of Offenbach's that he was able to rejoice when the corks popped at a gala supper celebrating the hundredth performance of some operetta.

There were plenty of other Boulevard journalists besides these; Albéric Second, for instance, the distinguished Henri de Pène, who considered it more flattering to be called a man of fashion than a journalist. Then there was Marcelin, the founder of *La Vie parisienne,* who perfumed himself like a woman, wore a white camellia in his buttonhole, and called Worth, the dressmaker, his friend.

Celebrities of an older generation moved tirelessly among these younger men. Théophile Gautier was still wearing himself out doing journalistic hack-work; Dr. Véron still gave select and epicurean dinners; Arsène Houssaye never missed anything that was on; and Nestor Roqueplan went from café to café coining clever phrases. It was he who compared the newspaper to a prison from which only a very few were able to escape. But did any of them try to escape? Most of them abandoned themselves without any resistance to the sweet burden of a life that bound them to fashionable Bohemia. Auber could not tear himself away. At the age of eighty-two he was regularly to be seen at the theater and at the Café Tortoni up to one o'clock in the morning; as if, a second Antæus, he were renewing his strength by contact with the Boulevards.

CHAPTER IX

HELEN OF TROY

OFFENBACH's operettas had started out on the conquest of Europe. Offenbach himself traveled a great deal, to ram the conquest home.

Every year he went to Bad Ems, which combined several priceless advantages. One of them was the springs. Offenbach conscientiously took the cure because of his rheumatism. But the cure did him no good, because it became ever clearer that the cause of the trouble was gout, from which he was destined to suffer for the rest of his life. Later on, it deprived him almost completely of the use of his legs.

In spite of the baths Offenbach would scarcely have chosen Ems as one of his favorite haunts had it not, like Wiesbaden, Homburg, and Baden, been a place of international repute. The irresistible attraction that these four German watering-places exercised upon the fashionable public was due to the fact that they were the only places in Europe where gambling was allowed. *Trente et quarante* and roulette flourished, outshining all the beauties of the scenery. Though Baden, " the pearl of the Black Forest," was indisputably outstanding, there was no doubt that the afternoon parade at Ems was extremely brilliant. Where such brilliance prevailed, you could be sure that the inspiration was Parisian. Sure enough, the Ems Kursaal was managed by a Parisian, M. Briguibouille. It was a branch of the big Kursaal at the cheerful neighboring town of Wiesbaden, which was under the management of the Duke of Nassau, who never wore anything but his field-marshal's uniform. In spite of the profound impression that this necessarily made at Wiesbaden, Bad Ems had even more brilliant uniforms to offer, because most of the German princes, with King William of Prussia at their head, were among its regular visitors. But it was not the uniforms that made Arsène Houssaye, for instance, feel at home there.

"I thought I would be lonely among all the water-drinkers," he wrote home to his wife with evident satisfaction, "but I have met many Parisians here, Aurélien Scholl, Pontmartin, Béchard, Albéric Second, Wolff, Villemessant, Aubryet. . . ." If the *boulevardiers* streamed to a place, it needed no further recommendation.

In short, Offenbach had good reason to like the atmosphere of Ems, and as the theater provided a suitable background for operettas, he produced one or two there every year. One of them, *Les Bavards,* was produced there for the first time. This was in 1862, just about the time when Dostoevski suddenly appeared in Wiesbaden, having come straight from Russia, and drove straight from the station to the roulette-table, in the vain hope of extricating himself for ever from his financial troubles.

The libretto of *Les Bavards,* by Nuitter, was based on a comedy of Cervantes. After a perfect orgy of talk in one scene, the next was played in complete silence, and the contrast was extremely comic. The little work was enlarged and expanded before being produced in Paris, and Mme Ugalde made her debut in it at the Bouffes. Saint-Saëns called it a little masterpiece.

During his stay at Ems in the following year Offenbach once more showed his astonishing flair for discovering new talent. A girl he heard singing at the theater at Bad Homburg immediately made a great impression on him. Her name was Zulma Bouffar, and she was only twenty years old. In spite of her fair hair and blue eyes she was of southern French origin. She was indeed an artist. Her whole childhood had been spent among traveling players, and her father had given her singing lessons. At the age of twelve she had been engaged at Lyon by a troupe of German traveling musicians, who took her to Cologne. The troupe played in one of the restaurants at which Offenbach had appeared as an infant prodigy, and chance willed it that one of the regular visitors to the restaurant should be Albert Wolff, who was himself a youth at the time. He said that Zulma's father ate at the restaurant every night and raved about Paris and its marvels all the time, only stopping when his little daughter appeared on the platform and started singing risqué French songs, which fortunately nobody understood. " Bravo! Bravo! " he would call out, and assure his neighbors that one day she would be a great artist. As soon as her number was over, " the little Parisian," as the diners called her, would go from table to table, collecting with a plate, and as a rule it would be piled high with coins by the time she had finished.

After Cologne she went on a long tour that took her through Belgium and Scandinavia and then back to Germany, where her father died at Hamburg. She continued touring without him and was eventually engaged by a theater in Brussels, where she remained for three years before starting on her travels again, in the course of which she played several Offenbach roles; and thus she had come to Bad Homburg.

She must have been extraordinarily attractive. Now she would be coquettish, like a lady of fashion, now she would be serious and intense, and it was hard to find a common denominator for her many moods. But underlying them all was the temperament of a gypsy. It was no mere coincidence that many years later she created the role of Carmen.

There is no doubt that Offenbach was first drawn to her because of the artistic potentialities that he divined in her; but that sort of attraction is apt easily to develop into love. The freedom of a summer holiday, as well as the innumerable memories they had to share, may well have served as a pander to their love-making; for it was inevitable that the girl should tell him of her early days of poverty in Cologne, which were bound to remind him of his own childhood, and of the eight bars of the waltz that still haunted him, though he had never been able to track

down its composer, Zimmer, in spite of all his efforts. Zulma
must unknowingly have conjured up a whole world of memories
and associations for him. Or was it only her young and very
present charms that so captivated him?

In any case, in that summer at Ems in 1863 Offenbach's powers flourished exuberantly, and he was given an excellent opportunity of demonstrating them.

After the first night of *Il Signor Fagotto,* in which he parodied
Berlioz and used every conceivable device, from animal grunts
and growls to the rattling of pots and pans, to ridicule false pomposity, a banquet was given him by his friends and admirers.
Applause and bouquets were showered on him, and he was even
given a torchlight parade. He was just in the mood to take on
a challenge of the kind that was put to him during the evening.
Somebody bet him that he could not both compose and produce
an operetta within a week. Offenbach eagerly accepted the challenge. As there was no lack of *boulevardiers* at Ems, there was
no difficulty in procuring a libretto. Paul Boisselot had one in
his trunk. The first night of *Lieschen und Fritzchen* took place
punctually just a week later.

The little one-act operetta, reminiscent of Hervé's *La Perle
d'Alsace,* extracted an infinite amount of drollery from its use of
the Alsatian dialect, and even today it betrays the brilliance of
Offenbach's inspiration at that time. Lieschen, a broom-seller,
and Fritz, a dismissed servant, meet in the street, sing, talk, and
flirt in a mixture of French and German. That is all, apart from
the charming interplay of thought and feeling. Was the opportunity it offered of coming yet further into contact with Zulma
Bouffar an additional inducement to accept the bet? At any rate
she seems to have played Lieschen at Ems, and not long afterwards she delighted Paris in the part with her charming miming
and her real German accent.

Fritzchen's and Lieschen's duet:

> *Je suis alsacien,*
> *Je suis alsacienne . . .*

became the rage at all the salons and with all the bands in Paris, and old Rossini applauded loudly when the little operetta was played in his house.

The program of a single day in the life of Offenbach at Ems in 1864 shows how he generally spent his time there:

6.30 a.m.	Offenbach takes the waters.
9 a.m.	He goes through the libretto of his new operetta, *Jeanne qui pleure et Jean qui rit,* with two of his players.
10 a.m.	He attends the dress rehearsal of *La Chanson de Fortunio.*
11 a.m.	He lunches, because he must.
Noon.	He attends a rehearsal of another operetta, *Le Soldat magicien.*
2.30 p.m.	M. de Talleyrand, the French Ambassador, calls upon him to introduce his wife.
4 p.m.	He takes the baths.
5 p.m.	He writes to his wife.
6 p.m.	He takes some time off for dinner.
7.30 p.m.	He attends the rehearsal of two new operettas at his hotel.

The question which was the most active, Offenbach or the springs of Ems, would certainly have been decided to the disadvantage of the latter.

If Ems was Offenbach's summer headquarters, Vienna soon became his second capital. In Vienna the ground was very well prepared for the operetta. Parodies of mythology had been traditional there, and because of political sympathies Paris had been very popular ever since the Revolution of 1848. It was therefore a perfectly natural ambition of Herr Nestroy, the manager of the Carltheater, to introduce Offenbach, the new idol of the Parisians, to the Viennese. He did so, however, in a highly unscrupulous fashion. Since the theater's shaky finances did not permit him to secure the dramatic rights in the proper and regular manner, he simply bought the piano score of *Le Mariage aux Lanternes* and patched together a German version, which, in spite of its imperfections, was enthusiastically received. This proved that the demand for Offenbach existed, so the Carltheater continued systematically to pirate his works, culminating in a production of *Orpheus,* with Nestroy as Jupiter, which introduced the *cancan* to Vienna.

The piracy only stopped when the actor Karl Treumann took

over the management of the Carltheater at the end of 1860. He immediately invited Offenbach to Vienna to produce three of his works in person and received him with honors worthy of an Oriental despot. Before rehearsals began, the awe-stricken women members of the cast presented him with a laurel wreath on a white satin cushion. On each leaf the name of one of the actresses was inscribed in gold letters. Offenbach conducted the performances of his three operettas before packed houses, and all the papers agreed that only now, with the composer's own instrumentation, was it possible to appreciate fully the "charming fragrance" of his music. Offenbach was in the seventh heaven of delight.

Eduard Hanslick, a distinguished musical critic and anti-Wagnerian, offered him his friendship, and Treumann's translations opened the world of the operetta to the German stage.

From that time onwards Offenbach returned to Vienna again and again. He became a positive cult there. In 1863 he was approached by the Concordia, a Vienna journalists' club, with a request for a waltz for their carnival ball. Apparently they did not tell him that they had approached Johann Strauss with the same request. Offenbach did not yet know Strauss. He could never refuse anything journalists asked him. He called his waltz *Abendblätter,* whereupon Strauss's waltz was promptly christened *Morgenblätter.* There was a friendly competition between the two waltzes at the Concordia ball, and the popular verdict, at any rate at first, went in favor of Offenbach. Not long afterwards the two rivals happened to find themselves sitting side by side at a restaurant. It was their first meeting, and Offenbach made a casual remark the consequences of which could not be foreseen. "You ought to write operettas," he said to Strauss, "you have the stuff in you." The words were casually uttered, but Offenbach was a European celebrity, and what he said carried weight. Later, when Strauss's operettas threatened to put his own in the shade, it could all be traced back to that chance conversation.

During the same year the management of the Vienna Opera House commissioned him to write a grand romantic opera. This was another bitter pill for Wagner to swallow, as the Vienna Opera House had just rejected him. What had Offenbach to do with grand romantic opera? The opera had always been his dream. He commissioned Nuitter to write him a libretto. It was faithful to the style of Scribe and Auber and contained all the familiar ingredients of German Rhine romanticism. Offenbach called it *Rheinnixen* (*Rhine Water-Sprites*), and, not content with elves and pixies, he put in any amount of soldiers, village maidens, and romantic ruins, to say nothing of plenty of moon-light. As soon as the first outline of the libretto was complete, Offenbach hurried to Breslau, to see Freiherr Alfred von Wol-zogen, who had been a great admirer of *Orpheus,* and asked him to undertake the German text. Wolzogen accepted, though he found the pixies rather odd. As for the music, Offenbach enliv-ened it with the " *Valse des rayons* " from his ballet *Le Papillon,* as well as the " Fatherland Song " he had composed in 1848. The latter was inserted in order to stimulate the necessary patriotic emotion. Nothing was omitted that would enhance the total effect. Offenbach's naïveté surpassed all bounds. It was possible to begin preparations for the production in September.

They lasted more than three months, in the course of which the gaunt, restless figure of Offenbach became one of the sights of Vienna. The Emperor granted him an audience, and the Carl-theater played his works continually and moreover had to face the competition of the Theater an der Wien, which also put him into its repertoire. " The war-cry here is: ' Offenbach forever! ' " Offenbach wrote home to Halévy in high glee. Forever? The first night of the *Rheinnixen* took place in February 1864, in the presence of the Imperial court, but it was withdrawn after only eight performances. Once more Offenbach had to abandon his dream of opera. There was a general consensus of opinion that he should stick to his own domain, the operetta. Nevertheless his " Goblins' Song " was highly praised. Hanslick said it had a

" lovely, luring sensuousness." It was destined to have a glorious revival as the " Barcarolle " in *The Tales of Hoffmann.*

Offenbach's headquarters, of course, remained in Paris, where, if possible, he was even more active than in Ems or Vienna. It was but a trifle, for instance, to compose a tune for Hortense Schneider to sing in *Le Brésilien,* a comedy by Meilhac and Halévy — it was their first work of collaboration — produced at the Palais Royal in 1863. The song earned Hortense Schneider enormous popularity. But that only made Offenbach's tedious and protracted struggles with the Bouffes the more vexatious. Varney, the manager, was mismanaging things so badly that he was heading straight for bankruptcy. His principal mistake lay in not playing Offenbach often enough. Offenbach felt that this damaged both his reputation and his purse, and when he saw Hanappier, Varney's successor, committing the same sins of omission, he promptly took legal proceedings against the theater he had himself founded.

When the case came up for trial, political tension was breaking through to the surface for the first time. The result of the 1863 elections revealed to the public that the dam which had hitherto protected the glamorous, delirious world of the Second Empire from the onslaughts of social reality had burst. Thirty-five deputies belonging to the opposition, including Berryer and Thiers, were elected to the Corps Législatif, and all Morny's skill was needed to steer the debates in the Chamber past all the dangerous reefs.

Meanwhile the public, who had no wish whatever to meddle in the turmoil of politics, tirelessly hummed, sang, whistled, or played a popular ditty which had appeared out of the blue, called *J'ai un pied qui remue,* and took enormous delight in pantomimes which presented plenty of the female form divine, particularly in *tableaux vivants.*

Offenbach provided for this fashion in his operetta *Les Géorgiennes,* produced at the Palais Royal in March 1864. An army of charmingAmazons under the command of Mme Ugalde, anticipating the parades of "Tiller girls," executed military maneuvers with great precision, singing a "*Marseillaise des femmes*," the refrain of which was "*A bas les hommes!*" Needless to say, these belligerent members of the fair sex ended by abandoning their desire for emancipation and allowed the male sex to resume its sway.

By now Offenbach's eyeglasses and side-whiskers were known all over Europe. He seemed to be everywhere at once, but there was only one place for him really, and that was at home. Herminie saw to it that he had as much rest as possible, entertained liberally to satisfy his craving for sociability, and looked after his four daughters, to whom in 1862 there was added a son. The unity and harmony of Offenbach's family made a great impression on his friends, all of whom had the greatest respect for Herminie, as had Offenbach himself. When she disliked anything he wrote, he promptly rewrote it. She had helped him in his hard times and she watched over him in his times of happiness.

His happiness was work. He was everlastingly composing — at home, at the theater, and on the way from one to another. Because of his gout he generally went about in a carriage. He led a life of strict uniformity, his only daily break being for lunch at the Café Riche, where he sat at a reserved table in the company of Villemessant, Tréfeu, Scholl, Rochefort, Aubryet, Crémieux, and others. This uniformity of existence had the effect of keeping his extreme sensibility in check, for he was full of compassion for human suffering and much in the grip of the past.

One morning when he was correcting proofs at his publisher's the latter mentioned in the course of conversation that a poor old composer had brought him a score which he had naturally been unable to accept, as the old man was completely unknown. Offenbach promptly took the musician's part and inquired his name. It was Zimmer.

"Zimmer?" Offenbach exclaimed. "Did you say Zimmer? Where does he live? Tell me quickly!"

Was he at last on the track of his childhood waltz?

The publisher replied that the man was returning next day to hear his decision.

"Do me a favor, a great favor," Offenbach said excitedly. " Publish the thing, pay him ten times what it is worth and put it down to my account, and send him to see me. I simply must see him."

He waited one day, two days, a week, several weeks, but Zimmer did not come.

When he gave a party he was as lavish to his guests as he was to the needy. When he was about, the money simply had to flow. On the occasion of the wedding of his eldest daughter, Berthe, to Charles Comte, he composed a mass specially for the occasion and invited more than ninety guests from Paris to the Villa d'Orphée, his house at Étretat. He put them all up for three days, and they ate at a great horseshoe table which took up four rooms.

The high pressure at which he lived was the result of a nervous tension that was intensified by his physical sufferings. Again and again he would blaze up when his librettists let him down or all did not go well at rehearsals. He knew about his liability to these lapses and would call on all his humor to help in smoothing things out afterwards. On one occasion he issued an appeal for clemency in advance.

"In his desire to remain upon the best of terms with MM. Meilhac and Halévy," he wrote to those two gentlemen, " the undersigned, Jacques Offenbach, musical composer, resident in Paris, in the rue Laffitte, asks the pardon of his collaborators in advance in case he should happen to offend them." It was impossible to bear him malice.

Nor was there anything objectionable even about his vanity. His vanity was not arrogance, but the unrestrained and candid expression of his pleasure at all the beautiful tunes that were constantly occurring to him. Why should he attempt to conceal the delight that they gave him? "I have finished the first act," he wrote in a letter to Halévy. "It is marvelously successful. The effectiveness of the finale is tremendous." The childishness of these ever recurring expressions is utterly disarming. Moreover, at least once he paid heavily for his vanity, as the following story shows. It is a story of which he might have made a first-rate operetta.

It occurred at a little town on the Rhine, which was just about to celebrate the unveiling of a monument. Flags and paper streamers were everywhere, and the whole town had put on its Sunday best for the occasion. The excitement reached its height on the morning on which the lieutenant governor was expected from Wiesbaden, which was not far away. He failed to appear, however. After a vain wait of two hours it was decided to send a deputation of six to fetch him. The crowd went on waiting, but the deputation failed to return. No news came till the afternoon, when the burgomaster received a telegram saying: " Deputation in trouble send money for fare home."

It was later discovered that the six men, having found the lieutenant governor ill in bed, had gone to the casino to console themselves by a harmless fling at the tables. The result was that they had lost all the money they had with them.

As it was known that they would return by the seven o'clock boat, the whole town turned out to greet them at the landing-stage, in spite of the late hour. Offenbach chanced to be on the same boat, on his way to Ems. The boat drew alongside to the strains of the famous quadrille from *Orpheus,* amid loud shouts of " Hurrah! " " They heard that I was coming and have prepared a reception for me," Offenbach promptly thought. In the meantime the members of the deputation frantically tried to make the crowd understand that the lieutenant governor was not on board, but their efforts were in vain. It was impossible to hear a single word in the tumult, and the crowd would have their lieutenant governor. And, lo and behold, there he was!

Offenbach, his face wreathed in smiles, walked down the gang-plank amid acclamation, graciously bowing to right and left.

Rapidly a procession was formed and made its way through

the gate of honor and the illuminated streets, to the ringing of bells, the blaring of the brass band, and the firing of a salute. White-clad maids of honor — the poor girls had been waiting ever since early morning — led the way, and the six deputies, with Offenbach in their midst, brought up the rear. The little procession stopped outside the town hall.

" My dear friends," said Offenbach, moved by this touching reception, " thank you, thank you a thousand times for this hearty welcome."

The burgomaster planted himself in front of him and started delivering a ceremonial address, beginning with a few observations about human progress and leading up to a request to the lieutenant governor to intercede with the high authorities and secure their sanction for the installation of gas-lighting in the town.

Offenbach had perhaps found it possible to put a favorable construction upon the references to human progress, but when it came to gas-lighting, it was obvious that he was the victim of a ghastly mistake; and while all the local celebrities hurried to the banquet he hastily slunk away under cover of darkness.

Depressed by the failure of his opera at Vienna, Offenbach's only ambition was to write a new operetta that should be an even more resounding success than *Orpheus*. Halévy wished once more to exploit the happy hunting-ground of Greek mythology, this time in collaboration with Meilhac. The result was that all concerned finally agreed on the promising subject of Helen of Troy.

While the libretto was being written Offenbach showed the great interest he took in the compilation of the text, in which he invariably collaborated, by writing and asking Halévy whether Homer could not be introduced into the plot as a war correspondent, and he also played with the idea of parodying *Tannhäuser*.

Letters to his librettists poured in from Ems, Étretat, and all sorts of other places, invariably raving about his music. The last letter, written at the end of September 1864, was from Vienna, where he was rehearsing *Les Géorgiennes* at the Carltheater; its mundane attractions were far more to the taste of the Viennese than the moonstruck gnomes of his grand opera.

Immediately after his return from Vienna the question arose of who should play the part of Helen. Hortense Schneider was the only conceivable choice. She had quarreled with M. Plunkett, the manager of the Palais Royal, because he had short-sightedly failed to appreciate the absolute necessity of yielding to her latest demand for an increase in salary. She was therefore free. But in her vexation at the fact that all the other theatrical managers did not immediately fall over each other's heels to make her offers, she had made an irrevocable decision to abandon the stage and go home to her mother at Bordeaux. What had Paris left to offer her? The Duc de Gramont-Caderousse was dying in Egypt and everybody else revolted her.

When Offenbach and Halévy went to see her she had already dismissed her servants and sold all her expensive furniture. They had to pick their way to her room through piles of packing-cases. As soon as they mentioned that they had come to talk to her about a part at the Palais Royal, she flew into an indescribable rage at the mere thought of M. Plunkett, but Offenbach sat down at the piano, which fortunately had not yet been packed, and played a few tunes from the new operetta. Hortense, sitting beside him on a trunk, was very soon humming the tunes as he played them, partly tempted and yet still resisting, like Helen of Troy herself. But her obstinacy got the better of her, and she really did go to Bordeaux. On her arrival she was surprised to find a telegram awaiting her, signed by Offenbach, Meilhac, and Helévy, announcing that the operetta was not going to be produced at the Palais Royal but at the Variétés. "I demand two thousand francs a month," she wired back. Within three hours there came a reply accepting her terms.

Cogniard, the manager of the Variétés, had accepted *La Belle Hélène* believing that the immediate future belonged to operetta. But in spite of his flair for what the public wanted, he had no sympathy for Offenbach's lavish tastes; in fact, he was mean to a degree, and when rehearsals began, in October, his niggardliness was so painfully evident that everyone's temper was frayed. Offenbach stormed at Hortense Schneider, and Hortense in turn was extremely irritated by her colleague, Mlle Silly. There was no denying that Mlle Silly, who appeared on the Boulevards in trousers, looked ravishing as Orestes with a monocle and, thanks to her wit, her talent for mimicry, and her bravura, gained effects that could only be achieved by a real star. The result was that one day Hortense Schneider gratuitously accused her of having stolen one of her lines, and threatened to withdraw from the cast. There was nothing for it but to let her have the line she wanted.

Meilhac was so nervous that he could not bear to have anyone in the audience during rehearsals except the Duc de Morny, who gladly sought respite from the Corps Législatif at the Variétés. Offenbach was certainly justified in calling Meilhac " *le grand dormeur* " and " *notre cher paresseux Meilhac.*" Nevertheless it was always he who outlined the skeleton of the plot and sketched the big scenes and situations, which Halévy filled in with witty comment and dialogue. Advance notices concerning the abduction of Helen appeared in *Le Figaro* regularly every day while rehearsals lasted, and Offenbach devoted his evenings to the work of orchestration.

" His children would be noisily playing, laughing, and singing all round him, and friends and colleagues would call to see him. Offenbach would talk and joke with complete freedom, but his right hand would go on writing, writing all the time." After Offenbach's death his original score for *La Belle Hélène* was found in Halévy's possession, and that is Halévy's own description of how it was written.

At the dress rehearsal the censor objected to the character of Calchas, on the ground that it was calculated to lower the prestige of the clergy, and insisted on the deletion of several sentences on the ground that they tended to undermine the authority of the state. The censor's objections were by no means without foundation, and it was only after Morny's intervention that they were withdrawn. Morny intervened all the more readily for having contributed to the libretto himself. Paris's song at the beauty contest of the three goddesses, of which great hopes were had, turned out to be a disappointment. Dupuis, who played the part of Paris, took this as a personal affront and hurried to see Offenbach at his home immediately after the rehearsal; but his indignation was promptly transformed into delight, because Offenbach had already rewritten the whole song on his way home from the theater.

The first performance took place on December 17, 1864, four days after the dress rehearsal.

An incident observed by only a few initiates took place during one of the intermissions, in the midst of the fashionable first-night crush in the corridors. Some time previously Henri Rochefort had so severely criticized the Duc de Morny's operetta that all Paris believed that his temerity would meet with condign punishment. Greatly to everybody's surprise, however, nothing of the sort occurred. Morny took a secret liking to his assailant, and the more his entourage tried to persuade him of Rochefort's literary insignificance, the more did his feelings towards Rochefort come to resemble those of a rejected lover. He would have liked momentarily to lay aside his rank and power and have a heart-to-heart talk with Rochefort, as between two friends, and if not to gain his love, at least to gain his respect. But Rochefort deliberately avoided being brought into personal contact with him, as though he feared he would find his personality irresistible. Morny, however, did not abandon the chase, but pursued him with an ardor that was entirely unworthy of a man of the world and was all the more touching for that reason.

On the first night of *La Belle Hélène* Daudet saw him bearing down on Villemessant, whose choleric countenance was visible from afar in spite of the crowd.

"Now you will introduce me to Rochefort immediately," he said to Villemessant.

" Certainly, Monsieur le Duc. We have only just been talking. He will be here in a second."

Villemessant dashed after Rochefort, but in that second he had vanished.

The reception of *La Belle Hélène* resembled that of *Orpheus*. The audience was perplexed, and most of the critics raised an outcry against the alleged desecration of antiquity. Though Jules Janin, wiser by experience, wrote more cautiously than he had six years before, he could not refrain from calling malediction down on the heads of the " perfidious " Meilhac, the " traitor " Halévy, and the " wretched " Offenbach. Not he, but Timothée Trimm, alias Léo Lespès, the popular editor of Millaud's popular paper, *Le Petit Journal,* this time became the laughing-stock of all Paris. Timothée Trimm informed his large, petty-bourgeois public that after seeing *La Belle Hélène* he had gone straight home to bury himself " in his old Homer " in order to take away the nasty taste that it had left in his mouth. He implied that he read Homer in the original with fluency and ease, but it turned out that in reality he did not know a single word of Greek.

The same causes produce the same effects. " We were wrong to attend the premiere," Prince Metternich said to his wife on leaving the Variétés. " Our name will be in all the papers, and it is wrong for a woman to attend a performance like that, to a certain extent officially." The Prince saw plainly that it was not remote antiquity but the very living present that the operetta was aimed at, and he could not fail to find it compromising, though he had no desire to admit how compromised was the society described in it.

From the standpoint of the frivolous observer, the mirror was held up to the contemporary regime in *La Belle Hélène* more unmercifully than ever. In fact it was shown up so pitilessly that its early end was made to look inevitable. *Orpheus* had contained no hint about the future, but *La Belle Hélène* was a prophecy of doom.

Offenbach's Helen is a fashionable woman who is bored with

L'ENLEVEMENT D'HELENE.

Paris qui par amour sur les dents s'était mis,
N'était plus guère bon qu'à fumer un cigarre
Hélène le savait aussi sans crier gare
Sur ses robustes bras elle enleva Paris.

(Enéide travestie par Mr Fion.)

THE ABDUCTION OF HELEN

Lithograph by Daumier, 1842, in the Bibliothèque Nationale

LUDOVIC HALÉVY
Drawing by Degas, from the collection of Daniel Halévy

life and longing for a change. She would need but little encouragement to lead the life of a courtesan. An entry in the Goncourts' diary, dated October 1864, states: " A young woman said to me: ' One is only happy when dancing or sleeping.' " At that time, when the intoxication of the Second Empire was beginning to wear off, society, in the face of the reality that was remorselessly rising up to meet it, was becoming increasingly filled with a sense of the vanity and futility of things. That is Helen's situation entirely. Nauseated by her surroundings, there is nothing she would like better than to fall in love. So she falls an easy prey to the handsome and experienced seducer, Paris.

The other characters are shown in anything but a flattering light. The Greek kings are contemptible figures, and the soothsayer Calchas is the representative of a priesthood that does not think it worth while even to keep up a pretense of piety. That explains why they are all on such excellent terms with the world of frivolous pleasure-seeking represented by that nice little *cocodès* Orestes, who parades his hetairai on the Boulevards of Sparta and confides to Calchas:

> *C'est avec ces dames qu'Oreste*
> *Fait danser l'argent à papa;*
> *Papa s'en fiche bien, au reste,*
> *Car c'est la Grèce qui paiera.* . . .

What a change since the time of *Orpheus*! In *Orpheus* Jupiter was still concerned with public opinion. But in *La Belle Hélène* all such inhibitions are cast aside.

The reason is that everyone is aware of inexorable fate approaching. The word " fate " is constantly on Helen's lips, and when unspoken, it remains in the background all the same. All the characters are perfectly well aware that a catastrophe is inevitable. Greece has forgotten all sense of duty and honor, and the refrain of the song in which Agamemnon describes the orgies to which the country is a prey is:

Tu comprends
Qu' ça n'peut pas durer plus longtemps.

And the end of the whole thing is the proclamation of the Trojan War.

The plot is developed with a frivolity that takes the whole range of satire in its stride. In fact, the frivolity is even more pronounced than it was in *Orpheus;* for at the time when *Orpheus* was written, reality was still hidden behind a cloud. But in the meantime it had become visible, and consequently the demand for frivolity had become all the more urgent; and as the reality that was looming was heavy with impending doom, the melancholy with which John Styx had lamented the vanished past is absent from *La Belle Hélène.* Helen is a charming, roguish creature, and all the other characters are similarly drawn. The frivolity reaches its climax when Helen's adultery is justified for reasons of state — a fantastic jumble of right and wrong that passes straight over into delirium. But the delirium lacks the carefree note that it had in *Orpheus.*

"*Il faut bien que l'on s'amuse,*" the chorus sings while Helen and Paris are together; and Paris, as high priest of Venus, preaches to the people: "*Je suis gai, soyez gais, il le faut, je le veux!*"

Much has changed since the days of "*Evohé! Bacchus est roi!*" The intoxicating revels of *La Belle Hélène* are accompanied by a presentiment of doom. Let us eat, drink, and be merry, it seemed to say, for tomorrow we die. This admixture of gloom substantiated the operetta's revolutionary function.

The frivolous ambiguity of the libretto enabled the music to be at once humorous and lyrical. "Really I do not know any music on earth which contains such a striking mixture of extremes," wrote Camille Bellaigue. "It is impossible to choose between the sentimental Offenbach and the other, or even to know them from each other, they are so completely fused." It was perfectly natural that they should be fused. For it was not mere pleasure in destruction that drove Offenbach to satire and parody; he destroyed only to make room for natural, unfeigned humanity. His mockery was the result of his sincerity and at the same time gave his sincerity greater scope.

Success came to *La Belle Hélène* just as it had come to *Orpheus*. After ten to fifteen performances the box-office receipts started increasing, and favorable notices written by Rochefort and Jules Vallès, both of whom appreciated the operetta's damaging implications, helped. Léon Halévy, Ludovic's father, came forward as its doughty champion. Léon Halévy had an unrivaled knowledge of the ancient Greeks, and he wrote a poetical epistle demolishing the arguments of those who held that the piece was a desecration of antiquity. Did not Offenbach put gods and men into ecstasy? he asked. Was not that in the best classical tradition? The skeptic and Voltairian Lucian, he added, would have been much astonished at finding heathen altars defended by present-day Christians.

Gradually *La Belle Hélène* became the rage. It allowed the accent to be put on eroticism and the gospel of pleasure. Not only fashionable Bohemia but the faubourg Saint-Germain started flocking to the Variétés. Hortense Schneider was a brilliant success. Her form had grown fuller in the course of years, and she was now a Rubens beauty. Auber said that her singing was a delight to the ear. Even more marvelous than her singing was the skill with which she managed to say the most daring things and yet get away with them. What could not be said she suggested by innuendo, and ran through the whole gamut of nuances without the slightest effort. When her smile meant yes, it yet left one in fear, and when it meant no, it yet left one in hope. That, at any rate, was what Meilhac said of her.

In 1865 the whole of France was singing:

> *Dis-moi, Vénus, quel plaisir trouves-tu*
> *A faire ainsi cascader, cascader la vertu?*

A terrible heat-wave broke out at the end of May, but it did not affect the box-office receipts at the Variétés. A gala supper was held to celebrate the hundredth performance, at which Hortense Schneider, in all her diamonds, presided, sitting between Offenbach and Villemessant. Her health was proposed by Offenbach. He had every reason to be satisfied. He had won his lawsuit against the Bouffes, which was now compelled to play his operettas regularly.

La Belle Hélène appeared in Vienna and Berlin during the same year. Europe was at Offenbach's feet.

CHAPTER X

LA VIE PARISIENNE

EVER since his seizure of power the Emperor had done all he could to promote the development of trade and industry. For if the bourgeoisie were doing good business they would continue to accept his political tutelage without demur; moreover, the prospect of millions encouraged the general glamour that was so essential for the maintenance of his regime. But the remarkable thing about the economic glamour was that it was in entire harmony with the economic situation. In encouraging it the Emperor was not, as in other spheres, creating phantoms, but showing himself a thorough realist.

Thanks to the impulse that he imparted, the latent potentialities of the economic situation were unrestrainedly developed. The credit system was widely extended, and French capital flowed to every foreign market. From 1852 to 1865 France lent four and a half billion francs abroad. The Emperor's free-trade policy, though it certainly earned him the hostility of the big industrialists, worked in the same direction. One of his chief helpers was Michel Chevalier, a product of Saint-Simonism, who recognized world exhibitions to be a mighty spur to economic development.

The Emperor's initiative in the economic sphere, however, rather undermined than strengthened his regime. If his destiny can be described as tragic, it is because those of his acts which were most in accordance with the needs of his time ultimately destroyed him. He let loose economic forces solely for the sake of the glamour that was one of their by-products, but failed to take into account the fact that those very forces were pregnant with a liberal, democratic spirit that was hostile to his dictatorship. The conclusion of trade treaties, the growth of financial and commercial bonds between the nations, and their permeation by capitalism were all triumphs of economic liberalism, which necessarily awakened the need of corresponding political forms. With every advance of capitalism it became more evident that this was the foundation of all social life, and the more peremptory became the question of whether or not there was any real need to have an Emperor at all. From the beginning of the sixties onwards, the Empire became more and more an anachronism.

The exiled revolutionaries of 1848 had faithfully kept the republican flame burning, but it was not till now that a broad economic foundation for republicanism came into being. Henceforward students, young artisans, minor officials, all those who knew Victor Hugo's hymn of hate against the Emperor by heart, openly displayed their sympathy for republicanism. A whole new generation, which honored Gambetta as its leader and was alienated by the intransigence of the old generation of revolutionaries, rallied to the support of the republican opposition elected to the Chamber in 1863. The opposition hated the Emperor as the man of the *coup d'état* and fought tooth and nail in the Corps Législatif against the Mexican expedition, which was undertaken at Eugénie's behest and with the support of Morny, actuated by sinister financial motives. The expedition met with disaster after disaster, and cost immense sums of money and the sacrifice of thousands of lives. The dynastic glamour that was lent to this adventure by the fact that the Archduke Maximilian went to Mexico as Emperor made it even more abominable in the republican opposition's eyes.

The workers were even more directly affected than the bourgeois republicans by economic developments. The consequence of the trade treaty with England and the unemployment in the cotton industry caused by the American Civil War inevitably made them realize their own dependence upon the international economic situation; and as economic expansion had already led to a number of international congresses and alliances, the idea of international combination for the purpose of securing better conditions for themselves naturally occurred to them. A delegation of workers, sent to the Great Exhibition in London in 1862 with the Emperor's assistance, caused the idea to spread abroad. Thus within the very bosom of capitalist economy there were formed the forces directed towards its abolition.

How consciously the workers aimed at emancipation was shown by their attitude at the elections in 1863. Instead of allowing themselves to be deceived by marks of Imperial favor, they rallied behind the republican bourgeoisie, who, in gratitude for their support, secured for the working classes the satisfaction of some of their most pressing needs and obtained schools and libraries for them which served to meet the proletarian demand for education. In order to win the masses back to him, the Emperor reconciled himself to making great concessions, which did not, however, have the desired effect. His most important concession was to grant them, with Morny's consent, their long-demanded right of association and with it the right to strike. Another considerable advance on the part of the proletariat in the autumn of the same year was represented by the foundation in London of the First International, which soon came under the guiding influence of Karl Marx.

The economic trends that led to the growth of opposition also affected the governing plutocracy. If the working class was internationally minded, the plutocracy was cosmopolitan. Ever since 1855, the year of the Universal Exposition, Paris had been swarming with rich foreigners who, apart from their business activities, devoted themselves predominantly to pleasure; and society, in harmony with the official economic policy, readily came forward to meet them. The Empress attracted foreign women to the court, and the Duc de Morny associated a great deal with the Russian colony. A more tangible expression of the mood of friendliness towards foreigners that was prevalent in high circles was the great ball arranged by the Minister of Marine at the beginning of 1866, the chief attraction of which was a " procession of the four corners of the earth," in which representatives of all countries and climates took part.

The brilliant social life led by the interlocking circles of foreigners, the world of fashion, and the aristocracy was the result not only of the stimulus given by the Emperor but also of the increased self-consciousness of a plutocracy intoxicated by its own economic achievements. In fact the latter was probably the most important factor. There was something of the conquistador about them. The procession of horsemen and horsewomen and elegant carriages to be seen every afternoon in the Bois was an incomparable pageant of wealth. At some of the Boulevard restaurants the display of luxury and magnificence was no less impressive, at the Maison d'Or, for instance, and, above all, at the Café Anglais.

After the closing of the Café de Paris in 1856, the Café Anglais came to occupy a position in the Second Empire corresponding to that of the Café de Paris in the reign of Louis-Philippe. It was a tall, white building with a maze of corridors and innumerable public and private rooms. Its European fame attracted practically every foreign visitor to Paris. However, if a stranger, knowing no better, entered it at midday he would be disappointed to see the dining-room occupied only by a number of elderly gentlemen, brokers and bankers, scanning the latest Bourse quotations over their noon meal. In reality the Café Anglais never awoke from its slumbers until dinner-time, when it would be packed from top to bottom. The greatest activity reigned in the cellars, which contained hundreds of thousands of bottles, which were sent to the tables on a miniature railway. On special occasions the cellars were transformed into Bacchic grottoes. Innumerable branches of vine and clusters of grapes dangled from the vaults and the pillars and in the recesses.

But things only really began to hum at the Café Anglais at midnight, when the fashionable world streamed in after the theater. For year after year the leading spirit was the Duc de

Gramont-Caderousse, who would resort to a room on the first floor known as the *grand seize,* where he and his uproarious clique would have supper parties, now with actresses, now with courtesans. For fear of explosions the two categories were kept rigorously apart, in so far as any really rigorous distinction between them was possible. Supper would rapidly develop into a carousal, to which the Duc de Gramont-Caderousse would often give the required impetus by throwing the crockery out of the window.

He himself cracked up just like the crockery. He returned from Egypt at the beginning of 1865 in a state of deathly exhaustion, but tried to resume his old life and appeared everywhere with Hortense Schneider as before — she was still playing the part of Helen of Troy. But as poor Gramont-Caderousse could not help realizing that he no longer had anything in common with the Trojan Paris, during the summer he betook himself to the Pyrenees alone. He could not bear the solitude, however. He saw Paris once more or, rather, not Paris, but the inside of his room in Paris, from which he could no longer move. In September he died, with only one friend at his bedside.

His death did not diminish the tumult at the Café Anglais. Night after night it was filled with the popping of champagne corks and the strumming of pianos and the inevitable ditty *J'ai un pied qui remue,* mingled with the music of Offenbach and the sound of cries and laughter coming from every room, while curious sightseers mingled with the society men from the *grand seize* and roamed about the vaults below. These orgies brought in money. Eighty thousand francs' worth of cigars were sold every year, and the chef drew an annual salary of twenty-five thousand francs.

The Duc de Morny was quicker than anyone else in authority to detect the lurking danger from the republicans. All his efforts were directed towards coming to terms with the Left opposition. He possessed unusual insight into economic trends and necessities, and his statesmanlike flair made him perfectly well aware that the democratic spirit with which the times were pregnant could no longer be suppressed and that the only hope of saving the Empire lay in unhesitatingly recognizing the fact. .

Not that Morny was interested in the blessings of democracy. He was a cynical realist, and cared nothing for it. All he was interested in was the maintenance of the regime and with it his own power. No sooner had the workers been granted freedom of association than he started working out a scheme of widespread reforms, aiming at the liberalization of the Empire, for which he hoped to secure the Emperor's consent. He wished to extend the privileges of the Chamber, restore the freedom of the press, and take the republican Émile Ollivier into the Cabinet.

Perhaps Morny's influence might really have delayed, if not prevented, the Empire's collapse. But before there was any chance of putting his reforms into execution he suddenly died, at the age of fifty-six, as the result of an attack of bronchitis which his tired constitution had no power to resist. A *grand seigneur* to the end, he never mentioned the objectionable word " death," though fully conscious that it was approaching, but only spoke of his imminent " departure," as though he were about to take a journey.

He died on March 10, 1865. Ludovic Halévy said he had loved and lost him, and felt completely shattered. " M. de Morny would have done more for me if I had wished him to, if I had asked him," he wrote in his diary, " but I had only one thought: to complete my career at his side and never to leave him. Never to leave him."

Without Morny, Halévy felt lost and robbed of his support in the Corps Législatif. He believed that the Second Empire had now been deprived of its prop.

As if to strengthen him in this belief, political tension increased after Morny's death. During the month in which he died there appeared a pamphlet attacking the Emperor, *Les Propos de Labiénus,* which caused a sensation in republican circles. The Government condemned its author to five years' imprisonment for contumacy and started imposing fines on Rochefort. It made no difference.

Prosper Mérimée, an old friend of the Empress Eugénie — she was invariably called " the Spaniard " because of the Mexican affair and her reactionary outlook — made the acquaintance of a republican student at about this time, and on the strength of this contact declared that there was something bitter and threatening about the republican section of the younger generation, not, however, without adding that another section of the same generation consisted of empty-headed young wastrels.

There was something threatening about the young generation. The observation was correct. Early in December 1865 the Goncourts' *Henriette Maréchal* was produced at the Comédie Française. As the students had discovered that it had been accepted at the express wish of Princess Matilda, they ruined the first night with their booing. The same occurred on succeeding nights. The ringleader was a young man whom Jules Vallès christened Pipe-en-bois, because the shape of his head was like a wooden Tyrolese pipe. The name of Pipe-en-bois assumed a revolutionary significance and became a bogy to the bourgeois. Its owner later took part in the Commune, escaped, and died in obscurity.

The Emperor did little to check the dissatisfaction. He was tired and ill and had so completely lost his bearings that a capacity for aimless and ineffectual intrigue was all that was left to him. He hamstrung the liberal reforms, and his foreign policy was disastrous. Under pressure from the United States he was compelled to liquidate the Mexican expedition and abandon the Emperor Maximilian to his fate. What was more serious, he allowed Bismarck's Prussia to gain the hegemony in Germany by wars against Denmark and Austria. Instead of seizing his last opportunity and resorting to military intervention after the Battle of Sadowa, at which the Prussian victory was decided, he withdrew to the position of an umpire on the side-lines. But he exercised this role with such weakness that he gained the friendship neither of Austria nor of Italy. The result of his vacillation was that France was now confronted with two powerful neighbors. One of them, Germany, on the brink of achieving her national unity, boded France no good.

The Emperor did not, however, appear to be in the least seriously concerned. As his star was no longer shining, he watched the clouds instead. Clouds, though they sometimes gather threateningly, at other times scatter and disperse. For the rest he relied on his immense prestige. Though it had perceptibly diminished, it still kept his enemies in check.

In spite of the accentuation of hostility between the Left opposition and the Government, things did not yet come to a head. For the process of economic development had led to an assumption of democratic habits, customs, and appearances, and for the time being, this covered up the growing crisis. " Life threatens to become public," the Goncourts wrote as early as 1860; and in 1866 they wrote in their diaries that " the newspaper has killed the salon, and publicity has taken the place formerly occupied by society."

The democratic vogue was evident on every side. One example of it was the fashion for *café-concerts* that set in with the sixties. Entire families would go to them *en masse,* and very soon there was no part of the city without them. The mingling of classes was evident even in the fine new streets built by Haussmann. The most varied types were to be seen strolling there on Sunday afternoons. " Lovely creatures who stroll by in silk and satin . . . honest folk and rogues, elegant folk and old folk, artists and notaries, dandies with dainty mustaches, pimps with heavy sidewhiskers, famous whores and modest workmen, fathers of families with their wives and children. . . ." All these and more, according to Jules Vallès, made up the motley throng.

The world had become democratic, and the banker Millaud showed that he was aware of the fact by founding *Le Petit Journal* at the beginning of 1863. Its object was to cater for the petty bourgeoisie. These people, Millaud said to himself, were not interested in the finer points of politics, but wanted to be entertained and kept *au fait* with current affairs. *Le Petit Journal* cost only one sou, and it rapidly gained an enormous circulation, thus corroborating Millaud's estimate of the requirements of the man in the street. He knew instinctively every heart-beat of that still unexploited public, and the propaganda methods by which he captured it were extremely adroit. The offices of *Le Petit Journal* lay on the Boulevards, and brilliant illuminations would announce the beginning of a new serial story, while criers, like living loud-speakers, hammered the appropriate information into the brains of passers-by. Every window would be brilliantly lit, while magic lanterns flashed out allegorical scenes, and brilliantly illuminated letters flashed a message to the eyes that already had been dinned into the ears.

To meet this energetic competition, at the end of 1865 Villemessant founded a daily paper, *L'Événement,* which had Zola, Rochefort, and other Left writers among its contributors. The fact that Villemessant took such writers under his ægis shows how strong the republican movement must have become. Villemessant, as a royalist, of course belonged to the opposition himself, but he always allowed his contributors free expression of opinion, provided that they were not boring. A year later, when *L'Événement* was suppressed, he transformed *Le Figaro* into a daily.

The general democratic trend also, of course, influenced the behavior of the ruling caste. It was no accident that a new group was formed in the Chamber in 1866, *le tiers parti,* the leader of which was Ollivier. This group offered the Emperor its support on condition he granted the nation all political liberties. It was a hopelessly impractical proposal, but such attempts at compromise were in accordance with the mood of the moment. Under its influence the upper classes, snobbish as ever, started looking below them and sought to accommodate themselves to the modern democratic fashion. Characteristic of the new mood was the fame of Thérésa.

Thérésa first made her appearance in 1860 as a *café-concert* ballad-singer, and gained enormous popularity with a song called *La Femme à barbe*. The appearance of her autobiography, which she had no more written herself than Rigolboche had written hers, made her more popular still. Her success was undoubtedly due to the fact that she came from the people and was a complete embodiment of its idiosyncrasies. Her intelligent expression caused the banality of her features to be overlooked, and Théodore de Banville said of her voice that it combined the properties of a flute and a big drum, of a volcanic eruption and the song of a skylark. Banville also called her the embodied " revenge of romance," which adequately described her place in the scheme of things. As soon as she opened her mouth to sing, the emptiness and unreality of the drawing-room ballad became all too painfully manifest. But the very people at whose artificiality her songs were aimed flocked nightly to hear her at the Eldorado or the Alcazar. In 1865 and 1866 Thérésa had become practically indispensable to the *grande monde*. The Emperor invited her to the Tuileries, the smartest hostesses vied with each other to secure her services, and one highly respectable Victorian English lady who wished to open a salon in Paris actually engaged this *café-concert* artist in the hope of enhancing her social prestige.

As long as the state of political equilibrium associated with this resurgence of democratic life was maintained, many intellectuals, artists, and fashionable Bohemians preserved their attitude of political neutrality. Many of them retreated into complete indifference, an attitude which was encouraged by the new democratic fashions, which were not the monopoly of any one party or class, but were manifested everywhere and in every sphere. Ludovic Halévy decided to cut himself completely adrift and abandon his career. But the prototype of indifference was Albert Cavé.

In his youth Cavé had given such striking proofs of his inclination to idleness that his family had despaired of finding him a suitable career. They had eventually prevailed upon him to enter the censorship department, and the only reason he ever consented was that the duties were confined to watching theatrical performances. He did his job with exceptional tact, but the mere fact that his visits to the theater were obligatory was enough to make him dislike them intensely. Therefore one day when the Ministry decided to give his position to somebody else and offered him the Legion of Honor into the bargain, he was very pleased. Now at last he could be as idle and free as he liked. He was entirely devoid of ambition, and became a kind of indifferent connoisseur, whose casually uttered criticisms were often remarkably to the point. This caused him to be considered an oracle by Meilhac, Halévy, Offenbach, Dumas, and others. "What does Cavé say about it?" was the first question asked by playwrights and actors. He constituted their ideal public; and though he was a supernumerary himself, he was nevertheless useful to those who took a real part in the theatrical life of the time.

In those years Paris was bathed in a uniform brilliance that was no longer based on the callousness of the bourgeoisie. Its essence now was fear of approaching catastrophe as expressed in *La Belle Hélène,* mingled with new hopes and the vast horizons opened up by the wave of democratic feeling. A glittering, deceptive light blurred the contours of things, shed an ambiguous glow over everything, and favored the appearance of daylight apparitions.

There were one or two apparitions surviving from a previous generation. Auber and Dr. Véron shared a box at the Opéra. They were two old men overcome with weariness, who went to sleep and snored in the middle of the performance; and the silent Persian, a little old man with a white beard, a black astrakhan hat, and a glittering diamond on his ring finger, still went to the Opéra too, to be gazed at curiously by the audience. There were other contemporary phenomena as well; for instance, a salesman who was very highly paid because he was able to imitate with his lips the rustle of new silks while showing his customers dyed ribbon.

Even more remarkable was Lambert, who did not exist at all. He turned up suddenly and as suddenly disappeared. " Have you seen Lambert? " everybody asked everybody else, and everybody knew somebody else who knew somebody else who had seen him. Timothée Trimm, the shining light of the *Petit Journal,* did exist, but in an unreal manner, because the public who were fascinated by his articles made a legendary figure of him. He encouraged this highly convenient fact by sometimes writing his daily article at a table in a busy café, and when he did so, people would gather in crowds outside it and watch awe-stricken while the great man had reference books fetched from his office, consulted them, filled sheets of paper with writing, crumpled them up, rewrote, crossed out, and revised; and finally a sigh of relief would go up when it was at last clear that the masterpiece had been satisfactorily completed.

Such was the Paris of that time. All classes of the population were caught up and carried away by the democratic swell, which released an abundance of extreme forces that at first kept each other in check. The city had become a cosmopolis. It lived in a kind of waking dream, the victim of a thousand enthusiasms, toying with a thousand dangers and hopes, vibrating and tense as though it were on the eve of some great event. Was it possible not to love Paris then?

" I am once more back in Paris," Halévy wrote, having returned on a hot August day from Étretat, where he had found the monotony insufferable, " and I am delighted to be home again. . . . I have seen Paris again, my home, my books, my china, my little balcony, my Boulevards, my Opéra, Paris. Yes, my Paris, it was with a childish pleasure that I set eyes on it all again." This was the city of which the revolutionary Jules Vallès wrote in retrospect: " I love this Paris with all the gratitude of my suffering. It was on its pavements that I fought so much and suffered so much. On the walls of its furnished rooms and on its paving-stones I left a piece of myself."

Before Offenbach sang the praises of his beloved Paris in his own way in his operetta *La Vie parisienne,* he wrote two other musical plays, of which the first, *Les Bergers,* produced in December 1865, was a failure. People went to the Bouffes to laugh, and *Les Bergers* was not funny enough for them. It was a pastoral, written entirely without satirical intention, placed in the time of Watteau and in the present, and thus it offered Offenbach an opportunity of composing in the style of the eighteenth century — like a little brook running between green banks.

An incident at one of the first performances illustrates the extreme tension of the political situation. Désiré, who took no pleasure in acting if he were not allowed to gag, made a cheap joke ridiculing " the principles of 1789," whereupon the republican papers promptly declared that the Government itself was behind his mockery of those sacred principles. The Minister of the Interior was compelled to fine Désiré in order to appease the excited opposition.

The second of the two pieces was *Barbe-bleu,* produced at the Variétés in February 1866. It was a complete and undisputed success. This time the Variétés was less stingy about the costs of production. This operetta, the libretto of which was by Meilhac and Halévy, was essentially one for the Parisian public, as its cooler reception in Berlin and Vienna showed. Nevertheless, even the Parisian actors at first thought it so daring that it was only with difficulty that Offenbach was able to persuade Dupuis to play the part of Bluebeard. What the actors found so shocking was the fact that Offenbach calmly burlesqued the grim legend of Bluebeard.

In *Orpheus* and *La Belle Hélène* he had taken a corrupt regime and handled it satirically, but in *Barbe-bleu* he made a comedy of real horror. It was precisely this sleight-of-hand, by which horror was abruptly transformed into uproarious comedy, that pleased the public; for they were only too anxious to make light of the terrible catastrophe that they dimly felt was hanging

over their heads. In spite of their forebodings they allowed themselves to be carried away by the democratic feelings that prevailed
on every side. A further reason for the operetta's success was
that it allowed plenty of scope to those democratic feelings. They
were expressed in the part played by Hortense Schneider — that
of Boulotte, a simple peasant girl, whose unceremonious, almost
rebellious attitude to King Bobèche shocked the court very
greatly. " She played and sang her role with incomparable wit
and talent," Halévy wrote after the first night. Bluebeard himself went so far as to assert that by his association with Boulotte
he was introducing a new era, in which " palace and cottage "
were united and made indistinguishable. Side by side with all
this and underlining it is a satire on court life, the gay impudence
of which was such that it almost led one to assume that such a
thing as a court could only really exist in fairy-stories. The song
beginning: " A courtier must bow his shoulders . . ." became the
rage in 1866. In addition to this witty and epigrammatic tune
there were others which showed that it was merely second nature
to Offenbach to ridicule the diabolical character of Bluebeard.
Nothing pleased him better than poisons that were really sugared
water, and murdered women who cheerfully survived. Such miracles were after his own heart. His music in such passages as
that in which the murdered women are resurrected and happiness
triumphs over evil is particularly delightful.

La Vie parisienne, that most enchanting of all pæans of praise
that have ever been written to any city, differed from the previous *offenbachiades* in an essential particular. Instead of hitting
at the present through the past, Offenbach for the first time
used the present as his raw material. Previously Offenbach had
used gods, mythological figures, and medieval heroes to cast light
on the life of his own contemporaries, but in *La Vie parisienne*
he made an operetta out of the contemporary scene. Hitherto he
had revealed the present by means of the past, but now he constructed a realm of fantasy out of the present day. During the
rehearsals the fancies that he spun out of topical themes seemed

so boring and stupid that the actors grumbled, and Meilhac and Halévy looked forward to the first night with trepidation. Offenbach, delighted by his own music, was the only one who had absolutely no doubt whatever about its success, and he was right, as he had been in the case of *Les Deux Aveugles*. The first performance, which took place on October 31, 1866, at the Palais Royal, had a reception which exceeded even his expectations. *Barbe-bleu* and *La Belle Hélène* were put in the shade. The whole of Europe was enraptured by this glittering vision of Paris life.

Offenbach, developing one of the themes of *Barbe-bleu*, plunged into the midst of the modern democratic society by which the dictatorship had already been undermined. In *La Vie parisienne* there is no tyrant and there is no more mention of the court. Instead of these half-vanished phantoms we are presented with a series of characters belonging to contemporary, cosmopolitan Paris, which is a center of world economy and world entertainment. One of them is the Swedish Baron de Gondremarck, who wishes to plunge headlong into the vortex, and another is a Brazilian who desires to squander his substance on courtesans. Their wishes drive them into the world of fashionable Bohemia, with pictures of which the piece abounds.

But the key to the operetta was by no means the world of fashionable Bohemia alone. What made it really typical of his time was the picture given of the social turmoil produced by liberal capitalism. The cobbler Frick and the little glove-maker Gabrielle — the part created by Zulma Bouffar — are called upon to do great things, the head waiter Alfred shows himself to be a diplomat and a consummate judge of human nature, and domestic servants have no difficulty in aping the manners and behavior of high society; and the whole thing is presented in a manner which certainly does not give the disadvantage to the lower classes.

There was no doubt about the democratic feeling upon which the operetta was based. Moreover, it reflected very accurately the peculiar balance of forces prevailing at the time. But first of all it expressed the irony and skepticism with which Meilhac and Halévy regarded all the rival political creeds. This skepticism, to which human sincerity alone was sacred, had hitherto manifested itself in the frivolous treatment of tyrants, heroes, and gods. Now, in its treatment of modern democratic society, it put the frivolous world of fashionable Bohemia in the center of the stage and made the action revolve round the courtesan Metella and two little *cocodès,* Bobinet and Raoul de Gardefeu.

The ball is set rolling by an incident typical of this frivolous world. Gardefeu is waiting for Metella at the station, but she dismisses both him and his friend Bobinet. This disappointment, added to their financial embarrassments, causes the pair to decide to return to the salons of the faubourg Saint-Germain and fall in love with an heiress. But before leaving the station Gardefeu hears of the arrival of Baron Gondremarck and his wife. Obviously he immediately decides to set his cap for her. He presents himself to the Baron as an envoy sent specially to meet him by the Grand Hotel and takes the couple to his house, which he passes off as an annex of that establishment. The Grand Hotel had only just been erected. This promising beginning results in the most comic situations. There is, for instance, a hurriedly improvised dinner at which Frick and Gabrielle take the places of honor, and a *soirée* at which Gardefeu's servants pretend to be highly placed personages. " All these fancies . . . are crazy," Sarcey wrote after the first night. " But they are crazy after the fashion of a dream. The most unlikely and unexpected accidents divert their progress, and the result is a fantastic figment of the brain that has only the most dim and distant connection with the original idea. But there is always logic at the back of it, though it is subterranean and uncontrolled."

All this hilarious confusion is bound up with satire — nay, is the satire itself. However serious the intentions of Bobinet and Gardefeu may be, the fantastic chaos they cause show that they are not to be taken too seriously; and when Frick, Gabrielle, and

the domestics imitate the behavior of polite society, their imita-
tions are parodies too. Incidents scattered throughout the plot
reinforce the same effect. Alfred, the head waiter, knows all there
is to be known about the patrons of the Café Anglais, and
Bobinet has to admit that the young women of the faubourg
Saint-Germain are just as mercenary as the cocottes.

As usual the satire, as well as all the improbabilities of the
plot, is developed in an atmosphere of rapture. Foreigners are
enraptured on arriving in the intoxicating atmosphere of Paris,
we are shown the delirium of the fashionable world that haunted
the Café Anglais, and as a consummation the delirious scenes
that characterize the servants' party, ending with song:

Tout tourne, tout danse.

Offenbach, a specialist in this rapturous kind of music, took
an active part in constructing the libretto of this scene, in order
to give himself scope for all the musical effects at which he aimed.
Jules Claretie somewhat reluctantly declared that *La Vie parisienne* made him laugh so much that somebody might have been
tickling the soles of his feet; and he added that the effect was as
if the whole house had been taking hashish. It was a kind of
dionysiac orgy, no longer based, as it had been in *Orpheus,* on
the bourgeois craving for a narcotic, but on the exciting feeling
that a new day was dawning. This time the delirium differed
from its predecessors; it was awakened by the birth of democracy,
conceived in Paris, great, cosmopolitan Paris, in which the shape
of things to come was already being revealed. Servants, artisans,
a society man, and a distinguished foreigner all fraternally drink
each other's health at the servants' party.

As the general delirium does not cover up and conceal reality
but rather celebrates it, the satire is not, as in former *offenbachiades,* more or less submerged by it; this time the satire is corrected
by a sympathy in which all the characters are bathed, all of them
being members of a democratic society. Bobinet and Gardefeu
turn out to be charming young men at heart, and as for Metella,

she is a real fairy-tale courtesan. Her feelings for Gardefeu border on love, and she is sufficiently *au fait* with things to sing the *grand seize* song, the words of which described the " hangover " which generally followed carousals at the Café Anglais. But even the *grand seize,* with its *cocodès* and *cocodettes,* was just another part of the general life, which, whatever it was like, was undergoing a happy renewal.

Meilhac and Halévy put all this into perspective by letting contemporary Paris be seen through the spectacles of memory. The contemporary scene is preserved, like a specimen in a glass case, in a letter of recommendation to Metella given by Baron Stanislaus de Frascata to his friend Baron Gondremarck. The writer, tied to the " cold country " in which he lives, sighs for the champagne suppers, Metella's sky-blue boudoir, the songs, the glamour of Paris, the gay and glittering city, throbbing with warmth and life, in which differences of station are abolished. Metella reads the letter to the strains of Offenbach's music, which surrounds it with a yearning melancholy, as though Paris were paradise lost, and at the same time with a halo of bliss as though it were the paradise to come; and, as the action continues, one is given the impression that the picture given in the letter is beginning to come to life.

Sarcey called the operetta dreamlike, because of its improbability. But he is refuted by the recently deceased Karl Kraus, a fanatical champion of Offenbach, who fought passionately for his resurrection and wrote the most penetrating analysis of *La Vie parisienne.* In this operetta, Kraus wrote, " life is nearly as improbable as it really is." For it is true that *La Vie parisienne* did not exaggerate, but if anything remained behind reality.

Was there a head waiter like Alfred at the Café Anglais? There was. His name was Ernest, and he was a big, handsome man of inimitable correctness. If he condescended to sweep crumbs from a tablecloth he did so in the manner of a *grand seigneur* instructing a new and inexperienced member of the staff. The Alfred of the operetta showed the Swedish Baroness into a room at the Café Anglais reserved for married women. That room really existed too. It had its own staircase connecting it with the street, and the ladies that used it believed that they did so unobserved. They were mistaken, however, for thanks to a cunning arrangement of mirrors, their comings and goings could easily be watched from the big dining-room, and one evening one of its patrons had the mortification of seeing his best friend making for a private room in the company of his wife. The Brazilians who ruined themselves and the foreigners who made fools of themselves in Paris really existed too. " It seems to me that the whole city of Paris is my mistress," Khalil Pasha said to Arsène Houssaye, looking at the Boulevards. The Bobinets and Gardefeus really existed too and caused all sorts of mischief.

The following story is told by Meilhac, and it certainly was not pure invention. A Baroness who wanted to take part in some amateur theatricals wrote to a well-known actor, B., whom she did not happen to know, even by sight, asking him if he would give her lessons in acting. B. duly called on her and she promptly fell in love with him. Soon afterwards she went to a theater and discovered that her lover and the real B. were different persons. It turned out that her letter had been picked up at the porter's lodge by a young actress who no longer remembered which of the many gentlemen of her acquaintance had read it and followed up the opportunity. There were not many real courtesans in Paris who possessed the wit with which Halévy and Meilhac endowed Metella, but they were certainly adepts at intrigue.

All the ingredients of Offenbach's operettas existed in reality. That did not prevent the majority of his contemporaries, like Sarcey, from believing that the world into which it plunged them was a dream-world. Had their eyes been opened, they would have recognized that *La Vie parisienne* held up a mirror to the fantastic life they were actually leading.

CHAPTER XI

SUNSET GLORY

1867, the year of the Universal Exposition, was ushered in by a debut and a resignation.

The debut was that of Cora Pearl. As her ambitions remained unsatisfied even by the liaison she had recently entered upon with the young Prince Napoleon, she decided to sample a new sensation, that of acting, and to appear as Cupid in a revival of *Orpheus,* by which it was hoped to rescue the Bouffes from its financial plight. As a love-goddess of Cora's exalted rank could not possibly be expected to put up with an ordinary theatrical dressing-room, Prince Napoleon took a flat for her in a house next door to the theater, from which he had a special staircase built allowing her direct access to the stage door. One evening a Cupid who looked like a walking jeweler's shop came tripping down the staircase and on to the stage, with diamonds in his hair, diamonds studding his shoes, diamonds glittering all over him. "Bravo, Cora!" the house roared. The diamonds glittered brilliantly, but Cora herself had such a severe attack of stage-fright that she was scarcely able to stammer out the little song which she had so painfully learned by heart. And on the second night, when a crowd of students started making a disturbance, she packed up her diamonds and retired to private life and love once more.

A few weeks later Ludovic Halévy took advantage of the financial independence which he had by this time attained to resign from the Corps Législatif. Morny was dead, and a political career had no more attractions for him. He abandoned it all the more

readily because he believed politics at bottom to be nothing but
a game of chance, and in the political world he missed the genu-
ineness and sincerity without which he felt life was not worth
living. " All I carry away with me from the seven years I spent
in the midst of the representatives of my country is the most
profound political indifference," he wrote after his retirement.
" How much strife has raged over my modest head! But as for
genuine convictions, there were none, none whatever, either on
the Right or on the Left. There are only people who are nothing
and want to be something, and that is all."

It was the year of the Universal Exposition.

A huge building had been erected on the Champ de Mars, an
enormous, elliptical structure built of iron and glass, the general
effect of which was extremely ponderous. Contemporaries called
it the " Colosseum of Labor," or the " Industrial Tower of Babel."
When the Emperor, who was still personally popular, opened it
amid acclamation, most of the exhibits were still contained in
packing-cases. But the new Seine steamers were working, and it
was possible to go to the exposition in them. To reach the exposition grounds you passed through a tunnel. The grounds
contained an artificial lake, innumerable side-shows, and the
pavilions of the various nations. The Exhibition Palace itself, in
the center of which space had been left for an exotic garden,
consisted of seven halls radiating from the center, those at either
end being the highest. The Palace was the home of machinery.
Théophile Gautier went up to the ceiling in a crude hydraulic
elevator and imagined himself transplanted to an ancient arena.
He visualized gladiators doing battle and racing chariots thun-
dering over the metal floor below.

Opinions about the exposition differed widely. The exhibitors
complained about the high rents they were charged, while bourgeois idealists dreamed of universal peace and the abolition of
war. The democratic enthusiasm to which they had all fallen a
prey caused Victor Hugo, whose perspectives, in both space and
time, had become noticeably shortened in exile, to rise to heights

of ecstasy. " In the twentieth century," he wrote in the *Paris-Guide* for 1867, which visitors to the exhibition carried about with them like a Bible, " there will be an extraordinary nation. It will be a great nation, which will not prevent it from being free. It will be astonished at the respect with which conical projectiles are now regarded, and it will only be with difficulty that they will be able to tell the difference between an army commander and a butcher. The capital of that nation will be Paris, and its name will be not France, but Europe."

It was the year of the Universal Exposition.

At the Variétés Offenbach's latest operetta, *The Grand Duchess of Gerolstein,* was being rehearsed at high pressure, the aim being to have it ready for the opening of the exposition. The little that was known about it stimulated widespread curiosity. It was said that it was only out of consideration for the censor that Meilhac and Halévy had placed the action in the eighteenth century, in one of those fabulous little German states which Eugène Sue had invented for his *Les Mystères de Paris*. The operetta was said to be a satire on militarism; it was also said to be a satire on the Russian court and Catherine the Great and to be teeming with topical political allusions. Eighteen military bandsmen actually appeared in it, and so on and so forth. *Le Figaro* simply reveled in it.

At the dress rehearsal Hortense Schneider, whose salary had now mounted to the dizzy height of four thousand five hundred francs a month, suffered one of her most grievous disppointments. She had devised for herself a superb ribbon of an imaginary order to be worn diagonally across her bosom, and her whole heart was set on wearing it. But it upset the censor so severely that he insisted on its being removed. The authors instantly altered a sentence in which the censor perceived an allusion to the Austro-German War, but they found it far, far more painful to break the news to Hortense Schneider that she must sacrifice her ribbon. She sobbed bitterly when she heard the dreadful news and swore that she would never act again. But as soon as the orchestra struck up at Offenbach's bidding, she dried her tears, smiled again, and took her place at the head of her army. Next year she was able to show visitors to her salon a picture of herself in the full glory of her costume as the Grand Duchess of Gerolstein, proudly adorned with the forbidden ribbon. Thus she avenged herself pictorially.

Courtesans, bankers, diplomats, Imperial dignitaries, everyone of any consequence in the *grand monde* or the *demi-monde* attended the first night at the Variétés on April 12. It was an audience after Hortense Schneider's heart. One thing that it proved was that the day of the crinoline was over; because all the ladies, with the Princess von Metternich at their head, appeared in straight skirts. They were all dressed in the shade of brown which was then fashionable — it was known as " Bismarck color " — but a bright contrast was provided by the brilliant red corals they wore in their hair, on their ear-rings, round their necks and on their sleeves. The gentlemen of the Jockey Club who pronounced judgment on the scene from their orchestra seats had prominent side-whiskers and enormous shirt-fronts and had recently taken to wearing square monocles.

The first night left the most experienced theater-goers in doubt as to whether the operetta would be a success or not. About the first act there was only one opinion; it was an unquestionable success. The Jockey Club laughed immeasurably at the tirades of General Boum, and when Hortense Schneider, with a fur over one shoulder, a Hussar's cap over one ear and a riding-whip in her hand, sang at her first entry: " *Ah! que j'aime les militaires . . .*" she brought the house down. The satirical song " *Voici le sabre de mon père!* " increased the general enthusiasm almost to the pitch of frenzy, which was maintained well into the second act, the first half of which contained the heartfelt lines with which the Grand Duchess's ladies-in-waiting accompany the reading of letters from the front, as well as the Grand Duchess's love-song:" *Dîtes-lui qu'on l'a remarqué,*" the music of which Halévy called a jewel. Hortense Schneider scored an immense triumph. The public did not know which to admire most, her singing or the malicious language of her eyes, her reckless daring or her finesse. She had become a brilliant star in the firmament of operetta. But as for the piece itself, there was no doubt that it fell off perceptibly after the middle of the second act.

Offenbach was not surprised, because after his first reading of the libretto he had complained of its lack of humor and un-dramatic construction and had proposed numerous alterations which had nevertheless not been carried out. The third act, with its complicated palace intrigues, was a still greater failure. Sarcey called it " a vulgar farce."

Fortunately the authors promptly recognized the operetta's weaknesses. They cut out the parody of *Les Huguenots,* recognizing that operatic parodies of this kind no longer accorded with the taste of the times, and made innumerable other altera-tions, with the result that the third act was saved and the second became as successful as the first. In its new version, which was presented as early as the third night, the operetta became a tri-umphant success. Offenbach, Meilhac, and Halévy had every reason to be pleased. During the last two and a half years *La Belle Hélène* had had three hundred performances, *Barbe-bleu* about one hundred and fifty, and *La Vie parisienne,* which was still in the repertoire, nearly two hundred. Nobody doubted that *The Grand Duchess of Gerolstein* would break the record.

Its amazing popularity had a great deal to do with the fact that Bismarck was the man of the hour. Bismarck's policy had brought war near, and this operetta was about war. The threat of war dominated public life and exercised a hypnotic fascination; the Mexican fiasco was well remembered, and the superiority of the Prussian needle-gun was well known. But instead of taking France's weaknesses to heart — the frank recognition of which might certainly have caused a panic — the general public pre-ferred to gloss over the seriousness of the situation and not bother about such things as wars. Was not war an anachronism, which nowadays had no justification whatever? That was the kind of

thing that men were saying at the time of the Universal Exposition, which seemed a guarantee of the irresistible advance of the
democratic unity of the peoples.

The Grand Duchess of Gerolstein gratified the universal inclination to treat the subject of war frivolously. Its hero was the
bombastic General Boum, whose unparalleled stupidity was only
equaled by his valor. Instead of taking snuff like a civilian, he
fired a pistol and inhaled the smoke that came from the barrel;
and at a council of war he produced a plan of campaign which
revealed the involuntary humor of many real plans of campaign.
He pined for a war without taking the slightest interest in the
reasons or the lack of reasons for fighting it. And war is declared
in *The Grand Duchess of Gerolstein* because Baron Puck, the
Grand Duchess's adviser and former tutor, desires a distraction
for her.

Before the Austro-German War, when it was rumored that
Napoleon III was preparing a new war, Prévost-Paradol expressed the opinion (and Halévy agreed with him) that in view
of the spread of the liberal movement a war would be very welcome to the Emperor. " The idea . . . of distracting men's minds
and diverting them with the hope of territorial aggrandizement
is unfortunately only too natural, and everybody knows that it
is generally absolute governments that choose this way out of
difficult situations."

Sure enough, absolutism as well as militarism is parodied by
Offenbach. The Grand Duchess promotes the fusilier Fritz to
be a general because she falls in love with him, then reduces
him to the ranks again because he prefers to remain faithful to
his Wanda. Mischievous favoritism of this kind not only reminded the Parisians of the Tuileries and the Winter Palace,
but called up pleasant memories of the little German states —
the Duke of Nassau in his field-marshal's uniform, for instance,
and the innumerable princes of the Confederation at Baden and
Ems.

In short, the operetta made fun of everything there was to

be made fun of — not forgetting the court gossip in the news-papers, haunted castles, and the icy demeanor of diplomats. It was mainly the music that stripped the gilt off the gingerbread of military bombast and pretentious autocracy. And all this " de-bunking " was done for the benefit of the quick wits of demo-cratic townsmen, who reveled in it. The common sense of decent, reasonable people is throughout exalted at the expense of out-moded and obsolete political institutions. The Grand Duchess is a real young *parisienne,* who is not easily taken in, and grace-fully leads Prince Paul, her dull-witted suitor, by the nose, and Fritz, a youth of the same stamp, remains insensible to courtly glamour, while his ready wits win a battle which General Boum would certainly have lost.

1867 was the year of the Universal Exposition. Or was it the year of *The Grand Duchess of Gerolstein*?

The Emperor himself saw it as early as April 24 and smiled at the strategical skill of the operetta general, twisting the ends of his mustaches, although he must certainly have been reminded of some painful memories. But appearances had to be kept up. Thiers, was, of course, enthusiastic in his admiration of *The Grand Duchess,* the allegory of which he, the Emperor's political opponent, was in a better position to appreciate than anyone.

Towards the end of May the Prince of Wales, a perfectly dressed young man who united the virtues of the English fam-ily man with those of the Parisian dandy, arrived in Paris. As the Variétés, which had long since been sold out, attracted him far more than the Universal Exposition, he applied to Hortense Schneider, whom he did not know, on the very day of his arrival, asking her if she could not secure him a proscenium box. Hor-tense started frantically rushing from agency to agency and eventually found him a box, though not one of the best ones, and he duly appeared in it with the Duke and Duchess of Man-chester and the Marquis and Marquise de Galliffet. He very soon felt a desire to pay homage to the Grand Duchess of Gerolstein. After the second act he accordingly presented himself in her

HORTENSE SCHNEIDER
in The Grand Duchess of Gerolstein

HORTENSE SCHNEIDER'S DRESSING-ROOM AT THE VARIÉTÉS, 1867

Water-color by Louis Morin, from the collection of Daniel Halévy

dressing-room, accompanied by the Duke and the Marquis, and a motley company met his eyes: Hortense's hairdresser; the actor Couder in all his glory as General Boum, with his plumed helmet on his head; Albert Wolff, the journalist; two adjutants; and Ludovic Halévy. Halévy afterwards reported that Hortense Schneider nearly burst with pride and kept repeating " Your Royal Highness " in every other sentence. As for the Prince, he enjoyed himself so thoroughly behind the scenes that it was with a sigh that he returned to his box and the somewhat elderly Duchess of Manchester. He would very probably have sighed much more during his stay in Paris if Hortense Schneider had not consoled him for the tedium of all his official duties. In gratitude he returned to London with a large pile of photographs of her, which he showed to everyone, never failing, however, to sing the praises of General Boum as well.

The Czar Alexander was due in Paris on June 1, but was too impatient even to wait until his arrival and telegraphed his Ambassador from Cologne asking him to secure him a box at the Variétés immediately. The Czar's haste was obviously due to rumors of certain resemblances between the court of Gerolstein and that of St. Petersburg which had penetrated as far as the Neva. Three hours after his arrival in Paris, he was seated in his box at the Variétés. His motive may have been to check the truth of the rumors for himself, but very soon after the curtain went up he had forgotten all about them and was captivated by Hortense Schneider's charms. Unfortunately his son Vladimir was equally captivated, with the result that all the little Boulevard papers came out with descriptions of a lively scene that took place between the two when the performance was over.

A few days later there arrived the representatives of the new great power, Prussia — King William, the Crown Prince Frederick, Moltke, and the eagerly awaited Bismarck, whose white cuirassier's uniform and enormous boots caused the Parisians great amusement. All these, with the Czar and twenty other princes and potentates, attended a parade in the Bois next day, with which Napoleon III tried to impress upon his visitors the fact that the military might at his disposal was greater than that of the Grand Duchess of Gerolstein. *" Ah! que j'aime les militaires!"* the latter could have sung with the greatest possible conviction if she had been present at the review of sixty thousand men with flags recalling the Crimea, the Italian campaign, Syria, China, and Mexico. When the parade was over and the Emperor and the Czar drove back together in their gala carriage, several pistol-shots rang out, but they did no harm. The Emperor said politely that the bullets must undoubtedly have been meant for him, but they had been fired by a Pole, aiming at the Czar.

As for Bismarck, after the parade he doffed his uniform and donned his evening dress and went to see *The Grand Duchess of Gerolstein*. It gave him the greatest possible satisfaction, for it seemed to him to be a proof that the French military spirit was in an advanced state of decay; apart from which it put into the pillory the petty German states which he proposed shortly to liquidate. The satire on miniature courts and petty princelings visibly amused him. *" C'est tout-à-fait ça,"* he said in the best of humor to Moltke, who shared his box. Moltke, as usual, was silent. Perhaps he may have been considering how closely the character of General Boum approximated to reality. Both he and Bismarck had seen through the Emperor's weaknesses. Bismarck called him an *" incapacité méconnue,"* while the observant Moltke noticed " the dead look in his eyes."

On the evening of July 1, the day on which Paris had been celebrating the arrival of the Sultan, crowds of people were strolling as usual in a popular concert garden in the Champs-Élysées. It was a fine summer evening, like any other. The stars were shining, the air was mild, and everyone seemed instinctively to be talking quietly, in order the better to enjoy it all. Suddenly a terrible piece of news started spreading through the grounds. The Emperor Maximilian of Mexico had been shot by order of Juárez. An Imperial orderly officer entered the garden and confirmed the information. In a second a crowd had gathered round him, pressing him for details. " Oh, how terrible! " women's voices exclaimed again and again. Then deep silence fell. The spell was only broken half an hour later when an unsuspecting theater-goer arrived with two witticisms he had just overheard in Hortense Schneider's dressing-room. These spread round the garden like wildfire too, the orchestra struck up, and everyone felt happy again.

The shooting of Maximilian was a dramatic ending to a disastrous undertaking. It put an end to all the official celebrations in honor of the Sultan, quite apart from the fact that it caused a number of crowned heads to sleep uneasily in their beds. But there was at any rate one sovereign who had no need to worry: the Grand Duchess of Gerolstein. Her power was more firmly established than ever. She accepted the homage of the kings of Portugal, Bavaria, and Sweden; and every evening she received in her dressing-room princes from countries great and small. Her dressing-room was papered in pink, and apart from the princes and her indispensable maid, Josephine, invariably contained several dogs. Hortense Schneider doted on her dogs, of whom she possessed no fewer than eight. They were called Love, Pugg, Vicky, Mimi, and so on, and were allowed to be taken for a drive in the Bois every afternoon. While their mistress was on the stage, they kept guard over a leather trunk which contained an iron casket full of diamonds — presents from various princes to the Grand Duchess of Gerolstein.

For her the differences between operetta and real life were visibly obliterated. On the stage she amused herself with wars; in real life she amused herself by keeping a rich young man as a kind of pet. His name was Xavier Feuillant, and he may have reminded her slightly of the Duc de Gramont-Caderousse. He had served in the African Chasseurs, could read if it was absolutely necessary, and was very fond of fighting duels. Actresses and courtesans petted and spoiled him, because he was so nice and useless. He was one of Hortense Schneider's lap-dogs. That he was not entirely devoid of intelligence was shown by some of the jealous tricks he played on Hortense in spite of all his devotion to her. When the Grand Duchess was on the stage she liked playing to the right-hand proscenium box, which was generally occupied by Ismail Pasha, the Viceroy of Egypt, who had been one of her favorites for years past. One evening Feuillant put on a fez and took up his position in the proscenium box on the opposite side, so that from the stage he looked exactly like the Egyptian and caused the poor Grand Duchess, casting bewildered looks from side to side, to believe herself to be suffering from hallucinations. Not satisfied with that, he took an apartment opposite Hortense's house, and whenever she granted a private audience to any princely admirer, had the windows illuminated and the whole place decorated with the visitor's national colors.

But neither practical jokes nor Mlle Silly's spiteful phrase: " *C'est la passage des princes que la Schneider* " altered the fact that practically all the princes and potentates went and paid homage at Hortense Schneider's feet.

One day during the summer a lady of striking elegance drove up to the exposition gates. The carriage was stopped. It was explained to her that only royalty were allowed to drive round the exposition.

" Make way! " the lady called out. " I am the Grand Duchess of Gerolstein! "

The officials bowed respectfully, and Hortense Schneider, smiling graciously, passed through.

During her reign the world made pilgrimage to the great exposition and learned to recognize itself. At the exposition the Goncourts had the feeling they were walking in a dream. It was a dream made up of fragments from all over the world. Domes and minarets mingled with huts from northern climes, the massive solemnity of Egypt was cheek by jowl with the neatness of Holland, and Russia bordered on the Tyrol. It was delightful to wander through this dreamlike landscape, which was as pret-

tily colored as a picture-book. Inside the Exhibition Palace the
picture-book gave way to a grammar, the confusion to a sys-
tematic survey of the accomplishments of European civilization,
extending from Krupp's guns to the war of science against deadly
bacteria, from Millet's pictures to the new light metal, aluminum.
As a result of the current democratic trend, special attention was
paid to labor problems and to the efforts being made to raise the
standard of living of the lower classes. Here and there statistical
information was impressively displayed, showing that even then
the gift of turning such material to the purposes of government
and industrial propaganda was well developed.

The innumerable cafés and restaurants that surrounded the
Exhibition Palace employed orchestras of every nationality, as
if to drown the noise of the machines. One of them was a Prussian orchestra, which played Viennese waltzes and was conducted
by Johann Strauss. He was still so little known that no one paid
any particular attention to them. In order to help him Princess
von Metternich invited him to play at a ball at the Austrian Embassy, which was attended by the Imperial couple and the whole
Gerolstein court. Strauss played his waltzes to the light of lamps
shining from flower-baskets suspended from the ceiling, while
an artificial fountain played over rocks that were wreathed in
roses. In spite of this it is unlikely that he would have come to
the top had not Villemessant chanced one day to enter the restaurant where he was playing. *"Elle est bien bonne,"* Villemessant said to himself, listening to the music. He was at the zenith
of his power and had his finger in every pie. He took the leading
members of his staff up in a captive balloon, turned Baden-Baden
upside down, and lent brilliance to the fashionable life that was
beginning to flourish upon the Riviera. It was a mere trifle for
him to launch Johann Strauss. A few articles in *Le Figaro* and a
soirée in honor of his new protégé, to which he invited people
like Flaubert and Turgeniev, and the thing was done. The world
was at Strauss's feet. Encouraged by this success, Strauss was em-

boldened to present his *Blue Danube Waltz,* which had met with a disappointing reception in Vienna. Paris received it with enthusiasm and called it " the waltz of waltzes."

Paris was full of music. Another Viennese who had arrived in time for the first night of *The Grand Duchess of Gerolstein* was Offenbach's friend Eduard Hanslick. He had come to judge the international musical competitions held in connection with the exposition. At Offenbach's house, to which he was a frequent visitor, he saw no trace of " the frivolity always mentioned in connection with his name." On the contrary, the impression that Offenbach made on him was that of an excellent family man. He was introduced to his daughters, who were grown-up young ladies now and had long since grown used to attending the traditional Friday evenings. Towards midnight they helped with the cold refreshments. They good-humoredly tolerated their father's raptures about the music of *The Grand Duchess of Gerolstein* and took a great interest in his collaboration with Meilhac.

" Offenbach would sit at the piano and sing to his librettist the music he had composed the day before. Now he would find there were four lines too few, and Meilhac would write them; now he would want two lines deleted, but Meilhac would maintain they were absolutely essential. When one was unwilling to sacrifice his music and the other his lines, the discussions were apt to become very lively. But they always agreed in the end."

The house in the rue Laffitte was one of the few oases in the midst of the tumult that *The Grand Duchess of Gerolstein* helped to swell. " It was impossible to open a paper without seeing accounts of banquets of every kind," a contemporary writer states; and, according to Rochefort, " Paris has been called the head of France, but all that it shows of France is — legs." Many of them gathered at a party in the Bois at which Cora Pearl and Julia Barucci were the leading spirits. Each female guest was greeted on arrival by the blowing of six hunting-horns, the orchestra alternately played selections from *The Grand Duchess of Gerolstein* and Strauss's waltzes, and a brilliant display of fireworks

GUSTAVE FLAUBERT
by Eugène Girard

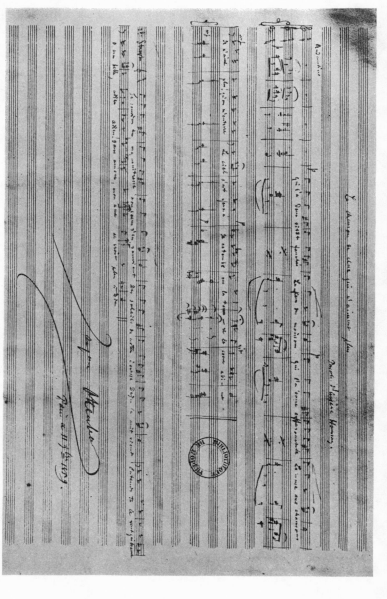

AUTOGRAPH AND MUSICAL MANUSCRIPT OF OFFENBACH

Courtesy, Rischgitz

took place while couples rowed on the lake in the darkness.

The Gondremarcks and the Brazilians had their money's worth. They were fleeced at the restaurants and robbed by the prostitutes, whose numbers had been increased by one-third owing to an influx from the provinces. The international medical congress for the combating of sexual diseases which was then in session in Paris had no cause to complain of lack of material.

La Païva, believing it to be her duty to entertain literary celebrities in her palace on the Champs-Élysées, kept away from the madding throng. When she inadvertently exposed herself to an unfavorable light, creases like black furrows appeared in her heavily powdered face, and her visitors felt they were in the company of a dolled-up corpse.

All this seething activity took place against the superb background of Haussmann's Paris. Foreigners never ceased admiring its perspectives and its monuments. Twelve avenues radiated from the Arc de Triomphe. Two lovely parks adorned the poorer quarters. On August 15, the national holiday, on which day the politically inconvenient *Grand Duchess* was compelled to cease its run, the pompous façade of the new Opéra, the erection of which the Emperor had commanded many years before, was unveiled. Plenty of other things were only façade too. Haussmann had developed such a mania for prodigality that the greatest sleight-of-hand was required to conceal the bankruptcy of the city's finances, and neither the twelve avenues nor the two parks were sufficient to reconcile the workers to the increase in rents and the rise in the cost of living that were the consequence of his megalomania.

1867, the year of the Universal Exposition, drew towards its close.

By September all the princes and potentates had departed, and Paris became the playground of the smaller fry, who arrived in multitudes from the provinces and abroad. They stared at the female mummy in the Egyptian pavilion, who was nearly two thousand five hundred years old and was no longer surprised at anything, swarmed over the Boulevards, the *quais,* and the places of amusement, and made a terrible noise everywhere.

About this time Dr. Véron died, but in the tumult nobody took any notice. He left two and a half million francs, a tidy sum earned mainly by his newspapers and the legs of the *corps de ballet.*

In October the Emperor Francis Joseph of Austria arrived in Paris, and, greatly to the vexation of Hortense Schneider, was the only monarch who failed to see *The Grand Duchess of Gerolstein.* He was in mourning for Maximilian, but he subsequently heard the operetta in Vienna.

The time for stock-taking had come. The Universal Exposition had been visited by about ten million people, including fifty-seven ruling monarchs and royal princes. But a bitter taste remained. An anonymous South German stated that the princes and people of Europe had had an opportunity of seeing how corrupt and demoralized the French Government was and that the country was in a state of ferment. There was a similar uneasy feeling among the Parisians themselves. " Everyone is afraid, without really knowing why," said Prosper Mérimée. Michel Chevalier, another victim of this feeling of uneasiness, said the exposition was like a bright meteor in a sky about to be rent by a thunderstorm. The Government felt uneasy too, but all it could think of was to take steps against the First International.

Hortense Schneider's stock-taking was more pleasing. She was now provided for for life, but she found the peace and quiet that descended upon her after the captains and the kings had departed so intolerable, though it was broken by a few tours, that she allowed the banker Raphael Bischoffsheim to give parties and dinners for her that were attended by the director of the Opéra and many influential journalists. She dreamed of still greater glory and still larger salaries, and the result of her dreams was her engagement at the Châtelet, where her salary was as fabulous as the pantomime in which she appeared. But as her voice was lost in the enormous auditorium and the very mixed audiences showed insufficient appreciation of her, this interlude in her career lasted only two months, after which, as mentioned before, she ruefully returned to the Variétés and the world of fashionable Bohemia.

Meanwhile Offenbach composed incessantly, without allowing the exposition to distract him. No sooner had he finished two *bouffonneries* (*La Permission de dix heures* and *La Leçon de chant*) for the little theater at Ems than he started writing a real comic opera, *Robinson Crusoe,* for the Opéra-Comique. It went one better than Defoe's version, and included a Hedwig Robinson, who follows Defoe's hero, only to fall into the hands of savages. During the rehearsals Offenbach had to be carried from his carriage to the stage because of a severe attack of gout. His enemies, who poured volleys of abuse upon the " offenbachism " by which Europe was enthralled, hoped it would be as great a failure as *Barkouf* had been. But they were disappointed, because the piece, which was produced at the end of November, was favorably received. Nevertheless, it fell far short of being the great success of which Offenbach had dreamed almost since boyhood. His revised version of *Geneviève* was produced at the Théâtre des Menus-Plaisirs in December, and at the year's end four revues extolled his triumph at the Variétés.

1867, the year of *The Grand Duchess of Gerolstein,* represented the last sunset glory of the Second Empire.

CHAPTER XII

VIVE LA RÉPUBLIQUE!

THE RISE of Offenbach and the beginning of the evolution of his genre, the operetta, had coincided with the Universal Exposition of 1855. With the Universal Exposition of 1867, in which the Second Empire appeared in all its glory for the last time before it collapsed, the decline of the *offenbachiade* began. Its heyday lay between these two events, both of which encouraged the international spirit. The operetta's zenith was inseparable from Louis Napoleon's dictatorship, and when the dictatorship collapsed, the operetta's day was over.

To be sure, Eugène Pelletan's protest against " the inferior art of the operetta," made in the Corps Législatif in the summer of 1867, when the exposition was in progress, seemed to die away ineffectually. *The Grand Duchess of Gerolstein* triumphed in New York, and in Paris Offenbach's name did not vanish from the boards. In the consciousness of his power Offenbach occasionally contented himself with calling on his reserves. If his operetta *Le Château à Toto,* a satire on the degenerate nobility, with words by Meilhac and Halévy, produced at the Palais Royal in May 1868, had a cool reception, it was because the music was already familiar. It was followed by a one-act curtain-raiser, *L'Île de Tulipatan,* which, with an old *bouffonnerie* he had originally produced at Ems, served to open the winter season at the Bouffes. This was minor work, as usual very popular. More ambitious was *La Périchole,* a comic opera produced at the Variétés on October 6. It was this piece that made it clear that times had changed.

The plot was suggested to Meilhac and Halévy by a one-act play of Mérimée's, *Le Carrosse du Saint-Sacrement.* The heroine was Périchole, a street-singer, who wanders about the country-side with her beloved Piquille, without any success at all. The Viceroy of Peru sees her and falls in love at first sight. But as the peculiar etiquette of his court prevents him from taking any but married women into his palace, it is necessary to find her a husband quickly. Périchole agrees to accompany him solely for the sake of getting a good meal. During the search for a suitable person to marry her, the Viceroy's emissaries chance upon Piquille, who, after receiving Périchole's letter of farewell, is about to commit suicide in despair. They ply him with drink and take him with them, and he fails to recognize Périchole in his drunkenness. The point of the whole thing is that in spite of all the piquant situations that develop, all ends happily and Périchole continues her journeyings with Piquille unharmed. It is all utterly remote from reality, and fresh charm is given to the traditional court satire by the play that is made with the comedy of royalty incognito. The people with whom the Viceroy mixes know exactly who he is and scrupulously refrain from telling him the truth.

Hortense Schneider was meant to play Périchole. After her unfortunate excursion to the Châtelet, she had played *La Belle Hélène* at the St. James's Theatre in London, to the delight of the Prince of Wales and other notabilities. From there she had gone to Baden, where it was the custom to dally and flirt in the park between dinner and going to the gambling-tables. One evening she found she had lost a bracelet, worth twenty thousand francs, and her laments were so grievous that all thought of flirting was forgotten. Lanterns were fetched, search parties were organized, and finally a Grand Duke found the bracelet lying on the grass in a distant corner. The ease with which he found it was, of course, considered very suspicious.

Hortense signed her contract with the Variétés on the express condition that Mlle Silly was never again to play in the same cast with her. The banishment of her hated rival did not, of course, prevent her from making the usual difficulties during rehearsals. Out of sheer caprice she refused to sing some of her lines aloud, and upon Offenbach's cleverly calculated threat to give her part to one of her rivals she threw her lines over the heads of the orchestra into the front seats and announced that she was going to Italy next day. Next day she was, of course, in her place again as usual.

The operetta was undoubtedly very successful, particularly the first act, although theatrically it was almost overloaded. Not a little of its success was due to the letter of farewell that Périchole wrote to Piquille, from which Hortense Schneider extracted every ounce of mournful sentiment. The music was reminiscent of Mozart, and the words were a versification of Manon Lescaut's letter in Prévost's famous novel. It can be compared only to the song of Fortunio or the letter to Metella in *La Vie parisienne*. It was no accident that Offenbach found inspiration in love-letters; for in these the beloved one, like paradise, is close and at the same time remote. The refrain of the duet: " *Il grandira, car il est espagnol*," was also memorable. The less dramatic second act had some slow passages, which were deleted immediately after the first night.

But in spite of all this, all was not well. Périchole's letter received more applause from the gallery than from the stalls, and there was no doubt that the world of fashion was a little reserved in its reception of the piece. They did not feel inclined towards emotion, nor did it suit them that Périchole turned away from frivolity to sing of faithful love. Finally, the eternal musical parodies which Offenbach apparently found indispensable were a trifle tedious. Parody of grand opera had lost its point, because of the democratic inroads made upon society, which was no longer a closed group centered on the Opéra; moreover, the operetta was becoming more opera-like itself, and thus the ground for its satire was cut from beneath its feet.

The existence of a critical undercurrent was shown by the friendly notice written by Tarbé, the implication of which was that Offenbach needed defending against the charge of repeating himself. " Offenbach's music is clothed in a robe of moirée, the colors of which are always changing. It is always the same robe, but never the same reflection," Tarbé wrote. Sarcey expressed himself less courteously, and his remarks betrayed that the public was beginning to tire of operetta. He said that court satire was somewhat outmoded, and summarily declared that the day of Offenbach's great operettas was over and done with and that all that would survive of it would be the one-act operetta, which was nothing but " our old friend the *vaudeville* adorned with a lot of new tunes."

Sarcey's words announced the decline of operetta. Indeed, in so far as the *offenbachiade* was a socially conditioned phenomenon, which to a large extent it was, after the Universal Exposition of 1867 it was bound to fade away. It had originated in an epoch in which social reality had been banished by the Emperor's orders, and for many years it had flourished in the gap that was left. Thoroughly ambiguous as it was, it had fulfilled a revolutionary function under the dictatorship: that of scourging corruption and authoritarianism, and holding up the principle of freedom. To be sure, its satire had been clothed in a garment of frivolity and concealed in an atmosphere of intoxication, in accordance with the requirements of the Second Empire. But the frivolity went deeper than the world of fashionable Bohemia could see.

At a time when the bourgeoisie were politically stagnant and the Left was impotent, Offenbach's operettas had been the most definite form of revolutionary protest. It released gusts of laughter, which shattered the compulsory silence and lured the public towards opposition, while seeming only to amuse them.

During the second half of Louis Napoleon's reign it became ever clearer that the operettas were something more than harmless pieces of entertainment. There was a threat behind the glitter of *La Belle Hélène,* and *The Grand Duchess of Gerolstein* earned the Emperor a painful reputation. The more the unreality of the Imperial structure was revealed, the more manifest the reality of the *offenbachiade* became, but the more superfluous it became as a political instrument. For, with the decay of the dictatorship and the growth of the Left opposition, social forces whose place had been taken by Offenbach's operettas came into play once more. The isolated social stratum in which it had prospered broke up into its component parts, and reality drove the operetta away.

From 1868 onwards this process could no longer be delayed. In that year the Emperor once more made concessions; he granted some of the workers' demands, he guaranteed the freedom of the press and freedom of assembly. It was too late. Economics dragged politics irresistibly in their wake, and the masses revived the republican aspirations for which they had longed and fought — aspirations renounced again and again during the past century.

Profiting by the freedom of the press, Rochefort's *La Lanterne,* which created great popularity for the republican cause, appeared as the vanguard of innumerable radical sheets. Villemessant helped to finance it, because Rochefort was too great a burden for *Le Figaro.* Was it political conviction that drove Rochefort, vaudevillist and gambler, into the revolutionary camp? His hatred of the Emperor equaled that of Victor Hugo and resulted in a remorseless onslaught of articles, epigrams, and reflections, illuminated by a gambler's passion and sharpened by a vaudevillist's wit. *La Lanterne* waged a guerrilla warfare on the Empire which damaged its prestige enormously. The paper's success surpassed all expectations. Its red cover was to be seen everywhere, in the street, in cabs, and in railway cars. After two or three months Rochefort made France too hot to hold him, and he fled to Belgium, from where he succeeded in smuggling the paper across the border, so that the flame was kept burning brightly.

The older generation of republicans remembered the battles they had fought for democracy in 1830 and 1848, and students became enthusiastic for the Great Revolution and made contact with the proletariat, which had started demanding the application of revolutionary methods. " Blood must flow again, you see," a workman said to Jules Vallès. And behind the political opposition, strengthening it, gathered all the dissatisfied people who hoped to avenge and compensate themselves for the hapless lives they led.

Once the revolutionary elements had been granted a limited freedom of speech, there broke forth torrents of argument and oratory at meetings that generally ended with curses for the Emperor and panegyrics for Socialism, notwithstanding the presence of Imperial police commissaries. Thus the soil was favorable for the reception of Eugène Ténot's book about the *coup d'état,* eulogizing the long-forgotten republican deputy Baudin, who had lost his life on the barricades as a pioneer of bourgeois freedom. Baudin became a martyr; and the newspaper *Le Réveil* opened a subscription fund to erect a monument in his memory. Other papers followed suit. The Government thereupon took proceedings against them, and there was a rich harvest of newspaper cases in the law-courts. Delescluze, the editor of *Le Réveil,* chose a thirty-year-old lawyer to defend him, and the defense turned into a public attack on Napoleon III. The lawyer's name was Léon Gambetta.

It would have been impossible for the operetta to have retained its old power in those agitated years. The circles which feared an upheaval had lost their former levity and high spirits, and the republicans had always wrongly regarded Offenbach as a representative of the Imperial regime. Now, when they felt things were really going to happen, they considered the operetta to be nothing but one of the Empire's evil products. From their point of view frivolity was immoral, and satire merely idle jesting, and from their point of view they were, of course, quite right.

The world of fashionable Bohemia was itself decaying. A new generation had sprung up that preferred the Maison Dorée to the Café Anglais, and the *grand seize* began to be neglected.

Offenbach was to feel the change, though not, perhaps, in *Vert-Vert,* a comic opera, with which he once more tempted fate at the Opéra-Comique on March 10, 1869.

The plot was laid in a boarding-school for young ladies, and, what with the charming music that Offenbach wrote for the dancing-lesson scenes, and its flappers, officers of dragoons, and romantic assignations, it was more favorably received than *Robinson Crusoe*. But it was only a seasonal success, and Offenbach was criticized for trying to elevate a *vaudeville* into a comic opera. This kind of criticism accorded with Offenbach's previous experiences at the Opéra-Comique and had nothing to do with the changed conditions of the time.

But the failure of *La Diva*, which opened at the Bouffes only two weeks later, came as a surprise. In *La Diva* Offenbach, Meilhac, and Halévy, keeping a promise they had made to Hortense Schneider, put her life-story on the stage. The plot concerned a little milliner who, after wanting to poison herself because of unrequited love, becomes a famous star of operetta, in whose dressing-room scenes take place such as occurred in that of the Grand Duchess of Gerolstein. So that the traditional tragedy of the comic actor's lot may be preserved, she has to renounce her love in the end. Two years earlier this operetta would have caused a sensation. Now its piquancies were received with yawns, and its allusions found no response among the public for whom they were intended. Perhaps because Mlle Silly was in the audience, Hortense Schneider herself was given a hostile reception, and her final lines were actually hissed. "I saw *La Diva* at the Bouffes," a reporter wrote in *La Vie parisienne*. "I did not laugh as I used to. We want something new. Ten years! That is a long time, when you come to think of it. What a lot of things Paris uses up in ten years!" Sardou's *La Patrie* was produced on the same evening and was a tremendous success, and not long afterwards Thérésa sang the *Marseillaise* at a private house instead of her usual popular songs.

In marked contrast to the decline of Offenbach was the harvest now reaped by other operetta-composers. Hervé, who had taken a back seat, wrote works such as *L'Œil crevé, Chilpéric*, and *Le Petit Faust*, which in spite of their satirical content played to packed houses in the years that followed the Universal Exposition.

Hervé had been Offenbach's predecessor in the *bouffonnerie,* but he showed his indebtedness to Offenbach in his big operettas. In Blanche d'Antigny he found an actress who seemed almost a new edition of Hortense Schneider, and this made it look even more probable that he would supplant Offenbach. She was an exuberant blonde with sapphire-blue eyes and a robust constitution capable of standing up to the greatest exertions. Like the heroine of *La Diva,* she had started as a midinette, and the first stage of her career was spent as mistress of a highly placed personage in St. Petersburg. One day she turned up in the Bois in a real Russian troika driven by a real Russian muzhik. Her ambition was to play in operetta. As she had not only a troika but some excellent letters of introduction, to say nothing of considerable native talents and an attractive personality, all doors were speedily opened to her. Nestor Roqueplan entertained her in his box at the Opéra, and Henri de Pène introduced her to the Palais Royal, where her debut in *La Château à Toto* was so successful that she made up her mind never to return to St. Petersburg. The high-spirited eccentricities of Hervé's operettas might have been specially created for her. Her Frédégonde contributed substantially to the success of *Chilpéric,* and her Marguerite in *Le Petit Faust* was a real triumph. She became the center of a clique of *cocodès,* who adored her because of the way she threw money about and because she swore like a trooper. In her rare moments of leisure she devoted herself to the pursuit of knowledge. Her favorite reading was a series of elegantly bound history books, which she studied in the belief that her impersonations of historical characters would benefit.

The fame which Hervé gained with his operettas right at the end of the Second Empire was mainly due to their farcical character. The nonsense in which they luxuriated was an irresistible attraction to the vulgar public, while the fundamental sense of Offenbach's operettas alienated them.

Another who scored his first real success in 1868 was Lecocq, whose rancor against Offenbach dated from the operetta competition in the early days of the Bouffes. The operetta he wrote now, *Fleur-de-thé,* the scene of which was set in China, was as devoid as all Hervé's were of that direct and critical bearing to reality that distinguished the works of Offenbach. Hervé's graceful and pleasant music left things as it found them; Offenbach's showed them up. Hervé, however, had the mortification of finding that he had a long way to go before dethroning his rival. He tells us himself that a lady in the audience at *Fleur-de-thé* exclaimed: "Oh, that Offenbach! Only he could write such music!"

A celebrity like Offenbach was not easy to dislodge. Did he himself realize that the situation had changed to his disadvantage? In any case he tried to adapt himself to it, with the same instinct with which he always responded to changes in his social environment. After *The Grand Duchess of Gerolstein* the form and content of his operettas altered. He started dropping contemporary satire and sought to approach the comic-opera form, thus tending in the same direction as Lecocq. *La Périchole* had shown the way that he was going. *La Princesse de Trébizonde,* produced at Baden at the end of July 1869, resembled it in style. In it he plunged into a fantasy world, something between a waxwork show and a prince's court, with tyrannical fathers and amorous sons and daughters, and music that really only he could have written. His comedy, his sensibility, his happy melodies remained, and thus he felt proof against catastrophe.

He was often to be seen strolling through the park at Baden on his way to rehearsals, in yellow trousers and waistcoat, a light-blue velvet coat, gray gloves, and a gray hat, looking like a grotesque character escaped from one of his own operettas. Friends came specially from Paris to see his latest work, and the applause sounded the same as in the past.

Encouraged by this success, which was to be repeated in Paris and Vienna, for a time it seemed to Offenbach that he would survive the changes going on around him unaffected. He went on happily composing as before and was full of plans. He seemed to be protected by a sure shield.

Of course he continually peeped out from behind it; with his impressionable temperament, sensitive to every wind that blew on the Boulevards, that was inevitable. Politics were in the foreground, so he, too, interested himself in politics. Not only did he start making political statements the hair-raising naïveté of which secretly caused Halévy the most intense amusement, but he actually started regular political intrigues. In order to help his brother-in-law Robert Mitchell, who was a journalist and a supporter of Ollivier's, he one day invited Ollivier to dinner. Ollivier accepted the invitation and sang his own praises the whole evening, talking as continuously as a waterfall. It was a real political dinner. The scene would have been worthy of an operetta.

Innocent as Offenbach was in political matters, he automatically tended, so far as his conscious political position was concerned, to side loyally with the bourgeoisie. He, who had done more than anyone else to destroy the Empire from within, now desired the maintenance of the very state of affairs that in his music he had continually undermined. Incidentally, a fact of which he could not possibly have failed to be aware was that he owed his world fame to the dictatorship and bourgeois society, and this made his aversion to the revolution all the greater; and this state of mind resulted in his collaborating with Victorien Sardou in a work of reactionary tendency entitled *Le Roi Carotte*. Its composition, however, was interrupted by the war.

The material for the libretto was taken from one of E. T. A. Hoffmann's tales, *Kleinzaches, genannt Zinnober*. Sardou's intention was to show the dangers resulting from Louis Napoleon's policy. King Fridolin, the hero of the play, whom he made very like the Emperor in some respects, tries to extricate himself from his very grave difficulties by favoring the radicals instead of the bourgeoisie. But no sooner are the radicals in power when they chase him from the throne and usurp the power themselves under the leadership of their Red King Carrot and of course lead the country to disaster. The moral was laid on very thick. Sardou, as a skilled dramatist, added a final climax in which King Fridolin, purified by exile, returns as his country's savior.

Fortunately Offenbach's family life remained unaffected by all this political excitement, and in August 1869 he celebrated his silver wedding at Étretat by an enormous dinner party, ending with a masked ball, for which he composed a march for forty reed pipes. Herminie and he appeared in the costume of a village bride and bridegroom. All his old friends were present, and there were fireworks and the night was filled with laughter and music. Even the gout did not desert him on this occasion.

That same summer Halévy saw a vision that deeply affected him and cast a light upon the darkness of the time. It happened in June.

Noisy demonstrations, the revolutionary character of which it was impossible to deny, took place in the streets in connection with the elections — the elections at which Rochefort and Gambetta gained places in Parliament. Dense masses of people, predominantly the rabble of the streets, surged along the Boulevards on evening after evening, and their attitude was so threatening that the smallest incident might have led to open revolt. On one of these evenings Halévy attended a performance of *Faust* at the Opéra, but was unable to pay attention to it because the tumult outside was still resounding in his ears. So he left his seat and went behind the stage and looked out into the street from one of the windows.

Below him was a forest of heads, which opened to make way for a shining regiment of cavalry hurrying to the Boulevards, and as though there were a secret connection between Gounod's opera and the events in the street, the music of the Soldiers' Chorus mingled with the noise of the horses' hoofs. A little later and it came to blows. Hats and helmets started flying, clothes and uniforms were torn to tatters, and in the midst of the mêlée a terrified woman started letting forth the most blood-curdling screams. Not being able to bear the sight another moment, Halévy returned to his seat. The boxes were filled with glittering diamonds and jaunty epaulets. The stage represented the interior of a sumptuous palace, in which sixty lovely girls were dancing. Halévy asked himself in dismay which was the illusion and which the reality.

Perhaps in his perturbation he recalled an episode of his childhood. In February 1848 he had been taken for a walk by his grandfather and had talked jubilantly about the proclamation of the Republic. His grandfather had sat down on a curbstone, and said: "You don't know what a republic means, my boy. I have seen a republic." Now he knew what it was that his grandfather had seen; and he also knew that the republican advance-guard was skirmishing again, and that once more the old forces that had so often gathered round the figure of Liberty were at work.

"Liberty leads the people." The old picture of Delacroix that had been acclaimed by the throng after the Revolution of July 1830 once more rose before his eyes. Which was the dream and which the reality? The fine palace and the elegant audience had been pushed out of the picture. It was no longer a picture, but vivid reality. The scene with all its characters rose almost tangibly before his eyes; Liberty, striding over the corpses and uprooted paving-stones, in one hand a musket, in the other holding aloft the tricolor; the smoke-blackened street-boy by her side with his two pistols, shouting: "*Vive la République!*" and on the ground the workman in blue blouse and red beret, gazing with dying eyes upon the figure of Liberty, who heeds him not, but goes forward to the assault, trampling diamonds and epaulets beneath her feet.

Halévy's vision at the Opéra was merely a crystallization of feelings and premonitions that had caused him two years previously to abandon the world of operetta and collaborate with Meilhac in writing a play, *Froufrou,* which did not, however, appear until the end of October 1869, at the Gymnase. "This success will no doubt cause MM. Meilhac and Halévy to renounce the intolerable genre of the comic operetta for a long time,"

Sarcey prophesied. This prophecy was not, however, fulfilled, although Halévy set *Froufrou* above all his operettas and was deeply gratified by its extraordinary success. *Froufrou* was the first important non-musical play written by the two librettists and was a serious attempt to cater for the seriousness of the times. *Les Filles de marbre* had introduced the age of the courtesan, and *Froufrou* marked its end.

Froufrou is a spoiled, frivolous wife who tries to escape from her real feelings and the difficulties that have arisen in her marriage by fleeing to Venice with her lover. But now comes the turning-point. The frivolity which was the *leitmotiv* of the operettas of Offenbach is abandoned, and it seems as though the marble daughters of joy of 1853 have melted at last. Instead of succumbing to the intoxicating charm of Venice, Froufrou breaks down under the perpetual, ever growing strain of knowing that her life is ruined, and finally she returns to her family, a dying woman. The grim and gloomy background of the Second Empire is laid bare and its self-destruction allegorically anticipated.

The Emperor and Empress went to see *Froufrou* in December. The Empress had just returned from Egypt, where she had attended the ceremonial opening of the Suez Canal and had been able to delude herself that the Empire was intact and the revolution only a nightmare. Did she perhaps identify herself with Froufrou and fear an early end herself? She sobbed so desperately that the rouge ran down her face, and she dared not show herself after the curtain fell.

With his thoughts still full of *Froufrou,* Halévy gave only a few words in his diary to the first performance of *Les Brigands,* which took place at the Variétés just before the new year. Apart from a few characters and episodes, it was not particularly original, but it was gay and certainly entertaining. If Halévy had not grown tired of operetta, he would undoubtedly have had more to say about this latest work of Offenbach, the libretto of which was once more by Meilhac and himself. For in *Les Brigands* the spirit of the *offenbachiade* shone at its brightest once more, in spite of the fact that it was not so much an operetta as a comic opera.

The change was noticed by the critics. *Le Figaro* described *Les Brigands* as " a marriage of convenience between comic operetta and the style of the Opéra-Comique," and attributed the development to the composer's intention of ennobling the genre to which he owed his popularity and success. That the change of style was deliberate is shown by Offenbach's instructions to his librettists to concentrate on scenes and situations as a whole rather than on dialogues and songs; in short, to write a libretto that lent itself to dramatic musical treatment.

" I want to put situations to music," he wrote to Halévy during the composition of *Les Brigands,* " and not to pile songs on songs as in *Toto* or *La Diva*. The public is tired of little tunes, and so am I." Since his first youth he had longed for the Opéra-Comique and aspired to dramatizing whole scenes with his music. It was only now that his longing was realized.

Les Brigands was by no means a complete departure from the *offenbachiade*. It was at once comic opera and operetta, the two living side by side on equal terms and in complete harmony. They were fused and intermingled in a remarkable manner. Operatic romanticism about brigands, of which the pattern and archetype is *Fra Diavolo,* is amalgamated with a satire typical of the earlier operettas.

The object of the satire is the world of finance. Pietro, former companion of the robber chieftain Falsacappa, starts telling a story of brigandage with the words: " Once upon a time there was a great financier." " Well, what next? " asks Falsacappa's daughter. " That is all," said Pietro. Everyone immediately thought of Mirès; and the *bon mot* let fall by one of the bandits, who said that " one must steal according to the position one occupies in society," was highly appreciated. The witticisms mainly centered in the fraudulent cashier whose peculations fail to bring him to disaster because most of the other " honorable " characters turn out to be just as great rogues as he is.

But all this jesting is overshadowed by the satire at the expense of the gendarmes, one of the most biting satires for which Offenbach was ever responsible. While the bandits celebrate an orgy, carabineers' footsteps are heard in the distance. " Tramp, tramp, tramp! " the bandits sing, now loudly, now softly, concealing themselves in the woods as the carabineers approach. When the guardians of the law finally appear, they themselves announce that unfortunately they always arrive too late. At this point the music becomes quite extraordinarily expressive. Not only does it make game of pompous officialdom and the hollow authority of the state, but it indicates the terror which the exercise of the latter can instill. The tramp of the carabineers' boots echoes like a ghostly refrain throughout the piece, and, as they are never on the spot where they are wanted, the effect is extremely comic. But at the same time the fact that they are always in the background raises an uneasy fear that one day perhaps they might be on the spot when they were wanted.

As Hortense Schneider was staying in Egypt with Ismail Pasha, whose attentions did not prevent her from turning the head of Theodore, Emperor of Abyssinia, Offenbach gave the part of the bandit chief's charming daughter to his favorite, Zulma Bouffar. Léonce, who had taken part in Offenbach's early *bouffonneries,* played the part of the cashier in this, the last real operetta. The march of the carabineers, who all wore boots of exaggerated size, made such an impression on people's minds that at a fancy-dress ball given by Jules Verne in 1877 the appearance of some " Offenbach's carabineers " created general amusement.

" Tramp, tramp, tramp! " Events followed one another in rapid succession, proclaiming now loudly, now softly, the coming of Nemesis.

The murderer Troppmann, whose bestial crime was regarded by the revolutionaries as a symptom of the moral degeneration caused by the Empire, was the talk of Paris for weeks. At the beginning of 1870 Émile Ollivier was entrusted by the Emperor with the formation of a Cabinet. His task was to complete the process of liberal reform and take the ground from under the feet of the revolutionary movement by setting up a parliamentary regime. It was one of those belated attempts to save the situation that always precede a convulsion. One of Ollivier's first acts was to dismiss Haussmann, one of the relics of the dictatorship. The Emperor parted with him with a heavy heart. Haussmann had preserved Paris from destruction by partly destroying it. *Rentes* went up, and Ollivier had the bourgeoisie behind him. Then a fateful incident occurred which roused new excitement.

Victor Noir, an excellent young man who was a follower of Rochefort, was shot by mistake by Prince Pierre Bonaparte, to whom he brought a challenge to a duel. Thereupon Rochefort started preaching armed revolt in his paper *La Marseillaise,* which was supported by the First International. No revolt, however, took place, and the storm died down.

Peaceful events held the center of the stage in the months that followed. One of them was a charity performance of *The Grand Duchess of Gerolstein* during the carnival at Nice at the beginning of February. Added glamour was given to this event by the fact that Hortense Schneider took part in it, having just returned from Egypt. Offenbach had been on the point of leaving for Vienna, but Hortense Schneider sent him a telegram, and he left at once for Nice, to conduct in person. When he took his place at the conductor's desk he reminded the spectators of Paganini, with his hair and side-chops billowing in the breeze from the cellos and his ill-fitting clothes hanging loosely round his gaunt frame. He looked as pale as a corpse and conducted as absent-mindedly as though he were suffering from a secret sorrow. Had he grown tired of comedy? Had *The Tales of Hoffmann* started haunting him?

The restlessness that drove him from place to place, from work to work, barely gave him time to breathe. Scarcely had he re-

turned to Paris from Vienna when he gave a gala supper at the
Grand Hotel to all the actors and actresses who had played in
his operettas. Hortense Schneider, Thérésa, and Blanche d'Antigny were present. After this festivity he devoted himself to the
composition of a comic opera, *Fantasio,* after Musset's comedy
of the same name, at Saint-Germain. He would presumably have
continued at this rate had he not broken down from exhaustion.
The doctors prescribed complete rest; and at Étretat he had to
give in and try to do nothing for a time.

About this time Halévy spent some months listening intently
to the tireless chatter in which the mothers of the ballet dancers
engaged in the labyrinthine corridors of the Opéra, and he was
greatly astonished at the things he learned — the mothers' naïve
pride at their daughters' aristocratic admirers; the curious attitude of the petty-bourgeois fathers, who as virtuous republicans
regarded extra-marital relationships with horror, but shut one
eye in order not to lose the material advantages derived there-
from; and the daughters themselves, trying out of filial affection
to placate their difficult fathers, while dreaming of a happy family
life with their protector of the moment.

Behind the scenes at the Opéra, Halévy discovered a world
with a morality of its own, a morality that was behind the scenes
of official, everyday morality. In the past he would undoubtedly
have used it as material for an operetta, but now he made a
story of it, which appeared in *La Vie parisienne* under the title
of *Madame Cardinal.* This was yet another proof that the operetta's day was done. In an operetta it would have been impossible for him to have restated his conviction, now reinforced by
his observation of these fathers, mothers, and daughters at the
Opéra, that it was not the façade of ideals that mattered, but the
real, human material behind. This conviction seemed doubly important to him in view of the political strife by which the country
was torn, and he wrote *Madame Cardinal* to point this moral.
That this kind of political indifference put a weapon into the
hands of the reactionaries was inevitable.

Nestor Roqueplan, who had been the idol of the Boulevards since the days of Louis-Philippe, died at the end of April. Not a few of Dr. Véron's cronies and former habitués of the Café de Paris had preceded him. Roger de Beauvoir had died paralyzed, neglected, and poverty-stricken in a dreary room. Lautour-Mézeray and Malitourne had ended by losing their reason. They and others of their sort learned that one cannot dine too well and drink too much champagne without paying the penalty. A premature and wretched death was the reward for the thoughtless squandering of their money and their spirit. The horror of their end equaled the brilliance of their youth. All these dandies and clubmen had drunk so heavily that their pockets were empty when the head waiter finally presented the bill. Those that survived might have been shocked for a moment at Roqueplan's death. But most of them, never having learned anything, were incapable of learning now. It was too late. They had just lived and mistaken life for one of the operettas that they loved. The ranks of the *cocodès* of the *grand seize* were already beginning to thin, as a result of illness and ruin which overtook many of them. Some had committed suicide, others were fighting in Africa, others were to eke out an existence at the gambling-tables. The war with Prussia was to give some of them a welcome opportunity either to disappear or to rehabilitate themselves.

Meanwhile there was no talk of war. On the contrary, if anything the horizon looked a little clearer. Once more fortune seemed to look kindly on the Emperor, as in the years of his seizure of power. He organized a plebiscite, asking the nation whether they accepted the liberal reforms and whether they wished to be ruled by him and his heirs. The favorable result of the plebiscite, held on May 8, seemed to rejuvenate and strengthen the regime.

Prévost-Paradol had such confidence in its durability that he became a supporter of the Imperial Government and went to Washington as French Ambassador.

No sooner had he embarked than the catastrophe began, in

connection with Prince Leopold of Hohenzollern's claim to the Spanish throne, and doom descended pitilessly upon the Emperor's head.

He had allowed Eugénie to have political influence, and enabled her to have the war she wanted with Germany. What was more important, he had allowed Bismarck, who required this war in the interests of a united Germany, to grow great.

" Tramp, tramp, tramp. . . ."

Paris no longer found the Iron Chancellor's big boots enormously diverting. During the first days of the war, news came from America that Prévost-Paradol had taken his life. He had learned of the declaration of war on landing and this, coupled with the terrible heat in Washington, had affected his mind.

Halévy's grief for the mentor and friend of his youth, whom he loved almost as his own self, was mingled with his grief for France. Sadly he walked through the feverish city. False rumors roused the people to heights of giddy enthusiasm, and the *Marseillaise* was sung at all the theaters. Then the truth started penetrating from the front, and enthusiasm changed to dismay. One theater closed after another. The foyer of the Variétés, in which *Les Brigands* was played until the last moment, was turned into a military hospital.

On September 2 the Battle of Sedan sealed the military defeat of France. The Emperor capitulated at the head of his army. After his surrender he was temporarily housed in the empty castle of Bellevue and was taken to Schloss Wilhemshöhe next day. When evening came he refused to have his room lit. He sat in his chair fully clothed, looking out into the darkness. The battle was over and there was no more firing. Suddenly the sound of music came through the night — a band playing tunes very familiar to the Emperor. A German regimental band came marching by, playing Offenbach. The Emperor broke down and wept.

On September 4 a Republic was proclaimed in Paris. Eugénie fled. The Second Empire was at an end.

Entr'acte 1870

ENTR'ACTE 1870

Upon the outbreak of war Offenbach rapidly returned from Ems, where he was taking the cure, to the greater security of Étretat. Execration followed in his wake. In 1862 he had composed a patriotic song, *Dieu garde l'Empereur,* which his publisher's business acumen now caused him to republish. A number of German papers, recalling his German birth, thereupon denounced him for composing war-songs hostile to the Fatherland. Offenbach indignantly repudiated having descended to any such infamy in a letter to *Le Figaro* on August 16, 1870. In spite of his gratitude to the land of his adoption, that was a thing of which he was incapable. The *Leipziger Allgemeine Zeitung* reproduced the letter, with the observation that Offenbach's real crime against his native land was having written his operettas.

Of far greater import to him was the change of mood in France, which caused him to fear that the fall of the Empire would wreck his own career. There was no denying the hostility of the republicans towards him, or the danger that threatened him from the passions that had been roused. Paris was besieged and on the brink of starvation, seething with lampoons against Napoleon and Eugénie, while outside the desolate Variétés lucky anglers offered fat pike for sale. All forms of entertainment were banned, and Blanche d'Antigny caused such a scandal by giving charity routs at which she sold embraces at so much each that she had to restrain her patriotic ardor.

Offenbach fled from the war and from himself. He went to Bordeaux, to Milan, and then to San Sebastian, where Herminie had gone temporarily with the children. He was perpetually haunted by the thought that no one had any more use for art and music. Whether that were true or not, he was temporarily outlawed. On the occasion of a performance of *La Princesse de Trébizonde* at the Bouffes in February 1871, many people were indignant at a work by the *Prussian* Offenbach appearing on a Paris stage. Perhaps the inherent flippancy of the operetta made them more indignant still. Lecocq prophesied that operetta would be killed by Prussian shells.

After the capitulation of Paris and the conclusion of peace the Champs-Élysées were temporarily occupied by the Prussians. All the houses on the Champs-Élysées were closed, with the single exception of La Païva's palace, which remained ceremoniously and ostentatiously open. She had zealously spied for Bismarck before the war, out of hatred for the Paris society which boycotted her, and she therefore now had redoubled reason for rejoicing at the triumph of German arms.

Meanwhile Offenbach had returned to Italy. He had been prostrate, mentally and physically, for months. A letter to his friend and librettist Nuitter proves that it was less his own personal fate than the national disaster that afflicted him. The letter also reveals all his naïveté. " I hope," he wrote, " that this William Krupp and his dreadful Bismarck will pay for all this. Alas, what terrible people these Prussians are, and what despair do I feel at the thought that I myself was born on the Rhine and am connected with those savages by a number of links! Alas, my poor France, how much do I thank her for accepting me among her children! "

Those phrases show how much he had grown part of the country which had been his adopted home for nearly four decades. The love expressed in this letter sprang from feelings vastly deeper than his somewhat awkward attempts to interpret the spirit of German nationalism in 1848, and they did not conflict with his internationalism, since France had been at the head of the international movement.

When the war with Germany was over, the civil war began.

Thiers, at the head of the Government forces, opened battle upon revolutionary Paris from Versailles. After his first vain attempt to disarm the workers, the Commune was formed, a coalition of Socialist revolutionaries to which there adhered not only the workers but all the tradesmen and little shopkeepers and artisans who were crushed by their debts and wished to prevent their creditors from returning. In 1848 they had fought for the revolution too. The population of Paris, inflamed by hunger and the roar of artillery, suspected treachery behind the hasty conclusion of peace, and reactionary resolutions passed by the National Assembly, which was predominantly monarchist, had driven them to revolt. Their aim was the annihilation of reaction and the continuation of the war. The Commune decreed the complete separation of Church and State and a whole series of incisive social measures, and among other symbolical acts ordered the destruction of the Vendôme column, which they regarded as a symbol of chauvinism and nationalism.

As long as the Commune lasted, its rule in Paris was absolute, for bourgeois society had fled, together with its retinue of flunkies, cocottes, men of fashion, and intellectuals. Among the very few who remained was the aged Auber, who died in solitude, and Edmond de Goncourt, who found some slight consolation in comparing the workers to the barbarians of old. Thanks to Thiers being reinforced by a large number of prisoners of war specially released for the purpose, the forces at the disposal of the Versaillese were so overwhelming that the war, which was fought with unparalleled bitterness on both sides, could have but one outcome. The shooting of insurgents led to the shooting of hostages, and when the heroic defenders of the Commune realized that they would be able to hold out no longer, they set fire to half Paris in desperation. The massacres perpetrated by the Government troops who entered the city lasted for days. The power of the bourgeoisie was re-established.

The old life rose again from its ashes. Before the shrieks of the wounded had died away, the cafés filled with absinthe-drinkers and billiard- and domino-players. Sensation-seeking foreigners swarmed into Paris on the heels of the returning bourgeoisie. Halévy saw an English family who were very disappointed because no smoke was rising from the ruins of the Hôtel de Ville and regretted not having come a week earlier. The insurgents were sentenced, and placards and *flâneurs* once more enlivened the Paris streets. A Cook's Tour advertisement gave Jules Verne the idea of writing a story about a record journey round the world. The problem of the day was whether France was once more to be a monarchy or not. Thiers, who wished to avoid a second civil war, inclined to a kind of conservative republic.

Meanwhile Offenbach traveled. In the course of the summer he stayed in his beloved Vienna to supervise the rehearsals of *Les Brigands*. Here, where life was continuing as usual, a mystery that had plagued him since his earliest youth was solved. Now that the shadows were about him, he was ripe for such revelations. One evening, he relates, he found the street through which his carriage was passing blocked by a crowd of people who had gathered outside a low-class dance-hall, a resort of workers and soldiers. A half-famished-looking old man, who was said to be employed in the place, was lying unconscious on the pavement. His name turned out to be Rudolph Zimmer. He had once been a teacher of music, but was now reduced to menial work in this establishment. Offenbach had at last found the composer of the waltz of his childhood.

He promptly took charge of the old man and saw to it that he was given proper medical attention. Eight to ten days later, Zimmer called upon Offenbach at his hotel to thank him. Offenbach played the eight bars of the waltz that had haunted him all his life. " So there is someone who still remembers me," the old man exclaimed, much moved, " and that someone is you! " Offenbach asked him to play the whole waltz, whereupon he sat down at the piano, played the eight bars, and stopped. He had forgotten the rest. That waltz contained his history, he said as he took his departure, and it was a very sad history.

That night Offenbach had suddenly to leave Vienna, and when he returned a month later he found that Zimmer was dead. He had left him a parcel, containing the waltz, a sapphire ring, a faded envelope, and a letter written in a trembling hand, in which he told Offenbach his story. It was a story of life, death, and constancy, rather like a popular ballad. The girl whom Zimmer had loved had died just before their wedding day, and in his sorrow for her he had sunk lower and lower. The letter ended with a request to Offenbach to keep the sapphire ring, which had been the engagement ring he had given the girl, and to burn the faded envelope, which contained a lock of her hair. Offenbach complied with the request, and had the waltz published into the bargain.

No sooner had peace been re-established in Paris than he resumed his old life there. During the summer he had been a guest of the Prince of Wales at Chiswick, and the return of the victorious troops to Berlin had been celebrated by a gala performance of *La Vie parisienne*. As Europe still prized him, he believed there might yet be hope for him in Paris.

At the end of August 1871 he attended a rehearsal of a revival of *Les Brigands* at the Variétés. The chorus sang the drinking song at the end of the first act with stiff gestures and wooden voices and gossiped during the intermission about their war experiences, which they found far more absorbing than this outmoded operetta. Offenbach, who was sitting on the forestage, crippled with gout, listened to the mutilated tempi in silence. Halévy saw that he was trembling beneath his thick fur coat. He told Halévy he had not slept and felt far too dispirited to interfere. But suddenly he rose to his feet, angrily shaking his stick. "What do you think you are singing, ladies?" he exclaimed. "Start all over again. The whole finale right over again from the beginning!"

" Offenbach strode over to the conductor at the piano and started conducting himself," Halévy's description of the scene continues. " He had suddenly regained his strength and was throbbing with vigor and energy again. His old ardor and excitement had been rekindled. He started singing and shouting and startled the singers in the back row from their sleep. Then he returned once more to the forestage and went over to the left of the stage to put life into the supers. . . . A minute before he had been shivering with cold, but now he was bathed in perspiration. He took off his overcoat, flung it down on a chair, and started giving the beat with all the strength that was in him. He struck the piano so hard that his stick broke in two. With an oath he flung its stump to the ground, snatched the violin-bow from the hands of the poor conductor, who was frightened out of his life, and went on beating time with incredible force. . . . He was no longer the same man, they were no longer the same players, the same singers. And as for the finale, it suddenly bubbled over with gaiety and cheerfulness and went with tremendous swing.

" Scarcely had the last note sounded when everyone, from Mlle Aimée down to the least important super, started enthusiastically applauding Offenbach, who sank back exhausted in his seat.

" ' I've broken my stick, but I've saved my finale,' he said."

He was the old Offenbach, but Paris was not the old Paris.

Part THREE

CHAPTER I

PANTOMIMES

" ONE still enjoys oneself, but it is not the real thing," Marguérite
Bellanger, who had once been the Emperor's mistress, said sadly
to Arsène Houssaye one day soon after the war. " It is the real
thing," Houssaye replied. All the same he could not help looking back regretfully to the nights at the *grand seize,* the receptions
at Saint-Cloud, and the first nights of Offenbach.

Life did not, of course, stop still. The gay, mocking Parisian
spirit and the old love of elegance revived when the year of horror was over. As early as 1872 four plans for theaters awaited the
approval of the prefect of the Seine, and carriages lined up in
the rue de la Paix outside the establishment of Worth, the fashionable Second Empire dress-designer.

But the real spirit of the times lay not in all these revived
manifestations of gaiety, but in a new seriousness that found the
Second Empire spirit of flippancy abhorrent and tolerated no
ironic smile. Resignation was the keynote among the intellectuals. " Out of resignation I am a republican," said Halévy, who,
of course, had not been a Bonapartist either. He did not feel any
hostility towards the people. On the contrary, his sympathies lay
rather with the elementary spirit of revolt embodied in the defeated masses, as his story *L'Insurgé,* published after the war,
showed. But he had too low an opinion of the worth of political
institutions of any kind to have any hopes of the Republic. If his
pessimism was based on an ingrained skepticism towards politics,
the pessimism of Flaubert, Taine, Renan, and other representative spirits was based on what they regarded as the disadvantages

inherent in a parliamentary system based on universal suffrage. They were both repelled and attracted by it — repelled because they feared that it would lead to the triumph of bourgeois mediocrity, attracted because they felt it preferable to the yoke of the Church, which a revival of monarchy would involve. They were in a comfortless dilemma.

More far-reaching in its effect than the nihilism of a small number of intellectuals was the need of moral regeneration felt by the bourgeois masses. Jules Simon denounced the corruption of the past regime, and it was felt that the Second Empire spirit of frivolity must be expunged by an era of hard and honest work. All the sins of the past era were of course put down to the operetta. " The brilliant theatrical era that opened with *La Belle Hélène* contributed, by its spirit of satire and disrespect, to the woeful work done by unbounded skepticism, triumphant materialism, and social decadence," wrote Victor Hallays-Dabot in 1871, completely ignoring the real tendency of Offenbach's work.

The moralists of the new era were also convinced that the war had been won by the " Prussian schoolmaster." A stirring faith in science, based on eighteenth-century rationalism and the industrial progress of the Second Empire, became the support and prop of the defeated country and consoled a generation under the spell of despondency. A conviction of the omnipotence of science made it possible to look forward to the rise of a new aristocracy not based on birth, and this served as a weapon against the clericals in the hands of Gambetta's republicans. In Zola's novels, which became typical of the new regime, science took the place that had been formerly occupied by morality.

The object of imitating the Prussian schoolmaster was to defeat him. Thoughts of *la revanche* were uppermost in everybody's minds, and patriotism became the order of the day. One evening during the early years after the war, La Païva, who had returned to Paris, having recently persuaded Count Henckel von Donnersmarck to marry her, chose to attend a performance of *La Périchole* in all the glory of her pearls and diamonds. Had her husband not been prefect of Metz during the war? And was she not now frequently received at the German Embassy? Indignant at the shamelessness of this mistress promoted to be a fine lady, the audience hissed La Païva, as she was still known, so persistently that she had to leave the theater early. The result, however, was a diplomatic protest on the part of Germany which compelled Thiers, the President of the Republic, to invite her to dinner. Thus she obtained her revenge.

In this strange post-war world Offenbach found himself at the circumference of things instead of being at the center. The spirit of the age was too sober to tolerate the scenes of intoxication he had offered the public of the Second Empire. Its mood was moral, and he seemed the personification of frivolity. Its increasing sense of patriotism was deeply wounded by *The Grand Duchess of Gerolstein,* and nothing was more repugnant to the zeal with which it paid homage to science and the idea of progress than the skeptical tone of the operettas and the glittering brilliance of the Boulevards. Though Napoleon III in his English exile continued until the day of his death to ask for Offenbach to be played to him, Offenbach as the creator of the operetta had lost all current interest.

Before the question arose of what he should do next, he was able to produce two pieces he had begun before the war. One of them, the " comic-opera pantomime " *Le Roi Carotte,* appeared on January 15, 1872 at the Gaîté. This theater lay in the commercial quarter, and since the last years of the Empire had successfully passed from the production of melodramas to the production of pantomimes under the management of Boulet. During the rehearsals Sardou altered all those passages likely to awaken painful memories of the recent past. He shifted the action from Germany to Hungary and was careful to see that monarchists, Bonapartists, and republicans all got their money's worth, which was a wise precaution in view of the mixed audience of such a large theater. Sure enough, the satire on the Second Empire delighted one section of the audience, while another applauded the implied criticism of radicalism. Sardou's real attitude was betrayed by his play *Rabagas*, which was produced at about the same time and raised the dust by reason of its satire on Gambetta and parliamentary government.

Le Roi Carotte was a big box-office success, and there was no doubt that this was in a substantial measure due to its lavish production. Offenbach himself inserted a scene called " Pompeii," which included any number of gladiators, street peddlers, courtesans, and processions. Paul de Saint-Victor said of Zulma Bouffar, who was one of the principal members of the cast, that she was like a cotton cap with a bird-of-paradise feather. This was a simile that could have been applied to Offenbach, with his perpetual oscillations between the opposite poles of paradise and a holiday fair. Another member of the cast was Offenbach's latest discovery, Mme Judic, who had recently been singing ballads at the Eldorado. The music contained hints of *The Tales of Hoffmann*. The hostility of a certain section of the public to their former idol was illustrated by Clément, who said that Offenbach, whose German origin he of course did not fail to mention, was still a tool of Bismarck as he had been before.

The second work of Offenbach's which had been interrupted by the war was his comic opera *Fantasio*, which was produced at the Opéra-Comique three days after the first night of *Le Roi Carotte*. The music of the first act was extremely successful, but apart from that it was found so tedious that it barely survived the first performance. This was apparently due to Paul de Musset's over-poetical version of his brother's play. After this failure no work of Offenbach was ever again to be produced at the Opéra-Comique during his lifetime. During the same year he traveled to Vienna with Villemessant, Albert Wolff, Aubryet, and other celebrities of the Boulevards who had been spared by the collapse of the Empire, in order to celebrate the launching of his comic opera *Der schwarzer Korsar*, the libretto of which he appears to have written himself. The critics united in condemning the libretto and criticized the music, which made excessive play with the amusing idea of an amateur orchestra which obstinately insisted on playing the wrong notes, for superficiality and excessive haste. As Vienna was starting to produce her own operettas on Offenbach's lines, he was losing ground there too. At the beginning of 1873 his operetta *Les Braconniers* was produced at the Variétés, but it was felt to be a pale imitation of *Les Brigands* and was a dismal and almost unnoticed failure. It seemed as though Offenbach's day was done.

Should he give up the struggle? He had no thought of it, particularly as the increasing stability of the regime made things more and more favorable for the theater. The National Assembly, which was heading straight for a monarchy, had overthrown Thiers and elected in his place Marshal MacMahon, who was by no means disinclined to a restoration. Under him the administration was promptly purged of republicans, and the Catholics were supported in every possible way. Meanwhile national reconstruction, favored by the astonishing wealth of France, got rapidly under way. A new era of economic prosperity seemed to be setting in. Thorough steps were of course taken to keep the proletariat in its place.

Two courses were open to Offenbach. One was to go in for elaborate productions in the style of *Le Roi Carotte*. His infatuation for the stage and his natural extravagance had always inclined him towards lavish stage-effects. The environment was now so hostile to his real talents that he had practically no alternative but to go in for the spectacular. The other course open to him was to continue along the lines of *La Périchole* — that is, to develop the operetta along the lines of comic opera. The latter was what Lecocq did. His historical operetta *La Fille de Madame Angot,* first produced in Paris in February 1873, could not fail to have an influence upon Offenbach.

Under the pressure of circumstances Offenbach chose to embark upon both courses. But it was impossible for him to embark upon a policy of spectacular production unless he secured a theater. Boulet having died, he took over the Théâtre de la Gaîté on

July 1, 1873. He was full of the most ambitious plans. He engaged two troupes, so as to be able to devote himself to operetta and spectacle at the same time, and dreamed of stage-effects that would put everything previously imagined into the shade.

What a difference there was between Offenbach the director of the Gaîté and the old Offenbach of the Bouffes! Eighteen years before, when he had hired a wooden hut in the Champs-Élysées, the world seemed to have been waiting for him to conquer it. Now he was a world-famous composer, haunted by the fear that the world had passed him by. Eighteen years before, his natural gifts had led him to create the operetta, which plunged him into the midst of the life of his time with the most unexpected consequences, and now he had to abandon the genre that had made him famous and be glad when he could capture general attention at all. In the old days he had gone forth like David with his sling to slay pretentious giants, but now the pretentious was his aim, and only the biggest good enough. Experienced old age often takes delight in signs and tokens. That is all that can be said in mitigation of this degeneration. Offenbach had grown old. Perhaps he had grown disillusioned and was tired of knocking down idols only to find that they were invariably put back on their pedestals again; and perhaps, too, he enjoyed lavish spectacles himself.

After taking over the theater, his first task was to have it renovated, and his second to negotiate with the Society of Authors, whose statutes contained a paragraph forbidding directors of theaters to produce their own works. He pointed out that this would mean depriving his colleagues of their livelihood, whereupon the clause was waived. He entrusted the management to his old friend and librettist Étienne Tréfeu, with Albert Vizentini to assist him. Vizentini's duties were those of principal conductor and maid of all work. This combination might have worked excellently but for the two men's incompatibility of temperament. For Vizentini immediately wanted to put into practice every wild idea that came into his head, while the phlegmatic

Tréfeu always delayed taking even the most urgent and pressing steps until the very last moment.

The Gaîté opened on September 2, 1873, with *Le Gascon,* a play by Théodore Barrière, for which Offenbach supplied the necessary music. It was a failure. It was not much consolation to know that some of his older *bouffonneries* were now in the repertoire of the Théâtre de la Renaissance, for Offenbach's fate was now bound up with the Gaîté. He therefore renounced such artistic projects as that of *A Midsummer Night's Dream* with Mendelssohn's music, or *The Ruins of Athens* to the music of Beethoven, and abruptly decided to produce *Orpheus* as a panto-mime. *Orpheus* had been his first triumph, and *Orpheus* must come to the rescue again.

In devoting himself to pantomime Offenbach yielded to a wide-spread taste of the time. Pantomimes had always been popular and had been given a second lease of life by the spectacular pro-ductions of Marc Fournier during the Second Empire. But dur-ing the immediate post-war period the public simply could not do without them. People wished at all costs to be distracted from politics and memories of the year of horror through which they had just passed. Pantomimes took them out of the banal, every-day world in which they lived, plunged them into a world of magic, and effectively prevented them from thinking by bom-barding them with lavish spectacle. So popular were entertain-ments of this kind that sagacious writers of the Boulevards like Ernest Blum were able to make a permanent and satisfactory living by refurbishing old pantomimes.

The libretto for the revised version of *Orpheus* was once more the work of Crémieux and Halévy. It consisted of four acts and twelve tableaux, and characters sprouted in dozens where there had been one before. Lavish stage-effects completely buried the plot, while innumerable ballets stifled the satire and the wit. There was a dance of Orpheus' pupils, a Ballet of the Hours on Olympus, a dance of the flies in the underworld. Ballets were introduced at every point on the slightest pretext. Offenbach wrote the additional music required in the south of France, and in a letter to Tréfeu and Vizentini said that Jacques was exceptionally pleased with Jacques. In reality, however, his new music was far inferior to the old. But was it the music that really counted?

What really counted was the lavish scenery and effects, for which Godin, the technical director, was responsible. Godin had worked in London, where he had become a master of stage illusion. He created a series of scenes that caused it to be said that *Orpheus* surpassed anything ever previously seen.

One scene represented dawn on Olympus. First there appeared the clock of heaven, a blue globe on which a woman stood swinging a pendulum. The clock struck, and a number glowed on the globe. Dreams started creeping slowly by, black, pink, gold, and silver dreams, passing through a series of artistic evolutions, until the gray clouds colored and slowly vanished and the marble hemisphere of Olympus appeared, with its gleaming arches and gigantic steps. The lavishness of the scenery and of the costumes, which were designed by Grévin, was on a scale that corresponded with the profusion of characters. There were one hundred and twenty members of the male and female choruses, and the *corps de ballet* consisted of sixty-eight dancers of the most various nationalities.

Owing to lack of space, the female supers had to be accommodated in a storeroom. Nothing was easier than to gather together a vast army of girls from factories and dressmaking establishments and the little furnished rooms in which they lived. They were only too glad to be able to earn an extra twenty or thirty sous, and when their naked limbs were exposed on the stage, their proletarian origin could not possibly be detected.

The pantomime was duly produced on February 7, 1874. The first night of this new *Orpheus* called forth sad comparisons with that of 1858. The latter, in spite of the slender orchestration, had been a fashionable event that touched the ruling classes to the quick. The *Orpheus* of 1874 was an attraction for the masses, padded out with chorus girls' legs and spectacular tableaux, and was remote from all reality. In 1858 Offenbach had been a great wizard, skilled in all the arts of disenchantment, but now he was robbed of his magic powers and had to fall back on the " stunts " of the technician to delight a public that was not his own.

That it did delight them was not to be denied. The pantomime ran to full houses for months. At the hundredth performance the audience had the special privilege of seeing Offenbach conducting in person, though he was suffering severely from gout. His appearance was an extra item in itself. He painfully swayed this way and that to the wailing of the oboe, but as soon as the trumpets sounded he suddenly darted forward and started gesticulating violently. The usual supper for the cast took place in connection with this gala performance, and Offenbach noticed that many of the players of the smaller parts were missing. No sooner had he discovered that the reason for their non-appearance was that they could not afford decent clothes than he ordered the stage manager to inform them that their salary was increased by one-third. He could be generous with an easy mind, because the total takings so far amounted to 1,800,000 francs.

This fantastic profit was made possible by the fact that elegance once more prevailed in Paris. The attempt at a restoration had failed, but the establishment of the President's term of office at seven years meant that the monarchists still had a chance. The nobles and the wealthy bourgeoisie were ruling the roost, and their interests were taken care of by *Le Figaro,* whose columns had nevertheless been opened to the much discussed Zola.

Offenbach seemed to possess an unlimited capacity for work. His pantomimes did not cause him to neglect his plans for operettas. Others would have found that the management of a big theater occupied all their time; not so Offenbach. He composed a number of operettas which more or less resembled comic operas. The best of them was the one-act *Pomme d'api,* which was produced at the Renaissance on September 4, 1873 and made it clear that as a musician Offenbach, though the times had passed him by, was as creative and full of ideas as ever. The little piece was specially written for Louise Théo, whom he discovered soon after Mme Judic at the Eldorado. Offenbach's first grand opera, *La Jolie Parfumeuse,* appeared at the Renaissance towards the end of 1873. It once more illustrated the value of Offenbach's extraordinary flair for discovering young, fresh talent at *café-concerts* and music halls, for it was mainly thanks to Louise Théo that the run of *La Jolie Parfumeuse* exceeded two hundred performances.

If Offenbach had reason to be grateful to her, she also had reason to be grateful to him; for he had been so certain of her talents that he had urged Halévy rather than the less deft Crémieux to write some realistic lines specially for her. She played the part of a young married woman seduced by a rich financier, whose mistress adroitly contrives to send her back to her husband safe and sound. This timely variation on the theme of *La Périchole* also gave Offenbach an opportunity of showing a picture of Parisian artistic circles. It did not approach the delightful absurdities of *La Vie parisienne,* however. Operetta behavior had now become far more prudent, like that of society itself.

The friendly reception given to *La Jolie Parfumeuse* with its gay and carefree music may have encouraged the Variétés to stage an expanded version of *La Périchole* early in 1874. It was like a resuscitation of the past, made the more complete by Hortense Schneider's agreeing to appear in it. Following a recent failure, Hortense had once more vowed never to return to the stage. She was a clever woman and was perfectly well aware that the end of the Second Empire had involved the fall of the Grand Duchy of Gerolstein, and she had had the wisdom to make provision in good time for any such eventuality. She owned a town house, two villas, priceless carpets and objects of art, and, above all, diamonds of every conceivable shape — a bodice brooch in the shape of a lily, a platinum clasp with twenty-two choice stones, a diadem studded with diamonds. But she could not resist the temptation to appear just once more as in the old days, when she had flaunted her wardrobe before an applauding public and paraded her glittering jewels before the eyes of visitors to her dressing-room. The past seemed to have been resuscitated, only this time the visitors to her dressing-room were not crowned heads. Offenbach, blissful at this resuscitation, attempted to persuade Meilhac and Halévy, who were perceptibly losing interest in operetta and obstinately refused to write new librettos for him, to change their minds.

" Believe me," Offenbach said to Meilhac one night behind the scenes at the Variétés, " people will still be talking about *La Périchole* when *Froufrou* is forgotten." But behind his words there was distress at the break-up of the old partnership.

Nevertheless he did succeed in persuading Meilhac to cooperate with Halévy and Millaud in the first act of *Madame l'Archiduc,* an operetta that was produced at the Bouffes at the beginning of the winter season of 1874. This operetta, which was the best of the post-war period, was apparently nothing but a repetition of the great *offenbachiades* of the pre-war era. But it only revived the court satire and intrigue and love of the past era in order to make sweet play with them. Fortunato, the court intriguers, the peasant girl who steps into the Prince's place, the Prince himself, who exactly resembles the Viceroy in *La Périchole,* all these characters, who had been extremely topical less than ten years ago, were now nothing but figures out of a fairy-tale. Even the dragoon scene, which was reminiscent of the " Tramp, tramp, tramp " finale of *Les Brigands,* had so far departed from its predecessors as to have lost all connection with reality. You could not tell for certain whether it was a pure product of the imagination or the last echo of a vanished age. It was an airy, impalpable creation that mocked gently at the smart clubmen and cocottes who once more populated the Bouffes and now seemed phantoms themselves.

This was not the first time that Offenbach had combined composing with running a theater. But the scale on which he was doing things now was incomparably greater, and it was only by working at incredible pressure that he was able to fulfill even approximately all the tasks he undertook. Before nine o'clock in the morning he would be seated in his office at the Gaîté, checking the box-office receipts, receiving a report on the previous night's performance, issuing orders for the day to be posted in the corridors, and attending to innumerable visitors in between. Crémieux or Halévy would look in, or Marcelin would come and ask for drawings of the costumes for his journal, *La Vie parisienne*. The busier Offenbach was, the happier he seemed to be. Moreover he liked doing things on a grand scale, provided that others had a share in them. On one occasion he invited his whole troupe to Étretat, not as their employer but as a kindly patriarch. He informed them through Vizentini that his servant would meet them at the station to show them to their quarters, and he urged them to bring warm clothing, because it was cold at night by the sea.

Beggars used to swarm round him like flies round a light. One day one of them pestered him so outrageously in the Champs-Élysées that, having no money with him, in order to get rid of him he took a sheet of paper from his wallet and scribbled some notes upon it, standing in the street, and over them he wrote " Beggar's Polka " as the title. " Any publisher will give you two hundred francs for it," he said to the beggar. A week later he met the same beggar in the street again and received a valuable lesson concerning the financial exploitation of his own works. The beggar confided to him that he had not, of course, been so stupid as to take his naïve advice, but that he had immediately asked all the leading music publishers for offers, by the clever manipulation of which he expected to obtain at least one thousands francs. Moreover, he also proposed exploiting the foreign rights, the rights for public performance at *café-concerts* and public balls, the cheap-edition rights, as well as the rights of selling it in the lobbies of the Bouffes and the Gaîté.

If Offenbach had made this financial genius manager of the Gaîté, the theater might perhaps have been saved. Instead he had to put up with the blunderings of the incompetent Tréfeu, who

PROGRAM, ROYAL ALHAMBRA THEATRE, LONDON

April 15, 1876

From the Gabrielle Enthoven Collection, Victoria and Albert Museum

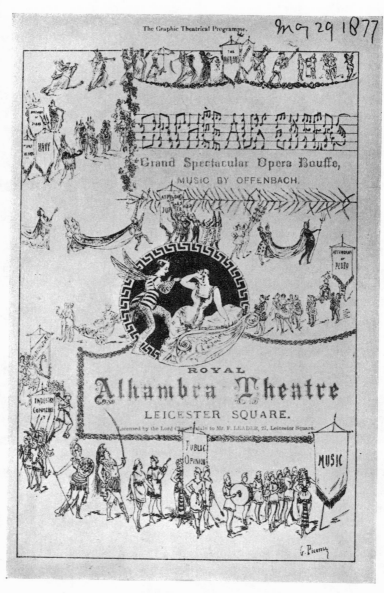

PROGRAM, ROYAL ALHAMBRA THEATRE, LONDON
May 29, 1877
From the Gabrielle Enthoven Collection, Victoria and Albert Museum

was guilty of one mistake after another. But however gross Tréfeu's mismanagement was, the real originator of the trouble was Offenbach himself. Not only did he more than readily submit to the influence of Sardou, whose heavy historical drama *La Haine* he felt would be a worthy successor to *Orpheus,* but he spent the enormous sum of 360,000 francs on staging it. The result of this expenditure was a hundred men in expensive medieval armor clanking aimlessly around the stage, while such dramatic tension as survived was effectively smothered by yards and yards of silks and satins. The first performance took place on December 3, 1874, and snow did the rest to keep the public away. When the fiasco could no longer be concealed, the mortified Sardou wrote a public letter to Offenbach announcing his irrevocable decision to withdraw his play from the indifferent public. In this way he at least assured himself a satisfactory exit. Offenbach, however, was left to bear the loss.

He was left in an extremely difficult position. He was faced with an enormous deficit, which he made frantic but vain efforts to meet by organizing matinees at the Gaîté, besides innumerable other things. Catastrophe seemed inevitable, and the fact that all London was enthusiastic about his ballet for the pantomime *Dick Whittington and His Cat,* which had just appeared at the Alhambra and for which he received 75,000 francs, failed to compensate him for the rumors about the Gaîté with which Paris was buzzing.

In the desperate search for a way out, Vizentini hit upon the brilliant idea of unfreezing the capital locked up in the medieval armor of Sardou's ill-fated play by reviving *Geneviève de Brabant,* the setting of which was also medieval, as a pantomime. Offenbach, who was at his wits' end, eventually agreed.

These must have been months of acute distress for Offenbach. The new *Geneviève,* which was produced at the end of February 1875, was a poor piece of work, hastily put together, shamelessly exploiting popular tastes. Hence it included innumerable nymphs and children's ballets, a diamond palace which sparkled with a thousand lights and colors, and plenty of stunts imported from London; to say nothing of Thérésa, who also appeared in the midst of this gorgeous display. But it was of no avail; the public stayed away.

Offenbach now drove blindly straight towards the abyss. Instead of profiting by experience, he involved himself with Sardou more deeply than ever and actually allowed him to try a new experiment on the stage of the Gaîté. Sardou had a play called *Don Quixote* in his locker and persuaded Offenbach to produce it as a spectacular pantomime, and, as though he were the bad fairy in the pantomime himself, he goaded Offenbach on to greater and greater expense. Some of the ideas mentioned in his correspondence with Offenbach were a flock of sheep surprised by a thunderstorm, a bull fight, a sunrise, and a sensational cloudscape. Both Offenbach and Sardou indulged in the most extravagant and fantastic dreams, and the estimates for scenery, costumes, and effects were even more extravagant and fantastic.

All these dreams, however, were interrupted by the theater's going bankrupt. At the end of May the company was liquidated, and by the end of the month Offenbach, who had wanted to go on alone, was forced to capitulate. He assembled all the players and employees of the theater — there were eight hundred of them — and gave them an unvarnished account of the situation, ending with the words: " You will be paid to the last sou, my children. If I have been careless, I shall at least remain honorable." Everybody wept.

The devotion of his players was shown by the way they celebrated his birthday. As he could no longer go to the Gaîté, the Gaîté came to him, in the rue Laffitte, where he was laid up with gout. The celebrations began with a firework display in the courtyard, after which they all entered his house, gave him an ovation, put a golden crown on his head, and filed past him one by one in a long procession.

His retirement, indeed, was as honorable as it could have been.

He surrendered all his property and three years' author's royalties to his creditors. His life lay in ruins about him.

To save himself from penury he sorrowfully accepted the offer of an American impresario, Bacquero, who invited him to go to America in the following year and conduct concerts at the Centennial Exposition at Philadelphia as well as in New York. He was nearing sixty and beginning to feel the burden of years. At the end of June the Gaîté was sold to Vizentini. The prospect of years of drudgery stared Offenbach in the face.

Alas, his material losses were not the only ones. A greater blow to him than any financial loss was the diminution in his fame, his bitter recognition of the fact that the times were leaving him behind. Other stars shone in the firmament, and other names outshone his own.

While he had been exhausting himself and prostituting his talents to save the Gaîté from ruin, *Carmen* had appeared, *Carmen,* by Bizet, who had developed in a far smaller world than he, with a libretto by his two old collaborators, Meilhac and Halévy. The conservative public, which now appreciated directness less than ever, were offended by *Carmen's* realism; but Offenbach knew that his friends' creation had conquered fields that must ever remain closed to him. Bizet's score filled him with an admiration that was entirely free of envy.

If Bizet showed him his own limitations, Johann Strauss beat him in his own domain, the operetta. Strauss had long been a prominent figure in Paris. Parisians judged the success of a ball at which he played by the number of violin bows he broke during the evening, and it was he who conducted at the first masked ball at the newly dedicated Opéra at the beginning of 1875. But his success as a conductor faded into insignificance beside the popularity he gained as an operetta-composer.

Just when the Gaîté was on the brink of bankruptcy and Offenbach had fallen so far back that *Les Hannetons,* a Bouffes revue that was full of his tunes, failed ignominiously, there took place the first performance of Strauss's operetta *Ali Baba and the Forty Thieves,* at the Renaissance. It was a great evening. Zulma Bouffar, the singer Offenbach was so fond of, played the heroine, and Princess von Metternich, who had been unable to resist the temptation of attending her fellow-countryman's first night, though she had to go on to a ball later in the evening, was in the royal box. A sensation of some sort could always be expected wherever the Princess appeared. So that the special applause she had for Strauss should not be drowned in the general acclamation, she leaned so far forward when the curtain fell for the last time that she nearly fell out of her box.

After *Ali Baba* the Renaissance produced *Die Fledermaus,* under the title of *La Tzigane.* Once more the heroine was Zulma Bouffar. No one in Paris but Offenbach, who was kept to his room by the gout, failed to see it. It became the rage of Paris, as *La Belle Hélène* had once been. Strauss's picture was to be seen in all the shop-windows on the Boulevards, and hats, ties, and socks were named after him. Offenbach's old friend Albert Wolff wrote one of his popular *causeries* about him. Nobody noticed how much *Die Fledermaus* owed to Offenbach and his epoch. Its libretto was based on *Réveillon,* a comedy by Meilhac and Halévy, and its music recalled the intoxicating quality of *La Vie parisienne.* Strauss, involuntarily using Offenbach's rhythms, conjured up the frenzied carousals of the Second Empire by which he had been surrounded in the year of the Universal Exposition.

However, the triumphs of *Die Fledermaus* had the result of bringing Viennese operetta into public favor — Viennese operetta, that feeble, middle-class caricature of the operetta of Offenbach, which substituted cosiness for gaiety, stupidity for nonsense, and idle prattle for wit. At the same time it banished satire and musically — apart from Strauss's own scores — served up nothing but stale dregs. The products of Vienna were to crowd the *offenbachiade* out of the world market for years to come.

What Offenbach himself felt at that time can be read between the lines in the introduction he wrote in 1874 for Arnold Mortier's *Soirées parisiennes*. In this book, the first of a whole series, Mortier started collecting the theatrical articles he had written for the *Figaro* in the course of the past year. Mortier did not concern himself with description or criticism of any of the plays he saw, but devoted himself entirely to light gossip. Offenbach in his introduction could not find sufficient words of praise for the work that Mortier was doing. By showing the manager in his office, the prompter in his box, the player before his mirror, he said, Mortier was preserving for posterity the innumerable incidents, details, and little events that were not mentioned in any theatrical history and were inevitably bound to perish unless someone took pity on them and preserved them. This observation of Offenbach's not only illustrated once more the perpetual attraction exercised over him by the surface ripples of the stream of life; it illustrated even more forcibly his fear of being forgotten and fading from men's minds. In the old days, during the years of joy and glamour, such a fear would never have occurred to him. But now the world was turning its back on him, and he trembled at the thought of being left behind and overlooked as something of no importance.

In 1874 Gaston Jollivet and Arsène Houssaye saw a venerable old lady outside the Théâtre de l'Odéon suddenly turn on an old gentleman and angrily rebuke him for treading on her dress. The old gentleman stammered an apology, and that was all. " They are George Sand and Jules Sandeau," Houssaye said with a smile. " They did not recognize each other." Once they had been married. Offenbach began to be haunted by the transitoriness of things, which this little story illustrates. The hastiness of time struck him with redoubled force because he was hasty himself.

Figure after figure disappeared from the forefront of the Paris scene. Some were reduced to poverty, like Cora Pearl, who lived, friendless and with no more beauty preparations, in a little room over a coach-house. Others had been clever enough to withdraw from the vortex before it was too late. Blanche d'Antigny died young. Anna Deslions enjoyed a secure old age, having saved and wisely invested the money given her by her former lovers. Not a few others who had enjoyed carousing with the *cocodès* were working behind shop-counters in small provincial towns or were ending their days in honorable matrimony in Italy, Russia, or Austria. Alas and alas! The music of Wagner was slowly creeping into fashion. And now that the word " Republic " had been put into the Constitution, the republican spirit spread irresistibly.

Offenbach was too old to change, so he clung to what he had. He preserved his quiet good nature, and his self-satisfaction remained invulnerable. Under a portrait of himself that hung in his house, he wrote: " To his best friend, Jacques Offenbach." The naïveté with which he allowed himself to be taken in by any joke that tickled his vanity was touching and absurd. After the failure of the Gaîté he went to stay at a hotel at Étretat — he had, of course, long since let the Villa d'Orphée — and some friends of his prepared a hilarious reception for him. They dressed up as operetta soldiers, planted themselves outside the door, and received him with full military honors. Albert Wolff, the ringleader, solemnly handed him the hotel key on a tray. " This is too much, this is too much," Offenbach murmured with a catch in his voice.

If anything was calculated to help him withstand poverty and the vanishing of the world to which he belonged, it was his happy family life. The same amateur theatricals still took place in his house in the rue Laffitte. One of them was a parody on Gounod's *Faust,* with Albert Wolff as Marguerite, and it created a sensation that went far beyond four walls. Friday evenings were still different from other evenings, and there would still be a party in his house after every first night, and his friends would invariably make a great noise on these occasions, which generally ended by several of them holding Offenbach aloft on their shoulders in his worn-out old easy-chair while the others danced around him.

This easy-chair was the gouty old gentleman's favorite. Nothing gave him greater pleasure than to sit in it, surrounded by his daughters. Every evening between five and seven o'clock he took a nap there, leaving half-open the door into the next room, where Herminie would be chattering with visitors, and when evening came, he would go to the theater where his works were being played.

Did Offenbach regret the Gaîté? Immediately after the crash he struggled stoutly to regain his old position, and Meilhac and Halévy came forward as loyal helpers. They wrote a libretto for him, *La Boulangère a des écus,* and promised to revive their old collaboration. A contract was drawn up, and Offenbach's hopes were so revived that he started dreaming of a return to the old days of *La Belle Hélène.* But his hopes were vain. The planned collaboration came to nothing, and *La Boulangère a des écus* remained the last joint work of the three old campaigners.

La Boulangère was played in eighteenth-century costume, and betrayed Lecocq's influence. During the rehearsals at the Variétés an incident occurred that destroyed the halo that had surrounded Hortense Schneider for so long. Bertrand, the director of the Variétés, had brought her back from St. Petersburg to play the leading role. But he had not counted on his beloved Mlle Aimée, who wanted to play the part herself. Following the example of the cunning mistress in *La Jolie Parfumeuse,* she found it the easier to get rid of her rival because Hortense Schneider herself gave Bertrand the desired opportunity. At one rehearsal, forgetting she was no longer a star, she announced she was throwing up her part. Mlle Aimée promptly seized her opportunity, and when Hortense innocently turned up at the theater again next day, she learned, to her astonishment and dismay, that she had been taken at her word.

As for the operetta, the first performance, which took place on October 19, 1875, was distinguished by the fact that Mlle Aimée tried to outdo her dethroned rival by covering herself with diamonds. It was praised by the critics and applauded by the public, but not rapturously.

If Offenbach was to satisfy his creditors, he had no time to lose. Not only did he lose no time, but he went about things like a maniac. He actually succeeded in having two more pieces produced in the five weeks that followed. One was a comic opera *La Créole,* which he composed for Mme Judic and which was a far greater success in London, as *The Commodore,* than it was in Paris. The other was a remarkable pantomime called *Le Voyage dans la lune.*

Offenbach only achieved these miracles of speed by never allowing himself a moment's rest. Anyone who chanced to look through his carriage-window as he drove from theater to theater would see the old man, wrapped in his fur coat, bending over a specially constructed desk, writing away incessantly. The carriage jerked forward, stopped, and rattled on again, but Offenbach went on covering the paper with notes, heedless of the traffic.

It seemed impossible that, working at this pressure, he should strike out on an original path. Nevertheless his pantomime *Le Voyage dans la lune,* produced at the Gaîté by Vizentini, was highly unconventional. It was taken from Jules Verne's novel of the same name. A dramatized version of Jules Verne's *Round the World in Eighty Days* had been a sensational success during the previous year. In his latest pantomime Offenbach once more proved his dramatic sense and his flair for topicality. In mixing science and fairy-tales and building modern Utopias into the traditional framework of the pantomime, he resurrected a genre to the destruction of which he had himself contributed. No doubt he was guided in this direction by the influence of one of his best friends, Aurélien Scholl. Scholl was one of the few journalists of the Boulevards who were progressive in their ideas after the war. He attacked the reactionaries who flourished under MacMahon for their presumption in coming forward as the sole champions of the " moral order," became a mighty champion of Zola's naturalism, and defended Jules Verne's pseudo-scientific novels on the

ground that they gave the masses valuable knowledge in an exciting form. Offenbach may have found his friend's views all
the more convincing because, thanks to Gambetta, republicanism
was perceptibly gaining the upper hand. Maxime du Camp wrote
at the time that bright, gas-lit streets and broad traffic arteries did
more to keep down murder and burglary than all the preachings
of the moralists. Technical progress had become a general watch-
word.

Offenbach paid his tribute to it with this pantomime. Its fantastic scenery and its topical interest drew crowds to the Gaîté.
Anticipating the publicity methods of the modern cinema, Vizentini had a large, flood-lit relief model of the moon erected on
the theater façade, and prided himself on its scientific accuracy.
The sensation of the first act was an enormous gun through
which the travelers were to be shot to the moon. So enormous
was it that it rested on mountains and stretched across valleys,
villages, and rivers. The second act showed the landscape of the
moon itself. One of its features was a tobacco plant which blossomed in a few seconds. But all these were trifles in comparison
with the volcanic eruption in the fourth act.

No sooner are the travelers to the moon sentenced to hard labor
in the interior of the volcano than there is a crash of thunder,
the earth quakes, lava flows, and flames rise everywhere. One of
the travelers takes refuge on an enormous rock. The rock is
struck by a ball of fire and flung into space. There is a shower
of ashes, then the devastated crest of the volcano is seen; and then
the earth, glowing brightly in the distance in the sky, starts growing bigger and bigger until it fills the whole scene.

The purely human plot was by no means overshadowed by
the astronomical scale of these events. It was filled with humorous and satirical incidents. Prince Caprice, played by Zulma
Bouffar, rouses very earthly feelings in the breast of Princess
Fantasia, who, like all the inhabitants of the moon, is incapable
of love. The love-affair between the two proceeds triumphantly
in the midst of all the technical wonders. So little, indeed, did

the latter predominate that there was actually room for a ballet of snowflakes and a ballet of chimeras.

What gave this pantomime its individuality was the magic of Offenbach's music. Indeed, it held forth a vision of a time when man should no longer be in thrall to technical invention, but should freely use and play with it.

CHAPTER II

SKYSCRAPERS

OFFENBACH set out on his trip to America on April 21, 1876. A whole escort — Herminie and the children and his sons-in-law and brothers-in-law and Albert Wolff and other friends — accompanied him to Le Havre, where he embarked on the *Canada*. The unusual size of this retinue was in accordance with the size of the ocean and its dangers. There was a heart-rending scene of farewell, and when the *Canada* began to move away and Offenbach saw his fourteen-year-old son Auguste standing waving to him, his heart misgave him just as it had when he himself had been fourteen years old and the mail-coach had clattered off with him to distant Paris.

During the crossing he tried to console himself by composing some lines for Mlle Théo to sing next winter in *La Boîte au lait*. Besides, he found acquaintances on board: Bacquero, his American impresario, and Mlle Aimée, who was also making an American tour. But the comforting Parisian theatrical atmosphere that Mlle Aimée brought with her was rapidly driven away by a rough sea that robbed him of all inclination to talk or to compose. A storm broke out, and Offenbach suffered agonies of fear. Even if he had been told that a no less uproarious storm of applause were surging round Thérésa in *La Boulangère a des écus,* the news would have had as little effect on him as Bacquero's and the captain's vain attempts to assure him that the storm was quite an ordinary one taking its ordinary course.

The *Canada* did not sink. As she drew slowly into New York harbor, a boat approached with musicians on board, playing selections from Offenbach's operettas to welcome him, though the effect was not as satisfactory as it might have been, because the pitching and tossing made them play out of tune, and every now and then they were so seasick that they had to stop altogether. Reporters came on board for the customary interview, and then the crossing was over.

A compensation for all its horrors was provided that same evening by the ovation that greeted Offenbach at his hotel, on the front of which an enormous plaque had been placed with " Welcome Offenbach! " on it. A serenade was played beneath his windows and attracted throngs of people in the street.

" T'ank you, sir! " Offenbach called down delightedly from his balcony.

The applause with which this, his first speech in America, was greeted proved to him that he would get on splendidly with the Americans.

No one could have been more susceptible than he to the innumerable new impressions that overwhelmed him on every side. He was full of admiration for the hotels, every bedroom of which, unlike those of Paris or Vienna, had a bathroom and lavatory attached. The hotels also contained shops at which one could buy almost everything under the sun, so that Offenbach remarked that one could arrive as naked as Adam and depart looking as elegant as the Count d'Orsay. After a few days he moved from his hotel to a boarding-house, in which he greatly admired the three electric bells provided on the ground floor. You only had to press the right button, and lo, a policeman, a porter, or the fire company would appear, whichever was required. As an old *boulevardier,* he strolled about the streets, noticed the innumerable birds in the foliage of the trees, the overcrowded street-cars and buses, the passengers of which always honorably paid their fares although there were no conductors to collect them, and the carriage parasols which served the double purpose of being used for advertisements and protecting the passengers from heat. Advertisements were to be seen in the most improbable places. One drug-store advertisement adorned a big drum, for instance, and the drummer had to make the most frantic efforts to hold the drum straight in order to allow the advertisement to be properly seen.

Gilmore Garden, in which Offenbach's concerts took place, was a huge pleasure-ground, which could hold eight thousand people. It also contained a collection of natural wonders. In one part of the garden there was a collection of tropical plants, in the middle of which was placed the platform for the orchestra. In a different part there was an artificial waterfall, intended to be an imitation of Niagara. When the thunder of the waters stopped, the thunder of the orchestra began. Consisting as it did of one hundred and ten musicians, it made at least as much noise as the waterfall. Offenbach speedily won the favor of the members of his orchestra by applying for admission to their organization.

Day after day he took his place on the platform, conducting selections from *Orpheus* or *The Grand Duchess of Gerolstein* and bowing to a crowd who were strangers to him and to whom he was a stranger. But was he not also a stranger to himself? When the fragrance of the tropical vegetation rose to his nostrils, he was oblivious of time and place. He might easily have been back in the Jardin Turc. Not he but the handsome Jullien might have been conducting, while he listened to his own waltz *Rebecca* to the accompaniment of the noise of the waterfall.

As he remained in New York for several weeks, he had plenty of opportunity to observe people and things. He always took pleasure in observing curious sights and curious people. In his book *Offenbach en Amérique. Notes d'un musicien en voyage,* which appeared in 1877, he did not fail to mention a senator, John Morrissey, who owed his advancement to that high rank purely to his skill as a boxer, to say nothing of a musical waiter, who whistled continually while he served; he whistled sad tunes when a dish was not to his taste, and merry ones when something was ordered of which he approved. When he whistled something from *The Grand Duchess of Gerolstein* in honor of a magnificent *"bombe glacée,"* Offenbach felt positively insulted. He thought his music was too good for ice cream.

Many of the things he noticed would have been noticed by any *boulevardier.* He observed, for instance, that the newspaper buildings on Broadway, one of which was actually nine stories high, were the highest buildings in New York; that the American women walked just as gracefully as the women of Paris, and so on. His book contains innumerable notes such as might have been made by any Parisian journalist, nor did he fail to mention the cult of the almighty dollar.

One day when he was out walking with a respected American citizen he noticed that the latter greeted the acquaintances he passed, now with an air of exaggerated respect, now with an air of superior condescension. Offenbach inquired the reason for these variations. " That musician whom I greeted so respectfully," the American replied, " enjoys a very honorable position in New York society; he is worth a million dollars. This one who is just approaching is only worth a hundred thousand, and therefore less well liked than the other. So I greet him with less respect." According to an article he wrote for *Le Figaro* while in America, Offenbach was forced to conclude that it was not so much love of music as awe of the dollar that attracted New York to his concerts. " This Offenbach must be a great musician," he heard somebody say. " He gets a thousand dollars an evening, just for conducting the orchestra."

Offenbach naturally took a great interest in the New York theaters. They were not to his liking. He did not approve of their amphitheatrical construction, nor of the practice of letting them for months, or often only for weeks. He found the versatility of the theatrical managers even more surprising. One of them combined theatrical management with commanding a regiment, besides being a director of a railroad company and a shipping firm. However, he ended by being murdered. Another, Maurice Grau, sometimes had more than five theaters at his disposal in different parts of America at the same time, unless he just

happened to have lost all his money. An American theatrical manager, Offenbach added with a touch of envy, could go bankrupt
three or four times without losing caste or having any difficulty in
finding new backers.

Such conditions had their effects. Offenbach attended a performance of Meyerbeer's opera *L'Étoile du nord* at Booth's
Theater, and he said of it that the chorus and orchestra were
never able to catch up with each other. It sounded like a medi-
ocre work of Wagner's, he added.

This taunt was no doubt the result of the fact that even in
America he could not help noticing that Wagner's influence was
spreading. For instance, the Lyceum Theater copied Bayreuth by
covering in the orchestra, the acoustic result of which was disastrous. Fortunately this was soon stopped. During one of the
performances clouds of smoke started spreading in the auditorium
and caused a panic. The cause of the trouble was that the orchestra had taken advantage of their concealment to light up their
pipes and cigars.

Offenbach was distressed at all these theatrical deficiencies, and
in gratitude to his hosts took it to be his duty to advise them how
they could be remedied. In Offenbach's view, the trouble was
that America had conquered in the material sphere, but not in
the things of the mind. The things that built the mind must
therefore be constructed afresh. Offenbach's advice to America
was not to remain satisfied as hitherto with inferior theatrical productions, but to raise a fund to create and maintain a permanent
theater. Furthermore he recommended the establishment of a
conservatory of music provided with first-class European teachers.
He also advised the Americans to build museums and academies
for painting and sculpture. It was a program that certainly bore
witness to Offenbach's far-sightedness. His only mistake was to
assume that America would not succeed in attracting the most
important European artists.

From New York Offenbach went to Philadelphia. A French
workers' delegation, sent to visit the Centennial Exposition, were

also at Philadelphia. The workers were in alliance with the bourgeois republicans at the time, and they were so little revolutionary-minded that such diversions were gladly allowed them. But it is very unlikely that these political enemies of Offenbach joined the enthusiastic crowd that filled the pavilion in which he conducted. This pavilion lay in a park that was a kind of miniature edition of the Gilmore Garden at New York, and, thanks to Offenbach's concerts, it became the rage of Philadelphia. Unfortunately the attraction could not be exploited to the full, as such earthly pleasures as operetta music were forbidden on Sundays. But the ingenious proprietor, who had already christened the place Offenbach Garden, found a way out by announcing a Sunday concert of religious music. Music was music, and dollars were dollars, and Offenbach would have been perfectly willing to conduct a mass for money. Offenbach sketched out a program, under the title:

GRAND SACRED CONCERT
By M. Offenbach and the Grand Orchestra
In a choice selection of sacred et classical music

Included in the program were not only such highly respectable items as Gounod's *Ave Maria* and the " Angelus " from his own operetta *Le Mariage aux Lanternes,* but other items of far less sacred intention. For instance, the Grand Duchess of Gerolstein's declaration of love was smuggled in as a " Prayer," and Helen of Troy's lament " *Dis-moi, Vénus,*" was disguised as, a " Litany." However, the authorities felt a little suspicious and refused to sanction it.

Offenbach's American tour drew to a close. Before sailing for home he made a trip to Niagara Falls and another short stay in New York and gave a big banquet for his orchestra and the many new friends he had made. He was presented on this occasion with an artistically decorated conductor's baton which was as big as a field-marshal's. But everything was on a big scale in New York. Two months before, he had only been able to stam-

mer out a helpless " T'ank you, sir," but now he was able to make
a full-blown speech, delighting everybody by his mixture of sentiment and wit. Six other speeches followed. The correspondent
of the *Courrier des États-Unis* stated that " few European artists
had been so highly honored in New York as the composer of *The
Grand Duchess.*" Indeed, his music made such an impression
that when Sarah Bernhardt toured the United States in 1880, the
only music ever played in the intermissions of *Phèdre* was selections from *La Belle Hélène.*

After a last concert in Gilmore Garden, Offenbach sailed for
home on July 8. This time the crossing on the trusty *Canada*
passed off with the elements in a gentler mood. But a storm of
political passion was unleashed, this time by Offenbach himself.
The farther New York receded into the distance and the larger
Paris loomed in conversation, the more oppressive became the
thought of once more having to face the attacks of the republicans,
who now had a majority in the Chamber. His forebodings of
difficulties to come made him talk indiscreetly, denouncing current political trends and praising the grandeur of the Empire at
the expense of the present day. Ill luck willed it that he unbur-
dened himself to a French republican Senator, who was so in-
censed by what Offenbach said that when he got home he
promptly incited the papers of the Left against him.

At last Le Havre came into view. The quay was crowded with
familiar faces — Herminie and the children, his brothers-in-law,
his sons-in-law, and friends. Embraces, kisses, and questions followed. Offenbach was home again. In America the anxious feeling that he was lost and uprooted had never left him for a
moment. Now it promptly vanished. In coming home he had
returned to himself.

" In France I became Offenbach again." Those are the words
with which he concluded his book on America. Albert Wolff
wrote an introduction for it, among other things defending his
friend against the absurd charge of having contributed to the
demoralization of France.

CHAPTER III

THE PACT WITH DEATH

WHEN Offenbach returned from America to France, he came back to himself. But a great change had taken place in him. He could not resume his former life. There was a barrier between it and him. Henceforward he was haunted by a thought that had never troubled him before — the thought that he, too, was bound to die. It robbed him of the happy-go-lucky light-heartedness with which he had previously lived, and his whole being was transformed. Under its influence the past rose up before him, and half-forgotten wishes and dreams were revived. All that he saw was colored by the pale light of death.

During the first two or three months after his return the Variétés decided to revive *La Belle Hélène,* and, lo, instead of being a fiasco, as everybody had expected, the old operetta turned out to be an evergreen that attracted even the younger generation, who were not tied to it by any memories. For three years nothing but tunes from *La Fille de Madame Angot* had been heard in the streets and cafés. But now everyone whistled or hummed tunes from *La Belle Hélène.*

Nothing could have been more calculated to stir Offenbach than this revival. Not only was it a painful reminder that for years past he had been but a shadow, but it drew him up sharply before the fact that he was famous only as a composer of operettas. This was the unkindest cut of all. Operetta no longer meant anything to him; it had become ancient history even to its creator. All the more desperately, therefore, did he ask himself whether it was only as a composer of operetta that he was worth anything.

In this state of mind it must certainly have cost him an effort to go on writing light music. But he had no alternative. Financial worries, apparently still in connection with the bankruptcy of the Gaîté, compelled him willy-nilly to continue with the production of operettas. There accordingly appeared: *Pierrette et Jacquot,* a little piece in one act; *La Boîte au Lait,* which he had started on the *Canada;* another scientific pantomime based on Jules Verne, *Le Docteur Ox,* in which the actor Dupuis and Mme Judic scored personal successes; and an operetta, *La Foire St. Laurent.* Though all these works contained charming numbers, their reception was relatively cool, as though the public could tell that Offenbach's heart was no longer in them.

In his gloom he was suddenly struck with an idea; it was to make an opera of material that had been familiar to him for a lifetime. *Les Contes fantastiques d'Hoffmann* had been produced as a play at the Odéon in 1851. The dramatic version was by Jules Barbier and Michel Carré, and one critic had said at the time that it would do excellently for a comic opera. Offenbach had once mentioned to Barbier that he would very much like to turn it into an opera himself. But he had been so much taken up with operettas that he had forgotten all about it. But now he remembered it again, and he knew, positively and certainly, that *The Tales of Hoffmann* belonged to him and to him alone.

Why had he not thought of it before? As if to punish him for previous neglect, the drama now resisted his advances. A libretto had already been written for it and entrusted to Hector Salomon, the chorus-master at the Opéra, who had nearly finished his score. It looked as though Offenbach was too late. That he did eventually secure the libretto was due solely to Salomon's unselfishness in withdrawing. Salomon must have felt that it was no mere whim but an irresistible artistic impulse that caused the older man to want the libretto so desperately. He must indeed have been an artist to have unhesitatingly acknowledged the priority of Offenbach's claim and to have agreed to sacrifice his own practically completed work.

" That Offenbach devoted himself so passionately to this material does not seem so inexplicable to his friends," Hanslick wrote. " Hoffmann's haunted world had always attracted him greatly. He himself in his last years looked like a transparent, pale, sadly smiling ghost from *The Serapion Brethren.*" But it was not the attraction of Hoffmann's haunted world that drew him to Barbier's drama. The reason why he coveted it so ardently was that he was now actually living in Hoffmann's ghost world. If in his youth he had looked like a character out of Hoffmann, it was because of the exuberant gaiety with which he had seemed to thumb his nose at evil, earth-bound spirits. As an old man doomed to die he resembled Hoffmann himself; like the latter, he, too, was now wrestling with evil spirits.

He was, indeed, a fallen Ariel, a spirit of the air brought down to live among the haunting spirits of earth. Once upon a time he had been able to mock at them and playfully skip over the obstacles with which they confronted him, without their being able to hurt him. But then his name had paled, his gout had grown worse, his son Auguste's health had deteriorated steadily, and after his return from America old age overtook him. It forced him to realize that he was no Ariel, but a human being, with death hanging over him; and he was perpetually haunted by the fear of his name perishing utterly.

" Everybody must have had the experience of being awakened at night by the slightest noise, which returns at intervals and drives all sleep away and increases one's inner fear until all one's senses are utterly dismayed," E. T. A. Hoffmann writes. " It has often happened to me to be suddenly awakened, whereupon I have felt an indescribable fear, as though I had had some terrible experience. It is as though some strange power has suddenly penetrated within us and taken possession of our hitherto clear senses."

Offenbach experienced this with incomparably greater force.

For he, as an Ariel, had not been familiar with such terrestrial hauntings and was therefore more exposed to their terrors now.

While he was at their mercy he discovered that he shared the fate of Hoffmann, the hero of the drama — nay, more, that he was Hoffmann's double. Like Hoffmann, who never achieved any of his three loves, Olympia, Antonia, or Giulietta, he had never attained the object of his love, grand opera. Like Hoffmann, he had been fooled by an evil spirit, who had estranged him from his true vocation. It seemed to him that he had blindly pursued false glory, and that he had wasted his precious gifts. He recalled his father's singing in the synagogue and his own day-dreams when he was an unknown young cellist at the Opéra-Comique, and the long years of fame and glory seemed so much dross.

The fear with which the passage of time filled him made him unjust to himself. If in the past he had underestimated the secrets of nature and the power of mysterious forces, he now underestimated the mission of his nature and no longer recognized the marvelous brightness it had spread. He walked abroad a " transparent, pale, sadly smiling ghost," convinced that he had irreparably wasted his life.

In writing an opera around the adventures of the unhappy Hoffmann he rendered an account of himself. He put his whole being into the music. In the Olympia act he portrayed the senseless, crazy activity of the Second Empire, its automatic gaiety, and the vanity of its champagne parties. That period had been seen through colored spectacles — he tore them away. In the Giulietta act, with the help of the " Barcarolle " taken from his *Rheinnixen,* he drew a picture of a debauched Venice, in which he once more, though more profoundly and cunningly than ever, conjured up the joy of the fleeting moment and the beauty of the passing day. But he only introduced this Venice to show the evil that lurked behind its gray façades. In *The Tales of Hoffmann* Venice was reduced to dust and ashes just as it had been in *Froufrou,* and Giulietta was no more than an unmasked Metella.

This opera was the judgment that Offenbach passed on himself; and the music, which is full of the panic of a child lost in the dark, betrays how many demons stormed in upon him during the process, in which his whole artistic existence was at stake.

Offenbach started negotiating for the production of the opera as early as 1877, but the Théâtre Lyrique, which wanted to produce it, went bankrupt, and the possibility of an early production went with it. Offenbach was not depressed by this. On the contrary, his gaiety and high spirits astonished his friends. The knowledge that he was writing a grand opera, creating the masterpiece which he had spent a lifetime alternately aspiring to and turning away from, buoyed him up; and the fact that he had had to grow old and condemn his whole past life in order to achieve this dampened his spirits not at all.

At the rehearsals of his operetta *Maître Péronilla* all the actors were struck by Offenbach's good humor. Instead of his usual nervous irritability towards his cast at rehearsals, he displayed a hitherto unknown gentleness. One day he mingled with the whirling couples at the end of the third act and, imitating the noise of castanets with his fingers, danced such a graceful fandango that everybody on the stage gathered round and watched him, entranced. *Maître Péronilla* appeared in March 1878.

Had it not been for the secret consolation of his opera, he would have had every reason to be downcast. Another Universal Exposition was due to take place in 1878, and he, the very heart and soul of the festivities in 1867, appealed vainly to the authors of *The Grand Duchess of Gerolstein* for a libretto. How deeply his two old colleagues' refusal hurt him is shown by a letter he wrote to Halévy, dated November 9, 1877, in which he reproached him and Meilhac for deserting their old comrade, with whom they had nearly always been successful, for " the Meyerbeer of the Renaissance." By " the Meyerbeer of the Renaissance " he meant Lecocq.

Offenbach did not exaggerate. In the course of years Meilhac and Halévy had become more and more closely associated with

Lecocq, who was now so much to their liking that it was for him and not for Offenbach that they wrote an operetta for the Universal Exposition. It was called *Le Petit Duc* and created a sensation, which was largely due to the libretto, which told a charming little story in comic-opera form. Henceforward Lecocq reigned as undisputed at the Renaissance as Offenbach once had at the Bouffes and the Variétés. As time was short and Offenbach did not want to be left out altogether, he swallowed his pride and tried to persuade Meilhac and Halévy at least to write him something for the Opéra-Comique. But Halévy told him he had no confidence in the Opéra-Comique, so all his efforts were in vain.

The opening day of the Universal Exposition was approaching, and Offenbach's name had vanished from the boards. He at least had the consolation of knowing that his name had not been completely forgotten, for several papers waxed indignant at his being left out in this of all years, and there was one sympathizer who called his dethronement a tragedy. " What anguish, what bitterness the aging master had to suffer! " wrote Max Nordau in an essay in Offenbach's memory. And Zola would not have been the man he was if he had remained indifferent to such a downfall.

" One has grown old," he stated during the exposition. " One has been blinded by the grossest flattery and dreamed the dream of eternal glory; and then one day everything collapses, the glory is a dust-heap, and one is buried before one is dead. I know of no more terrible old age."

However, it was Zola himself who had done more than anyone else to put Offenbach out of public favor. So intensely did he hate operetta that he called it " a noxious creature that should be strangled like a dangerous animal behind the prompter's box." Zola's anger, be it noted, was not directed at the slighter *bouffonnerie,* which he allowed validity within its limits, but to the big operettas that lasted a whole evening, of which he said that they surrounded stupidity with a halo of glory, encouraged vice, and diverted the public from serious things in a criminal manner. All these phrases Zola coined for Offenbach, though he had to confess that Offenbach's name would live in social history as the creator of the genre. It cannot be denied that under pressure of social conditions which Zola failed to take into account Offenbach stretched the framework of the operetta a little too widely and did work that was not free from traces of decadence. But the author of *Nana* put himself in the wrong when he held Offenbach responsible for the cheap and shoddy operettas that were produced one after another throughout the seventies and had nothing in common with the real *offenbachiades*.

The Universal Exposition, France's first international exhibition since the war, took place at a time of political calm. After the dissolution of the Chamber during the previous year as the result of reactionary agitation, the republicans had returned with a bigger majority than ever. This had encouraged powerful reactionary circles to try to persuade MacMahon to attempt a military *coup d'état,* but MacMahon had preferred to submit to Gambetta and Parliament. So the new Republic could feel secure. No wonder that on May 1, the opening day of the exposition, Paris was overflowing with happiness. There was dancing and feasting in the gaily decorated streets, and in the evening bands of workmen, artisans, and citizens walked arm-in-arm along the illuminated Boulevards singing Pierre Dupont's *Hymn to Peace.* Antagonisms of class and ideology that the Republic was later to reveal were still latent, so that, for the time being, the masses were able to delude themselves that their century-old dream had come true. It was as though the goddess of freedom had stopped in her course and were turning to the fighters following behind her and showing them the beauties of the territory they had conquered.

The beauties of the exposition attracted 250,000 visitors to the Trocadéro in the first week alone. The exotic splendor of that building, which has only recently been pulled down, may perhaps have been an expression of the republican wish for colonial expansion. The influx of visitors lasted until September, and, just as in 1867, the visitors included monarchs and princes. This time

they had to face the uncomfortable fact that France had become
a Republic, so they followed the example of the Viceroy in *La
Périchole* and traveled incognito. Hanslick was summoned to
Paris, just as in 1864. He waxed enthusiastic about the "fairy-
like" electric lighting of the avenue de l'Opéra, about the elevator in his hotel, about the telephone, which saved the expense
of messengers, and about a shop, close to the Bouffes, which had:
"Edison's Phonograph" on the signboard. "Monsieur le Phono-
graphe, as the demonstrator politely calls the machine, repeats the
notes of a trumpet played in front of it, and distinctly repeated
every word I spoke into it!" he reported.

The new times refused to be hampered with things of the
past. La Païva's career terminated abruptly in 1878. For years
past, her political ambitions had caused her to intrigue with her
husband for a Franco-German understanding, but their plotting
came to an end under circumstances that caused the Cabinet to
expel the compromising couple. They sold their French possessions and moved to Neudeck, in Silesia. Others who had also
been great in their time showed up like ruins in the bright light
of morning. Henri Herz, through whom La Païva had gained an
entry to the salons in the time of Louis-Philippe, a vain seventy-
two-year-old fop, tried to make up to a generation which had
never heard his name. And Roger, once the star of the Opéra-
Comique and the young Offenbach's patron, could be glad when
he was invited, out of sympathy, to air his aging voice in a private
drawing-room.

In the eyes of him who did not know about *The Tales of Hoffmann* Offenbach seemed to be one of the ruins too. A troupe of
Russian singers and dancers called Les Bohémiens de Moscou
played in Paris during the exposition, and some of the women
members of the troupe, catching sight of him during a visit to
the offices of *Le Figaro,* paid him the graceful compliment of
singing the "farewell letter" song from *La Périchole.* But *La
Périchole* lay ten years back. Things had come to the pass that
if Offenbach wished to recall the world to the fact of his existence,

he had to dig up his pre-war operettas — that is, if he could find a theatrical manager willing to produce one.

Fortunately, such a one appeared. Whether or no it was because M. Weinschenk, the director of the Gaîté, happened to be short of something new, he made up his mind to revive *Orpheus*. Offenbach jumped at the chance, and though it must have been against the grain to use *Orpheus,* which had already been played nine hundred times, once more as a public bait, he did all in his power to make it a success.

While the negotiations were in progress, he asked Hervé, whom he happened to meet in the street, to play the part of Jupiter. Hervé instantly accepted, but on condition that Offenbach conducted in person. They were two worn-out old artists, who had not met for years, and they were both far too crushed to recall their former rivalry.

Orpheus was duly produced on August 4, and everything went according to plan. Offenbach conducted the second act, Hervé played Jupiter, and the audience duly applauded. Apart from some provincial journalists and some minor actresses from the smaller theaters, the audience consisted mainly of foreigners, delighted at the opportunity of such a holiday treat. The processions, the ballets, and the stage-effects filled Léonce, who played the part of Pluto, with such an acute sense of discomfort that he yearned for the modest *Orpheus* of the Bouffes. " No," he said, shaking his head, " this is no longer my *Orpheus.*"

Nevertheless the production of *Orpheus* was less unfruitful than the production of *La Belle Hélène* had been two years before. It roused public curiosity for other works of Offenbach. Charles Comte, Offenbach's son-in-law, who was now director of the Bouffes, rescued *The Grand Duchess of Gerolstein* from oblivion, and Meilhac, Halévy, and Offenbach begged, beseeched, and implored Hortense Schneider to resume her abandoned throne. But Hortense remained adamant to all appeals. After her row with Bertrand, which had ended in her suing him successfully in the courts, she had once more yielded to the temptation of the floodlights and appeared in Hervé's *La Belle Poule,* but neither she nor the operetta had been a success, though the critics praised the quivering of her nostrils, which, so they said, were able to express what was inexpressible in words. Hortense thereupon vowed never to appear upon the stage again. As she remained obdurate, *The Grand Duchess of Gerolstein* appeared without her, or rather almost without her, for at the first performance she followed the acting of Paola Marié, who did her best to replace her, half-hidden behind the velvet curtains of her proscenium box, thus forcing the audience to divide their attention between the Grand Duchesses past and present.

Towards the end of 1878, as a result of his having to busy himself with his operetta, as well as many other things, Offenbach subjected himself to very dangerous strain. He had gone to Nice on account of his gout to work on his operetta *La Marocaine,* which was intended to be the next production at the Bouffes, when a telegram came from Weinschenck asking his permission to stage *Les Brigands* as a grand opera at the Gaîté, which made it necessary to compose a good deal of new music for it at once. On top of that, the Folies Dramatiques informed him that rehearsals for his comic opera *Madame Favart* were beginning immediately, and this involved the composition of still more music. For Offenbach it was impossible to resist these temptations. He forgot his gout, composed the required music in the twinkling of an eye, and returned hurriedly to Paris, where he divided his time so nimbly between the three theaters that each manager believed that he was working for him alone. Sometimes at rehearsals he was overcome with pain, but " I am just a little tired " was the sum total of his complaints.

Both *Les Brigands* and *La Marocaine* were distinguished by spectacular production. The former, in the true Gaîté style, reached its climax in a grandiose finale with more than three hundred people on the stage and was copied from an historical painting by Makart, while the latter indulged in scenes of Oriental magnificence that were really lavish for a place like the

Bouffes, but failed to make much appeal to the public. The *succès d'estime* earned by the comic opera *Madame Favart,* produced at the end of December 1878, is therefore to be rated all the higher. The plot is based on the diverting intrigues and confusion that result from a love-affair of Mme Favart, a celebrated singer, and the Marshal of Saxony, and enabled Offenbach to return to the style of his beloved eighteenth century. The melodious course of this " little brook running between green banks " contained a good deal that was typical of the operetta. Though it was not as successful as had been hoped, it was successful enough to gladden the hearts of those who admired the stoutness of Offenbach's struggle with adversity. He seemed to be living in the present again, but in reality he was so remote from it that he missed many chances that he might have taken.

In spite of the final triumph of the republicans, to whom the last stronghold fell with MacMahon's resignation, a period set in that was favorable to a renewal of the former light-hearted spirit of operetta.

As the faubourg Saint-Germain noticed that foreign monarchs did not hesitate to visit republican Paris, they ceased their sulking, as they had done in the time of Louis-Philippe, and started living luxuriously again. The winter season that followed the Universal Exposition was one of the most brilliant that Paris had ever seen. The reactionaries lived in a style of rococo magnificence, entertained princes of the blood to dinner, and in general used their wealth to keep the republicans in their places. These tactics failed completely in their object, for the simple reason that the republican bourgeoisie entered into vigorous competition with them. The sons of wealthy bourgeois took the place of the aristocratic rakes of the previous regime, life became more and more democratic, speculation increased alarmingly, and fortunes were made at scandalous speed. To all appearances, the Second Empire seemed to have returned. One of Worth's mannequins was specially deputed to show gowns designed to conceal the condition of pregnant women. Joy and glamour seemed to reign anew.

But Offenbach took no notice. He was a lonely old man, whose only ambition was to complete the work on which his heart was set. While Paris succumbed to *joie de vivre,* he buried himself in his opera, paying no heed to the tumult about him. He was deeply affected by the story of Antonia, who, if she sang, was bound to die. He sadly told himself that he had always succumbed to the temptation to sing in a fashion different from that in which he really should have sung; and by dint of incessant brooding about his supposed lifelong aberration he arrived at the conclusion that there was a secret connection between his work on *The Tales of Hoffmann* and the approach of death; that he, like Antonia, would die because in this opera he would really sing. Did he ask for anything better? He wanted to sing and die. Nevertheless he felt an infinite horror in the face of death, the horror of Ariel confronted with extinction at the hands of natural forces.

To Offenbach death was always strange and incomprehensible. He put death into his opera with the character of Dr. Miracle. He made Dr. Miracle rattle his medicine-bottles like the doctor who treated his sick son Auguste, and the music he wrote for him proved that he saw and heard Dr. Miracle everywhere. In April 1879 death robbed him of Villemessant, his friend and helper since the first days of the Bouffes. He would not have dedicated the opera to Auguste had he not known that his son, too, was doomed to die. There was no getting away from Dr. Miracle.

When his work on the opera was well advanced, as he wanted a quick decision about its fate, he arranged a concert at his home — he now lived in the boulevard des Capucines — on May 18, 1879, when fragments of the work were played. Among the guests were several people of great importance to him, besides the critics; among them Carvalho, the director of the Opéra-Comique, and Herr Jauner, of the Ringtheater at Vienna, who was said already to have made a favorable offer. The excitement that the music roused proved its power. The press announced that a descendant of Carl Maria von Weber had risen in the boulevard des Capucines, and Carvalho declared that he and no other must be the first to produce it. Offenbach did not hesitate for a moment, although he knew that artistically a production of his opera at Vienna would be superior. He gave *The Tales of Hoffmann* to the Opéra-Comique.

For him the Opéra-Comique was not just a theater, like so many others, but was rather the Promised Land. Hitherto he had always been chased away almost as soon as he had set foot in it. With *The Tales of Hoffmann* his feet would be planted in it firmly.

Time passed. During the summer he traveled once more to Germany, as though driven to follow the trail of his memories. At Wildbad, where he took the cure, he composed the ballad " You are as beautiful as a youthful dream." In Cologne he reverted from youth to childhood and was led by the eight bars of Zimmer's waltz to his parents' home. It had been pulled down, and most of the friends of his childhood were dead. Then he returned to Étretat, devoted himself once more to his opera, and, though bedridden by gout, composed an operetta, *La Fille du Tambour-Major*. Nobody could have guessed that every note of its gay and charming music had been composed in physical agony. Scarcely had rehearsals started when, in spite of the bitter cold spell at the beginning of December, he suddenly appeared in Paris at the Folies Dramatiques, promptly demanded more rehearsals, and, having learned by experience, restrained the blind enthusiasm of the manager, who wanted to overdo the spectacular entry of the Consul Bonaparte and his army into Milan at the end of the operetta. His old theatrical ardor had him once more in its grip.

Drums, military music, and patriotic tunes interspersed with gay, light-hearted rhythms were sufficient to assure *La Fille du Tambour-Major* a huge success. It was produced on December 13, 1879 and struck people as a daughter of *The Daughter of the Regiment*. The first-night audience was enthusiastic, and the whole house rose at the curtain representing the triumphant entry of the French troops. Offenbach once more became the idol of

LES THÉÂTRE ILLUSTRÉ. — LES CONTES D'HOFFMANN, opéra en quatre actes de MM. J. Barbier et Carré, musique d'Offenbach. représenté à l'Opéra-Comique. — Portrait d'Offenbach. — 1er acte : La Taverne de maitre Luther. — 2e acte : La Poupée automatique. 3e acte : Le Cabinet de Coppélius. — (Dessin de M. de Haenen.)

Courtesy, Mansell

SCENES FROM *The Tales of Hoffmann*

the multitude, but this time by exalting the very instincts and
ideals which he had once satirized. Was he a renegade? No, a
fallen Ariel, whose justification was *The Tales of Hoffmann*.

The huge success of *La Fille du Tambour-Major* was followed
by another, which gave Offenbach great satisfaction. Koning, the
director of the Renaissance, which was entirely devoted to the
cult of Lecocq, actually commissioned him, Offenbach, to write
on operetta. Offenbach told Koning that at last he would hear
real music again on his stage — a statement in which bitterness,
pride, and satisfaction were inextricably mingled. Offenbach
must have felt like a banished king hearing that his fickle subjects
were demanding his return.

Deeply gratified at this renewal of popularity, Offenbach, sum-
moning all his remaining strength, presided in March 1880 at the
traditional gala supper held at the Hotel Continental after the
hundred and first performance of *La Fille du Tambour-Major*. It
was given in honor of the Paris garrison. During the evening
the band played a quadrille made up from Offenbach's own
compositions. He listened and failed to remember from which
of his works some of them came. *La Fille du Tambour-Major*
was his hundredth work.

Time passed. When the warmer weather came he went to
Saint-Germain to revise his opera in the quiet of the Pavillon
Henri IV and to write the operetta ordered by the Théâtre de la
Renaissance. It was called *La Belle Lurette*. Rest did not exist for
him; now less than ever. At most he occasionally dropped his
score to read a life of Mozart, which he had read so often before
that he knew it practically by heart. Once when Victorin Joncières surprised him reading it, his eyes were full of tears, and
" Poor Mozart! " was all he could say.

No one disturbed him. Herminie was at Étretat with a part
of the family, and his only company was Mme Tournal, one of
his married daughters. But that was how he wanted it. For he
had made a pact with death, and he must therefore be alone.

" If you let me finish my work in peace, I shall be ready to follow you," he said. So conscientious was he in keeping to his part of the bargain that he seemed to compel death to keep it too.

Of course, no time limit had been fixed, and Offenbach was therefore feverish with impatience. " Make haste and produce my opera," he wrote to Carvalho. " I have not much time left, and my only wish is to see the first performance."

The cast was selected in June, and it was arranged that *The Tales of Hoffmann* should be the first new production of the winter season. Would he live until then? Sometimes he sadly stroked his big Russian deerhound, which he had called Kleinzaches after the legend of the first act. " Poor Kleinzaches," he sighed, " I would give everything only to be present at the first night."

The recluse was visited in his solitude by Meilhac, Halévy, and Albert Wolff, who came to stay for some time in the Pavillon Henry IV, because they knew that Offenbach's days were numbered, and felt drawn to him before he died. " It is terrible," his doctor told them. " There is nothing left of him, his body is completely exhausted." Indeed, so frail was he that in spite of his fur-lined coat he shut the windows for fear of drafts, though it was the middle of July, and when his friends called in the afternoon for a quiet game of whist they often found him lying motionless, like a corpse. When he realized their presence he would stir slightly, and the look he gave them seemed to come from another world. " What a lovely article Wolff will write about me after my death! " he sometimes said on these occasions. His friends lived in rooms on the first floor immediately over his head, and they would often hear tunes from *The Tales of Hoffmann* floating upstairs, mixed with terrible attacks of coughing. " Do you hear him? " Meilhac would say to Wolff. " Listen! The musician is at work! What an artist! When he is dead they will appreciate him."

It was a fine summer, which lured many Parisians to Saint-

Germain. Smart carriages and landaus passed by, and coaches full of laughing young people. But Offenbach remained insensible to the laughter and the cracking of whips and continued his battle with death in the Pavillon Henri IV.

Shortly before the middle of September he returned to Paris. The thought of the first night of *The Tales of Hoffmann* was the only thing that kept him alive. It had to be postponed, however, because of delay with the scenery, the costumes and decorations. Everybody knew that Offenbach could not wait, and in order to mitigate somewhat the agony of the delay, they took the dying man to the foyer of the Opéra-Comique, to enable him to hear parts of the opera. Poor Kleinzaches! But as though refusing to admit to what straits he was reduced, he unfolded his Ariel-like wings for the last time, and just before the end, played through his operetta to the Variétés artists who were going to appear in it during the winter season. His drawn face livened up, his eyes glistened, his gout-ridden fingers leaped like magic over the keys. On the afternoon of the next day, with his family around him, he looked over the sheets on which he had written out the last act of *The Tales of Hoffmann*. The piano arrangement was complete, and not a single bar was missing. He was still holding the manuscript in his hand when he had a sudden attack of suffocation, after which the death agony began.

"I believe tonight it will be over," he said in an interval of consciousness.

He was not mistaken. The end came at about half past three. Death had kept strictly to the pact. The first night had not been provided for in it.

It was October 5, 1880. In the morning Léonce, Offenbach's old comedian, called and asked the porter how he was. "Monsieur Offenbach passed away quietly, without knowing anything about it," the porter told him. "How surprised he will be when he finds out!" the comedian gloomily replied. The same day Albert Wolff fulfilled Offenbach's prophecy by writing a beautiful obituary notice for the *Figaro*. And many realized that day that the jester's work had been more serious than that of many whose seriousness was but a joke.

Two days later, wreaths and wreaths and still more wreaths were brought from the boulevard des Capucines to the Madeleine, where they were piled round the coffin, in the mortuary chamber. There were wreaths from the Paris theaters, wreaths from Vienna, from Brussels, from London, from Cologne. Then the funeral procession took place, which gave occasion to a real *offenbachiade*. Crowds of curious people, among them numbers of English tourists with their guides, thronged early to the church, in order not to miss the solemn event. They formed a solid wall, through which it was impossible for the mourners to pass, so that Halévy, Crémieux, Tréfeu, and other close friends were forced to listen to the service in the vestibule.

Famous singers took part in it, and even the most indifferent were not able to conceal their emotion when the song of Fortunio was sung, accompanied by the organ. The procession did not make straight for the Montmartre cemetery, but made a detour along the Boulevards, to allow Offenbach to take a final farewell of his theaters. He was not being played at the Bouffes or at the Variétés, but he was in his coffin and did not notice. Rain fell and thinned the ranks of those following, but one woman in black followed the cortège to the end. She was Hortense Schneider. This time she had no desire to flounce away in a huff.

Although Offenbach was unquestionably dead and buried, he did not yet disappear from the surface of life, to which he so obstinately clung. His operetta *La Belle Lurette,* which he had composed in the Pavillon Henri IV, was produced at the Renaissance a few weeks later. There was something shattering about its gaiety, wrung from a mind that was penetrated by the certainty of death; and never had his presence been so all-pervasive as at the ceremony organized by the *Figaro* on November 18, 1880, at the Variétés, when his bust was unveiled, and Léonce,

Mlle Théo, Dupuis, Zulma Bouffar, and all the others who had
to thank him for their success sang and acted selections from his
works. These tunes of the past three decades, including the " Barcarolle," were made even more effective by the innumerable
memories that were associated with them, though they sounded
as fresh and new as on the very first day. *Le Violoneux* conjured
up visions of the little wooden hut on the Champs-Élysées; the
duet from *La Vie parisienne* brought the whole Second Empire
to life again. The past, armed for a journey to posterity.

As soon as the last note had sounded, the bust was unveiled,
with Hortense Schneider standing next to it in the costume of
La Périchole, as well as Delaunay, who once upon a time, to the
despair of the young conductor of the Comédie Française, had
not been able to sing Fortunio's song. He recited Meilhac's lines
in praise of Offenbach:

> *Est il un seul coin sur la terre*
> *Où son nom ne soit pas connu?*
> *Dans l'un et dans l'autre hémisphère*
> *Est il un village perdu,*
>
> *Une bourgade abandonnée*
> *Où, sur quelque vieux piano,*
> *On n'ait dit l'Evohé d'Orphée*
> *Et l'amour de Fortunio?*

A month later Offenbach's ghost walked again. Blum, Toché,
and Wolff had together written a revue, *Les Parfums de Paris,*
and one of the three took it upon himself to ask Hortense Schneider to act in it. She of course abruptly refused. Her visitor, making for the door, remarked casually that it was a pity that she
should refuse on this of all occasions. Her curiosity was aroused,
and she asked him why. He behaved as though it were futile to
discuss the matter further. As she was so obviously unwilling to
return to the stage, what was the use? He kept her on tenterhooks for a long time before telling her that the revue included

an item that was a kind of Offenbach potpourri. But as she was not interested — his hand was already on the door.

" Wait! " Hortense Schneider exclaimed. " An item about Jacques — I will play in your revue! "

She did play in the revue, and it was as though she were singing about herself and Offenbach. Then she really vanished from the boards for ever.

Offenbach, however, did not vanish from the boards, but returned to them again and again.

The rehearsals of *The Tales of Hoffmann* were nearing their end. Ernest Guiraud undertook the instrumentation, in accordance with the family's wishes, and unselfishly consented to the postponement of his own opera, *La Galante Aventure,* so that Offenbach's opera might appear the sooner.

A drastic step was taken at the dress rehearsal. As it was feared that the length of the opera might be found wearisome, the whole Giulietta act, which should have been the last one, was deleted. But as it contained the " Barcarolle," which was indispensable, another drastic alteration had to be made, and the Antonia act was shifted from Munich to Venice. A less vital opera would never have survived such mutilation.

The first night was a big social event. It took place on February 10, 1881, in presence of the Minister Jules Ferry and many leading political figures; from which it could be concluded that Offenbach was no longer considered *le grand corrupteur* by the republicans. Herminie did not go to the theater, but an elaborate messenger service was provided by friends and members of the family, who kept her informed of everything as it occurred. The first messenger announced the loud applause that greeted the legend of Kleinzaches, the next reported Mlle Isaac's triumph as Olympia. When she patted away with the mechanical quickness of an overwound doll, the applause was so enthusiastic that her exit had to be repeated. Herminie was told all this and more. And when the last messenger arrived after the curtain fell, and visitors streamed in, bringing with them the jubilation of the

Opéra-Comique, her thoughts were with the husband who was the object of all this acclamation.

That was how the work was born on which Offenbach's fame was destined most securely to be established. He had always wanted to be recognized by the big critics. *The Tales of Hoffmann* was praised by them and given an honored place among the operas which he had once burlesqued.

All the same, this was not the most significant of his works. Others, like him, had wrestled with demons, but no one but he could have written the *offenbachiades*. They were not, as he himself imagined when his death was approaching, a betrayal of himself, but the reverse. *The Tales of Hoffmann* was a retreat. In writing *The Tales of Hoffmann* he betrayed his weakness. The importance of this opera was not that it went deeper than the operettas, but that it laid bare the dark foundations out of which the operettas had grown, and thus showed their depth. Not till *The Tales of Hoffmann* was it fully revealed with what airy lightness the *offenbachiades* had scared away the nightmares that continually oppress humanity.

The Paris premiere was followed by that at Vienna, which took place in December 1881. But the run was abruptly cut short because a big fire broke out in the crowded Ringtheater immediately before the curtain should have gone up on the second performance. This was an event that filled all theaters with a superstitious horror of *The Tales of Hoffmann* for years to come. It was as though the spirits of the opera were wreaking vengeance on one who now conjured them up after a lifetime of laying them. This catastrophe snapped a magic link that had for so long tied Offenbach to the land of the living, and he retreated into history.

Authoritative judges, like Saint-Saëns, believed that he would disappear with the times to which he had belonged and would soon be forgotten. They forgot that the works of Offenbach are not the whole of Offenbach, but that as creator of the operetta, he helped to express a unique attitude. It was because of this attitude that later generations could not help taking sides for or against him. Some have reproached him for profaning all great things and for contenting himself with the role of a futile entertainer. Others have loved him for those very traits which his enemies misjudged. Thus Nietzsche, for instance, had gone far too deep into the abyss of metaphysical speculation not to appreciate Offenbach's sense for the superficial. But no matter whether he is praised or condemned, acted or not acted, the mixture of gaiety and satire, revolutionary disintegration and backward-looking tenderness that permeate his operettas roused passions such as could only be roused by a great artist. Had he not been a middleman between time and eternity, he would scarcely have exercised the minds of posterity ever since.

Long after Offenbach had become history, individuals survived who had shone and worked with him. But they were isolated, and there was nothing to unite them any longer.

There was the ex-Empress Eugénie. She looked from the windows of the Hotel Continental at the gardens of the Tuileries, which looked remarkably empty without the Tuileries itself, and she walked the paths of the park of Saint-Cloud in the company of her memories.

There was Hortense Schneider. After her appearance in *Les Parfums de Paris* she sold her house and jewelry, prudently invested the proceeds, and married an Italian adventurer, named Émile Brionne, who pretended to be a French count. She discovered on her honeymoon that he was only interested in her money, so she returned to Paris, started divorce proceedings, and built herself a house in which she cut herself off from the outside world. As she grew older she grew miserly and extremely religious. She had a crucifix fixed over her bed and became more and more prudish. Like Eugénie, she survived the World War. They were two relics of a vanished epoch and survived till 1920.

There was Ludovic Halévy. About the time of Offenbach's death he retired from the theater, and from 1892 onwards confined his literary activities to encouraging young talent, besides devoting himself to his family, who also grew up in the Institut.

He had spent a happy childhood in the Institut building, and he dedicated the work of his old age to it.

Occasionally, when he felt the need for relaxation, he would go to the Variétés, take a seat, and listen to any rehearsal that happened to be in progress. The little actresses would wonder at the old gentleman with the handsome gray beard, why he looked on so seriously, and what he was doing there. Generally there would be one who was better informed than the rest, and she would reverently whisper his name. It would pass from mouth to mouth, and at the first opportunity a swarm of girls in costume would gather round the author of *La Belle Hélène*. And with all the girls around him, he would no longer look so serious, but smile in a friendly fashion, and give advice and encouragement to all the little supers and chorus girls and actresses who confided their troubles to the nice, gray-bearded old gentleman. And then they would disperse again and Ludovic Halévy would happily go his way.

SELECTED BIBLIOGRAPHY

A. BIOGRAPHIES

I. Offenbach

ARGUS: *Célébrités dramatiques: Jacques Offenbach.* Paris, 1872.

BEKKER, PAUL: *Jacques Offenbach.* (Vols. XXXI–XXXII, *Die Musik.*) Berlin, 1909.

BELLAIGUE, CAMILLE: " *Offenbach,*" in *La Revue hebdomadaire,* April 23, 1910.

BRANCOUR, RENÉ: *Offenbach. Les Musiciens célèbres* series. Paris, 1929.

HENSELER, ANTON: *Jakob Offenbach.* Berlin, 1930.

KRISTELLER, HANS: *Der Aufstieg des Kölners Jacques Offenbach. Ein Musikerleben in Bildern.* Berlin, 1931.

MARTINET, ANDRÉ: *Offenbach. Sa vie et son œuvre.* Paris, 1887.

MIRECOURT, EUGÈNE DE: *Les Contemporains: Auber. Offenbach.* Paris, 1869.

NADAR: " *Les Contemporains de Nadar: Offenbach,*" in *Le Journal amusant,* 1858, No. 155.

NORDAU, MAX: " *Der Pariser Aristophanes,*" in *Paris. Studien und Bilder aus dem wahren Milliardenlande,* Vol. II. Leipzig, 1881.

SCHNEIDER, LOUIS: *Les Maîtres de l'opérette française: Offenbach.* Paris, 1923.

SERVIÈRES, GEORGES: " *Offenbach avant l'opérette,*" in *Le Guide musical,* No. 33–6, August–September 1910.

WOLFF, ALBERT: " *Notice biographique,*" Preface to Offenbach's *Notes d'un musicien en voyage.* Paris, 1877.

——: " *Jacques Offenbach,*" in *La Gloire à Paris.* Paris, 1886.

II. Offenbach's Contemporaries

A la mémoire de Pierre Dupont. Lyon, 1899.

ALLOTTE DE LA FUŸE, M.: *Jules Verne. Sa vie, son œuvre.* Paris, 1927.

BOULENGER, MARCEL: *La Païva*. Paris, 1930.

CLARETIE, JULES: *Célébrités contemporaines: Ludovic Halévy*. Paris, 1883.

CURZON, HENRI DE: *Meyerbeer*. Les Musiciens célèbres series. Paris, 1911.

DECSEY, ERNST: *Johann Strauss*. Stuttgart, Berlin, 1922.

Friedrich von Flotow's Leben. Von seiner Witwe. Leipzig, 1892.

LABUSSIÈRE, PIERRE: *Louis Véron. (Thèse de doctorat en médecine.)* Paris, 1930.

LACOUR, LÉOPOLD: "*Meilhac et Halévy*," in *Gaulois et Parisiens*. Paris, 1883.

LOLIÉE, FRÉDÉRIC: *Le Duc de Morny et la société du Second Empire*. Paris, 1909.

MALHERBE, CHARLES: *Auber*. Les Musiciens célèbres series. Paris, 1911.

MIRECOURT, EUGÈNE DE: *Histoire contemporaine: Villemessant*. Paris, 1867.

MORIENVAL, JEAN: *Les Créateurs de la grande presse en France (Émile de Girardin, Henri de Villemessant, Moïse Millaud)*. Paris, 1931.

RECLUS, MAURICE: *Émile de Girardin*. Paris, 1934.

ROUFF, MARCEL, and CAZEVITZ, THÉRÈSE: *La Vie de fête sous le Second Empire. Hortense Schneider*. Paris, 1930.

ROUJON, HENRY: "*Ludovic Halévy*," in *Artistes et amis des arts*. Paris, 1912.

——: *Quelques mots sur M. Ludovic Halévy*. Paris, 1888.

SCHNEIDER, LOUIS: *Les Maîtres de l'opérette française: Hervé. Charles Lecocq*. Paris, 1924.

SÉCHÉ, LÉON: *Alfred de Musset*. Vol. I. Paris, 1907.

B. GENERAL REFERENCES

AUDEBRAND, PHILIBERT: *Un Café de journalistes sous Napoléon III*. Paris, 1888.

AURIANT: *Les Lionnes du Second Empire*. Paris, 1936.

BAUDELAIRE, CHARLES: *L'Art romantique*. Paris, 1925.

DAUDET, ALPHONSE: *Le Nabab. Roman de mœurs parisiennes*. Paris, 1877.

——: *Trente ans de Paris*. Paris, 1888.

DELVAU, ALFRED: *Les Lions du jour*. Paris, 1867.

FLAUBERT, GUSTAVE: *Éducation sentimentale*. Paris, 1869.

GIRARDIN, DELPHINE DE: *Le Vicomte de Launay*. 3 vols. Paris, 1856.

GUTZKOW, KARL: *Paris und Frankreich in den Jahren 1834–1874.* (*Gesammelte Werke,* I Serie, Band VII.) Jena.

HALÉVY, LUDOVIC: "*Pendant l'émeute. Notes d'un habitué de l'Opéra*" (signed A. B. C. in *La Vie parisienne,* June 19, 1869).

——: *Madame et Monsieur Cardinal.* Paris, 1872.

——: *Les Petites Cardinal.* Paris, 1880.

HEINE, HEINRICH: *Gemäldeausstellung in Paris 1831. Französische Zustände. Florentinische Nächte.* (*Sämtliche Werke,* Band VI.) Leipzig, 1912.

——: *Lutezia.* (*Sämtliche Werke,* Band IX.) Leipzig, 1912.

MEILHAC, HENRI: *Contes parisiens du Second Empire* (*1866*). Paris, 1904.

——: "*La Comédie du Cercle*" (Préface pour la 15ᵉ année des *Annales du Théâtre et de la Musique*). Paris, 1890.

MONTÉGUT, ÉMILE: *Essais sur l'époque actuelle.* Paris, 1858.

Muse populaire. Pierre Dupont: "*Chants et poésies.*" Paris, 1851.

NORDAU, MAX: *Paris. Studien und Bilder aus dem wahren Milliardenlande.* 2 vols. Leipzig, 1881.

——: *Paris unter der Dritten Republik. Neue Bilder aus dem wahren Milliardenlande.* Leipzig, 1881.

OFFENBACH, JACQUES: Preface to Vol. I of Arnold Mortier's *Soirées parisiennes.* Paris, 1875.

——: *Histoire d'une valse.* Paris, *c.* 1872.

——: *Offenbach en Amérique. Notes d'un musicien en voyage.* Paris, 1877.

RELLSTAB, LUDWIG: *Paris im Frühjahr 1843.* 3 vols. Leipzig, 1844.

SCHOLL, AURÉLIEN: *L'Esprit du Boulevard.* Paris.

VALLÈS, JULES: *Les Réfractaires.* Paris, 1866.

——: *Le Tableau de Paris.* Paris, 1932.

VEUILLOT, LOUIS: *Les Odeurs de Paris.* Paris, 1866.

WOLFF, ALBERT: *La Capitale de l'art.* Paris, 1886.

ZOLA, ÉMILE: *L'Argent.* Paris, 1891.

——: *Nana.* Paris, 1880.

C. MEMOIRS, LETTERS, ETC.

ADAM, MME (JULIETTE LAMBER): *Le Roman de mon enfance et de ma jeunesse.* Paris, 1902.

ALTON-SHÉE, E. D': *Mémoires du Vicomte d'Aulnis.* Paris, 1868.

AUDEBRAND, PHILIBERT: *Petits Mémoires d'une stalle d'orchestre.* Paris, 1885.

BASSANVILLE, MME LA COMTESSE DE: *Les Salons d'autrefois, souvenirs intimes.* 4 vols. Paris, 1862–6.

CAMP, MAXIME DU: *Souvenirs littéraires.* 2 vols. Paris, 1892.

CLAUDIN, GUSTAVE: *Mes Souvenirs. Les Boulevards de 1840 à 1870.* Paris, 1884.

DUQUESNEL, FÉLIX: *Souvenirs littéraires.* Paris, 1922.

HALÉVY, DANIEL: *Pays parisiens.* Paris, 1932.

HALÉVY, LUDOVIC: *Notes et souvenirs, 1871–1872.* Paris 1889.

——: *Trois dîners avec Gambetta (publié et annoté par Daniel Halévy).* Paris, 1929.

——: *Carnets (publiés avec une introduction et des notes par Daniel Halévy).* 2 vols. Paris, 1935.

HANSLICK, EDUARD: *Aus meinem Leben.* 2 vols. Berlin, 1911.

HOUSSAYE, ARSÈNE: *Souvenirs de jeunesse (1830–1850).* Paris, 1896.

——: *Les Confessions, souvenirs d'un demi-siècle (1830–1890).* 6 vols. Paris, 1885–91.

HUEBNER, GRAF JOSEPH ALEXANDER VON: *Neun Jahre der Erinnerungen eines österreichischen Botschafters in Paris unter dem zweiten Kaiserreich, 1851–1859.* 2 vols. Berlin, 1904.

JOLLIVET, GASTON: *Souvenirs de la vie de plaisir sous le Second Empire.* (*Bibliothèque Historia.*) Paris, 1927.

Journal des Goncourt. 6 vols. Paris, 1912.

LAN, JULES: *Mémoires d'un chef de claque.* Paris, 1883.

MÉRIMÉE, PROSPER: *Lettres à une autre inconnue.* Paris, 1875.

——: *Lettres à M. Panizzi (1850–1870).* 2 vols. Paris, 1881.

MEYER, ARTHUR: *Ce que mes yeux ont vu.* Paris, 1911.

NADAR: *Quand j'étais photographe.* Paris, 1900.

SCHOLL, AURÉLIEN: *Mémoires du trottoir.* Paris, 1882.

VÉRON, DOCTEUR L.: *Mémoires d'un bourgeois de Paris,* Vols. III–VI. Paris, 1854–5.

VIEL-CASTEL, COMTE H. DE: *Commérages en marge du Second Empire.* Paris, 1930.

——: *Mémoires du Comte Horace de Viel-Castel sur le règne de Napoléon III.* 3 vols. Paris, 1883.

VILLEMESSANT, H. DE: *Mémoires d'un journaliste.* 2 vols. Paris, 1867, 1872.

WOLFF, ALBERT: *Mémoires d'un parisien. La Gloire à Paris.* Paris, 1886.

——: *Mémoires d'un parisien. La Gloriole.* Paris, 1888.

ZED: *Le Demi-monde sous le Second Empire.* Paris, 1892.

Institut de France: *Académie Française. Discours prononcés dans*

la séance publique tenue par l'Académie Française pour la réception de M. Ludovic Halévy, le jeudi 4 février, 1886. Paris, 1886.
——: Discours de M. Halévy (Éloge de M. le Comte d'Haussonville).
——: Réponse de M. Pailleron, Directeur de l'Académie Française, au discours de M. Halévy.
——: Académie Française. Discours prononcés dans la séance publique tenue par l'Académie Française pour la réception de M. Henry Meilhac, le jeudi 4 avril 1889. Paris, 1889.
——: Discours de M. Meilhac (Éloge d'Eugène Labiche).
——: Réponse de M. Jules Simon, Directeur de l'Académie Française, au discours de M. Meilhac.
——: Publications diverses de l'année 1910. Paris, 1910.
——: Discours de M. Eugène Brieux, élu en remplacement de M. Ludovic Halévy (Éloge de Ludovic Halévy).
——: Réponse de M. le Marquis de Ségur, Directeur de l'Académie Française, au discours de M. Brieux.

D. HISTORICAL

BAC, FERDINAND: Intimités du Second Empire. Paris, 1931, 1932.
BAINVILLE, JACQUES: Histoire de trois générations (1815–1918). Paris, 1918.
BEAUMONT-VASSY, LE VICOMTE DE: Histoire intime du Second Empire. Paris, 1874.
BELLESSORT, ANDRÉ: "La Société française sous le Second Empire," in La Revue hebdomadaire, 1932, No. 4–15.
——: Les Intellectuels et l'avènement de la Troisième République (1871–1875). Paris, 1931.
BLED, VICTOR DU: La Société française depuis cent ans. Quelques Salons du Second Empire. Paris, 1923.
BULLE, CONSTANTIN: Geschichte des Zweiten Kaiserreichs. Berlin, 1890.
CHAMBRIER, JAMES DE: La Cour et la société du Second Empire. 2 vols. Paris, 1902.
CHARLÉTY, SÉBASTIEN: Histoire du Saint-Simonisme (1825–1864). Paris, 1931.
DÉMY, ADOLPHE: Essai historique sur les Expositions Universelles de Paris. Paris, 1907.
DUCHÊNE, GEORGES: Études sur la féodalité financière. La Spéculation devant les tribunaux. Pratique et théorie de l'agiotage. Paris, 1867.

GIDION, SIGFRIED: *Bauen in Frankreich. Eisen. Eisenbeton.* Leipzig, Berlin, 1928.

GORCE, PIERRE DE LA: *Au temps du Second Empire.* Paris, 1935.

HALÉVY, DANIEL: *La Fin des notables.* Paris, 1930.

MARTIN, GERMAIN: " *Histoire économique et financière,*" in *Histoire de la nation française,* Vol. X. Paris, 1927.

MARX, KARL: *The Civil War in France.*

——: *Class Struggles in France.*

——: *The 18th Brumaire of Louis Bonaparte.*

WEILL, GEORGES: *Histoire du mouvement social en France (1852–1924).* Paris, 1924.

ZÉVAÈS, ALEXANDRE: *Histoire de la Troisième République (1870–1926).* Paris, 1926.

E. THEATER AND MUSIC

ABRAHAM, ÉMILE: *Les Acteurs et les actrices de Paris.* Paris, 1852.

BOUTET DE MONVEL, ROGER: *Les Variétés 1850–1870.* Paris, 1905.

BRAZIER, NICOLAS: *Chroniques des petits théâtres de Paris.* 2 vols., nouvelle édition. Paris, 1883.

BUGUET, HENRY: *Foyers et coulisses.* 18 vols. Paris, 1873–85.

CROISSET, FRANCIS DE: *La Vie parisienne au théâtre.* Paris, 1929.

DUQUESNEL, FÉLIX: " *Les Grandes Premières: La Belle Hélène,*" in *Je sais tout,* December 15, 1906.

GINISTY, PAUL: *La Féerie. Bibliothèque théâtrale illustrée* series. Paris, 1910.

HALÉVY, LÉON: *La Belle Hélène. Épître à mon ami Paul Duport.* Paris, 1865.

HALLAYS-DABOT, VICTOR: *La Censure dramatique et le théâtre (1850–1870).* Paris, 1871.

LASALLE, ALBERT DE: *Histoire des Bouffes-Parisiens.* Paris, 1860.

MEYER, ARTHUR: " *Le Règne de l'opérette,*" in *Le Gaulois,* December 20, 1920.

MORTIER, ARNOLD: *Les Soirées parisiennes . . . par un monsieur de l'orchestre.* 11 vols. Paris, 1875–85.

RIEGER, ERWIN: *Offenbach und seine Wiener Schule* (Vol. IV in *Theater und Kultur*). Vienna, 1920.

SAINT-SAËNS, CAMILLE: *Harmonie et Mélodie.* Paris, 1889.

SARCEY, FRANCISQUE: *Quarante Ans de théâtre.* Vol. VI. Paris, 1901.

ZOLA, ÉMILE: *Le Naturalisme au théâtre.* Nouvelle édition. Paris, 1912.

*Hoffmanns Erzählungen. Ein Sonderdruck der Deutschen Buch-
gemeinschaft anlässlich der Max-Reinhardt-Inszenierung von
Offenbachs: " Hoffmanns Erzählungen."* Berlin.

F. THE BOULEVARDS AND PARIS LIFE

ARISTE, PAUL D': *La Vie et le monde du Boulevard (1830–1870).*
Paris, 1930.
BOULENGER, JACQUES: *Sous Louis-Philippe. Le Boulevard.* Paris, 1933.
——: *Sous Louis-Philippe. Les Dandys.* Paris, 1932.
DU CAMP, MAXIME: *Paris. Ses Organes, ses fonctions et sa vie dans
la seconde moitié du XIXe siècle.* 6 vols. Paris, 1879.
CHADOURNE, ANDRÉ: *Les Cafés-concerts.* Paris, 1880.
CHALLAMEL, AUGUSTIN: *L'Ancien Boulevard du Temple.* Paris, 1873.
DELVAU, ALFRED: *Histoire anecdotique des cafés et cabarets de Paris.*
Paris, 1862.
LAZARE, LOUIS: *Les Quartiers pauvres de Paris. Études municipales*
series. Paris, 1868.
SÉCHÉ, LÉON: *La Jeunesse dorée sous Louis-Philippe.* Paris, 1910.
SIMOND, CHARLES: *La Vie parisienne au XIXe siècle. Paris de 1800 à
1900.* 3 vols. Paris, 1900–1.
*Acht Tage in Paris. Eine Anweisung, alle Merkwürdigkeiten dieser
Hauptstadt in Zeit von einer Woche zu besuchen.* Paris, July
1855.
Paris économique. Paris, 1867.

G. PERIODICALS

Artiste, L'. Paris, 1843, etc.
France musicale, La. Paris, 1846.
Journal amusant, Le. Paris, 1855, etc.
*Journal des arts, des sciences et des lettres et de l'Exposition univer-
selle.* Paris, 1855, 1867.
Ménestrel, Le. Paris, 1836, etc.
Mercure de Bade, Le. Strasbourg, 1864, 1865.
Vie parisienne, La. Paris, 1866, etc.

INDEX